Nazi Propaganda Films

Nazi Propaganda Films

A History and Filmography

ROLF GIESEN

McFarland & Company, Inc., Publishers
Jefferson, North Carolina, and London

Unless otherwise noted, photographs are courtesy of
Filmmuseum Berlin–Deutsche Kinemathek.

LIBRARY OF CONGRESS CATALOGUING-IN-PUBLICATION DATA

Giesen, Rolf.
    Nazi propaganda films : a history and filmography / Rolf Giesen.
      p.   cm.
    Filmography: p.
    Includes bibliographical references and index.

    ISBN 0-7864-1556-8 (illustrated case binding : 50# alkaline paper) ∞

    1. National socialism and motion pictures.
    2. Motion pictures—Germany—History.   I. Title.
    PN1995.9.N36G54   2003
    791.43'658—dc21   2003006853

British Library cataloguing data are available

Cover photograph: Emil Lohkamp in the title role in *Hans Westmar*

Manufactured in the United States of America

*McFarland & Company, Inc., Publishers
  Box 611, Jefferson, North Carolina 28640
  www.mcfarlandpub.com*

Contents

Preface

This book focuses primarily on nationalist and propaganda feature films (and feature-length documentaries) made in Germany between 1933 and 1945, not short film productions and newsreels. Some of these films were *Staatsauftragsfilme*, i.e., films produced by order of and financed by the German Reich. These productions are marked in the respective list of credits.

It certainly is no easy task even for Germans to translate the Nazi phraseology, for it is bombastic and tautological to no end. I have tried, and the question is: to what degree did I fail?

Grateful thanks are due to my colleagues at Filmmuseum Berlin–Deutsche Kinemathek: Eva Orbanz, Uta Orluc, Gero Gandert, Peter Latta, Hans Helmut Prinzler, Dr. Holger Theuerkauf, Gerrit Thies; to producer-distributor Hanns Eckelkamp (Atlas Film); to Hans-Joachim Thunack for scanning the stills and illustrations; to the late cinematographer and effects specialist Gerhard Huttula, who had worked on several war films with director Karl Ritter; and to the late émigré writer Curt Siodmak, who once replied to a television interviewer's question to please briefly (as there was no time) sum up his experiences with the Nazis—"This is impossible to do in a minute and a half."

— *RG*

"…you are not dead,
you are alive in Germany."

—*Triumph of the Will*

Introduction: *All Quiet on the Western Front*

In his 1997 book *The Great Chessboard: American Primacy and Its Geostrategic Imperatives*, Zbigniew K. Brzezinski connects America's striving for a democratic world order and economical dominance after the collapse of the Soviet Union strongly with the idea of *Eurasia* and, looking for an ally in Western Europe, with one NATO junior partner especially: Germany, which by its new role shall be relieved of the stigma of twentieth century wars.[1]

Communications and propaganda films play prominent parts now and then: *Air Force One* and *The Patriot*, directed by Germans Wolfgang Petersen and Roland Emmerich, and *Collateral Damage*, starring Austrian Arnold Schwarzenegger who has become an American icon, are just a few examples. For this reason a book which offers a look back on Germany's own doubtful political efforts in the movie industry in World War II is more than a historical account in a world still shocked by the fatal terrorist attacks on the Twin Towers of the World Trade Center. It deals with Adolf Hitler and his invasions of Western and Eastern Europe in order to create another version of *Eurasia* which had to be founded on bygone racist terms. And it also deals with Hitler's victims who were either sentenced to the gas chambers or, as true German *Volksgenossen* (national comrades), blinded by intellectually stupid but emotionally powerful propaganda, sent to the front.

My father, born in 1924, was a member of the Hitler Youth and in 1939 took part in the anti–Jewish pogroms and riots of the *Reichskristallnacht*, smashing the windows of a shop owned by Jewish proprietors. A few years later, he faced death many times on the Eastern Front and never could forget it. He used to tell me about it with a strange mixture of sheer horror and burning enthusiasm (perhaps because it was the only time he left his small home town and saw a little of the world he was ordered to conquer). In an almost hypnotic state of magnetic attraction, he religiously went on holiday each year to Berchtesgaden in the Bavarian Alps, where the Führer once resided like an eagle in his Berghof residence. If you are a German writing about that subject, you cannot write as an innocent party even if you were blessed by a late birth as one German chancellor stressed. You are living, so to speak, with the dead who are not really dead. Their spirit, unfortunately, is always with us. As a German you are part of Teutonic history, culture and nature. How could that be changed? My father, a tiny wheel set in motion to create a world-wide Aryan ice age, was a life-long film buff. So was Adolf Hitler, who set the seal not only on Germany but on UFA and the German film industry, neither of which ever recovered from his fixed idea of world leadership.

In 1931, UFA, short for Universum Film Aktiengesellschaft, Germany's largest movie outfit, founded during World War I as part of General Ludendorff's propaganda efforts, released *Der Kongress tanzt* (*Congress Dances*) starring Willy Fritsch, Lilian Harvey and tall, gaunt Conrad Veidt as Metternich. Though it wasn't that evident in this movie full of esprit, Metternich had been a visionary politician and diplomat: "My private belief is that the old Europe is at the beginning of its end. I, who am determined to go down with it, shall know how to do my duty. The new Europe, on the other hand, is still in an unrealized state; between end and beginning there will be chaos." Two world wars exemplified that chaos. Many Germans wouldn't accept the defeat of World War I. Oswald Spengler, a philosopher with a sharp intellectual mind as well a detester of democracy, saw in it "the economic collapse of the white world" and "the economic destruction of Germany": "Since then the world has been ruled by the low shortsighted thought of the vulgar man who has suddenly come into power. *That* was the victory! The destruction is complete, the future is almost hopeless, but the spirit of revenge upon society is appeased."[2] How pathetic these words sound, but the tragedy of the second war was born out of the first, and the vulgar man manifested himself in one unknown private from the Western Front, Adolf Hitler. For World War I, as Spengler saw it, Serbia was the stimulus, Austria was the urging, Germany was the reason, and the powers of the entente were responsible. Afterward, the originators of the Versailles Treaty, inspired by an intransigent Clemenceau, were stupid enough to make the peace almost unbearable and thus unwillingly sowed the seed of the Nazis.

It clearly was Hitler's goal to correct the results of World War I, but in starting another war he wanted to avoid what he considered the reason for Germany's defeat. So the Nazis had to create a "national unity of support," as it would be called today. They called it *Volksgemeinschaft* (national community), and it was linked by anti–Semitism. Everybody knew that Hitler's policy would provoke another war. In his book *Der Fragebogen* (The Questionnaire), published in 1951, Ernst von Salomon, who occasionally worked as a screenwriter, cited Captain Ehrhardt, who after World War I led an infamous nationalist volunteer corps: "There will be war, that is certain. And we will lose that war, that is certain, too. I am going to risk everything to explain to the English that after that [first] war the madness of Versailles must not be repeated."[3]

On December 17, 1930, *Völkischer Beobachter*, edited by Adolf Hitler, published a denunciation signed by several leading Nazis, among them Dr. Frick and Dr. Goebbels, of what they regarded as propaganda films infiltrating Germany: For months via German cinemas a flood of for the most part foreign film products has been pouring out into the public. These are designed to discredit Germany's reputation abroad, to poison the German people's accepted standards, to trample on the honor and dignity of German women, to paralyze the spirit of resistance of the German people. Above all they exhibit the tendency to encourage the undermining of German defense, so essential especially in this time of other states' armament, the nationalist feeling and the general Christian social norms by postulating a shameless propaganda of abortion. We refer primarily to films like *10 Days That Shocked the World, Two Worlds, Battleship Potemkin, The Dreyfus Affair, The Blue Express, Women in Need, Frauenglück — Frauennot, Cyankali* and most recently, above all, the movie *All Quiet on the Western Front*. That last American Jewish product deals with a nasty and mean denigration of German front soldiers who are demonstrated to the audience in a bizarre and distorted manner. And this fact carries weight as the film was made by American Jews and cast with American actors who are partly Jewish. Berlin's German conscious population has given its view on this movie in spontaneous repulsion in big mass demonstrations.

Erich Maria Remarque had published *All Quiet on the Western Front* as a novel that accurately depicted the depressing effect of the great war on the individual young soldier who enthusiastically volunteered from the classroom to the front. In 1930, film rights to *All Quiet on the Western Front* were acquired by Carl Laemmle, Jr., production chief of his father's Universal City Studios in Hollywood. Out of the deal came a superior movie, directed by Lewis Milestone — and a chance for Dr. Joseph Goebbels, then gauleiter in Berlin, to sabotage the opening in the German capital and make it into the headlines of the newspapers.

All Quiet on the Western Front opened at Berlin's Mozartsaal cinema at Nollendorfplatz on December 4, 1930.

> Seldom was a Hollywood movie expected with such anticipation in Berlin since the pros and cons of this film have been debated so livelily.
>
> For it is not only a picture play — it is magnificent.
>
> The question of German war experiences has been touched on by Hollywood — after the German Remarque book there certainly is extreme danger of offending, of insulting with the resurrection of all that horror.
>
> At both premiere screenings the movie left the deepest impression. There was no disruption, no opposition. The incomparable power of the moving art of picture and sound, of sound film itself, renewed inevitably the most terrible hours of war.[4]

The Nazis, however, titled it a *Juden-Schmutzfilm* (a Jewish smear-film) and used it for their propaganda machine. They tried to sabotage screenings and protested outside of Mozartsaal chanting "*Deutschland, erwache* (Germany, Awake)!" Initally there were only 40 to 60 demonstrators but they got what they wanted when the police were called in in strength.

> The National Socialists bought some hundred tickets. Soon after the screening began the well-prepared action against the movie was launched.

It started with nationalist and anti–Semitic interruptions. Stink-bombs were thrown, and white mice were released.

Present were several National Socialist *Reichstagsabgeordnete* (members of the German parliament), among them Dr. Goebbels and Pastor Münchmeyer who encouraged their followers by shouts and directed the scandal.

The screening had to be interrupted.

This led to brawls with those patrons who turned against the terror. The police, summoned for help, meanwhile had to forcibly clear the auditorium.

The demonstrators had the impertinence to ask for the admission fee back because the screening had been broken off. They shattered a pane of glass in the box office and threatened the lady cashier. Outside at Nollendorfplatz the demonstrations went on.

The management of Mozartsaal was forced to call off the 9:00 p.m. screening.[5]

In *Völkischer Beobachter*[6] the Nazi editors ran a "reader's letter" by a war injured "front soldier" who signed with *Heil Hitler!*:

Herr Remarque a.k.a. Remark doesn't hesitate in his shoddy effort to portray the German front soldier as a man who has been shitting himself. With this he supports those convictions on which one can only spit. For this there are simply no words!

It was not the German front soldier who had been shitting himself but those social democratic comrades who, bribed by French money, organized festivities and caviare orgies at home till they had made a mess not only in their pants but in the spittoon.

I have served as common soldier in the West as well as in the East in a regiment that fought at the very front but never ever have I noticed in my comrades the condition insinuated by Herr Remark. This I can take on my oath at all times with a clear conscience.

Reverently I commemorate the heroic greatness in which our German brothers silently knew how to fight and to die. Unforgettable for myself is the storm night in Zlow where our battalions attacked superior forces like lions.

Indelible honor to their memory! They died so that Germany might live!

On Wednesday, December 24, 1930, *Völkischer Beobachter* ran a story with the headline "The Beast of Berlin," reminding its readers that Carl Laemmle, the same "film jew" whose company distributed *All Quiet on the Western Front*, had already been responsible for an anti–German film, Lon Chaney's *The Kaiser, the Beast of Berlin*, made in 1919. The Nazi paper cited the ad for the movie: "A story of mad, ruthless ambitions, a Shocking expose of the Secret Instincts of the Wickedest Human Being in all History." The Hitler paper complained that Jew Laemmle was still an honorary citizen of his so-called "home" village, Laupheim in German Swabian near Ulm.

The Nazis applauded when that "smear-film," masterminded by "impudence and scorn of Film Jew Laemmle," was eventually forbidden and gleefully quoted the reasons given by the *Filmoberprüfstelle* (Superior Board of Censors) under the Cabinet Council's Dr. Seeger: By no means could this pacifist movie cope with the emotional state of war participants; it was not a movie of war but one depicting German defeat and therefore was anti–German.[7] The film, it was speculated, would be able to damage Germany's reputation in foreign countries.

What Nazis in turn expected from German movies, Hitler, three days after his seizure of power, demonstrated by personally attending the premiere of UFA's submarine drama *Morgenrot* (*Dawn*) starring Rudolf Forster, fresh from his success in the movie version of Bert Brecht's *The Beggar's Opera/The Threepenny Opera*. Forster played lieutenant commander Liers, who successfully navigates his U-boat in World War I against the British until the enemy tricks his vessel into surfacing. An apparently harmless sailing ship turns out to be a camouflaged British armed merchant ship which telegraphically summons a destroyer to its aid. The destroyer rams the U-boat, which sinks to the bottom of the sea. In the end, one officer and an ordinary seaman shoot themselves and sacrifice their lives to save the remaining eight, as there are only eight life-saving devices on board. (By the way, the submarine was loaned to UFA by the Finnish government as Germany wasn't allowed any such boats by the decree of the Versailles Treaty.) At Hitler's side sat Dr. Alfred Hugenberg. Hugenberg not only was then head of Universum-Film A.-G., he was also the Silvio Berlusconi of his days. He had been quite instrumental in the *Verbot* (withdrawal) of *All Quiet on the Western Front*. A former leader among Ruhr industrialists, he later built up a press and media concern and used this for political power. In 97 Ufa theaters spread over 47 cities he tended to run the nationalist films that he preferred. He regarded himself the "Lord of Press and Film." He was a co-founder of the Pan-German League and DNVP (*Deutschnationale Volkspartei*, German National People's Party) and was a strong supporter of the national opposition that came to power in 1933. He was Reich minister of the economy and Reich minister for food and agriculture in the first Hitler cabinet, and a member of the unholy "cabinet of national concentration." His objective was to be "economic dictator," and he freely volunteered to remodel Germany.

"…Hugenberg's social Darwinism attested to the continuance of the radical nationalist tradition from the 1890s through 1933. Such nationalism was not a cultural cement uniting men of the same language and customs, but a badge of racial superiority entitling a dynamic state to expand. Inaction was inferiority; imperialism characterized progressive states. Energized by national capitalism, Germany would find her 'place in the sun.' Any citizen willing to accept these ideals and work for the fatherland could call himself a German…. The rejection of political liberalism, the condemnation of socialism, the glorification of militarism, the manipulation of propaganda, the demand for colonial expansion, the call for a strong national leader — all of these themes are documented in Pan-German literature."[8] Diminutive administrator Hugenberg and his friends strongly believed that they could use Hitler as a mere front for their own aims because the "Lord of Press and Film" was by no means a charismatic. He never became a popular figure; as a grandfatherly type he never was worshipped by the women who went on to elect Hitler in masses. Five months later, Hugenberg had lost his political power and was no longer needed by Hitler and the Nazis although, at least for the next few years, he remained in control of Scherl-Verlag and UFA. Ultra-conservative Hugenberg and the "Green Shirts" of his party were buried in a brown sea, unable to control the Pandora's Box they had helped to open.

Rudolf Forster (right) in *Morgenrot*.

The late emigrant author Curt Siodmak told this writer that he met *Morgenrot*'s director, Gustav Ucicky, again after the war in Switzerland. "Where have you been?" Ucicky innocently asked Siodmak. "At least, I wasn't in one of your blast furnaces," Siodmak replied sarcastically.

Here is a list of film artists who, like the Siodmak brothers Curt and Robert, decided to leave Germany after Hitler's assumption of power (and saved their lives in the process): actors Gitta Alpar, Betty Amann, Siegfried Arno, Albert Bassermann, Elisabeth Bergner, Trude Berliner, Felix Bressart, Ernst Deutsch, Tilla Durieux, Martha Eggerth, Friedrich Fehér, Alexander Granach, Oskar Homolka, Oskar Karlweis, Fritz Kortner, Franz Lederer, Albert Lieven, Peter Lorre, Lucie Mannheim, Fritzi Massary, Grete Mosheim, Karl Huszar Puffy, Walter Rilla, Camilla Spira and Szöke Szakall; directors Ludwig Berger, Kurt (later Curtis) Bernhard, Erik Charell, Ewald André Dupont, Karl Grune, Fritz Lang, Anatol Litvak, Joe May, Max Neufeld, Max Ophüls, Max Reinhardt, Artur Robison, Reinhold Schünzel, Detlef Sierck (Douglas Sirk in Hollywood), Wilhelm (William) Thiele, Friedrich Zelnik; screenwriters Robert Liebmann, Franz Schulz (Spencer), and Billy Wilder, a decade later one of Hollywood's best directors; producers Seymor Nebenzahl and Erich Pommer; composers Werner Richard Heymann and Friedrich Holländer; and cinematographer Eugen Schüfftan (Eugene Shuftan), who finally was recognized with an Academy Award for his work on the Paul Newman vehicle *The Hustler*. (In January 1938, Julius

Streicher's virulently anti–Semitic magazine *Der Stürmer* demanded the death penalty for producer Joe Pasternak and director Hermann Kosterlitz, who in Hollywood had his name changed to Henry Koster and later directed the first CinemaScope epic, *The Robe*.) Others who were not able to leave the country in time were murdered in concentration camps, notably in Auschwitz: Hans Behrend died in 1942; Kurt Gerron, Marlene Dietrich's partner in *Der blaue Engel* (*The Blue Angel*), in 1944; Paul Morgan and Willy Rosen in 1943.

In front of those who stayed back, club-footed Dr. Joseph Goebbels, future "*Schirmherr*" (patron) of German film, Minister of Propaganda and Public Enlightenment (whatever that meant), in his speech in the Kaiserhof hotel, Berlin, on March 28, 1933, portrayed himself as a "passionate lover of film art": "I can further add in my favor that I have seen most films made at home and abroad. Therefore I have a certain fund of knowledge and experience, so that I am in a position to give a judgment on things that are in any case of substance." He cited Fritz Lang's *Die Nibelungen* (*The Nibelungs*), Luis Trenker's *Der Rebell* (*The Rebel*), the 1928 silent melodrama *Anna Karenina* starring Greta Garbo (an idol of Hitler's, too) and — Sergej Eisenstein's revolutionary *Battleship Potemkin* which was quoted in Goebbels's diaries as early as June 30, 1928: "In the evening we saw *Potemkin*. I have to say that this film is fabulously made. With quite magnificent crowd scenes. Technical and landscape details of succinct power. And the hard-hitting slogans are formulated so skilfully that is is impossible to contradict them. That is what is actually dangerous about this film." In spite of his admiration for "Jewish" American and "Bolshevik" Soviet movies Goebbels regarded himself primarily a "man who had never distanced himself from the German film": "For many years I have recognized to what heights German film can be led by the power and the ingenuity of the German spirit. One should free oneself of the belief that the present crisis is a material one; on the contrary, the crisis of movies is a spiritual one." While he despised *Der blaue Engel*, which was based on a novel by Heinrich Mann, he seemed to be impressed by *M* with Peter Lorre as child murderer: "Saw *M* by Fritz Lang. Fabulous. Against humanist stupidity. For the death penalty. Well made."[9]

The death penalty would become the rule in Nazi Germany.

CHAPTER 1

"Martyrs" of the Nazi Movement

One of the first genuine Nazi movies, *S.A.–Mann Brand*, was considered by its maker, director Franz Seitz, as a *Heimat film* (home film) with folksy traits. The film begins with a Communist attack on an SA (*Sturmabteilung*) meeting place in Munich, which the police quash. As Fritz Brand leaves and heads home at night, lurking Communist thugs want to shoot him, but fail because Anni Baumann, a Communist worker's daughter, accompanies and warns him. That was the *Schulterschluss* (solidarity) of the young ones dreaming that National Socialism really consisted of the two parts of its name: nationalism and socialism. At home, too, Brand confronts a generation gap and clashes with his father, an unemployed Social Democrat; but his mother is receptive to her son's visions of a liberated Germany.

> MOTHER: Fritz, be reasonable. Is this "association" worth gambling your life for?
>
> FRITZ: It's not an "association," mother. It's a movement — yes, a freedom movement. Our fight concerns something very important — Germany's freedom. A life doesn't count for much where a whole nation is concerned.

Meanwhile, Alexander Turrow, the secret Russian Communist leader (*Heil Moscow*), asks Anni at the KPD (Communist Party) hangout to win Brand over to their side, otherwise Brand will die. Turrow then arranges for Neuberg, the Jewish supervisor, to fire Brand from his job as a tractor operator. Again Anni warns Brand of the plot, and Brand pretends to be a Communist. Cleverly, he arranges for the transport of weapons from the KPD warehouse by his Nazi comrades. But Turrow remains

9

suspicious. Brand is shot during this venture but recovers. Finally, Hitler becomes Chancellor. In this moment, everybody, including Brand's father, converts to the Nazi movement. Only Neuberg the Jew is forced to seek a train to Switzerland while the SA men wildly celebrate their victory.

At the premiere, it was discovered by one SA führer that the posters for *SA-Mann Brand* were painted by a Polish artist. He and other SA and SS members left the cinema in protest.

"To a film like this, the reviewer had to apply strict standards, even though it's in a good cause," as critic Dr. Fritz Olimsky saw it:

> The reviewer gained the impression that in this case some parts fall under the category *Konjunkturkitsch* [kitsch dependent on economic trends]. A film director who for about 1 decade directed cheap mass-produced films has taken economics into account and has chosen a National Socialist subject. The writers S. Dalman and J. Stöckel are mixing heroic pathos with bare-faced, tear-glanded sentimentality, but for a change the "humoristic lights" (so popular with the film people) are not forgotten, in short, all in all the proven mix of feelings with public appeal guaranteed comes into being. The characters are essentially drawn in gross black and white manner: here hundred percent heroic SA people, there hundred percent villainous communists. If a real poet would have tackled with this subject — and only a real poet should have dared to write an SA film epic — everything would have looked different, for sure, but here both writers in their goal to achieve something worthwhile become at many points unusually clear in a way that is rather embarrassing.
>
> That does not make for a good movie yet the joined efforts of writers and director succeed at several points in laying on the audience's agony. Such films we have always called *Rührkitsch* [over-sentimental kitsch] and we have no hesitation in doing so in this case, too. That so experienced men, keen on a big commercial success, this time selected a patriotic subject to which they brought no qualification whatsoever makes the case actually even worse."[1]

In his role as *Gauleiter* (district leader) Goebbels, who by the way found *SA-Mann Brand* "not as bad as I feared,"[2] had struggled to conquer the streets of Berlin. As they knew from the example of early Christianity, after which the Nazi movement was clearly patterned, the Nazis were looking for martyrs to turn their movement into a semi-religious order with the quality of a death cult that prepares others to die for the cause. Two acclaimed propaganda heroes, murdered in the street fights during the final years of the Weimar Republic (mainly against the Communists), were Horst Wessel, a member of the SA, and Hans Norkus, a Hitlerboy. Just a few months after the Nazis' seizure of power, filmmakers, in order to bow and scrape to the Hitler party, went on to transform these legends into movies.

UFA's prestigious Hans Norkus project (directed by Hans Steinhoff) was based on the 1932 best-selling novel *Der Hitlerjunge Quex* by Karl Aloys Schenzinger, who also collaborated on the screenplay with Bobby E. Lüthge, and was strongly supported by *Reichsjugendführer* Baldur von Schirach himself, leader of the Hitler Youth. Hitler honored the project by attending the world premiere at Munich's Phoebus Palace on September 11, 1933, with von Schirach addressing the audience of the gala affair:

Heinz Klingenberg (left) and Max Weydner in *SA-Mann Brand*.

My Führer, German Comrades! There is little I can say about *Hitlerjunge Quex*, for this film speaks for itself. I can only draw your attention to the young comrade whose fate will be immortalized ... for he is no longer with us.... It was at the time of the worst terror, as I stood before 2,000 Hitler Youth members who had responded to the general "call-up" in Berlin. I spoke to them of the sacrifice that was required; of the Führer and of heroism. An oppressive atmosphere hung over this assembly, we had a premonition of a terrible event.... I said that

Manfred Kömpel-Pilot (right) and Heinz Klingenberg in *SA-Mann Brand*.

tomorrow there might be one whom I would not see again. And I said to him, be thankful for having had to take this fate upon yourself and for having the honor, among millions, of bearing the name of the Hitler Youth. Next morning, Herbert Norkus fell at the hands of the Marxist terrorists. In the place where the little Hitler Youth fell there now stands a Youth movement of one and a half million. Each individual knows the spirit of sacrifice and comradeship. I would like us in this hour to raise ourselves to his memory. Let us continue his battle, let us fight with his unyielding spirit. Heil Hitler!"[3]

Then it became dark, and the movie began.

In the presence of Chancellor Adolf Hitler and a great number of the members of the German Government, high officials, army representatives and leaders of the national organizations,[4] UFA released its big national screen epic *Hitlerboy Quex* in one of Munich's finest theatres on Monday. The international press was fully represented. The film tells the story of a boy of fifteen who was brought up in communistic ideas and who, in time, recognized the errors of his way and finally joined the ranks of the national socialistic organisations. The film ends with the tragic death of this boy who dies, a martyr, for the new idea of German national freedom.

A big picture, full of human interest, dramatic tension and action. Excellent acting, direction and story, wonderful photography and settings. Although this picture is of outspokenly national socialistic tendency, it will be viewed with

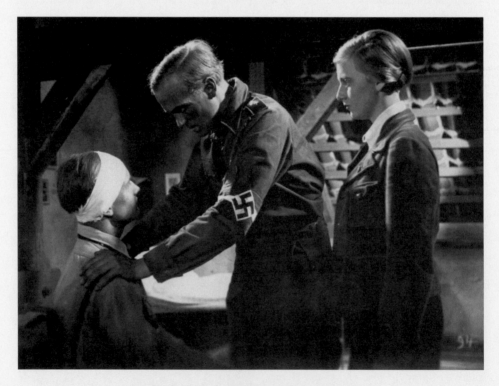

Claus Clausen (center) in *Hitlerjunge Quex.*

decided interest beyond the German border line, because its story will interest everybody, no matter what his political viewpoint may be. Besides it constitutes the best means of information in regards to the real conditions and the real spirit of the new national Germany. The Munich premiere of *Hitlerboy Quex* was the biggest success in years. The audience raved with enthusiasm."[5]

Several days later, thousands of Hitler Youth in uniform lined the entrance to Berlin's biggest premiere cinema, the Ufa Palast am Zoo.

"In the novel, the fictional Heini Völker, a.k.a. Quex, is a separate individual from Herbert Norkus, a real-life Hitler Youth who died in the hands of the Communists. The novel directly refers to Norkus's death and makes the Hitler Youth a conscious role model for Heini.... Steinhoff's film, as well as its reception by the NSDAP, conflated the real-life Norkus and the fictional Völker. The film eventually was widely celebrated as the biography of the fallen Norkus, butchered by a Communist gang."

Fifteen-year-old Heini Völker, a printer's apprentice in left-wing dominated Beusselkietz, somewhat resembles Fritz Brand's sixteen-year-old Hitler Youth friend Erich Lohner, son of a war widow, who is fatally shot during an SA march to a Communist district and will join "my father in heaven." Heini's father, too (Heinrich George, a formerly leftist actor in his first but not last part in a Nazi film), is unemployed like Brand's and, even worse, he is a Communist. When Heini, the song of the Hitler Youth on his lips, enthuses about the Nazi Youth's true comradeship in front of his mother (Berta Drews, George's real-life wife), his father in the next room overhears and comes in furious, boxing the ears of his son, with each slap issuing

Hitler Youth gathering in *Hitlerjunge Quex*.

a line of the Internationale. Although his father signs him into the Communist Youth (supervised by one agitator named Stoppel), Heini remains faithful to Hitler Youth comrade Fritz and his sister Ulla, a proper Hitler Girl. They invite Heini to come to the opening of the new Nazi club room. Heini warns them that the Communists harbor a secret arsenal. To the police he blabs about Stoppel's intention to attack the Nazi hostel. Leaving the police station, he is spotted by some Communists. Stoppel, accusing Heini of being a traitor, harasses Heini's mother by threatening to kill her son. She resolves to kill both herself and Heini by leaving the gas turned on overnight. She perishes, but Heini is rescued. While he is recovering at the hospital, Fritz and Ulla cheer him up with the gift of a brown Hitler Youth uniform. Despite Stoppel's repeated efforts to lure Heini away from the Nazis, Heini, utterly fearless, willing to die, distributes NS fliers in Beusselkietz where he is surrounded by the Communist gang and knifed to death by Wilde, its fierce chieftain, in a deserted fairground tent. When Kass, the *Bannführer* (youth leader) and other Nazi *Pimpfe* (i.e., members of the *Jungvolk*), surround their expiring comrade at a hospital bed, Heini stammers out the words of von Schirach's "March of the Hitler Youth." Upon his demise, in a final flickering of life, multiple dissolves of marching columns carrying swastikas resound with the song's refrains. Baldur von Schirach didn't allow the announcement of the youthful actor's name who played Heini, claiming that the boy didn't want to become a professional actor but wanted to pursue his joiner's apprenticeship. When he appeared two years later in another movie, *Wunder des Fliegens* (*Miracle of Flying*), it was finally revealed that his name was Jürgen Ohlsen. Originally signed for the part of the Hitler Boy, however, had been Hermann Braun, son of *Kammersänger* Carl Braun, who couldn't accept (to his own regret) because of illness. (The ideological mechanism of transforming youth into a prepared semimilitary squad has been the same throughout history: the "Education for the Death.") Many Germans are best characterized as longing for a short intense life and then expecting death. National Socialism was like that, like a religious order or death cult.

Emil Lohkamp in the title role in *Hans Westmar.*

"All those at UFA who collaborated in the making of this film," said Ernst Hugo Correll, in charge of production at UFA, "have achieved great merit, not only in developing German film art, but also in the artistic presentation of National Socialist ideas. Those of us who attended the film's premiere and saw just how moved and shaken the audience were at the death of Hitler Youth Quex, must realize the unlimited possibilities of the truly German film, and the enormous tasks awaiting us."[6]

The Horst Wessel project, which should have been the flagship of that trio of premier Nazi films, was adapted from his own novel by Hanns Heinz Ewers, a writer who in 1913 had scripted Paul Wegener's dual role in *The Student of Prague* and whose antifeminist nightmare novel *Alraune* was filmed three different times. Wegener, the screen's first *Golem*, not only played in the first of these versions, he joined his friend Ewers in the Wessel film and loaned his almost Slavic features to the Muscovite, Kuprikoff, who decrees Wessel's martyr death. He is an "Asian Commune Golem." According to National Socialist propaganda, the original Horst Wessel (1907–1930), leader of an SA sturm in Berlin Friedrichshain, was shot by the Communists; but actually the murder was not politically motivated. In fact, Horst Wessel, sort of a pimp, was killed by a conman, the lover of his landlady.

Coming from waltz-loving Vienna, young Korps student Horst Wessel, in Ewers' film played by Emil Lohkamp, is shocked at the decadence of Berlin's nightlife where he hears a negro jazz band rendering "Die Wacht am Rhein" and indifferently dishonoring the memory of the slain soldiers of World War I. Giving up his studies, he devotes himself solely to SA activities and becomes a manual worker in order to convert as many of his fellow workers to National Socialism as possible. "I'm telling you, all Germany is at stake down there on the streets. And that is why we must get closer to the people; we cannot stand aloof anymore. We must fight side by side with the workers—it's all or nothing!" He even leads a protest march past the KPD headquarters, the Karl Liebknecht house, which results in the obligatory street fights of the 1920s. Finally, when the "Jewish-Bolshevist" KPD is losing votes (and members) in the important Berlin district Friedrichshain, the Muscovite (Moscow) wire puller decides that Wessel must die. Although the SA leaders don't want him to go back to his appartment in Friedrichshain (instead he is supposed to continue his studies in Greifswald), he does so and is betrayed by a neighbor. Riddled with bullets, Horst Wessel passes away at a hospital. His last word is "Deutschland." His last convert, who joins the Nazi movement, is former Communist Camillo Ross. And here the so-called "Horst Wessel Song" wells up:

> The Banner High! Tightly closed are our ranks
> SA is marching with its solid tread
> Comrades shot by the Red-Front and the Reaction
> Are, in spirit, marching with us.
> Clear the street for the brown battalions
> Clear the street for the man from the SA
> Millions look upon the swastika full of hope
> The day of freedom and for bread begins to dawn.
> The alarm is sounded for the last time
> We are all ready for the battle.
> Soon the Hitler flags will hang above all streets
> Servitude will last only a little longer.
> The banner high! Tightly closed are our ranks

Above: Mathias Wiemann (left) and Walter Franck in *Togger. Below:* A scene from *Togger.*

SA is marching with its solid tread.
Comrades who were shot by the Red-Front and the Reaction
Are, in spirit, marching with us.[7]

Unfortunately, not only did the audiences dislike these trio of movies, the Nazis themselves ordered at least the Horst Wessel film re-edited after a closed screening on October 3, 1933, and canceled the premiere which should have taken place on October 9. In a communiqué it was stated that the movie "neither does Horst Wessel and the National Socialist movement, foundation of this state, justice nor is his (Wessel's) historic personality adequately portrayed. So the film endangers the life interests of this state and the reputation of Germany." Involved in the making of the film was Dr. Ernst ("Putzi") Hanfstaengl, an early associate of Adolf Hitler and then the party's foreign press chief. Hanfstaengl had composed the score.

"I showed Hitler and (photographer) Heinrich Hoffmann the rough cut and they seemed to like it well," Hanfstaengl said, "but I had reckoned without Goebbels ... The premiere was arranged. The invitations had gone out. Everyone in Berlin society from the Crown Prince down was to be present and suddenly Goebbels forbade the film to be shown.

"This was too much. A lot of money had been tied up in the project and now ruin stared us in the face. I stormed in to see Hitler and then Goebbels, but the little man had invented a thousand excuses why it was not to be shown, although his real reason was jealousy. It was too bourgeois in approach, emphasized Wessel's Christian background too much, was not full of the National Socialist revolutionary spirit, was trite — everything was wrong."[8] Some time later Hanfstaengl left Germany and became an advisor on Nazi affairs to President Roosevelt.

Two months later, with only a section about the origin of the "Horst Wessel Song" removed, the film finally opened under the new title *Hans Westmar, One of Many*. Despite the enormous publicity the movie was poorly received by Berlin audiences, which were quickly developing a total resistance to political films. (The stage receipts for *Hans Westmar* totaled RM 62,200,[9] while more successful films like *Die vom Niederrhein* [RM 25,400] or *Schwarzwaldmädel* [RM 33,600] cost only a third or half of that sum. Since the film industry wasn't eager to lose money by supporting politics, it canceled further feature film experiments in Nazidom.) Eventually, the SA *Sturmabteilungen* (SA Storm Troopers), the "revolutionary" NS laborers' phalanx modeled after similar left-wing organizations (the Fritz Brands, so to speak), were deprived of power and politically put out of the way in 1934 during the "Night of Long Knives." The "revolution" devoured its children.

Another rare NS film of this time was *Togger*. It dealt with one of Goebbels' favorite subjects: the press. Togger, chief editor of *Neuer Tag* (*New Day*), strongly opposes the sale of his paper to the foreign Reuger trust. In his editorials he decries the damage which he believes results from the Reuger people's machinations. Reuger is going to cancel its advertisements; it plots a strike among the type-setters and even conspires with the paper's copartner who is in need of money as his mistress, a singer, turns out to be wasteful. But Togger remains steadfast. On January 30, 1933, Togger's persistence is generally acknowledged. The press is going to be nationalized. The movies will follow soon...

CHAPTER 2

Triumph of the Will: The Odd Case of Leni Riefenstahl

Producer Thomas Schühly, who had worked with Rainer Werner Fassbinder after an ill-fated Terry Gilliam movie (*The Adventures of Baron Munchausen*) and in between dreaming of an *Alexander the Great* project with Oliver Stone, became interested in another, more contemporary "great," Adolf Hitler. He considered the Hitler story a drama of Shakespearean proportions and hoped to have director John Milius on board, who had proved his "Prussian soldier's nature" by directing *The Red Flood* in which Soviet troops out of the blue invade a rural, peaceful American countryside. After the *Hitler* project folded, at least temporarily, Schühly became aware of what noted German t.v. documentarist Guido Knopp in a series termed *Hitlers Frauen (Hitler's Women)*.[1] So he went out to propagate the idea of a movie version of Leni Riefenstahl's lengthy, blatantly pro–Nazi memoirs. Phoning this writer, Schühly called Leni one of the most outstanding female artists of the 20th century and regretted that jealous people had transformed her into kind of a witch.

"What could I possibly have known, I was only a girl then," explained Leni, working on her post-mortem fame at the opening of an exhibition devoted to her work at the former Communist Potsdam film museum in December 1998. Bitterly she complained that for years she had been pursued like a witch in medieval times although she always had been totally unpolitical, just interested in art for art's sake.

So, was she one of *Hitler's* (potential) *women*? There is newsreel footage in which she denies that, and in her autobiography there is no hint, at least no *direct* hint—

"…(In 1935) I asked Hitler, 'How did you spend Christmas Eve?' There was sadness in his voice: 'I had my chauffeur drive me around aimlessly, along highways and through villages, until I became tired.' I looked at him, amazed. 'I do that every Christmas Eve.' After a pause: 'I have no family and I am lonely.'

'Why don't you get married?' (It sounds like a proposal on Leni's part; or at least, that is what she wants to suggest.)

'Because it would be irresponsible of me to bind a woman in marriage. What would she get from me? She would have to be alone most of the time. My love belongs wholly and only to my nation...'"[2]

Leni Riefenstahl started out in the film business in Arnold Fanck's alpine films, some of which were produced by Henri Richard Sokal, for some time one of Leni's obviously numerous lovers. In his unpublished autobiography Sokal, who passed away in 1979, vividly remembers that time:

> Although her abilities as actress were limited, her personality matched the part and was translated by the screen. Furthermore I hold her in high regard as collaborator, she was mentally and artistically inspiring. This is the reason why I made in succession further movies with her.
>
> Our personal relationship mattered no more. Her many love affairs and tragedies became for myself (as long as this didn't happen during my movies) a fountain of constant amusement. Sometimes they lasted only a few days, but during these days Leni was overcome by the respective partner, absolutely convinced that she loved him. Till the next lover would confine her interest. The partners always were the best in their field: no matter if producer, director, actor, skier, tennis-player, they all were champions and leaders. Her nymphomania, if one could term it that way, had élitist features. Her unmistakable instinct for what suited her let her fall in love automatically with the champion most beneficial according to the particular circumstances. It would be too easy to equate this instinct with calculation. People who are obsessed by themselves, by their urge for self-realization and sense of mission, like Riefenstahl, are interested in the whole world. They are interested in men only as a tool which has to serve this self-realization. They are playing it in a virtuoso manner.
>
> This explains Riefenstahl's later relationships with Nazi rulers.[3]

So how did Leni, a professional dancer and an "obscure" film actress under director Dr. Arnold Fanck, titled "box-office poison" by Sokal and not possessing the slightest sense of humor, become affiliated with the Nazis? By her own will, we might say: by her own will to go out only with champions. Nevertheless, every German living in those times later likes to emphasize that he or she was forced to do something by order. In her wordy autobiography, Frau Riefenstahl suggests that she was forced, too; that Hitler pressurized her into making *Triumph of the Will*— the title taken from the Nürnberg Party rally of 1934 — which became a cinematic epic of small and mass parades.

"...I was determined to resist taking on this assignment." "Speeding to Nürnberg" in her car, she had only one thought in mind: "to free myself from this project." Thus is, allegedly, what she said to Hitler when she met him on his Mt. Olympus:

> "...I am afraid I cannot make this film."
> "Why not?"

"I am completely unfamiliar with all the subject matter. I can't even tell the SA (*Sturmabteilungen*/Stormtroopers) from the SS (*Schutzstaffel*)."

"That's an advantage. Then you'll see only the essentials. I don't want a boring Party rally film; I don't want newsreel shots. I want an artistic visual document. The Party people don't understand this. Your *Blue Light* proved that you can do it."

Obviously, Hitler, who considered himself an artist, appealed to the artist in Leni. She felt flattered. However, one might assume she downright provoked being flattered and wooed. It had an effect and broke any "resistance" she may really have had. But how could *Das blaue Licht*, Riefenstahl's Fanck-influenced film legend about a young girl from the mountains, prove that she and nobody else was able to handle the assignment of political propaganda (although we have to concede that this particular movie had beautiful visuals)? *Blue Light* was Riefenstahl's only directorial attempt up to that time. Her memoirs continued.

"That wasn't a documentary. How am I supposed to know what is politically important or unimportant, what should or shouldn't be shown? If my ignorance makes me leave out some personality or other, I'll make a lot of mistakes."

Hitler listened attentively. Then he said, smiling, but in a resolute tone, "You're too sensitive. You're just imagining all these obstacles. Don't worry, and don't force me to keep asking you. It's only six days you'll be giving me."

"Six days?" Again I interrupted him. "It's going to take months. The main works starts in the editing room. But quite apart from the time factor," I pleaded, "I could never take responsibility for such a project."

Then Hitler became insistent. "Fräulein Riefenstahl, you have to have more self-confidence. You can and you will do this project." It sounded almost like an order.[4]

There it is: in Germany, the so highly popular term *order* which excuses everyone and everything. *Ein Befehl, jawohl, mein Führer, stillgestanden — attention!* Not fulfilling an order meant *Befehlsverweigerung* (refusal to obey orders). Of course there is no way to prove what really was discussed between Hitler and Fräulein Riefenstahl. It is doubtful that an *order* was given, but to speculate that she was lacking in self-consciousness is absolutely ridiculous.

"You, Leni, will photograph me in Nürnberg. This year the Nürnberg congress in *Mein Reich* will be a mass celebration." Does that sound like a harsh order? At least that is what we read in Ernst Jaeger's articles.[5]

In 1939, the *Hollywood Tribune* published a series of articles on the occasion of Leni's visit to the American movie industry's Mecca: "How Leni Riefenstahl Became Hitler's Girlfriend" was written by an insider — and, perhaps, one of Leni's ex-lovers. Ernst Jaeger, once editor-in-chief of *Filmkurier*, the Berlin trade paper, had known her since 1925. Jaeger had accompanied Miss Riefenstahl on her trip to the U.S.A. in the capacity of "business manager" and had decided not to return to Nazi Germany. Hollywood's anti–Nazi league gave her a lukewarm response. "There is no room in Hollywood for Leni Riefenstahl. There is no room in Hollywood for NAZI AGENTS!" the *Tribune* screamed.[6] Leni had to return. One part of Jaeger's series[7] is characteristically titled "A Valkyrie Flies to Valhalla."

What Ernst Jeager wrote wasn't always based on facts but often on what Leni had told him. And so it seemed that not Leni but Hitler was the first to approach the actress. Jaeger claimed that Hitler had amired Leni since 1925 [*sic*], since he saw her on the silver screen in Fanck's *Der Heilige Berg* (*The Sacred Mountain*). He also claimed that Hitler saw *The Blue Light* on several consecutive evenings and that he was fired "like a high school boy"[8]:

> Did Adolf Hitler intend to marry the woman he admired and loved: Leni Riefenstahl? Did the furious tempo of the world politics destroy a romance which had already begun before Adolf Hitler became the dictator of Europe?
> Leni Riefenstahl's career symbolically reflects the swashbuckling fortunes of the Third Reich. Highflown romanticism and unscrupulous intrigues, both masked behind a brilliantly maintained camouflage, surround the rise of Riefenstahl to the position of the most enviable woman in Hitler's domain."[9]

Jaeger let us participate for instance behind the curtains of the second meeting she had with the Führer. "'That night ended at dawn,' Leni later told a friend. 'We sat in front of the fireplace. He said he would bring about situations which would cause all the statesmen of the world to come to him in Germany. The new world-order would be determined by him. He has reason to consider himself the greatest statesman in the world, and I, too, believe that of him. I have never seen him so upset and excited. He stood before me as though on an invisible pulpit, his hair flying.'"[10]

We learn that the Führer didn't usually keep Leni waiting a minute: "When she didn't hear from him for a day, she was frantic with anxiety. But when she finally received a message from him to come to a distant suburban street of Munich, she realized that all her fears were distorted fancies."[11]

"It wasn't my intent originally to become a director," Leni Riefenstahl declared. "I wanted to be an actress." Thus she came together with Adolf Hitler, who once remarked to one of his aides: "I suppose *I* am Germany's greatest actor."[12] Leni shared Hitler's artistic leanings. A witness quoted by Guido Knopp's staff remembers that Leni appeared almost on a daily basis, first at Goebbels's place; then she was seen in the *Reichskanzlei*, and finally she got the assignment to do a short of the party rally of 1933 that was named *Sieg des Glaubens* (*Victory of the Faith*), a blueprint for *Triumph of the Will*. That film was produced by the Ministry for People's Education and Propaganda, by Reich minister Goebbels. And through that project Riefenstahl became acquainted with Goebbels's superior, Hitler himself, which made Herr Goebbels very jealous. What had started as promising in the beginning, with Goebbels courting Leni (in her memoirs Frau Riefenstahl quips that she had to hold up her hands to ward the minister off[13]), cooled down afterwards. Everything looks like it was carefully planned by Leni: "The watchdog of his master [Goebbels] was determined to let any woman get only as near the Fuehrer as he deemed safe."[14] There even were some rumors spread by enviers that Frau Riefenstahl might not be Aryan but those were deliberate attempts to mislead. According to a report from September 6, 1933, she was registered Lutheran in the files of *Zentraleinwohnermeldeamt* (local government office for registration of residents) on her father's side to the great-grandparents, on her mother's side to the grandparents: Therefore her "Aryan origin" was beyond any shadow of a doubt.[15]

According to Riefenstahl's memories, she suggested another filmmaker for *Triumph of the Will*, the Communist documentarist-turned-Nazi Walter Ruttmann, who once made an impression by making *Berlin, Symphonie der Grossstadt*. In his footage for *Triumph of the Will*, Ruttmann employed outrageous trick photography to illustrate a prologue of World War I; the hated Treaty of Versailles; unemployment, inflation and economic misery; Hitler's unsuccessful "Beer Hall Putsch"; his imprisonment in Landsberg prison, writing the personal bible of *Mein Kampf*; first copies of the book rolling off the printing presses; and finally, the victory of the movement. The distinct Ruttmann style, however, didn't fit with the aesthetics of unsophisticated Nazis, who were more on the track of Arnold Fanck and Luis Trenker and what they called *Bergfilme* (alpinist films). They didn't go for Ruttmann's artificial kaleidoscope of history that started with shots of the frenzied German stock market in 1923, a flood of worthless paper money. According to Riefenstahl, "it was a chaos. He evoked the historical by use of headlines and such. You cannot create with paper in that way. The wind blew paper — poof! And the headlines were revealed. Hopeless, hopeless, hopeless. It was awful. He tried to shoot great heroic shots from underneath — you know, like Eisenstein. It was not successful. I couldn't use a metre."[16] Ruttmann's symbolism was considered too "intellectual": surfing sea and surging people made ecstatic to the point of orgasm by the Führer's seizure of power were too heavy, too obvious. In any case, it was never in Riefenstahl's mind to have Ruttmann direct the whole *Triumph of the Will*. He was assigned to parts only, particularly the prologue. To Paul Falkenberg he confided in 1934, "Well, I am a whore, I have sold myself to Riefenstahl."[17] With cameraman Sepp Allgeier he filmed in all parts of Germany and tried to finish his work in October in Babelsberg. Riefenstahl's change of mind about using Ruttmann seems to have something to do with Hitler visiting her in the cutting room on December 6, 1934. From then on *Triumph of the Will* was no more a record of the movement but a national document. In the end the prologue was abandoned completely.

Interestingly enough, Riefenstahl had cannibalized her former lover Fanck and taken away some of his best cameramen like the aforementioned Sepp Allgeier, and his ideas. She had used him to further her career. She was jealous of Marlene Dietrich, of course, who had become a "*Weltstar* [international star]"; there was a rivalry between the women that lasted till Leni's old age. After finishing another of Fanck's ventures, *SOS Iceberg*, she wanted to prove herself in a *real* feature film that required some acting (and not only surviving in the mountains). In 1933 she proposed to UFA *Mademoiselle Docteur*, a story suggested by Fanck, who had worked with that character of German espionage. It certainly should outdo Greta Garbo's *Mata Hari*. Although Leni was not the greatest actress on the screen, she was in real life. She belonged to that rare breed that was able to cry on demand.

"But then I got a telephone call from the Reich Chancellery asking me to be there the next day at 4 p.m.; the Führer wanted to see me. I didn't have the courage to say no."[18] We also could assume she had no interest in having that courage — just the opposite.

Leni Riefenstahl would have worked for practically any political regime. If she had lived in Soviet Russia she would have found a way to the Kremlin and into Stalin's inner sanctum; in Italy she would have embraced boastful Duce Benito Mussolini;

in Britain she would have joked with cigar-smoking Winston Churchill. German post-war actor Mathieu Carrière, sitting with a depressing Helmut Berger, compared his fellow actors with prostitutes, thus sharing Ruttmann's sentiments. So Leni Riefenstahl seems to have been only interested in three things: in power — in money — in her own career. And that was exactly what Hitler promised her: "You will have a villa, such as you never even dreamt of. You will have your own film studio. Nothing, neither expense nor lack of money can obstruct my plans!"[19] As a first gift she received a deluxe leather edition of *Mein Kampf*. Leni was able to immediately capitalize on big displays of emotion and generosity. And that was exactly what Hitler gave to her; at least she remembers it that way. "I would like to make you an honorable offer, consistent with your talent. As you know, Dr Goebbels, as Minister of Propaganda, is responsible not only for the press, but also for theatre and cinema. But since he has no experience in the area of films I thought of you. You could work at his side and be in charge of the artistic aspect of the German cinema." German cinema, the whole film industry being offered to her on a silver platter! "These words made me dizzy." Bravely Miss Riefenstahl resisted the tempting offer. "'My Führer,' I said, 'please forgive me, but I do not feel that I could take on this honorable task.'"

Unbelievable that she should, that she could have resisted. Or didn't Hitler court her enough? (It needed hours to "convince" Romania's wire-puller, Elena Ceausescu, a similarly self-willed person to Leni, who ended being shot with her husband in 1989, to take on a leading position in the Communist state.) Riefenstahl even refused to do a "faithful" film version about Horst Wessel's life, and later, while visiting Goebbels, declined to make a movie about the Propaganda Minister's pet subject about the press called *The Seventh Great Power*. Instead her most ardent wish was to play Kleist's *Penthesilea*. She ended up doing a short film about the fifth party rally in the history of the National Socialist German Workers' Party, the above mentioned *Victory of Faith*. Why did she refuse all biggies and consent to do only a tiny bit? Might it be that her memory about certain incidents fails her? Might it be that actually all the hard work on her part could only get her the short film assignment? She had nothing in the wings. UFA had cancelled the *Mademoiselle Docteur* project. The Ministry of Defense wasn't interested in spy films at all. Nevertheless Riefenstahl was fortunate, because out of *Victory of Faith* grew the seed of a much bigger "documentary" about the next Nürnberg party rally.

"There is little doubt, however, that no director or producer could have made a film such as *Triumph of the Will* without having an avid interest in the subject: Hitler and the Nazi party. Moreover, *Triumph of the Will* could not have been turned into the outstanding film that it is, if the director had not also been an artist. Riefenstahl's skill as a filmmaker is as evident in the production as her homage to Hitler. As a matter of fact, the well-known (late) German actress, Hildegard Knef, recalls having heard Riefenstahl say that she had a vision when she first listened to Hitler speak. 'I saw the surface of the earth as a semiglobe,' Riefenstahl reportedly said. 'It opened up, and a huge fountain gushed forth into the sky and fell right back to earth. It was as if the entire surface of the earth was being whipped by a storm.'"[20]

The film opens with a title card that it was produced by order of the Führer:

On September 5, 1934,
20 years after the outbreak of world war,
16 years after Germany's woe and travail began,
19 months after the start of Germany's rebirth,
Adolf Hitler flew once more to Nürnberg to muster his
Faithful followers…
1934, the Party Congress.

Christ-like, Hitler is descending from the skies by airplane. "Some day in the future you will make a film for me against the Catholic church," Hitler once had announced to Leni. He had explained to her his hatred of the power of the Catholic church: "The church paralyzed the might of the state; it folded the hands of men in prayer instead of clenching their fists for fighting. He abused all the movie producers who ended their pictures with silly and clumsy bowing and kneeling before the Madonna and the saints. The converted Catholic had a willing pupil in the Lutheran girl who never went to church or felt the need of prayer. The coming Germany would not bow to holy images. It would bow to and honor and have faith in the principles and leaders of the party — in him. The glitter of the holy mass and altars would disappear from the screen and be replaced by pictures glorifying the party."[21] Although we do not see the Führer (because he wasn't at all in that particular plane), everybody seems to feel his presence. Siegfried Kracauer in his study "From Caligari to Hitler" even went so far to compare Hitler, flying through the "marvellous clouds," with "a reincarnation of All-Father Odin, whom the ancient Aryans heard raging with his hosts over the virgin forests." While the plane's shadow passes over the columns that march through the old streets of Nürnberg, the "Horst Wessel Lied" is played. Walter Frentz's hand-held camera is behind Hitler riding in a limousine. (Frentz eventually became the Führer's personal cameraman. We will hear more of him later.)

Later, as night falls over the city, a mob of thousands of fanatics gathers. "In front of the Führer's hotel the crowd pushes forward in the dark night. The army marches up. Torches and searchlights break through the evening darkness. In large, beaming lights a welcome shines from the hotel: 'Heil Hitler!' The army band groups in a ceremonious circle, the grey steel helmets gleam in the dazzling light. The conductor raises his baton. On up to the starry sky there rise the festive melodies of the tattoo. Again and again the Führer appears at his window, again and again he is cheered by the cheerful and exalted people on this festive, happy evening."[22]

Next day, city and masses awake:

Youngsters, roused by drums and bugles, wash at a hewn trough, spray each other with hoses, help one another to spruce up. They give the cooks a hand to stoke fires under huge cauldrons of porridge, retrieved boiled puddings and vast bunches of frankfurters from scalding pots, and line up for breakfast with their billycans. It is very jolly, like a Scout jamboree, with laughter and brisk businesslike music. Horsing around, they wrestle on piggyback, hold mock chariot races, toss one another of their number sky high from a blanket. Comradeship is the message here; and they are clearly having a lot of fun. A five-minute folk parade follows — all lederhosen, dirndls and concertina music — then the Horst

Wessel anthem breaks through again as Hitler arrives to review a troop of flag bearers before being swept on. Once more we see the crowds, and never far away the children, straining for a glimpse of Hitler, the young girls, all good honest folk. The air is one of hope."[23]

In Ray Müller's film about *Die Macht der Bilder* (*Leni Riefenstahl—The Power of Images*), Leni Riefenstahl denies that her movie is a documentary. One of the reasons is that there are only a few selective speeches filmed in the Luitpold Hall. It opens with what the Deputy Führer, Rudolf Hess, in storm trooper dress, had to say to a beaming Hitler: "*You* are Germany! When you act, the nation acts; when you judge, the people judge!" He finishes ecstatically, "*Heil Hitler! Sieg Heil! Sieg Heil! Sieg Heil!*"

There follow brief, empty excerpts from the speeches of twelve other Nazi leaders: Adolf Wagner, district leader (*Gauleiter*) of Bavaria; Alfred Rosenberg, Reich leader of the Foreign Policy Office and commissioner for supervision of ideological education of the NSDAP, author of *The Myth of the 20th Century*; Otto Dietrich, Reich press chief; Dr. Fritz Todt, general inspector for the German road system; Fritz Reinhardt, head of the official NSDAP School of Orators; Walter Darré, Reich Minister of Agriculture; Julius Streicher, district leader of Franconia, publisher of *Der Stürmer* (The Stormtrooper), who insists that a nation that does not value its racial *purity* will perish; Robert Ley, leader of the Reich Labor Front; Hans Frank, Reich Minister of Justice (and once Hitler's personal advocate); and Dr. Joseph Goebbels. Finally, Konstantin Hierl introduces the men of the Reich Labor Service, Germany's answer to unemployment, the misery of the Great Depression—fifty thousand of them. Each man carries a spade as if it were a rifle.

Hitler greets them, "Heil, worker volunteers!"

The corpsmen answer, "Heil, my Führer!"

Shots of Hitler and Hierl watching the demonstration.

"Here we stand. We are ready to carry Germany into a new era. Germany!" thousands of throats promise.

There follow close-ups of several worker individuals.

"Comrade, where are you from?" one of them asks.

"I come from Friesia," a young worker replies.

"And you, comrade?"

"From Bavaria."

"And you?"

"From Kaiserstuhl."

"And you?"

All parts of Germany united in the *Volksgemeinschaft*: Pomerania—Konigsberg—Silesia—the coastlands—the Black Forest—Dresden—the Danube—the Rhine—the Saar.

"*One People, one Führer, one Reich!* Today we are all workers together and we are working with iron."

ALL. With iron.
ONE. With mortar.
ALL. With mortar.

ONE. With sand.

ALL. With sand.

ONE. We are diking the North Sea.

ALL. We greet you, German worker.

ONE. We are planting trees.

ALL. Forests everywhere.

ONE. We are building roads.

ALL. From village to village, from town to town.

ONE. We are providing new fields for the farmer.

ALL. Fields and forests, fields and bread — for Germany!

SONG. We are true patriots, our country we rebuild. We did not stand in
the trenches amidst the exploding grenades but nevertheless we are soldiers.

VARIOUS. From one end of Germany to the other. Everywhere, in the
north, in the west, in the east, in the south, on the land, on the sea, and
in the air. Comrades, down with the Red Front and reaction.

"Its artificiality appears awkward to modern eyes, and it is not easy to resist
comparison with Hollywood's Seven Dwarfs as the young men shoulder their shov-
els and march off to work, singing."[24]

"Comrades, by Red-Front and reaction killed ... you are not dead, you are
alive — in Germany." Germany, the order of a death cult, populated by work *soldiers*
who haven't forgotten the battlegrounds of Langemark, Tannenberg, Liège, Verdun
and others.

Triumph of the Will is, in great parts, a male movie, as the Nazi movement was
a male one featuring certain anti-women aspects, but a movie schizophrenically made
from the viewpoint of a female. This is a contradiction only at first glance since the
party had been elected massively by women who, as female national comrades, wives
and mothers, were supposed to sacrifice themselves in favor of husband and children and see such sacrifice as the greatest good (this phenomenon is depicted in Gustav Ucicky's 1939 production of *Mutterliebe*). (Hitler himself, according to some
historians, might have been a crypto-homosexual; at least he was a Narcissus, who
absolutely believed in his prophecies and saw himself as Germany's savior. In his attitude towards women he was pre-pubescent.) *Triumph of the Will* reflects much of
the Nazis' and Hitler's personal sado-masochism. A torchlit rally of SA storm troopers ("People, take your guns!") is addressed and placated by their leader, Viktor Lutze,
who succeeded the unfortunate SA leader Ernst Röhm (who was a declared homosexual), a victim of Hitler's hatred, which rendered the once powerful SA
insignificant: "Comrades! Many of you who are here tonight know me from those
first years of our movement when I marched with you in your rank and file as an SA
man. I am as much of an SA man now as I was then. We SA men have known only
one thing: fidelity to, and fighting for the Führer."

American journalist William L. Shirer, an eyewitness, remembers the feeling of
the event more clearly than Riefenstahl's cameras. "Hitler faced his S.A. stormtroop-
ers today[25] for the first time since the bloody purge. In a harangue to fifty thousand
of them, he 'absolved' them from blame for the Röhm revolt. There was consider-
able tension in the stadium and I noticed that Hitler's own S.S. bodyguard was drawn

up in front of him, separating him from the mass of brownshirts. We wondered if just one of those fifty thousand brownshirts wouldn't pull a revolver, but no one did."[26]

Then there are sunlit scenes of masses of Hitler Youth on the Champ de Mars, the future cannon-fodder for the *Wehrmacht*, observed in their fatal act of education. Hitler is introduced by Baldur von Schirach: "My Führer … we experience the hour that makes us happy and proud … a young people is facing you … that does not know class or caste … you are the example demonstrating the greatest unselfishness in the nation, this young generation wants to be unselfish, too … you embody the concept of fidelity for us, we want to be faithful, too."

Satisfied Hitler looks over the army of boys. "We shall pass away, but in you, Germany will live on… You are flesh of our flesh, blood of our blood. Your young minds are fired with the same spirit that fires us. As the great columns of our movement march victoriously through Germany today, I know you are among them. And we know that Germany is before us, within us, and Germany follows us."

Ten years later, Walt Disney, a producer whom Hitler as well as Goebbels had admired, made a short animated film, *Education for Death*, from the book by Gregor Ziesemer, with marching rows of Hitler Youth, transforming first into soldiers, then into crosses on graves. This short scene is the best comment on what Leni Riefenstahl began. Riefenstahl herself very often claims to have been interested only in art and technique. With the emphasis on dynamic rather than static tasks, she even had the cameramen practice rollerskating. "Such effects were seldom employed in those days. Abel Gance, in his *Napoleon*, was the first screen director to use the mobile camera successfully in a feature film, but documentaries did not employ such mobile photography. I wanted to try it and so I built rails and tracks wherever I could at the rally site. I even wanted to install a tiny lift on a 140-foot-flag pole in order to achieve intensely visual effects. At first the city fathers refused to grant me permission; but with Albert Speer's help it was finally installed on the flagpole."[27]

So she was able to single out Herr Hitler amidst a forest of flags, 180,000 party members and 250,000 spectators and laid the contrast between these masses and Hitler's godlike presence. "The Lord," who has created Germany, speculates Hitler consequently has called him to lead this nation.

Perhaps the most memorable images of *Triumph of the Will* show Hitler, Lutze and SS chief Heinrich Himmler walking down a wide aisle to the war memorial where they are supposedly to lay a wreath. The watchers are squared away into rectangular shapes that symbolize utmost discipline. After this ceremony, Hitler reviews the parade of 97,000 SA and 11,000 SS men and participates in a flag ceremony clutching his personal banner, "his blood flag." Remembering Röhm ("neither the SA, nor any other institution of the party, has anything to do with this shadow"), he utters a clear word of warning: "If anyone sins against the spirit of my SA, this will not break the SA but only those who dare sin against it."

Further parades confirm the idea of Germany as a massed, marching column of men. The closing scenes show the final party congress in the crowded Luitpold Hall which is dominated by a large illuminated eagle. Hitler's entering with Rudolf Hess is accompanied by the tunes of the Badenweiler March and the Führer gives, for a Riefenstahl film, a relatively long speech:

The Sixth Party Congress of the movement is coming to its close. What millions of Germans outside our party ranks may have considered only a most impressive display of political power has meant immeasurably more for the old fighters; it is the great personal and spiritual meeting of old fighters and comrades-in-arms. And perhaps one or the other among you, in spite of the compelling grandeur of this troop review of our party, was wistfully recalling those days when it was still difficult to be a National Socialist. Even when our party had only seven men [*sic*], it already voiced two principles: first, it wanted to be a true ideologically conditioned movement; and second, it wanted, therefore, to be, without compromise, the sole ... and only power in Germany. As a party, we had to remain a minority because we had mobilized the most valuable elements of fighting and sacrifice in the nation, which, at all times, have amounted not to a majority, but to a minority. And because these men, the best of the German race, in proud self-confidence, have courageously and boldly claimed the leadership of this Reich and nation, the people in ever greater numbers have joined this leadership and subordinated themselves.

The German people are happy in the knowledge that the constantly changing leadership has now finally been replaced by a stabilizing force, a man who considers himself representative of the best blood (*which, of course, he was not*), and knowing this, has elevated himself to the leadership of this nation and is determined to keep this leadership, to use it to the best advantage, and never relinquish it. It will always be only a part of the nation which will consist really of active fighters, and more will be asked of them than of the millions of other fellow countrymen. For the fighters, the mere pledge "I believe" is not enough; instead they will swear the oath "I will fight!"

The party will for all time to come represent the élite of the political leadership of the German people. It will be unchangeable in its doctrine, hard as steel in its organization, supple and adaptable in its tactics; in its entity, however, it will be like a religious order. But the goal must be that all respectable Germans will become National Socialists. Only the best National Socialists are fellow members of the party.

In the past our adversaries, through suppression and persecution, have cleaned the party from time to time of the rubbish that began to appear. Today, we ourselves must do the mustering out and the discarding of what has proved to be bad and, therefore, inwardly alien to us [i.e., *Ernst Röhm*]. It is our wish and will that this state and this Reich shall endure in the millennia to come. We can be happy in the knowledge that this future belongs to us completely. While the older generations could still waver, the young generation has pledged itself to us and is ours, body and soul. Only when we in the party, with the cooperation of everybody, represent the supreme embodiment of National Socialist thought and spirit, will the party be an eternal and indestructible pillar of the German people and of our Reich. Then, eventually, the magnificent, glorious army — those old proud warriors of our nation — will be joined by the political leadership of the party — equally tradition-minded — and then these two institutions together will educate and strengthen the German man, and carry on their shoulders the German state, the German Reich.

At this hour tens of thousands of party members are already leaving the city. And while some of them are still reveling in reminiscences, others are already beginning to prepare the next meeting — and again people will come and go, will be moved anew, be pleased and inspired, because the idea and the movement are a living expression of our nation, and therefore, a symbol of eternity.

Long live the National Socialist movement! Long live Germany!

During this speech, Hitler shouted himself, as always, into hysterics which must have had a comic effect on foreigners (just remember what Chaplin made out of it in *The Great Dictator*, a movie Hitler saw twice). Then Hess finishes the party rally by exclaiming the Führer's motto, "The party is Hitler, but Hitler is Germany: just as Germany is Hitler. Sieg Heil! Sieg Heil! Sieg Heil!"

The film ends with the infectious singing of the "Horst Wessel Lied."

To coordinate all this, a monumental task, Leni Riefenstahl claims to have had only ten days of preparation. Everybody who knows a little bit about filmmaking will realize that this would have been utterly impossible. No, Riefenstahl prepared carefully and extensively, assisted by district leader and *Frankenführer* Julius Streicher, Albert Speer and the cameramen she partly had taken away from her former "mentor" Arnold Fanck. Leni later, in 1977, saw it as a "pure[ly] historical film…. It reflects the truth as it was then." So truth is changing, and also motives are changing. In fact, *Triumph of the Will* was a declaration of love to Hitler (and was announced that way in the official release papers). With Riefenstahl and Hitler it was two hysterics coming together.

Ernst Jaeger, who had helped Leni with "writing" the show, indirectly denied that there were only ten days of preparation when he confirmed that everything was carefully rehearsed, like a big stage play.

"Nürnberg 1934… Ceaselessly Hitler and Leni Riefenstahl examined every hall, every staircase, every platform. He approved the position of the loudspeakers where he would appear, he determined how the movie cameras would follow him. At these rehearsals he learned to smile again. What no one else dared to tell him, she would prescribe in the matter of fact tone of the director: We will have to use some stuff to keep your hair in place; we will have to cut your hair shorter… The often caricatured cowlick was to be shortened two and a half inches by the shears of this Delila. 'And that dreadful cap must go,' she told him. Hitler was adamant. The visored officer's cap was part of the official uniform. But he promised to take it off, as often as possible."[28]

Hitler "rewarded her with one of the most pompous premières Germany had ever witnessed. All the government officials, all the foreign representatives were in the theatre. Then, Hitler made an appearance with light-footed nonchalance, on the wide balcony of Germany's largest theatre. Before he entered his box he paused. Sitting in the next loge he saw the much-whispered-about mother of Leni Riefenstahl, from Russia. Before 2300 people he went to her seat, bowed, stretched out his arm toward the astonished woman, drew her fingers to his lips and kissed them. Behind 2300 electrified gasps there was but one thought—'Queen Mother!'"[29]

On May 1, 1935, Goebbels awarded Miss Riefenstahl the National Film Prize for *Triumph of the Will*. "This film represents an exceptional achievement in the film production of the past year. It is closely relevant to us because it reflects the present: it describes in unprecedented scenes the gripping events of our political existence. It is a filmed grand vision of our Führer, who is shown here for the first time on the screen in the most impressive manner. The film has successfully overcome the danger of becoming a mere propaganda feature [!]. It has lifted up the harsh rhythm of our great epoch to eminent heights of artistic achievement. It is a monumental film, thundering with the tempo of marching columns, based on iron principles redhot with creative passion."

Obviously, Hitler himself addressed Leni on that occasion and thanked her for much needed inspiration, for being his muse:

> I have struggled just as you have. You with a film and I to rearm the German people.
>
> The apparent confusion of high politics is quite as simple as the film industry.
>
> The generals, the experts, the professors, the research men, all laid before me thick reports on the new armament laws. Naturally, they remarked that their reports were not final; they still had to be reconsidered; the time was not yet ripe. Our foreign diplomacy stood in the way.
>
> One Friday night it suddenly struck me. That night I had to push it through once and for all. I said to myself — "now you will do it just like Leni did."
>
> I took my scissors and began to snip off parts of the drafts and reports. The entire armament law, which again introduces general compulsory conscription despite the provisions of the Versailles Treaty, I cut down to a bare quarter page in the book of laws. "Every German is liable for conscription" and a few more such sentences and the numbers of the paragraphs besides. It pleased me very much.
>
> It was 2 o'clock in the morning. I ordered my airplane for Berlin. I telegraphed ahead to gently prepare the members of the cabinet to be ready for a meeting on Saturday.
>
> I went at them, one after another. First came Dr. Goebbels. Ach, he was an easy mark, he went over to my side very quickly. Then Goering, Frick and the Army. Then, after I had them all lined up, I had my Foreign Minister Herr von Neurath sent in.
>
> "Why do you want to hold out against me, Herr von Neurath?" I said. "All my men agree on this new armament law and want to close it today. Why should I wait still another year or two? Now you too will say yes!"
>
> What could he do? One has to use such tricks to take them by surprise, and I knew there would be no war...[30]

All those who still deny that Riefenstahl created a propaganda piece and claim it was a documentary or who see the result "somewhere between the two," like David B. Hinton or Richard Corliss, who termed *Triumph of the Will* "a sympathetic documentary of a propaganda event" (Richard Corliss, "Leni Riefenstahl: A Bibliography," *Film Heritage* [Fall 1969], p. 30), should read the expensive souvenir program, "Hinter den Kulissen des Reichsparteitagsfilms," which is pure propaganda. Riefenstahl compares the rhythm of editing to dancing. Having been a ballet dancer, she absolutely felt prepared for this tough job. In cutting the miles of footage, sixty-one hours, in a tiny barrack in Berlin S.O., Leni sealed herself off from the outside world, talking to none, "not even to my mother." The first week she worked twelve hours a day, the second week fourteen, then sixteen. She worked so fanatically that some of her employees became ill. During the making of this movie, Leni found out "that I had a definite talent for documentaries," and so, while still considering herself to be another Marlene Dietrich (and starring in *Penthesilea*) and after finishing *Day of Freedom*— a short to placate the military who felt short-changed in *Triumph of the Will*; it depicted nothing other than army exercises and tanks— she went on to shoot the two-part 1936 *Olympic Games* movies for her own company, the Olympia Film Inc., which meant prestige as well as big business for her. In those films, Hitler was reduced to just an extra, a prominent spectator. (During these days, Leni had exchanged her "lover" Hitler for American athlete and 1938's Tarzan Glenn Morris.)

War wasn't the time for Fräulein Riefenstahl. Now she herself was reduced to a prominent spectator and labored on a feature film, *Tiefland*, which was released after the war. *Tiefland* by Eugene D'Albert was Adolf Hitler's favorite opera, and Riefenstahl's movie was sort of a last declaration of love and farewell to the dictator. Then, in 1948 and 1949, came *denazification*. Proudly, Leni Riefenstahl in her memoirs cites a passage from the statement of justification which insinuates in her favor that she couldn't possibly have been an anti–Semite.[31]

This from the decision of the Baden State Commission for Cleansing, Decision Chamber Freiburg (1949):

> It is formally established that Frau Leni Riefenstahl was not a member of the Nazi Party or any of its divisions; consequently, there is no suspicion of guilt under Directive 38. However, it remains to be examined, if and to what extent Frau Riefenstahl promoted the National Socialist tyranny in other ways through her cooperation with the party or its divisions; or, if she emerges as a beneficiary of the same. For this part of the examination, the accused must not be presumed guilty, but on the contrary, full proof of guilt must be established.
>
> The investigation into the relationships of Frau Riefenstahl with leading personalities of the 'Third Reich' proves that, contrary to the many widespread rumors and assertions made by the public and in the press, no relationships were established that went beyond what was necessary for the execution of her artistic undertakings. In particular, no proof could be found to justify the claim that a close personal, or even intimate, relationship with Hitler existed. The completed investigations of the American and French occupation authorities have produced the same results. There was not a single witness or piece of evidence to prove that a close relationship existed between Hitler and Riefenstahl. Furthermore, this conclusion is supported by numerous sworn affidavits, several of which are from Hitler's immediate circle. The interrogation of Frau Riefenstahl conducted by the chamber did not shake the chamber's conviction, but rather, strengthened it. Frau Riefenstahl proved herself to be a thoroughly honest [!] and believable [!] witness, and even where her own statements could have been unfavorable to her, she did not hold back or try to vacillate in her responses....
>
> Frau Riefenstahl never strove to, nor did she exercise any influence upon the political decisions of the rulers of the 'Third Reich.' She had absolutely nothing to do with politics either before or after the Nazi takeover of power but rather was completely involved in her artistic concerns. To produce propaganda for the Nazi Party was far removed from her thoughts [!].
>
> ...Frau Riefenstahl at first emphatically refused to accept the commissions and undertook them only upon the repeated and irrevocable instructions of Hitler; therefore she lacked the clear intentions of consciously producing propaganda for

the Nazis. Her efforts were aimed at producing a documentary film rather than political propaganda. After the film was critically received as a very important piece of film art [!], it is not the fault of the creator that the Nazis decided to exploit it for propaganda purposes at home and abroad. None of the presumptions necessary for a *dolus eventualis* can be accepted. The prizes earned by the film and its rating by international juries and press reports show that the film was not regarded abroad as propaganda. The extreme hate with which Riefenstahl was pursued [!] by Goebbels and members of the Propaganda Ministry is proof of the fact that she was never recognized as a propagandist for the "Third Reich" by the regular party circles. Frau Riefenstahl never agreed to make propaganda or agitation films such as *Jud Süss*, even though such offers had been made to her (the Horst Wessel film and the Grossmacht-Presse film). In this connection, it must also be pointed out that at the time of filming of the Party Rally film, the anti–Semitic Nürnberg laws had not yet been passed and the Jewish pogroms had not yet taken place. Also, the war preparations of Hitler were not yet known by outsiders, and the true nature of the movement was still disguised. For that reason, a guilty sentence on the promotion of the Nazi tyranny cannot be reached. It contradicts the facts to say that Frau Riefenstahl was an "indisputable propagandist for the National Socialists." She had, moreover, maintained friendships to the last moment with Jews, and during the Nazi regime had employed non–Aryans in her film work and had protected them from Nazi persecution. The "Heil Hitler" greeting was not customary in her circle....

To examine to what extent her competitors in the film industry were involved in the propagation of misleading rumors about Frau Riefenstahl is not the business of the court; the task of the court was only to examine the veracity of the rumors, and the court's findings were negative. In order that no formal or material incriminations against Frau Riefenstahl shall emerge, the court with a majority vote hereby declares Frau Riefenstahl to be "not in violation of the law."[32]

Nonetheless, due to the protest of the French military government, six months later she was classified in absentia as a fellow traveler. "And I preferred that," she said. She went on to fight against being "robbed" of her copyright by filmmakers like Erwin Leiser, who had used scenes from *Triumph of the Will* in his Swedish documentary, *Mein Kampf.* Doing documentaries about the African tribe of the Nuba and deep-sea diving, she waited for her star to rise again and rehabilitate her and wreck the efforts of the witch hunters. What counted for her, was what posterity thought about her being "one of the supreme artists of the cinema, the greatest woman film maker ever,"[33] not being accused, incorrectly, of being Hitler's former mistress, although she certainly had played the coquette with that false rumor.

"Leni had never seriously spoken of marriage before. If in 1933 she would not have confirmed the possibility of marriage to Adolf Hitler, neither would she have dismissed the idea. But from the moment the self-confessed Fuehrer became the Fuehrer in actuality, she knew she could never domesticate the Dictator. This despite the fact that Nazi Number 2 Hermann Goering had married an actress [Emmy Sonnemann] and the people on that occasion smilingly joked that now 'he' would marry 'his Leni.' Yet Hitler never spoke of marriage. She remained his good friend, his consoler, but the days of her consort-ship were over. Leni, always astute in woman's intelligence, knew that if he were to maintain the illusion of superman, he could never again lose himself in a woman."[34]

Leni had to console herself with the insight: "Marriage would have brought the Dictator down to the level of the men he ruled. The mysticism of his personality would have been destroyed by marriage and the accompanying brightly-lit living room-and-bedroom."[35]

"With certainty she is no political being, for this she is too naive," resumed her former producer H. R. Sokal.

> But Hitler finally offered her the means adequate to her excessive ambition for self-realization. So she blindfolded herself for what would have disturbed her, she suppressed what she didn't want to know and found in her almost brilliantly ego-istic intuition the only passable way to serve equally herself and the Nazi regime: the way of a high priestess of beauty.
>
> The beauty of body, the beauty of power, the beauty of desire for freedom, the idea of self-realization of a people without room she glorified in her *Olympia* film, in the Party rally films—and young "beauty-stricken" men set off following this banner into a war out of which they didn't return.
>
> Can one blame Riefenstahl therefore? That is the question to be asked. It is the question about the political responsibility of the artist. Film is an eminently polit-ical medium reaching the masses, transporting ideas which leave an effect sub-cutaneously. So the question about the political responsibility of the filmmaker must be asked. Riefenstahl however withdraws herself above all doubt, to the sublime purity of her high priesthood, into her Holy Grove of beauty and naive Nuba, politically naive cineasts and magazines and publishers acting politically deaf like Riefenstahl, worshipping her and personally benefiting from the cult. Her not coming to terms with the past is so perfect as the life-long illusion of Leni Riefenstahl.[36]

"Leni Riefenstahl came up with numerous untruths after the war," Felix Moeller remarks. "She has already been faced with the contradictions between her statements and Goebbels' notes with a camera rolling in Ray Müller's film documentary *Leni Riefenstahl—Die Macht der Bilder* (*Leni Riefenstahl—The Power of Images*). This included in particular her constant social contacts with the National Socialist lead-ers, which began even before the 'seizure of power.' However, it certainly seems she has so internalized the version of innocence she has upheld over the years that she actually believes it today, without being aware that she was wrong."[37]

> On December 9, 2001, Frank Jensen in the Berlin newspaper *Der Tagesspiegel* reported the theft of valuable Nazi film materials from a cellar in Neukölln. Hanns-Peter Frentz stated that thieves had made off with 98 large-format pho-tographs (duxochromies) of Hitler, Göring, Goebbels and other high-ranking Nazi officials; 20 film reels; and a 16mm projector from the 20s. "Everything I had from my father is gone," said Hanns-Peter Frentz.
>
> Hanns-Peter Frentz is the son of Walter Frentz, the photographer who became the Führer's personal cameraman. Frentz first caught the Party's attention after serving as one of the cinematographers on *Sieg des Glaubens* and *Triumph des Wil-lens*. In 1941 he won a permanent commission as Hitler's cameraman, with the duty of filming the Führer for newsreels and other publicity materials.

Despite Walter Frentz's standing in the party, only one of the stolen films was a Nazi propaganda work, the film *Hände am Werk* (*Hands at Work*). The dux-ochromies, however, were an invaluable record of Nazi history — which the thieves most likely knew. Hanns-Peter Frentz has theorized that dealers in military or Nazi memorabilia were behind the theft; he notes that he had already rejected several dubious offers to purchase the photographs.

According to the *Der Tagesspiegel* article, Walter Frentz, now in his nineties and living in a nursing home, had not been made aware of the theft. The article continues:

How did his father concern himself with his role in the Third Reich? His son hesitates a little. "He has dealt with the subject in similar ways as Leni Riefen-stahl." The father takes the view that he had only documented "what others had done." Walter Frentz was aware of more than just the propagandist self staging of the Nazis, though. He had filmed the production of V1 and V2 weapons in the Thuringian concentration camp Mittelbau-Dora, as Hanns-Peter Frentz knows. And his father became a witness to the SS shooting thousands of Jews in 1941 in Minsk. "He was totally horrified," says the son. However, into his 70s, the father had honored the ban on speaking about the atrocity which he had been subjected to by a general after the massacre.

In the meantime Leni Riefenstahl was preparing for the celebration of her hundredth birthday in August 2002 and finishing her documentary, *Impressionen unter Wasser* (*Impressions Under Water*), part of the legend and testimony of a Riefenstahl Renaissance. She has become an icon of the pop culture.

CHAPTER 3

The Eternal Forest: Blood, Soil, and Euthanasia

The semidocumentary *Ewiger Wald* (*Eternal Forest*), an "allegory of our history and life," was produced under the instructions of the NS Kulturgemeinde (National Socialist Culture Group).

"It must be stressed that the NS Kulturgemeinde is not only concerned with the encouragement and preservation of art; no, it is much more a group for the promotion of a new heroic art.

"The NS Kulturgemeinde will show in *Ewiger Wald*—a film about our forests— just how well prepared it is for such a task! Our ancestors were a forest people, their God lived in holy groves, their religion grew from the forests. No people can live without forest, and people who are guilty of deforesting will sink into oblivion... However, Germany in its new awakening has returned to the woods. All the laws of our existence make reference to the wood. The film *Ewiger Wald* sings this exalted song of the unity that exists between people and the forest from traditional times to the present."[1]

The prologue postulates the subject of nature's eternity, an eternal cycle of Death and Rebirth!

The pathetic commentary compares eternal forest with eternal people, thus representing the German racial stock as imperishable, an eternal forest constantly renewing its youth:

Ewiger Wald — ewiges Volk.
Es lebt der Baum wie du und ich,
Er strebt zum Raum wie du und ich.
…
Volk steht wie Wald in Ewigkeit.
Eternal forest — eternal people.
The tree lives like you and me,
It reaches up towards space like you and me.
…
The people, like the forest, will stand forever.

In several historical episodes (augmented by primitive lyrics) the synonymous bond between forest and people is illustrated: "It's from the forest that we come, and we live like the forest."

A confrontation with Rome is portrayed. Legionaries occupy the forest areas and are defeated in the battle in Teutoburg Forest.

"Als der Süden waldlos lag, zog Christentum dem Walde nach." ("When South lay without forests, Christianity followed forest.")

We see lumberjackers at work. The felled timbers are removed by carts and shipped by rafts alongside half-timbered houses.

Majestic trees are superimposed as the towers of mighty cathedrals: *"Als den Glauben wir verloren, der den Vätern heilig galt, hat deutsche Art ihn neu geboren in der Dome Allgewalt."* ("When we lost our fathers' faith, German kind gave birth to it again in almighty cathedrals.") (—"From the height of these masterpieces, it's the forest, the face of Germany, which looks upon us and which speaks to us.")

The peasants' revolt is perverted into a national farce. It is explained not by social origin and conflicts but solely by the felling of timbers: *"Der Bauer tot, das Volk in Not."* ("The peasants dead, the people in need.")

Frederick the Great, King of Prussia, wants new forests to stand up like soldiers! After each winter there is another spring. The forest grows and with it its people:

"Du blühst, Blume der Romantik, von den Bildern deutscher Maler unvergänglich wunderreich." ("You are blooming, flower of the Romantic period, in the paintings of German artists immortally and miraculously.")

The industrial revolution brings renewed turmoil into the contemplative eternity of the Teutonic woodland gnomes. Sawmills clear the forest of trees. *"Hört nur, wie die Stimme schallt: Die Industrie braucht Wald!"* ("Listen to the sound of the voice: Industry needs forest!")

Dark clouds announce new misfortune: the First World War. Artillery fire fells trees en masse. At the same time it is a Christmas tree which gives the soldiers warmth and security in their shelter.

After the war, watched by colored French soldiers, the Versailles Treaty reclaims what was left of German forests which therefore are heavily threatened by an influx of African blood: *"…von fremder Rasse durchsetzt: Wie trägst du, Volk, wie trägst du, Wald, die Last?"* ("…infiltrated and undermined by an alien race: You people and forest, how do you bear the burden?")

But since everything is Death and Rebirth summer returns inexorably. National

Rebirth is the final gift to the unshakeable German people. A Maypole is decked with swastika flags.

"Volk steht wie Wald in Ewigkeit." ("The people, like the forest, will stand for ever.")

But through German soil (and through the forests), like a bitter irony, leads the *Reichsautobahn*, the asphalted freeway the Führer built. Director Robert Adolf Stemmle depicted the work on this freeway in 1938's *Mann für Mann* (*Man by Man*):

> This film allows us to see the great work of the *Reichsautobahn* from the viewpoint of the worker. It shows how comradeship proves to be the soul of the joint work and remains grand beyond all temptations of private passions. Man for man, the army of unnamed German workers, fighting everywhere, on the *Reichsautobahn* as well as representative buildings, in order to realize the ideas and visions of the Führer and his engineers.
>
> Locations are a *Reichsautobahn* camp and primarily a bridge caisson in which hand-picked workers have to lay the air-pressured foundations of pillars. An earth tremor damages the caisson in which are six men. An enormous squad of comrades does a most difficult job to rescue them out of the muddy grave. So strong is the belief of the audience in the final victory of comrade help that one only rarely has the feeling during the rescue operation, which is outlined impressively in many memorable scenes, that the accident could cost lives."[2]

To keep forest, freeway and countryside *rein* (clean and pure) Hitler and his cohorts implemented a so-called euthanasia program, launched to kill tens of thousands of the mentally ill whom they considered "life unworthy of living."

From the clean and pure all dirt and impurity had to be excluded, washed away. (Hitler himself was fanatically clean; he permanently washed his hands, even after touching his beloved shepherd dogs.) In 1941, Wolfgang Liebeneiner directed a movie from the novel of a writing physician, Hellmuth Unger, by the title of *Ich klage an!* (*I Accuse!*) dealing with the subject of euthanasia in a very subtle way. The movie focuses on a researcher, Professor Heyt (Paul Hartmann), who performs a mercy killing on his wife (Heidemarie Hatheyer), a pianist, who is suffering from multiple sclerosis, by administering a fatal injection. Having been betrayed to the police, the doctor is tried for murder — and it is left to the spectator if he should be convicted.

> "Gentlemen, I have entered this trial hoping to leave it as a free man in order to return to my research of the terrible disease that has killed my wife. I have believed that my case is just an individual one which I have to sort out by myself but in the course of the trial I have learned otherwise. Only by chance have I become a researcher and not a general practitioner. Because of this circumstance the problem of euthanasia hasn't affected me earlier. I am convinced I would have done for other patients what I did for my wife. For the physician has to love all people unconditionally. I am not afraid. Today's science is tomorrow's error. Whoever wants to have successors must proceed. There was a time when physicians were the priests of nature. For them illness and health represented ebb and flow inside the human body, related to the interaction of the stars and the universe's streams. Then physicians learned to reckon and measure. Physicians became doctors; people who cured others became researchers, like myself. Today, however, with mankind setting off to new frontiers and dropping the mental, moral, social,

and religious chains that superseded eras imposed, medicine returns to its origins: from the materialist point of view to the acknowledgment of a special vitality and to holistic medicine. We researchers, too, are constantly aware that there are no illnesses but only sick people; that a good physician must command the same qualities as a thousand years ago, the most important being love — like the first and greatest German physician, Paracelsus, has taught us: "Medicine is love."

Therefore I do not want to be released in order to save myself for my special discipline. I want the law used against me which was formed by the past and which is still effective. Here I stand, Karl Thomas Heyt, and confess that I have released my wife, who was incurably ill, in accordance with her own wish. Here I stand, the accused, but I accuse myself. I accuse the prosecutor of superseded perceptions and outdated laws. This doesn't concern just myself but hundreds of thousands of those hopelessly suffering whose lives we are forced to extend against nature and whose tortures we are forced to increase into the unnatural ... and it concerns those millions of healthy people, because everything ... has to be consumed in order to let beings live whose death would be a release and a liberation for mankind... And now, honorable judges and jurors, I ask for your judgment![3]

Tobis distributors asked exhibitors not to trivialize this serious "art film" by a tasteless publicity campaign or reduce the high ethical value by announcing a sensational thriller: "A short time after its release everybody is talking about this film which doesn't need boosted craving for sensation."

Thirty years after the war, in a letter to *Der Spiegel* magazine,[4] Wolfgang Liebeneiner responded to his movie being termed a euthanasia film by saying the charge was correct but a misunderstanding:

That has to do with the term "euthanasia" itself. In the *Clinic Dictionary* by Psychrembel (177-122 edition, 1958) it is defined as "longing to die, easy death; support of e. with pain-relieving means when death is inevitable." According to our criminal law it is a punishable offence — if it leads to death before an illness would have ended life — just as murder and, if executed at the wish of an ill person, as "manslaughter on demand" (section 216). This difference, which is crucial for the sentence, is often forgotten in common language, and since this foreign word became first known to us in connection with the euthanasia practiced on thousands of mentally ill persons, who definitely didn't ask for their death, your phraseology could evoke the impression that I would have provoked murder with my euthanasia film. My film however deals exclusively with euthanasia on demand of an ill person.

The problem of euthanasia on demand is as old as medicine itself, if not older. Every general practitioner is confronted with it. It was investigated in depth in numerous philosophical, theological, ethical, legal and medical studies, and portrayed in novels and stage plays.

The film was to test if one would accept in Germany a law which would allow "euthanasia on demand" under certain medical and legal provisos. It evoked a general discussion during which the rumor about the killing of mentally deranged persons changed from a punishable horror tale into a public scandal — a then unique occurrence which helped prompt the calling off of the action. The proposed law was dropped for the response was negative, too. Maybe the audience feared not so much the law but the chance that a bad government might misuse a basically good law. This fear — born out of the bitter experiences of the NS time — has had a lasting effect till today.

However, from a Secret Police report (*SD report*) we know that "its (the movie's) main theme is a discussion of the problem of voluntary euthanasia for people suffering from incurable diseases. A secondary theme deals with the question of the elimination of life which is no longer worth living."[5]

One has to know that *I Accuse!* was under the overall control of the "Führer's office" and its director, Goebbels' friend Philipp Bouhler, who was one of those responsible for mass murder by euthanasia, from the very beginning. Goebbels first mentions "liquidation procedures for lunatics" at the same time as planning for the film began, in June 1940. A February 14, 1941, entry in Goebbels' diary reads: "Talked to Liebeneiner about some new film material on euthanasia. A very difficult and tricky subject, but an urgent one as well. I gave Liebeneiner some guidelines." Felix Moeller wrote:

> Goebbels' aims were clear: moral taboos and resistance from the Christian churches were to be broken down for cinemagoers by discussions that are started quite harmlessly. *I Accuse!* served as a kind of reaction test, making it possible for the regime "to soften people's inclination to reject euthanasia without showing itself in its true colours." But the film had to be revised. After the invasion of the Soviet Union and a much-quoted sermon preached on 3.9.1941 by Clemens August Graf von Galen, the Bishop of Münster, who came out strongly against annihilation, it was "downgraded to suggestive hints" by extensive toning down. Both the people's response to the sermon and also advances in the east, which were halting at first, made Goebbels feel that his intended propaganda for euthanasia was no longer appropriate: "I must ask the Führer to look at the question of whether he actually wants a public debate about the euthanasia problem at the moment. We could probably link such a debate with the new Liebeneiner film *Ich klage an*. I am against this, at least at the present time. A debate like this would only make feelings run high again. This would be extraordinarily important during a critical period of the war." (15.8.1941) After Goebbels spoke to Hitler again, there was only vague talk of his agreeing to defer "all home subjects" that could "distract from the aim of victory." Thus the "heated discussions" that Goebbels still welcomed in June were no longer desirable because of the state of the war and the church's protests. Consequently the press were instructed to refrain from discussing *I Accuse!* from then on and "in no case to bring up the problem of euthanasia in this regard."[6]

In the end *Ich klage an!* "no longer seemed to have much to do with the murder of the mentally ill, as obvious connections had been cut, the main problem had been shifted towards death on request and because of the requirement that euthanasia should be correctly treated in legal terms, it could be shown a few weeks after the uproar about the Galen sermon."[7] This change in plot and structure perfectly served as an excuse for Liebeneiner in the post-war era. *Ich klage an!* was seen by 18 million people: "Just how much film enters the realm of serious observation and discussion was clearly illustrated by the special showing of the great Tobis masterpiece, *Ich klage an...* A celebrated gathering of experts were invited for this showing ... but above all, doctors had been invited. The chiefs of Breslau's hospitals were seen together with the country's best-known specialists. This signifies that both laymen and specialists are recognizing the achievement of films, which would not have been conceivable a few years ago. The most influential circles are now fully reconciled to the belief that film must be accepted as a 'witness for our time.'"[8]

CHAPTER 4

Hitler Youth: Soldiers for the Führer

Viktor de Kowa, then well known on German screens as a charming lover and married to a Japanese, directed *Kopf hoch, Johannes!* (*Chin Up, Johannes*) from a script by Toni Huppertz, Wilhelm Krug and West German Chancellor Konrad Adenauer's later government spokesman Felix von Eckardt. The 14-year-old son of a German landowner has grown up outside Germany when his mother leaves with him for South America. After the death of the *auslandsdeutsche* (Argentine) mother Johannes is brought back to Germany by his aunt. But father and son don't get along. Johannes is spoiled, grown up in female luxury, the father embittered and pig-headed. The only solution: a Nazi Political Educational Institution, Castle Oranienstein in Westerwald. There, surrounded by 200 Hitler Boys of the same age, the temperamental and capricious but nevertheless decent son matures into a splendid fellow. In the beginning he resists discipline and community spirit, but a dramatic experience transforms him into an honest and reliable national comrade. Johannes even succeeds in pairing off father with aunt. Happy ending.

This was what one and a half centuries ago Hegel, Fichte and Jahn were longing for: a fearless and disciplined German youth which is living, fighting and working enthusiastically for the fatherland, not for a fee's sake, but in joyful devotion to the people. Today a young generation matures which fits Nietzsche's words: "Where I found life there I heard the language of obedience, too. Everything that lives obeys." This youth which was raised in the ethos of obedience and in the service on the whole is the objective of the Majestic film released by Tobis which has found its competent director in Viktor de Kowa, the versatile and always personable actor and director of outspoken young nature....

41

Among the audience in the packed theatre were many young faces. They were glowing from enthusiasm. Young hearts were beating higher: in the picture — a splendid reflection of a time which primarily and most deeply is their time — they found meaning and the contents of their life confirmed. Perception of and fulfillment in the world are grouped around the three great terms of honor, courage and discipline. The struggle for life which this youth is being schooled in in the National Political Educational Institutions begins with the struggle for oneself....

This youth is soldierly. It knows the term comradeship not as a moral postulate but as a most natural experience deep inside. It grows up in order and in the great freedom of integration and subordination unter the highest principles of man's social existence, not in the narrow parlors of decaying drill institutions, not in the constraints of pathetic commitment but in nature and sun, in all seriousness and dignity, a personal sense of responsibility and clearly recognized aims, including games, sports and exuberance, in a world which had been opened up for them and in which they shall acquire their merits as fit for service.[1]

In the pressbook we read under the headline "Das Gesicht unserer Jugend — The Face of our Youth":

...according to the intention and the spirit of the man who loaned them his name this youth stands already in the big front of a sworn community, inflamed by the greatness of their time and prepared for the most noble service for the fatherland. And so it shall be: hard as Krupp steel, tough as leather and fast as the greyhounds they mature for the very tasks which are waiting for them, introduced to and prepared for a life full of fighting spirit by their own organization.

Nowhere else and never before has been done more for our youth than today in youth hostels founded in big numbers, in National Political Educational Institutions forming the young German man mentally and physically, and in *Ordensburgen* [castles of the order] educating the *Führernachwuchs* [upcoming leaders]. The face of this German youth is already chiseled in its proud shape...

Their work is fight. It praises peace but not for the leisureliness of life. Their peace is victory.... It knows the ethics of observance, of action and of service to the whole. Everything that lives obeys.[2]

In 1941 Tobis produced another Hitler Youth film, *Jakko*. It seems very odd that Hitler Youth isn't mentioned at all in the Tobis notes to their business partners and exhibitors:

The happy liveliness of our youth is portrayed by this film.
Conflicting worlds are confronted true to life and with strong dramatics, filled by interesting atmosphere and delightful colorfulness.
The colorful life of the circus ring, the world of the traveling people in the unreal glamour of a small circus with its light and shady side.
The settled, quiet life of a wealthy merchant house in an old Hanse town with its cultured traditions, its sense for law, common decency and cleanness.
The world of bars with its dubious characters, weak and unrestrained criminal natures.
The magnificent, healthy world of our boys! Through these worlds the fate of

A poster for *Kopf Hoch, Johannes!*

our film's hero leads: the orphaned artist boy Jakko. The brutality of an unscrupulous circus director forces the boy to flee. In a friend's house he finds a second home.

However the uneducated boy has difficulty fitting into the new home. Being a child of nature he regards order as an enemy. Little misdeeds, real silly pranks, a rash deed committed out of selfless but wrong helpfulness and the knowledge of a theft throw him into great confusions and into conflicts with his benefactors and the police.

Only after heavy inner fights in which his young comrades remain true to him does the boy find the way into the community and to faithful performance of his duty.

In contrast, the Navy Hitler Youth, which opens the path of duty until death to young Jakko, is hailed in the contemporary reviews:

Here we actually feel this reality of youth comradeship of which the boys tell their parents and relatives with glowing eyes. Livelily and impressively, Fritz Peter Buch who based the screenplay on a novel by Alfred Weidenmann has directed the transubstantiation of a joylessly rising youthful circus rider into the new comradeship. We thank the director that he doesn't portray this way as a "conversion." With satisfaction all see how one is won not by force but by gradual conviction, particularly one of those who firmly resists giving up his little high-handed manner and his disobedience born out of wrongly understood fatherly legacy ("never bow!"). And what do all boys glean when they see this fresh, sportingly thinking comrade of the Navy Hitler Youth? They are delighted to see how wonderfully natural the new generation is living in a world which doesn't know anything about the educational severity and intolerance of yesterday. Enthusiastically concentrated are all young actors, especially the boyish unspoiled Norbert Rohringer as Jakko and young Rüdiger Trantow.[3]

The next Hitler Youth movie was directed in 1942 by Alfred Weidenmann himself: *Hände hoch* (*Hands up*):

The film opened the youthfilm hours 1942–43 which were introduced by speeches of Reich Minister Dr. Goebbels and *Reichsjugendführer* [leader of Hitler Youth] Axmann....

This film created for the youth and with the youth is an image of the life of German boys aged 11 and 14, an image which in its straightforwardness, not being made-up, is a fine testimonial of their zest for life. It shows the boys in all their exuberance and with the lust for boyish adventures, but behind the cheerful events of this film we feel that splendid fellows mature in these boys— and this results always absolutely casually and naturally out of the entertaining to and fro of the movie without pointing this out accentedly.

One feels: This movie could only be created by a film enthusiast who himself rose in this circle. By one with whom the boys gathering around him stick through thick and thin, one who commands their language in every little detail and who knows and understands the joy of boyish experience.

Such a man is the creator of this movie, Alfred Weidenmann, author and director in one person. One day he appeared with other film people in a *Kinderlandverschickung* camp [kids from the bombed cities were evacuated to the rural countryside] in Slovakia and shot this film of the world of youth. Because they participated with sheer enthusiasm, and because this film didn't ask for anything else than things should be allowed to take their course of nature, zest for life, and thirst for experience the film creator managed to make a movie in which there is no wrong sound, no fabrication, and no stiff behavior. He never shows up with turned phrases and with thoughts which are not in accordance with our youth.[4]

HIMMELHUNDE

Spielleitg.: **Roger v. Norman**

Dialogleitung: Ulrich Erfurth

Drehbuch: Philipp Lothar Mayring nach einer
Idee von Hanns Fischer - Gerhold / Bauten:
Hermann Asmus / Kamera: Herbert Körner

**Malte Jaeger / Waldemar Leitgeb
Erik Schumann / Albert Florath
Berta Monnard / Georg Vogelsang
Claus Pohl**

Herstellungsgruppe: Eduard Kubat

An ad for *Himmelhunde*.

The following is from a report about movies screened in spring 1943 at Central Cinema Quadrath where *Hands Up* was shown with a "documentary," *European Youth*:

April 7, 1943

Hände hoch

A party event which was very well attended. The film introduced one to the life and bustle in a *KLV.* camp at *Hohe Tatra*. Very skillfully constructed, spiced with suspense and humor, the film had an extremely enlightening impact on those parents who could separate only with difficulty or not at all from their opinion to keep their children with them. For this reason the propaganda effect should have been positive.

Albert Florath in *Himmelhunde*.

Europäische Jugend[5]
    A fresh lively film about the state of building of the national youth in all European countries. Entertainingly the awakening of Europe's Youth establishes itself under German leadership as an invincible barricade against Bolshevism and Plutocratism. This film was generally well received and found the right expression in the hearts of the viewers by its instructive format.[6]

Announced by Ufa as *13 Jungen* (*13 Boys*) this 1941 movie was released just as *Jungens* (*Boys*), directed by Robert Adolf Stemmle from a screenplay by O. B. Wendler, Horst Kerutt and Stemmle himself. "While Steinhoff's *Hitlerjunge Quex* took as a theme the shift of views and selfless fight of German Youth, Stemmle portrays in this film the serving action, the proving of this youth at the building of the German national community. The setting of the movie is a small fishing village at the Kurische Nehrung [a sand-bar on the East Prussian coast]. A purposeful Hitler Youth Leader succeeds in gathering the youth of the village enthusiastically around him. They expose an inhabitant as people's pest and gas smuggler and put him out of action as well as clear things up for the sake of the whole community."

    At that time many former Hitler Boys were old enough to become pilots, to conquer and rule the skies for their Führer. As early as 1935, in a Terra movie titled *Wunder des Fliegens* (*Miracle of Flight*), Heinz, a young boy who wants to become a pilot, meets World War I flying ace Ernst Udet, a friend of Hermann Göring's and Leni

Riefenstahl's. Udet, who committed suicide when war broke out, was the basis for the title character in dramatist Carl Zuckmayer's play *The Devil's General*. Heinz' mother, however, is against the boy's ambition because her husband was shot down in that horrible first war. But the boy's spirited enthusiasm is not to be stopped. Inspired by Udet, Heinz joins a glider club, flies over the Zugspitze in the Bavarian Alps in bad weather and crashes. His flying friend Udet rescues him as the Führer needs courageous boys like him. The boy was played by nobody else than Jürgen Ohlsen, famed for his title role in *Hitlerjunge Quex*.

Another Terra production, *Himmelhunde* (*Bloody Dogs*), directed in 1942 by Roger von Norman, focuses on a Hitler Youth glider flying group in a camp in the Suabian Alb. The subject is the need for absolute discipline. The boys

Waldemar Leitgeb in *Himmelhunde*.

secretly repair a damaged glider of novel construction in order to enter a forthcoming competition. Eventually they win the first prize; nevertheless, Werner, the boy who is mainly responsible, is punished by Kilian, the group leader, who strictly forbade their entering the competition. The gliders bear the stamp of the swastika. Incidentally, most of the boys were original Hitler Youths selected from 3,000 contenders: "See the young pilots at fight with the elements as well as in their examination of the conflicts that are evoked by disregarding of an order."[7]

What began with high aspirations of the youth ends pitiably. With the war already lost (and not too many planes available for them to crash-land) the last Hitler Boys volunteered as anti-aircraft auxiliaries during the allied bombardment of Germany and defended the German capital in the senseless struggle of *Götterdämmerung*.

CHAPTER 5

The German Film Academy

On August 3, 1937, Goebbels noted in his diary that action would be necessary to counteract the mediocrity of German films. Whereas officially he had claimed that the drain of talent in the film industry by emigration or extermination of so many Jewish artists was no problem at all, actually it was: "The Führer has had enough, too. I get new forces. Young talents to the front. Remove the old reactionaries. Fresh air and milieu more human. No false scene romanticism."

As Goebbels envisioned it, the German Film Academy should become the training ground for new cadres: a cadet school for filmmakers. Besides education by chosen experts like art director Erich Kettelhut, who had worked on the Utopian sets of Fritz Lang's silent *Metropolis*, the students of the first term were also instructed in the *Weltanschauung* (world view) of National Socialism:

> Essential features of National Socialist Weltanschauung.
> The struggle of Nordic man for his perception of the World.
> (Ancient wisdom of India and Persia. The Greek philosophy of nature. Our knowledge of outer space.)
> About the eternal laws of life.
> (Nature and man. The miracle of life. The laws of genetics. The eternity of genotype.)
> The Nordic man's way into history.
> (The North, Germanic and European migrations.)
> Our Germanic inheritance.
> (Racial foundation: The Germanic people's species and Weltanschauung and their significance for our time.)

The transformation of Roman Universalism into Germanic lebensraum.
(Chlodwig, Bonifatius, Pipin, Karl the Franconian.)
Kings and priests in their struggle for world domination.
(Heinrich I, Otto, Heinrich IV and Gregor VII, Friedrich I and Alexander III, Friedrich II and Innocenz III.)
The fight of the Germanic power in late Middle Ages.
(The settlement of the East. The Hanse and Order of Knights. Reformation and Counter-Reformation.)
The Prussian model and the development of the Bismarck Reich.
The powers of degeneration in the 19th century.
(Liberalism, capitalism, Marxism, confessionalism.)
Judea's shadow over the world.
(Nature and Effect of World Jewry.)
The fight for power of the National Socialist movement.
The building of the National Socialist Reich.
The necessity of National Socialist population policy.
The racial legislation of the National Socialist state.
Germany's rise to world power.

Ideologically, the program of course was turned backwards: justification in history. Thus it was the conclusion that Germany's bright future was that of *Herrenrasse* (master race) and world power, if not world leadership.

As president of the academy, Goebbels didn't select a movie expert but one of his cohorts, Wilhelm Müller-Scheld. Peter Pewas, who later became a promising film director, belonged to that premier élite of hand-picked students: "The criteria of the selection were strange. The head of the Academy, Herr Müller-Scheld, a former dramatist, was looking for the big talents, naturally, but among National Socialist offspring he found more *Gesinnung* [convictions] than real talent. Later only a handful of graduates could catch on." Dr. Oskar Kalbus, a leading employee of UFA's distribution arm and lecturer (after the war, he became director of the German releasing division of Columbia Pictures), described the selection:

In the beginning only girls and boys from wealthy families let themselves register in the Film Academy, but Goebbels categorically demanded that working-class children should be educated to become film stars, too. So the President drove straight to the Ruhr [Germany's industrial area] and brought a girl from a miner's family who had a speech impediment which on the tape recording of test takes became even more evident. The faculty of film art suggested to send the disappointed girl as soon as possible back to her parental home. The President, however, took the disappointed girl to Berlin's Charité hospital where she was operated on at the expense of the Academy, but that operation didn't help in working miracles creating a suitable voice for sound films. After that the desperate President went to the seaside resorts of the Baltic and the North Sea where workers spent their holidays sponsored by [the organization] "Kraft durch Freude." Here the talent scout with an expert eye studied bathing youth in order to motivate the most beautiful girls to enter Film Academy. The Strand Police which didn't know of the worries of sorely tried Presidents of Film Academies debated if the uncanny visitor might be a white-slave trader and if it

should grab him for the sake of youth. The President left the seaside without having achieved anything.

Three years after its founding the Film Academy was closed. Official reason: the
outbreak of war. In fact, it was a failure from the very beginning. One cannot con-
fuse art with (reactionary) convictions.

Chapter 6

Baptism of Fire: Nazi Germany at War

In Johannes Meyer's *Dreizehn Mann und eine Kanone* (*Thirteen Men and a Cannon*), the first picture devoted to German artillery, starring Alexander Golling, a declared Nazi actor from Munich, we learn that in the summer of 1916 a German Army corps on the Eastern Front is in a precarious position, outnumbered by the Russian enemy. They can get no reinforcements, but at least they receive a special battery with a long-distance gun 500, manned by 13 gunners, which has already proved its worth on the Western Front. This battery successfully shells the rear of the enemy to such an extent, that a planned offensive has to be postponed. One gunner, however, a Russian, who has disguised himself, tries to sabotage the military efforts.

Ludwig Schmid-Wildy, known to many Germans as an elderly grandfather on the Bavarian stage, at the turn of the last century started as the original Munich Kindl and in 1934 co-directed and starred in one of the first national war films, *Stosstrupp 1917* (*Shock Troop 1917*), produced by an Aryan Film Company on the sound stages of Bavaria Studios in Geiselgasteig. The movie depicts the heroic fighting on the Western Front from Easter to Christmas: battles with the French, the night of 15th to 16th August 1917 in Flanders, the English breakthrough at Cambrai with hundreds of tanks. Finally, under the umbrella of a Christmas tree, a captured British soldier dies in the arms of German soldiers. The Teutonic tragedy of the First World War as depicted in films like these offered continual twists to inject Nazi militarist and nationalist propaganda. The same company went on with director Hans Zöberlein, a fanatical Nazi, to film another epic about the early post-war years: *Um das Menschenrecht* (*For the Rights of Men*). The plot deals with four Bavarian soldier friends,

Hans, Girgl, Fritz and Max, who in 1918 return to a Germany that is plagued by chaos and revolution. Max, an artist, is beguiled by the charming Petratka, who unfortunately is a Russian agent. Fritz, too, is taken by Socialism. Girgl on the other hand is worried about the new *Zeitgeist* (spirit of the age) but has retreated to the country somewhere in the mountains. Hans, who doesn't want to watch idly as Germany is ruined by the Bolshevists, joins a volunteer corps and fights the Lefties in the streets. (These corps partly consisted of formations of the old Army, partly of volunteers. They were brought into action against Communists, and against Bolshevists in the Baltic in 1919 and in Upper Silesia in 1921.) Suddenly he confronts Max and Fritz face to face but sets them free. Fritz and Max find a hide-out on Girgl's farm; in the end Girgl is charged with aiding and abetting high treason. There is a happy ending only for Hans and his fiancée, Berta.

"*Urlaub auf Ehrenwort* [*Leave on Word of Honor*] is a film about moving human fates in the final year of war in metropolis Berlin. Without doubt this movie which erects a harmless memorial to the unknown gray German soldier belongs to the best of German film industry." Film critic Fritz Olimsky wrote: "To say it right away, concerning the idea and the whole kind of execution, this film is such an outstanding piece of work that it will be short-listed for the state prize; of course, today we do not know how many more valuable films will be released before May 1, but from what has been shown until now this one stands in first place in the candidacy. This was the general impression at the magnificent premiere in Berlin's Ufa Palast am Zoo which was introduced by the overture of 'Rienzi' [the Wagner opera that especially impressed young Hitler] played by the High School Orchestra of the Air Force conducted by the *Luftwaffe*'s musical stage manager, Prof. Hufadel.

The subject could be summarized in one line from the dialogue: '*das verdammte Pflichtbewusstsein*' ['that damned duty consciousness.']"

Fifteen years after the lost war, Germans were beginning to look back more proudly on the "*Heldenkampf unbekannter Soldaten*," the heroic struggle of unknown soldiers. *Im Trommelfeuer der Westfront* (*Constant Barrage of the Western Front*) was a semi-documentary rolling up "*Geschütze aller Kaliber* [big guns of all calibers]," *feiertagsfrei*; it was passed by the censors for screenings on public holidays and religious festivals. Religion means: recollection, retrospective view, regression. At least parts of the German nation in their religious zealotry were going to correct the events and the defeat of World War I in the prospect of a second war. Everybody knew it. There were posters, however leftist: *Hitler means war*. But nobody seemed to care, and those who cared did agree.

In 1937, Karl Ritter produced and directed *Unternehmen Michael* (*The Michael Action*). Set during the first World War, the film shows the German armed forces hard at work on a secret offensive called "The Michael Action." When the action is launched, the Germans experience heavy losses, but they persevere against the British nonetheless, capturing many British lines. Eventually the German troops find themselves confronting the so-called British "Labyrinth," a cement and barbed-wire fortress. The taking of this Labyrinth by the 37th German Storm Battalion becomes the focus of the movie. When the Storm Battalion's commander, Captain Hill, is severely wounded, a heroic staff officer, Major Zur Linden, assumes command and leads the troops against a fierce British counterattack.

13
Mann
und eine
Kanone

UFA-PALAST AM ZOO

An ad for *13 Mann und eine Kanone.*

As described by Roger Manvell in *Films and the Second World War*, the action proceeds to its glorious and tragic end:

Major Zur Linden receives orders to retreat, but he refuses. He calls for concentrated artillery fire on the village which means sure death for himself and his men. With a heavy heart the general, fully understanding the sacrifice the

13 Mann und eine Kanone

Ein Film d. Bavaria-Filmkunst
nach einer Idee von G.Forzano

Friedrich Kayßler

Otto Wernicke

Alexander Golling

Regie: Johannes Meyer

Another ad for *13 Mann und eine Kanone*.

Major is prepared to bring in order to ensure the ultimate success of the offensive, issues the necessary orders. In a matter of minutes the village has become a hell on earth. The major and his few remaining men defend their lives against overwhelming odds to the end. The storm battalion occupies what is left of the village and push forward to the "Labyrinth." The major's sacrifice was not

in vain — but in the interests of the "Michael Action" and of his Fatherland.[1]

All brave combat efforts, however, had been in vain. Didn't the audience of 1937
know from history that that war was lost in the "long" run, eventually, and that the
remaining "heroes" had to surrender in 1918?

This from a contemporary review[2]: "Here we have amongst the many war films
for sure the most honest and respectable.... Major Zur Linden who risks his life to
execute his plan is played by Mathias Wieman with a deeply stirred white heat and
obsession, with seething and power which transform him above his part into a
preacher of terms like duty, responsibility and comradeship. Heinrich George is the
commanding general. His performance is outstanding. He doesn't deliver his lines,
he really *is* the character. When he has his great outbreak, because the absence of
heavy batteries evokes the greatest of dangers for the success of the Michael Action;
when he addresses the storm battalion like his own comrades; when he brings the
difference between front and general staff home to the major; even when at the end
he consults the dead Zur Linden, his experience and immediate mediation of this
experience weigh like a ban, like a colossus on the audience."

To prepare for a new war (and create, as Goebbels noted in his diary on April 23,
1940, not "films about marriage" but "manly, heroic films"), it was necessary to control the German film industry even more. Right after the seizure of power the Nazis
still used the mechanism of *Volkszorn* (people's wrath) against pictures not in favor
with them, thus following the example set with *All Quiet on the Western Front*. But
then, step by step:

> Control of the industry was ensured in a number of ways — at the top, increas-
> ing economic control of the raw materials of the film industry and its flow of cap-
> ital, and by the establishment of strict control not only of subject matter through
> censorship (regularized by the Reich Film Law of February 1934), but of distri-
> bution and exhibition at home and abroad. At studio level, control was exercised
> by bringing all workers in the industry, artistic and technical alike, into line
> through the establishment during 1933 of a Reichsfilmkammer, or State Film
> Chamber, which controlled everyone participating in film production, including
> investigation into their racial origin. All Jews were automatically banned, and
> they were precluded, though other state chambers for the arts, from working in
> the fine arts, music, the theatre, authorship, press, or broadcasting. All workers
> had to become members of the only recognized trade union — the Deutsche
> Arbeitsfront; all previous unions were abolished. Goebbels even controlled film
> criticism; while politically "undesirable" films ... were banned outright, politi-
> cally "desirable" films were expected to be praised in the press for their patrio-
> tism."[3]

But that was not enough. It was intended to have the whole film industry *gle-
ichgeschaltet* (brought into line), the same as the press. By 1937, old man Hugenberg
was no longer in charge of UFA. After complex negotiations, the privy councilor and
his allies were forced to sell their shares (although in 1943, on the twenty-fifth
anniversary of the founding of UFA, Goebbels consoled him by presenting him with

the Order of the Eagle for his work with Germany's leading film company). Tobis, by the way, already had been "nationalized" in 1935.

Like the political parties, independent production outfits had to disappear in order to gain full political control and make German films "*kriegstauglich*" (fit for war). To execute this mission Goebbels had selected a discreet, highly experienced and efficient financial expert, Max Winkler, who had done similar duties with the press through his Cautio Trust Company. The situation was ripe: In the mid–'30s German film industry had been run into the ground by government and was isolated and cut off from foreign trade. It sounds ironic that the Nazi state, which had destroyed its prospects, should take over most of film production and distribution. At the end there was almost total nationalization of German film. The most important of the surviving film companies (Bavaria Filmkunst G.m.b.H. in Munich, Prag Film A.G. located at Barrandov Studios in Prague, Wien-Film G.m.b.H. in Vienna, Tobis-Filmkunst G.m.b.H., Berlin-Film G.m.b.H., Terra-Filmkunst G.m.b.H., and Ufa-Filmkunst G.m.b.H. in Berlin) were subsumed under one giant holding company, Ufa-Film G.m.b.H. (Ufi), so called because UFA was the most prominent name in German movies. In charge of Ufi was a *Reichsfilmintendant* (Reichsfilm director-general) whose duties were production development, political orientation of artistic and mental *Gesamthaltung* (attitude) and artistic operation of personnel as well as promotion of new talent. Appointing managers and approving contracts of employment with a monthly fee of more than RM 2,000 were also functions of the director-general. To guarantee technical development a *Film-Technische Zentralstelle* (Film-Technique Center) was founded by Ufi, with sections for construction; camera equipment; sound equipment; stage technique; post-production; color film technique; re-recording; television; and inventions.

In 1941, the usual, medium-sized film (called *Mittelfilm*) was scheduled for 53 days on the sound stages, more costly films (so-called *Grossfilme*) for 80 days. Directors at that time commanded from RM 10,000 to 80,000 for their services, writers from 8,000 to 35,000, cinematographers about 20,000, stars up to RM 100,000.

One of the biggies, which united the fact of a lost war with the new goal of loving and breeding animals, was Arthur Maria Rabenalt's ... *reitet für Deutschland* (*Riding for Germany*) starring Willy Birgel as Rittmeister (Cavalry Captain) Ernst von Brenken, who in 1918, after Germany's defeat, returned heavily wounded to his estate. Von Brenken's disillusioned, punished condition clearly resembles that of Germany after the war:

> He, whose second nature was riding, is condemned to a wheelchair. Given up by the physicians he resisted death. Now he resists permanent infirmity — and succeeds with enormous energy and a belief in his mission which nobody can deny and take away from him.
>
> The property is heavily mortgaged; nobody fully understands horse-breeding in these days. Brenken remains silent and acts. Marten, his former non-commissioned officer, has joined him feeding the animals. With him Marten has brought the horse Harro that saved Brenken's life in Russia, and that was auctioned and believed lost. Brenken pins all his hopes on that noble animal — he rides to it and gets it nominated, although everybody declares him nuts, for the

Great Prize of Europe at the riding event in Geneva. The only ones who believe in him are Marten and Toms, the sister of von Brenken's friend.

In Geneva there is a true tumult as Brenken appears in the riding arena. German riders and horses have not appeared at a riding event since the end of the war. German riding as a sport should have been destroyed forever, as well as German horse-breeding, because the country was robbed of its best horses. There is an extremely dramatic fight between Brenken and the other participants, then a jump-off between the three best to whom Brenken belongs. Brenken representing the German colors is the winner, and the German anthem is played, which wasn't heard at this place for years."

Von Brenken's role was modeled after Baron von Langen "who after the World War for the first time led the German colors to victory in an international riding event and broke the ban into which the world of Versailles had cast German horse-riding. Germany's equestrian sport had been crushed by the treaty for the best horses had been taken away from it. The German rider seemed to be cast out forever from international competitions. Unexpectedly, a German announced his entry — on top of that a man who not long ago had recovered from a bad war injury. There was a response of doubt, scorn and derision: this German riding in tournament is less treated with hostility than ridiculed. Amongst numerous uniforms of foreign countries he entered the fight as the only one in civilian clothes and — won…. No, the Versailles Treaty wasn't torn apart by this victory. It was not a genuine political action which he accomplished. But he acted in opposition to the unholy spirit of Versailles which only could survive in a defeated Germany, and which only could wrinkle its nose at a powerless Germany in order to rule it. And so this deed of Baron von Langen was an outspoken political deed, a national deed by which he claimed a place of honor, and not only in the hearts of friends of the tournament. Many a breach had to be overcome, many a trench had to be stormed until Germany lined up for the final storm. But this Baron von Langen set a glowing example which started to fruit. A political example which at that time seemed to be so far away from all things political. His deed is an example for the political impact of true achievement. Every effort serves the fatherland because it makes it stronger and helps its reputation. For that reason this Baron von Langen is an example to all of us … and a confirmation of our own activities. It doesn't count if we stay here or there, on this or on that position. It counts if we fill our place, that we fulfill the mission that we are able to.[4]

(When … *reitet für Deutschland* was re-released after the war in West Germany by Prisma Filmverleih it was done so with slogans like "Forbidden for years, finally passed by the censors!" or "Millions have seen this film, millions will see it again.")

The so-called "New Germany" needed its sons back from all over the world as a new war was in the wings. This was the message of director Jürgen von Alten's *Das Gewehr über* (*Shoulder Arms*): A German settler in Australia, who believes his son is becoming decadent through democracy, sends him with a friend back to Germany for military service. After initial difficulties both young men learn to value Teutonic discipline and the "romantic" ideals of a National Socialist Germany ruled by a Führer, who, throned like an eagle in the Bavarian Alps, hatched World War II in lonely isolation. Easy to understand that Dr. Goebbels called this in his diary (entry of November 16, 1939) "a bad *Wehrmacht* propaganda film. Came close to a ban."

In the beginning militarist movies were camouflaged behind the "harmless"

Willy Birgel is riding for Germany in ...*reitet für Deutschland*.

mask of what Germans understood as comedies. Toni Huppertz, who wrote the screenplay for *Kopf hoch, Johannes!*, in 1935 directed *Soldaten — Kameraden (Soldiers — Comrades)*. The film is to be seen as part of the policy of German rearmament: Two young men are called up for military service. Willi comes from a rich family and is rather spoilt while Gustav is a hard-working youngster with character.

Gustav soon learns to appreciate the need for strict army discipline and becomes an exemplary soldier, whereas Willi sulks continually and performs mean acts against his fellow soldiers. In time, however, Willi begins to recognize the error of his way. When a fire breaks out in a nearby village, Willi saves a child trapped in the flames of a burning building. Gustav climbs up a ladder to help him, and the two become the best of friends:

> In Tempelhof Toni Huppertz is directing a movie titled *Soldaten — Kameraden*. This is the first feature film that focuses on our new Wehrmacht; it should become a comedy for general audiences. Four writers supplied ideas, G. O. Stoffregen, R. Schneider-Edenkoben, Hans Helmuth Fischer, and Toni Huppertz himself. In the leads we will see several young actors of the rising generation.
>
> These days the press was invited to a maneuver ball which took place on the Tempelhof soundstages. About sixty 'regular' soldiers of our Berlin guards took part, too. For all shall look as authentic as possible; military advisors supervised the shooting to avoid one of those dull military comedies we remember from the past.
>
> If one looks closer, there is no difficulty in distinguishing the real soldiers from made-up extras. The ladies of this maneuver ball, of course, were professional movie extras. Our soldiers seemed to enjoy this 'film service.' Filled with enthusiasm they waltzed with their respective partners while a camera was moved among the leads, Franz Niklisch, Hans (*sic*! Franz) Zimmermann, Günther Vogdt, Herti Kirchner, Vera Hartegg... Today's recruit life is presented in a somewhat coarse but always tasteful manner.[5]

Comradeship was written in capitals in Werner Hochbaum's *Drei Unteroffiziere* (*Three NCOs*), made in 1938-39 and starring Albert Hehn, Fritz Genschow, and Wilhelm H. König: Various episodes show the story of three warrant officers and their service in peacetime. One of the three falls for a young actress neglecting his Army service completely, but the other two save this national comrade from himself. A short time later war would begin.

Harald G. Petersson was a useful screenwriter in the 1960s when he scripted a highly successful Teutonic western series suggested by Karl May's trivial novels (the novels inflamed most young boys then, even a young Adolf Hitler), starring the noble Apache chief Winnetou (Pierre Brice) and his white blood brother Old Shatterhand (Lex "Tarzan" Barker). But he had already proved his worth in 1939 with his script for *Blutsbrüderschaft*, a comradeship between two young men that started in World War I. In the post-war period one has been sabotaging the Occupying Powers all these years while the other has become director of a factory, unfortunately controlled by the English. But on September 1, 1939, both leave to serve their country once more, together. Petersson also cowrote *Wetterleuchten um Barbara* (1941), which showed Tyrolean peasants before Austria much too voluntarily joined the German Reich and transformed itself into Ostmark fighting for the cause of Adolf Hitler. The pressbook emphasizes the fanaticism of these peasants who jeopardized for National Socialism what their ancestors had built up.

The ideal combination of the resulting romantic mountaineer films à la Arnold Fanck and Luis Trenker and war films was *Spähtrupp Hallgarten* (*Hallgarten Scout-*

ing Patrol), a film about the actual fighting experience of mountain soldiers in Norway in 1941:

> The fifth company of the Marienwald mountain soldiers was ready to march. "Today we move out for a big field exercise — it is the first which doesn't take place in our home mountains. You will have to prove yourself at another place — do not bring disgrace on the tradition of our regiment...!" These were roughly the words which the company commander addressed to his troop.
>
> These words fighter Hannes Hallwachs remembered, just at the moment when he and his comrades brought to the waters of a mountain river a rubber dinghy. Everything they had experienced until they moved out and left their garrison in the Bavarian mountains was practicing what had become their second nature during the training.
>
> They had pursued the enemy for days, but hadn't got to see him scarcely. Everything went on like a big exercise. The comradeship which bound them for more than a year proved itself superbly.
>
> Mountain soldier Hallgarten sunk the paddle into the light green, foaming water. The ones who sat in front and behind him in the boat, did the same. They were filled by the incredible suspense of the hour, which should bring them the first combat with the enemy. Mountain soldier Hallgarten was wondering about the thoughts that occurred to him. Everything was as usual but in a quietly exciting way totally different. What was it really? Hallgarten did his movements mechanically. He helped to make a bridge, carrying timbers, wielding the axe, filling plank to plank — everything went like clockwork.
>
> Suddenly there was the rolling echo of a firing and the howling in the air and the grenade splinter hitting a rock. It was a shot aimed too short, Hallgarten thought. Then everything went in quick succession. The enemy was on the other side of the narrow ridge which cut like a knife into the blue sky. Immediately guns were ready to fire, the pieces of equipment aimed accurately on target, and shot after shot left the barrels. The barrage had to be exact. Well covered, the mountain soldiers waited — but there came nothing more.
>
> The bridge was ready and served its use. Soon mountain soldier Hallgarten was on the other bank, soon he was climbing up the steep rocks together with his comrades, on the advance that nothing could halt.
>
> In the next letter home during a rest somewhere in the forest he wrote about this first encounter with the enemy. The mountain soldier, however, didn't find the correct words to describe the experience of the fight in detail.
>
> These are things one has to fight for himself. In words it could be indicated at best.[6]

Contradicting the common view, there was no romanticism anymore in the once peaceful mountains.

At the beginning of the war, the most popular weapon in Germany was the small U-boat (to his personal regret, Hitler didn't command a great fleet) as seen in director Günther Rittau's *U-Boote westwärts* (*U Boats Westwards*).

> As mysteriously as a legend from primordial times this film commences: a whirlpool is forming in the slightly wavy silver streak of the sea above which a heavily shadowing evening cloud is hanging; ... with a drip-spraying tower and

A scene from *U-Boote westwärts.*

a body as narrow as a lancet a big submarine surfaces. A heavily armed war ship
is gliding now where a moment before nothing has been. Whoever will see this
image announcing the outstanding work of cinematographer Igor Oberberg and
director Günther Rittau, who comes from the camera side himself, in its burning overture will feel what an eerie effect the surfacing of such a steel swordfish
must leave on an enemy trade ship. He will grasp, too, why submarines are being
called "terror of the sea."

The willingness to learn a little bit about life on board a submarine is the higher
as even today the fog of a carefully kept secret floats above the action of this invisible weapon of destruction, which already in World War [I] was bathed in the
light of legendary fame. Today it carries again a big deal of our attacking energies against the island empire. This UFA film, which was made with the support
of the High Command of our Naval Fleet and with the participation of commanders of the submarines and by officers, non-commissioned officers and crews
of the U-boat weapon from a screenplay by Georg Zoch, has none other hero
than the submarine itself: the fate of all these men either touches people's hearts
in novella form or introduces only anecdotally some variety that remains in the
background as it is in reality, too. The submarine itself leaves an impact like a
heroic personality, and the crew in its body of iron seems to be forming an integrated whole.

Two voyages in between a few but crucial hours of shore leave are told in brief
images. The adventures which are experienced on these voyages are typical: danger and success are in the closest interaction. During the first voyage the submarine's barrels don't meet any "*grosse Brocken* (big opportunities)," but the

second time a huge convoy is being tracked down and for the most part destroyed. After that there is a hail of British depth charges in heavy rows upon the deeply diving U-boat. And these seconds, in which the thunder of detonations shakes the walls and in which the glasses of the measuring instruments crack, the light goes out and the danger of sinking too deep is parried with cold calmness, form the dramatic highlights of the movie. The camera moves from face to face and shows the utmost strain of doomed boldness: this leaves such an intense effect on the viewer because he doesn't realize that in the confinement of the U-boat interior, where everybody in the face of highest danger has to remain resolutely silent at his place, motion-packed scenes are impossible.

Fearsome for example are those scenes with the camera showing a torpedo's detonation within the body of a British destroyer, when the crew jumps overboard in wild panic, when the overheated valves hissingly pour out white steam clouds and finally the bubbling waves devour the ship listing to one side.

In the crew of our U-boat there is no "star"; none of the faces has become too familiar to us through long loving acquaintance. Thus a whole group of fellow actors profits equally from the play: all of this is part of the structure of this film full of fighting spirit and couldn't be different. We see Herbert Wilk as a lieutenant-captain who has been matured above his years by the early seriousness of responsibility, Heinz Engelmann as the first lieutenant who fits with an especially effective attitude of reserve into the framework of the plot, Joachim Brennecke, the type of youthfully enthusiastic hero who is granted the honor to suffer the *dulce et decorum* death for the fatherland with believingly glowing soul, E. W. Borchert as the engineer who is only fascinated by his machines, and Josef Sieber as the juicy mate. Carl John, married by proxy on board, is released from his sorrows as expectant father, Herbert Klatt and Willi Rose represent humorous parts, and Clemens Hasse as a diver in location shots is at the mercy of the troubled waters, when he quickly loosens a fishing net tangled up in the ship's starboard propeller, in a dutifully efficient way. These are the parts where *Soldatentum* [being a soldier] and *Schauspielertum* [being an actor] are touching in mutual duty. The short scenes in the homeland — in the screenplay a little longer and, regarding the inner coherence, maybe allowing the film to be more easily understood — unite the submarine men and the women: Ilse Werner, Carsta Löck, and Agnes Windeck.

Rittau's direction, to say it again, overcomes many problems which result from the condensed space in which to move and the special kind of duty...[7]

Fifteen years before, Günther Rittau had helped Fritz Lang enormously in the making of *Metropolis*, creating a city of the future through paintings, miniatures and stop-frame animation and a machine woman cloned to life in an alchemist's chamber. They didn't know then that his movie perfectly well expressed what exploded years later in aggressive Nazis' minds: an unholy mixture of medieval ideology and modern militarist inventiveness. Science and superstition.

In the original manuscript of his autobiography, *Unter Wolfsmenschen*, one of the extras of *Metropolis*, writer Curt Siodmak, called popular German actor Heinz Rühmann "*Hitler's Schosshündchen*" ("Hitler's pet"). The editors omitted that remark, but Rühmann's affinity with the Nazi movement proved somewhat embarrassing for the popular actor after the war. Although he made no definite NS film, his comedy *Quax, der Bruchpilot* (*Quax, the Crash Pilot*) was sublime propaganda for his pilot friend Hermann Göring's *Luftwaffe*. In this movie, the first rule is to keep an aeronautical order (*"Fliegerische Zucht und Ordnung steht über allem!"*). Quax, a rather forward person, has won a flight course, flying lessons somewhere in Bavaria, and after some trial and error becomes an outspoken flying genius.

"...*Quax, der Bruchpilot* is a war film. The plot follows the standard formula of dozens of war films, German or American: a misfit becomes a hero when he learns to overcome his individuality for the sake of a greater whole. Although the film takes place in 1928 with no overt references to war, a military atmosphere pervades the flight academy where the majority of the scenes take place. The instructor declares that pilots form a 'stormy front' that 'fights for the idea.' They fly, he promises, not into the sky but into 'world history.'"[8]

After being the Condor Legion in the fierce prologue of the Spanish Civil War, the *Luftwaffe*, shaped by Göring and his then aide, Ernst Udet, entered "universal history" in Poland. Hans Bertram's "huge documentary about the suppression of Poland from the air," *Feuertaufe* (*Baptism of Fire*), describes the action of the German Air Force in the Poland campaign. "Distressed, holding our breath here we experience the conquest of Polish airspace by our irresistible *Luftwaffe*, its intervention defeating the Polish army near Kutno and in the Bzura curve and causing the suppression of Warsaw by our fighting pilots. Truth and reality of the facts are depicted by this film; it is a report that was made possible by the utterly fearless action of German cameramen. This is a warning document of the German pilot's spirit towards our enemies." "Germany's flying sword destroys the first enemy. The thrilling movie report of the fights and victories of our *Luftwaffe* in Poland. Reconnaissance planes and fighter aircraft conquer the airspace. Combat planes and nose diving bombers chop up the deployment area, streets and airports, destroy the surrounded armies near Kutno and force the surrender of Warsaw." "Shot during the battle actions. Faithful and plain are the images, serious and hard as war itself. As a contribution to the history of Pan-German fight for freedom this film shall be a document for living and forthcoming generations."[9]

Following is a contemporary synopsis of *Feuertaufe*[10]:

> The experience of the autumn days of 1939 rising in front of us: Poland, incited by England, is employing force against the Reich.
>
> All the world is in a fever of war.
>
> Only Germany remains calm; in the final hour the Führer tries again to save peace.
>
> But Great Britain will not tolerate *Grossdeutschland* at her side, and the West European Plutocracy (free masons and Jews!) has thrown down the gauntlet to National Socialism.
>
> Whoever wants peace must be prepared for war!
>
> Adolf Hitler's *Wehrmacht* has lined up for *Grossdeutschland*'s fight for freedom, and...
>
> ...like a sword from the sky our air force is ready to take-off.
>
> On the night of September 1st Polish artillery opens fire on the City of Beuthen within the German Reich.
>
> At 5.45 a.m. orders are given for a counter-attack.
>
> "From now on bomb is repaid with bomb!"

It is the task of both air fleets brought into the Polish campaign to first destroy the enemy's airports, to smash the Polish air force, to hit military targets, to disrupt railroad networks and bases, and prevent the enemy's deployment, supply and retreat.

On September 2nd the German Air Force already dominates the entire Polish space absolutely. The German advance has thrown the Polish army from a standing position from East Prussia up to Galizia; pursued Polish divisions are surrounded near Radom; here flying squadrons are used for support of the army.

After the collapse of the Polish combat unit near Radom follows the catastrophe of the main unit near Kutno.

In the great battle of encirclement at the curve of the River Weichsel our Air Force then intervenes in the final fights. At the Bzura it prevents the breakthrough of nine Polish divisions and contributes to the increased dissolution of the strongest Polish combat unit which contains a quarter of the enemy's army.

And again the German Air Force gets the task to force a fast decision when it comes to the final battle for Poland's capital. In spite of the repeated warnings of the German High Command, the commander of the city forces the civilian population in almost criminal lunacy to armed resistance and therefore transforms the open city of millions into a fortress. [Just the same happened when war returned years later to Germany and Hitler ordered German cities to become fortresses, the last being the city of Berlin.]

Warsaw's resistance is broken in 36 hours by planned bomb attack; here the JU 52 came once again to honors of engagement.

Whoever in a circular flight above the mass of houses registered the impact of weapons from the air in its whole extent will recognize the gigantic guilt that England has when London broadcasts misleading and false reports and empty promises.

England has betrayed Poland.

On September 27th the fortress of Warsaw surrendered unconditionally [as Berlin would six years later] with 130,000 prisoners and an immense booty of guns and baggage trains.

In 18 days the campaign was finished; but it shouldn't enter history as the smashing of a weak host by a modern giant army.

The German soldier has fought a well-equipped adversary, and often, as with mobile warfare, our fast troops faced superior forces.

Thanks for the success of this great victory without serious losses once again are to be given to our Air Force, which blinded the enemy's reconnaissance, tore apart the railroad network and shattered the strategic display of the enemy.

General Field Marshal Hermann Göring acknowledges the immortal deeds of the German Air Force by stating: "The promise the German Air Force has made in Poland, it will keep in England and France. The flying army today is standing from the Rhine up to the sea prepared for new action. We will prove to Mr. Chamberlain that there are no islands anymore. Every pilot's heart beats faster when clearance for take-off is given: We are flying against England!"

Feuertaufe introduces the infamous song and march "Bomben auf Engelland" [Bombs on England] by Norbert Schultze, whose lyrics by production manager Wilhelm Stöppler exhort the listener:

A poster for *Feuertaufe*.

Hört ihr's in den Ohren klingen:
Ran an den Feind!
Bomben! Bomben!
Bomben auf Engelland!

Do you hear it ring in the ears:
Go at the enemy!

> Bombs! Bombs!
> Bombs on England!

Proudly the Tobis pressbook quotes rave reviews from a press forced into line:

> Millions will see *Feuertaufe* and experience the blow from the hammer that whacked up Poland out of its megalomaniac dreams. Millions will become inflamed at the reflection of *Feuertaufe* and walk off with rich profit for their own life"—*Völkischer Beobachter*.
>   We have seen much cinematic productions about the Poland campaign. What we see now, *Feuertaufe*, communicates the strongest thought one can imagine at all... This film contains images which are breath-taking"—*B.Z. am Mittag*.
>   The great experience: *Feuertaufe*. The huge film about the fearless action and grand victory of the German Air Force in Poland"—*Berliner Nachtausgabe*.
>   Images one will never forget"—*Der Angriff*.
>   The images ... lead the spectator right into the zone of death... One roars nose-diving with the camera mounted onto the wing into the firing batteries of the *Westerplatte* [a Polish fortress]... One is present when in the destructive battle in Kutno a never-ending rain of bombs is dropped onto the Polish divisions at the Bzura retreating to the East... One observes the fastness and precision of the bomber crews arming the returning machines for the next start... With the camera one pans the effects of bombs on the earth... The image of terror experiences its final increase in the hell of Warsaw which must be blamed on the madness of the Polish defenders and the unscrupulousness of the malicious English agitators... Images of frightful beauty"—*Berliner Börsenzeitung*.
>   Right from the beginning the tempo of the film is so breath-taking that only in retrospect one will recognize how an exemplary concentrated use of word and image could make so burningly perceptive the events of those days... Nothing is faked and nothing invented, nothing rehearsed and nothing superimposed. The screenplay was written by war itself, war was directing, and the story is about the war in all its austerity and demoniac power respectively.... The final scenes are deeply shocking and powerful, a portent for Germany's enemies"—*Berliner Lokal-Anzeiger*.

For his achievements in *Feuertaufe* director Hans Bertram received congratulatory telegrams from both Hitler and Göring.[11]

From Poland it was only a stone's throw to the Victory in the West. *Sieg im Westen* was the title of a documentary covering the campaigns in Belgium, Holland and France in May and June of 1940. It resumed the propaganda line of "two centuries of uninterrupted unfairness of all the European powers to Germany," the most innocent power of them all which couldn't even harm a fly. According to the narrator, Adolf Hitler appeared as Christ-like savior of this innocence in the film's introduction:

> On three great rivers, on the Rhine, Danube and Vistula, lies this beautiful land, for which we must fight again and again — Germany.
>   In 1648, after the Thirty Years War of brother against brother, in the peace of Westphalia, the first German Reich was shattered. France and England exploited the disruption of the German people to establish themselves as world powers.

After more than 200 years, Germany, in recognition of the general danger, welded the majority of German states together into the second Reich under the brilliant leadership of Bismarck.

This newly won unity brought a peaceful development and a growing prosperity to the German people. Colonies were acquired, if only a fraction of the possessions that England had at its disposal.

An army that was ready for action and a strong fleet protected homeland and colonies.

England feared for its world domination. Politicians and merchants pressed on with the encirclement of Germany. The result was the World War.

For four and a half years Germany fought against almost the whole world. The German Army was winning on all fronts.

England waged another war, the hunger blockade against women and children, and drove a wedge between the front and homeland.

The political weakness of the German regime was its undoing. In the shameful treaty of Versailles, Germany was violated. The tribute extorted by the enemy, inflation and unemployment, brought the German people the bitterest misery. Exhausted, worn down and leaderless, they drifted toward destruction. The enemy used this weakness.

In this time of decline, Adolf Hitler, the common soldier of the World War, founded the National Socialist German Worker's Party. His idea was a beacon. It was carried forward by the Storm Troopers. From a seven-man following grew a powerful political army.

And the light of the German army burned bright from the time of collapse. The 100,000-man army guarded the inheritance from the old glorious army, and gave the Führer the foundation for the rebuilding of a new people's army.

In place of the forbidden weapons, all the Army had was dummies, cardboard tanks and wooden cannons, but behind them was the burning will to smash the treaty [of Versailles].

French threats cannot stop the growth.

January 30, 1933 marks the turning point in German history. The new political soldier clasps the hand of the Reichswehr soldier. The fellowship of the trenches in World War I finds its fulfillment.

The new construction begins.

But England arms. Disarmament proposals of the Führer are rejected.

Two years after the seizure of power, the Führer announces general compulsory military service.

The armament industry and the German worker work without pause to catch up with the advantage of the heavily armed western powers.

The Führer unswervingly pursues his great political goal. He shatters the chains of Versailles and takes back what is German.

The Rhineland.

Austria.

The Sudetenland.

The plan of the Western powers to use Czechoslovakia as an airbase is thereby frustrated.

As a protection against the mounting threats of invasion voiced against Germany, the Führer builds the Westwall. Fortress engineers, construction troops, the Labor Service and the Organisation Todt work hand in hand and in no time at all stamp the great work out of the earth.

The Czechs place themselves under the protection of the German nation, and so drop out as a vassal of the western powers.

Only Poland remains as a hope for England and France.

The Germans in Poland undergo the most severe terror.

To solve the corridor question, the Führer makes repeated liberal offers.

The Warsaw administration answers these proposals with military demonstrations, with harsher and harsher terror against the German population. The English and French diplomats struggle feverishly for war.

On the first of September, 1939, the Führer announces in the Reichstag: "Last night for the first time, Poland attacked us with its regular troops. Since five forty-five we have been shooting back."

After 18 days, the enemy is completely beaten.

Warsaw surrenders.

Germany's eastern border is now free.

Now, long transports roll westward to strengthen the assembling forces in the defense of the Westwall.

In the unshakeable willingness for peace and in the knowledge of his strength, the Führer extends an offer of peace to the western powers, which is interpreted as a sign of weakness and rejected.

On the contrary, the enemy seeks to create new bases of operations in Scandinavia.

The Führer steals a march on this plan on April 9, 1940. Ten hours earlier, German troops occupy Denmark and Norway. The German Navy knocks all the trumps out of the hands of the English Navy. The cooperation between the three branches of the armed forces is exemplary.

From Narvik to Basel, an unbroken front stands against the west.

The soldier on the Westwall has a hard winter behind him. He waits for the enemy attack.

The trust of the army and of the whole German people belongs to the Führer, in whose hands the fate of Germany lies, who alone knows when the hour of the great decision will strike, but who also knows that this people in arms stands in true love behind him, and is ready at his call to start toward the Great Decision!

The defense rests and pleads that Germany is not guilty. No, the Führer didn't break all contracts, didn't provoke the war with Poland. It all came out as preventive war to rescue and save suppressed Germans' lives all over the world.

Now for the main section of *Sieg im Westen*:

This film was shot by the cameramen of the reporting staff of the commander-in-chief and troops of the Army Film Unit, side by side with the fighting forces, with casualties. The enemy side is shown through captured English and French film.

On the night of 10 May 1940, the Führer made the following proclamation to the German people:

> "Soldiers of the Westfront!
> "'The hour for the decisive battle for the future of the German nation has come. The German people have no hatred towards the English or French people. It is a question today, however, of whether it [the German people] will survive or be destroyed. What we have

seen as a great danger for several months has come about. England and France are attempting, by use of a gigantic diversionary maneuver in southeastern Europe, to attack the Ruhr through Belgium and Holland. Soldiers of the Westfront! The hour has therefore come for you. The battle beginning today will decide the future of the German nation for the next thousand years."

In Nazi minds nothing is done for less than a thousand years.

What follows now is an account of military actions against France and the British Expeditionary Force.

To justify the German attack the fabricators of the film claim that British and French troops already had violated Belgian neutrality, marching out and ridiculing Germany's Westwall with the song "We're Going to Hang out our Washing on the Siegfried Line." Now by violating Belgian neutrality themselves German troops manage to group in the back of the French and to outflank the heavily armed, "invincible" Maginot Line. This was a strategic idea left from World War I — the so-called Schlieffen plan which allowed a *Blitzkrieg* strategy similar to the Poland campaign.

On June 14, Paris falls as a ripe fruit into German hands as a result of careful strategy.

Generals von Bock and von Küchler review the troops.

Iron crosses and assault badges are the merited awards of the men who have marched, fought and attacked for five weeks.

…the National Socialist soldiers, who are filled with enthusiasm for the Führer and his idea, are victorious over technology, machines and material.

Almost 2 million French prisoners, commanders of six French armies, 29,000 officers, the complete armaments and equipment of more than 130 divisions, as well as the material from fortresses and countless stores of weapons, munitions, equipment, supplies, raw materials and prefabricated materials fall into German hands.

The French regime draws the only possible conclusion from the collapse: it asks for an armistice. Compiègne will be used as the showplace of this historic event.

On behalf of the Führer, the Chief of Staff of the Armed Forces, General Keitel, will lead the negotiations in the historic railroad car where the armistice was signed in 1918.

After the victory in the West, the Führer and Commander-in-Chief of the Armed Forces gave his appreciation of the deeds of the army with the words: "The German soldier has himself to thank for the success of this masterly campaign in world history. In all situations in which he was placed, he proved himself to be of the highest quality."[12]

In contrast to the victoriously heroic northmen, we are shown "barbarian" Senegalese troops fighting for French colonial power and "instinctively" know how it was possible to overwhelm what the Nazis called *Rassengemisch* (mix of races).

Several cameramen had been assigned by Lieutenant Colonel Dr. Kurt Hesse, who had been put in charge of the Armed Forces Propaganda Section V — one of them Hans Ertl, a mountaineer, who had worked with Leni Riefenstahl on *Olympia*. Ertl was present when the film was screened for the Führer and described the scene.

"A few minutes before the special showing of the film in a projection room of the Reich Chancellery on January 20, 1941," Ertl said, "we (that is, Lieutenant Colonel Hesse, First Lieutenant Welter, Svend Noldan, Sepp Allgeier, Heinz Kluth and I) were introduced to the Führer by Colonel von Wedel. Hitler greeted each of us very warmly with a handshake and asked us where we were from and what particular tasks we had accomplished in connection with the film. He talked with Sepp Allgeier more freely as he already knew him from the Nuremberg films as a member of Leni Riefenstahl's team... A few comfortable chairs were placed in the natural wood and red brick projection room, which was built like a staircase. We sat — Hitler in the middle — in the first row. Behind us sat SS guards. In front of us, SS orderlies lounged on the chairless steps. Hitler was visibly impressed by the film. He especially favorably, even enthusiastically observed those scenes that showed everyday experiences in various locales which reminded him of his own time as a soldier in the First World War."

Sieg im Westen was released abroad, too: in Spain, Finland, Argentina, Sweden, and Japan. Tokyo press chief Major Mabuchi is quoted as saying, "Over and above the material equipment, the spiritual upbringing of the entire nation to engender a fighting, soldierly outlook is not to be forgotten. In this sense, the Japanese people have much to learn from this film."

This from a report to the General Staff of the Army (Attaché Section I/Pr.; No. 2238/41 g) dated July 1, 1941 and signed by V. Mellinthin:

> In summary, the following can be stated: the film *Sieg im Westen*, in European countries as well as countries outside Europe, by means of the Attachés' influential military propaganda, has contributed a great deal in showing pictorially the high renown of German warfare, the combined strength and the destructive effect of the German Armed Forces, and in heightening this effect by the most widespread propaganda means. Thus it had a unique success.
>
> It must especially be mentioned that through the placing of press criticism in neutral as well as friendly foreign countries, a longer-lasting (and in this case extremely favorable) indirect German military propaganda was carried out. In this connection, it should be added that it turned out to be absolutely correct to hold back the commercial exploitation of the film through film companies: only in this way the representatives of the German Army, the German Military Attachés, had the chance to put the magnificent success of the German conduct of the war and the German Army in their proper framework of military propaganda.

This from a special brochure published for the release of this movie[13], on the history of early war films:

> "Reviewing this film it is interesting to recall the origins. Since 1897 soldiers and seamen have cared for films documenting their work: effect of bullets, scattering, launchings, *Kieler Woche* [a weekly nautical event in Kiel]. And as early as September 9, 1897, the permanent secretary of *Reichsmarineamt* [naval office] wrote "that the photographic record and portrayal of ship launchings promises to deliver material that could be examined scientifically."
>
> Since even before the invention of film animated movies were known and pop-

ular (Reynaud's Praxinoscope), it is not surprising that animation very soon depicted battles. For instance, the French produced a filmed overview of the battle of Austerlitz, which caused enormous attention because it clarified the connection of operations on both sides. These first works were followed by many more; they were reserved, however, for small circles of experts. The need of cinemas couldn't be satisfied with those. In the cinemas war was regarded merely as sensation. In many short feature films there were battle scenes reconstructed from historic paintings. In 1907 and 1908 Pathé frères had dragged the Prussian Ulanes of the 70s War into the first political smear-film, *The Grandfather*, and made such a big business with it that they believed the connection of war and a political smear campaign must always be rewarding.

The film advertisements of those years before 1914 again and again deliver references to a piece of war, which serves as background and highlight, whether [of] a sentimental love story of Theodor Körner (1912) or *Queen Luise* or *Unter dem Doppeladler* ("greatest war play from the German-Danish war 1864–66"). The scenes from the battlefield are always especially emphasized.

In 1912 Pathé frères announced full-page in German film trade reviews:

> "We
> had the most favourable place as you can judge yourself
> from the accompanying illustrations
> The same is true for
> the next shots, too
> The Emperor in Switzerland
> September 3–8, 1912 (60 Pfg. per meter)
> September 9–14, 1912 (60 Pfg. per meter)."

This was difficult enough to tolerate in the case of newsreels, but the advertising lines sounded even more horrible announcing the first real war scenes. On October 17, 1912, the first Balkan War had begun on the Serbian and Bulgarian border.

The "Nordisk Films Co." announced:

> "We sent special photographers to the locations of war and will deliver in the next time weekly about 200 metres of footage of interesting events. From now on we accept your advance orders."

"Express Films Co." in Freiburg/Br. increased the promotion efforts during the second Balkan war with its advertisement from January 3, 1914:

> "If you want to give your theatre the aura of an
> *Educational institute*
> then of course you have to present to your audience the film
> *Mit der Kamera in der Schlachtfront*
> (*With the camera in the battle front*).
> This film recorded on command of His Majesty the King of Greece,
> in the fighting ranks of Greeks and Bulgars made in the greatest
> mortal danger, shows you excellently clearly all horrors and dangers
> of modern war.
> *Resounding*
> in the annals of film art these highly interesting shots will be

Giant success

and will not fail to materialize because all are interested in such world-shaking events.

The film was screened for His Majesty Kaiser Wilhelm II and found the highest of praise of His Majesty.

Ask immediately　　　*Grand promotion material*
For release offer　　　*at your disposal!*
Express-Films Co., G.m.b.H., Freiburg i. Br.
Editor and Distributor: The Day in Movies."

Finally the "art" of public relations surpassed itself. American press reviews were quoted as shouting:

"*A giant success in the New World!*"
The Morning Telegraph in New York reported on February 1, 1914
5,000 people stormed "Weber's cinema theatre"
in which our film
Mit der Kamera in der Schlachtfront
(*With the camera to the battle front*)
was screened!

At the opening the crowds were that enormous that a huge force of police was needed in order to allow the proper attendance at the theatre.

Everybody, who has seen the highly interesting and educational film, said that these images of a lifelike war *surpass all expectations* and that until then no such formidable play had been presented that even offered the advantage of reality, and for that reason it will be immeasurably valuable.

So and in a similar way enthusiastic reports run, which we receive from the country of progress and intelligence. Therefore don't miss out on immediately asking for your release offer from us because without any doubt this film will cause an *enormous sensation* in Europe, too.

Splendidly brilliant shots taken right next to the action!
Great promotional material!
The film can be viewed at the office of our representative,
Mr. Albert Löwenberg in Berlin W 66, Mauerstr. 93.

In the World War, film records were entrusted at first to private film reporters. In 1915 France built up an army film service of 10 cameramen. Austria and Russia regulated matters of film officially. The German perception was issued at the beginning of the year 1916 by the head of the Cinematographic Department, Major Schweitzer, in an introductory essay for the magazine "Der Film" on January 1, 1916:

"The present war is the first in which *cinematography* appears as a link in the chain of means by which one tries to notify outsiders of events from the war scene. The *moving image* is very well suited to bring back to the ones who stayed at home, livelily and clearly the deeds of their brave troops at land and at sea. And not only this: in foreign countries, too, the cinematograph shall and can show impressively and irrefutably the accomplishments of German armies. So the film becomes for us an *excellent means of propaganda*, *propaganda of truth and justice*, and proves wrong all malicious rumors (which our enemies in their own countries and abroad so masterfully and eagerly manage to spread) often [in a] better and more cutting [way] than the printed letter.

"Besides that film is useful from a *military* standpoint, too. Here are moments recorded, which in their entire peculiarity become fully evident first by the moving image and remain so in memory.

"The *High Command*, in recognition of the good services which cinematography is able to render also in war, from the very beginning tried as much as possible to found at all costs an institution for the whole organization of news and reporting of events. Besides war correspondents and photographers, cinematographers were allowed as well to spend some time in the respective theatres of war and take footage.

"Suggestions of all kind were already made to *fundamentally* reorganize *cinematography* as far as it concerns military purposes, particularly in a case of war. Alas, until now all of these measures have proved less suited and not useful.

"In Austria-Hungary and Russia the High Command has taken cinematography in its own hands, all footage is shot by officers and their crews. This system in itself offers indisputably certain advantages because the officer and his men have free access everywhere and the High Command's military reservations towards civilians are removed. So footage is taken, which would be impossible to shoot under other circumstances. The German High Command, however, has shut itself off until now from the same thought because on the other hand it doesn't wish that *private film industry*, which *especially* in Germany has *developed that splendidly,* shall be excused from its duties for the purpose of war."

The French work was excellently organized, strongly supported by Poincaré, the "Cinema Marshal," especially in circulation abroad, and expanded by the American film world, and they deliberately used the 'sensation' of war, even took wild brutalities, and counted on inflaming hatred even against better knowledge. More in a report from the year 1918:

"Whoever at this time attends a French cinema will gain the strangest and most horrible impressions about the usually highly acclaimed good taste of the French. In the cinemas things are screened, which one would not believe if he saw it with his own eyes. French soldiers are portrayed as especially heroic and brave in French cinema reports; war newsreels, however, could be entirely different. A short time ago a series of war reports was shown, a film produced by Pathé Frères, which presented a *Zeppelin* that was shot down over the Thames. Actually that would be not that serious. But after this image follows another series of exceptional brutality. Seeing the downed Zeppelin there is a second title that reads: '*Les cadavres Boches.* [The German bodies.]' These images show perfectly clearly the useless rescue attempts, the struggle in death and the dead bodies of our heroes, who had died in the catastrophe of the airship. This film was the biggest sensation (!!) on the French cinema market and eliminated those bloodthirsty English horror films the English film

industry swamped the French film market with. This film, which is
forbidden to be shown even in England, is screened in each French
cinema, from the most elegant Paris theatre down to the most miserable village dump."

German resistance culminated in the work of *Bild- und Filmamt* (*Bufa*). Hundreds of films, which we thank it for and which were brought home by military
film troops, could be valued as honest footage, as pictorial documents of the
events. But only rarely was it possible to combine them in a way that a continu-
ity of film resulted, which gave an impression of the *real* action. Often the shots
became a ridiculous triviality after 10 or 25 years, and today a good portion of
the effect and therefore approval is missing. A picture like *Höllenkampf an der
Aisne* (*Hell Fight at River Aisne*) doesn't manage to deliver an image of what was
achieved in those days by hundreds of thousands. That is because of the technique — to watch images in such a manner is alien to us. Primarily, it has to do
with a certain trivialization. For many feet of film one somehow suspects that the
most important footage was shot on a training ground, on a maneuver area, and
that the hissing white and gray clouds are not the result of enemy fire but the
effect of fireworks, which wouldn't harm anybody. That didn't prevent many of
these films since 1923, when they were passed by the censors, leaving a great
impact in closed screenings for former war participants, at least when they were
introduced by a passionate speaker, who observed gravity and was accepted so
to speak by most as an expert during the course of the event.

The time between both wars brought a great number of attempts of all kinds
to capture those martial events in film (feature films, educational, culture and
training films). The battles of Friedrich the Great, the battles of the liberation
wars, especially Leipzig, Waterloo, Königgrätz, the fights of 1870, the colonial
wars, finally the World War, were again and again dealt with in feature films or
testimonial movies or films to be screened in schools. It could happen that in an
absolutely sentimental feature film plot like that of *Sklaven des 20. Jahrhunderts*
(*Slaves of the 20th Century*) — German prisoners in France — the story became
particularly lively when, between terribly staged kitsch shots from the files of
Bild- und Filmamt, appeared scenes of the German artillery bombarding the
trenches of the enemy.

Most attempts at *staging events* have failed because they were inadequate either
in preparation or in the means. An old Bismarck film fought the battle of Königgrätz involving a single company. One saw Prussian troops vaguely behave as if
they lined up as Egyptian catapult warriors in a Pharaoh movie against Nubian
marksmen somewhere in the mountains at the Nile. The fact that the old wish
the military expert and historian might have a word to say in such features, even
more in serious films about the war events from 1914 to 1918, is easily understood
in the face of so many failures. There were not only children but above all girls,
who often laughed shouting for joy when some of the approaching infantry fell
and lay flat. Only a few realized that it was the bitter dying of soldiers who had
done their duty that was being depicted.

Serious men attempted in the 20s to make a three-part film about the World
War out of animated maps and reconstructed scenes. All conscientiousness didn't
prevent some uniforms being too good and too new, some trenches not being
damaged enough and too green. All this produced the poisoned word that this
World War actually had been fought on the lot of Neubabelsberg. One minor

detail served in making the whole film out to be untrustworthy: the troops that marched in August 1914 along streets lined by trees with bare branches were obviously filmed in October or November. It is part of the attitude of that time that such a film in the 20s was not welcomed by the officials. Many men of those days wished that films about war would demonstrate what had really gone on, and yearned for them to be used to fight the indifference, which was present in many circles, especially with the young generation, which was largely ignorant about war. Lastly, the rejection of such films was intensified by the younger generation not knowing the context of the war: they couldn't learn anything about the failure of the older generation just from a movie. Similar things happened concerning slides about the war of 1914–18: what was selected by devoted and brave publishers had no chance of being used.

That attitude has changed since. This time from the beginning it was considered vital, for instance concerning slides and film, that the photo and film documents of the present war were timely collected by the film troops of the Army, by film reporters, and propaganda companies as well as by special forces of the High Commander of the Army. During the France action the reporting staff of the High Command of the Army was brought into action and contributed an important part of the film footage. Additionally among the English, French and Belgian spoils of war, there were films to be found in different stages, which could be used in this film for different purposes, too. What once left a strong impact in a film about Verdun, real French footage of the life in the fortress and of French supplies, was used throughout the film.

"The other side" voluntarily joined in, the Poilu, the Tommie marched up and fought, firing out of the big armed fortresses, batteries and machine-gun positions on the attacking enemy. The war machine of the allies presented itself without brightly polished disguise and those behind the front, in the cities and villages, got to see them freshly from the sound stages of "war films" and newsreels.

How did these moving images of the enemy get into German possession? Very often that happened accidentally. Methodically all spoils were examined. The departments, which got the task, found rich footage, which the enemy could not destroy or save.

Goebbels, who attended the Berlin premiere of *Sieg im Westen* on January 31, 1941, at the Ufa Palast am Zoo (which was covered with Iron Crosses and war flags), was less satisfied and more critical. "The film still has a mass of defects, but the material is so strong that in the end it overwhelms one. The public, mostly officers, was deeply moved." He did what he could do against the film, which was made by the Wehrmacht and therefore was out of his hands. The Film Review Board, run by the Propaganda Ministry, only gave the film second rank certificates. The upset Hesse, of course, demanded the highest certificate. Goebbels wrote, "Hesse has written a letter, in which he tries to extort a better certificate for his film. I summon Wedel and Martin immediately and refuse any further collaboration between my ministry or myself and Hesse…"

Goebbels found an ally in Reich Marshall Göring, who was himself not satisfied with what he saw in *Sieg im Westen*. The Luftwaffe's eminent role in the Victory in the West was only shown in an extremely sketchy fashion, different from the way it was portrayed in *Feuertaufe*. By February 21, Goebbels was able to record in his diary:

"I talk over a few things with Göring… He has had some problems with Brauchitsch about his stupid propaganda. The Führer is also very displeased about it. Brauchitsch is supported by Hesse. The Führer has a very low opinion of him.

"I come to an agreement with Göring about the Propaganda Companies. He is willing to place operators at my disposal but not at the Armed Forces Chief of Staff's. He totally rejects Brauchitsch's Western Front film…"

On March 5, 1941, Goebbels wrote: "The Hesse matter is fast becoming a Brauchitsch matter. Keitel is for Hesse's dismissal. Brauchitsch is holding on to him. I have Hesse barred from the press and radio. Now we will see what comes of it. In any case, I shall not give in. I am now handing all the material over to Göring for his information."

The Nazi state was descending into rival satrapies. Hitler not only tolerated this rivalry, it was part of his personal politics of "*Divide et impera* [Divide and rule]." Hesse had to take his hat or his cap or what else. Göring had struck Brauchitsch, giving Goebbels a hand in taking over at least more war propaganda. Now he had high hopes of getting his own films out of this agreement with another satrap, not only documentaries like *Baptism of Fire* but whole feature films. The time was ripe now that Germany was going to bomb Britain into extinction.

One of the leading producers of German war films was a man we have already come across— Karl Ritter, the producer of *Hitlerjunge Quex, Rivalen der Luft* (a picture about the comradeship of youthful glider pilots, directed by Frank Wysbar who

Otto Wernicke (looking through window) in *D III 88*.

in Ritter's own words was not very well suited for this task), *Unternehmen Michael*, and—by personal order of the Führer (on January 27, 1939)—*Im Kampf gegen den Weltfeind*. Ritter was a participant in World War I and an early National Socialist. "In our cinemas we want to see nothing else than convinced National Socialists," Ritter said. "The path of German films will lead without any compromise to the conclusion that every movie must stay in the service of our community, of nation and our Führer." Ritter's name was associated with the genre of air war films, which was developed in the second half of 1930s.

> It was no easy task in the years before the seizure of power by the Government of National Socialist Revolution until the outbreak of World War II, which was provoked by England, to communicate to the German people an image of the revival of the German air force, of its tasks and aims, of its strength and combat-readiness. For up to March 1st, 1935, only under cover of a camouflage that although safe demanded much denial, could the basis of a new German air force be built up. In the years to follow, too, the protection of the strictest observance of secrecy had to cover particularly the youngest and most progressive part of the army. The same kind of restraint was exercised in the movies. Thus the fact explains that the newsreels then contained only rare footage of the many and diverse areas of the air force and that only a few documentaries were released, with *Flieger, Funker und Kanoniere* by Rikli (Ufa) the most remarkable and at the same time most comprehensive.
>
> In feature films, however, a well-formed line began. In *Pour le mérite* (Ufa) the heroism of pilots was developed from 1914 till the gray November days of 1918, the severe experience in the political and economical disturbances was shown until the time was ripe for the best and most energetic to return to their beloved air force. In this new air force *D III 88* is staged; here are the events and aggravations of the everyday life of flight, besides the portrayal of air and military service which offer the chance for building up a real feature. Part of this series is without doubt the film *Feuertaufe*, too, which is, although a documentary, highly impressive and lively. It tells of the first trial of the German air force in the Polish action. In *Kampfgeschwader Lützow* the men known from *D III 88* fly against Poland and England: out of the flight, male conflicts and fates the plot was created for a feature film. Then the Ufa film *Stukas* depicted the fight of a group in the Western action, which was brought on against many different targets, made up from very different men, but indissolubly united in their comradely feeling.
>
> What all of these films have in common is that for the air force, flying, is not a sideline or background but a dramatic highlight; yes, the air force, flying, basically is the focus of the feature film plot. Besides these projects numerous other feature films were made, exclusively or partly dealing with air force protagonists or locations, which couldn't be defined however as genuine flight films, like *Verräter, Unternehmen Michael, Über alles in der Welt, GPU* or *Wunschkonzert*.[14]

In *Über alles in der Welt* (*Over Everyone in the World, 1940*) Karl Ritter turned to his beloved episodic format of moviemaking.

> "On September 2 [*sic*; September 3] 1939, England and France declare war on Germany. In England, France, and on the high seas, Germans are hunted down, persecuted, and imprisoned. The Colombes Stadium in Paris has been turned into

a concentration camp where Germans and Jews are confined. Two of the prisoners are Fritz Möbius (Fritz Kampers) of the Siemens-Schuckert factory and Dr. Karl Wiegand (Carl Raddatz), a German correspondent in Paris. Escape seems impossible, but Wiegand is freed and attempts are made to enlist him in anti–German propaganda activities. Wiegand pretends to be interested in the proposition and vouches for Möbius. This is their only possible way to regain freedom and return to Germany.

Both men flee, Möbius during an air attack. Wiegand goes to the front, accompanied by Leo Samek (Oscar Sima) of the League for the Human Rights, and a girl, Madeleine Laroche (Maria Bard). The three observe the battle of an Austrian battalion. In the heat of the battle, Samek and Madeleine lose their heads and run away, but Wiegand remains steadfast and makes his way across the battlefield to join the German ranks.

At the same time, the members of a Tyrolean musical group are dragged from a London stage into a concentration camp. Samek and Captain Stanley of the Secret Service (Andrews Engelmann) try to free them and enlist their services. Three members of the band pretend to be interested. They are taken to France, watch the same attack which made it possible for Wiegand to escape, and also make it across the lines to Germany.

At the outbreak of the war, the German tanker *Elmshorn* is on the high seas in the Atlantic. The ship is pursued by an English destroyer. The captain of the tanker directs his crew to sink and abandon the ship so that it will not fall into British hands. The crew is picked up by the British destroyer *Arethusa*. Soon afterward an explosion on the destroyer causes cries of "German submarines!" And indeed, a German submarine emerges from the sea, takes the Germans off the British destroyer, and deposits them at Vigo, Spain, from where they make their way through friendly Italy to Germany.

On a Pommeranian airfield, German planes are ready to go into action. They attack the Polish hinterland. One of the planes does not return, but has to make a forced landing in enemy territory. A German plane flies to the rescue. Braving enemy fire, the plane lands on Polish soil, picks up the German crew and brings them back to their home base. But the rescue plane is hit, and the crew tries to save itself by parachute. Among them is Hans Wiegand (Hannes Stelzer), Karl's brother. The group flees across the forests and mountain passes of France and reaches the Italian border.

On board a German minesweeper stands the captain and one of his officers. They scan the air with their field glasses. The Germans down 37 of 45 enemy planes. The radio announces: "This is our answer!"

The film closes with a symbolic apotheosis of Germany's invincible strength. The five unconnected episodes, all showing Germans overtaken by war in foreign lands or on hostile seas, prove the great sacrificial love Germans hold for their fatherland which they will rejoin regardless of danger."[15]

The scenes dealing with the *Luftwaffe* are clearly the best and most exciting: 45 Vickers-Wellington bombers are met by German fighters over the North sea, and 37 are shot down. Ritter was a man of the air and was joined by process specialist Gerhard Huttula in creating miniature work and background projection (from plates shot by aerial cinematographers). Huttula's model aircraft were made from plywood and in different sizes, to suggest depth and perspective when attached to fine wires and

Director Karl Ritter (left, in uniform) on the set of *Über alles in der Welt*.

hung in front of a process screen onto which the transparencies were projected. Some of the more detailed foreground models were equipped with tiny motors, fed with electricity by the supporting wires, while models in the back were flat cut-outs. All trick shots had been laid out before shooting in storyboard form, which was extremely rare for German movies, particularly at that time. Similar techniques were employed by Japanese (Eiji Tsuburaya, later in charge of the *Godzilla* series) and American (A. Arnold Gillespie) effects specialists. In their next collaboration, *Stukas*, Ritter and Huttula even faced a bigger technical challenge.

> Karl Ritter's films are grown in an entirely male mental climate. Comradeship and fight are the subject of *Stukas*, too. It is a movie with no important roles for women. Background is the days of the German victory in Holland, Belgium, and France. Three squadrons of a Stuka group are brought into action against Liège, Dunkirk, Tirlemont et al. The life between fighting actions following each other in rapid succession is hardly less strained than the hours of flight, the minutes of dogfights, the seconds of nose-diving. Sheer enthusiasm transfigures the danger. Faithful comradeship proves its power when one comrade after another, after an emergency landing has to be bailed out middle of the enemy. Out of this comradeship the life of each one continuously receives a stream of power. Faith takes away the fright of death. The emotion becomes more intense in the festive heights of Hölderlin's hymns and Wagnerian music.
>
> *Stukas* is a film about people, not machines—however much the nose-diving birds of steel themselves are an expression of the will to fight and a daring confidence in victory. In the screenplay which he wrote in association with [Felix]

Carl Raddatz addresses his crew in *Stukas*.

Lützkendorf, Ritter has outlined the characters and temperaments of each man with striking conciseness. The dialogue obviously learned from listening to life strikes exactly the tough but warm note that characterizes such a young flying squadron. In spite of the uniformity of this pilot's type, every figure is sharply drawn and unique. There men stand with mighty vitality besides nondescript introverts, the quietly reserved, the culturally smoothed; lucky devils besides the unlucky ones; wild daredevils besides the iron restrained calculating shrewdly; dreamy artist types beside clear-headed realists. This mosaic of characters is carefully thought out and artistically put together using many voices to sound the chorus of fighting comradeship.

Right casting then letting the actors freely express is one of the trademarks of Ritter's directorial art. Never does one feel a *"Drücker* [pressure]," meaning that the director never asks for something which the actors' ability is not able to provide. Thus the efforts seem fresh and unaffected. Carl Raddatz as group commander deserves high praise: he is a man for whom his subordinates would go through hell and high water, because he sets them an example as if it were the most natural thing in the world what he is demanding from them. At his side, with gentle, soft agility, there is Albert Hehn: a *Lebenskünstler* [person who always knows how to make the best of things] and a precise adjutant. O. E. Hasse plays the medical officer with cultivated weight: a superior conversationalist, a friend of the good things of life, older and more serene and yet carried away by the fire of youth around him. Marvelous is the dark but naive seriousness with which "Patzer" played by Ernst von Klipstein observes his persistent misfortune, curs-

Three airmen in one bed in *Stukas*.

ing it so long until the sun shines for him, too. Wild and quick-tempered, working himself up into a state of feverish delirium, is the dashing leader of the Bull's Squadron, Hannes Stelzer: For him fight is like intoxication, while for the squadron's captain of the "cavaliers," the insatiably vital Karl John, it is the elixir of life; for the captain of the Ninth, Herbert Wilk, it is spirit, distance, concentration. A sympathetic newcomer, Johannes Schütz, plays the "chick[en]." Josef Dahmen gives an outstanding portrayal of the plain mechanic, who is in love with his machine. This is only a selection of those who are acting well and effectively.[16]

"...every comrade is equally representative of the feared Stuka weapon, which itself is growing into a giant symbol with the destruction of the enemy, his pilots, his tanks, and with the panic-evoking pursuing and bombing. Restlessly, day and night, every time standing by, composed even after the greatest of dangers, constantly in the mood for tough jokes—so every man stands his ground with marginal deviations of his temperament.

"The effect of all things technical is grand, the battling noise is breathtaking. The advance in France, the enemy catastrophe of Dunkirk are given much attention. One cannot easily imagine how and where these shots were taken, as they are dragging the spectator actually and directly into all details and into the enormous tableau of battle actions."[17]

The story structure, however, was less impressive. Howard K. Smith reviewed

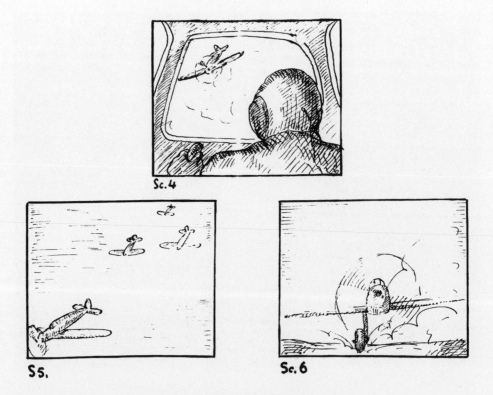

Storyboard excerpt for model shots to be filmed by Gerhard Huttula for *Stukas*. (*From the personal files of the late cinematographer Gerhard Huttula.*)

the movie after having viewed it in Berlin. "It was a monotonous film about a bunch of obstreperous adolescents who dive-bombed things and people. They bombed everything and everybody. That was all the whole film was—one bombing after another. Finally the hero got bored with bombing and lost interest in life. So they took him off to the Bayreuth music festival, where he listened to a few lines of Wagnerian music; his soul began to breathe again, he got visions of the Führer and of guns blazing away, so he impolitely left right in the middle of the first act and dashed back and started bombing things again, with the old gusto."[18]

In the end, after their victory in France, the Stukas prepare to attack England:

> *Viel schwarze Vögel ziehen*
> *Hoch über Land und Meer,*
> *Und wo sie erscheinen, da fliehen*
> *Die Feinde vor ihnen her.*
> *Sie lassen jäh sich fallen*
> *Vom Himmel tief bodenwärts.*
> *Sie schlagen die ehernen Krallen*
> *Dem Gegner mitten ins Herz.*
> Refrain:
> *Wir sind die schwarzen Husaren der Luft,*
> *Die Stukas, die Stukas, die Stukas,*

Immer bereit, wenn der Einsatz uns ruft,
Die Stukas, die Stukas, die Stukas.
Wir stürzen vom Himmel und schlagen zu.
Wir fürchten die Hölle nicht und geben nicht Ruh',
Bis endlich der Feind am Boden liegt,
Bis England, bis England, bis England besiegt,
Die Stukas, die Stukas, die Stukas!
Wenn tausend Blitze flammen,
Wenn rings sie Gefahr bedroht,
Sie halten stets eisern zusammen,
Kameraden auf Leben und Tod!
Wenn Beute sie erspähen,
Dann wehe ihr allemal!
Nichts kann ihren Augen entgehen,
Den Stukas, Adlern gleich aus Stahl!
Refrain:
Wir sind die schwarzen Husaren der Luft
Tod säen sie und Verderben
Rings über des Feindes Land.
Die Spuren sind Trümmer und Scherben
Und lodernder Himmelsbrand.
Es geht schon in allen Landen
Ihr Name von Mund zu Mund.
Sie schlagen die Werke zuschanden,
Die Schiffe schicken sie auf Grund.
Refrain:
Wir sind die schwarzen Husaren der Luft, etc.

Translation:

Many a blackbird is flying
High above country and sea
And where they appear, there
The enemies flee in front of them.
They let fall themselves steeply
From the sky to the depths of the ground
They sink their iron talons
Right into the enemy's heart.
Refrain:
We are the black hussars of the air,
The Stukas, the Stukas, the Stukas,
Always prepared and ready to attack,
The Stukas, the Stukas, the Stukas.
We dive from the sky and throw a blow.
We don't fear hell and don't keep quiet,
Till finally the enemy lies on the ground,
Till England, Till England, Till England is defeated,
The Stukas, the Stukas, the Stukas!
When a thousand lightning streaks are flaming,
When danger threatens to encircle them,
They stick together like iron,

A scene from *D III 88*.

Comrades by the devil!
When they catch sight of the prey,
Then woe betide it any time!
Nothing can escape the eyes
Of the Stukas, like eagles of steel!
Refrain:
We are the black hussars of the air
They sow death and destruction
Around the enemy's country.
What is left is ruins and broken pieces
And burning sky.
In all countries already their name is passed
From mouth to mouth.
They wreck the fortresses,
They send the ships to the ground.
Refrain:
We are the black hussars of the air, etc.*

Tobis on the other hand had Hans (*Feuertaufe*) Bertram and *Kampfgeschwader Lützow* (*Fighting Squadron Lützow*), which, as mentioned earlier, was sort of a sequel to *D III 88* in which the World War I tradition of fighter aircrafts was transferred to the then present day by Lieutenant Colonel Mithoff: "We have not lost our faith. We

*"*Stukalied*," music by Herbert Windt, lyrics by Geno Ohlischläger, ©1941 Ufaton-Verlagsgesselschaftmbtt. Reproduced by permission of BMG Music Publishing, Germany.

A pilot in the cockpit in *D III 88*.

have worked and rebuilt. And we have hammered the spirit of the fighter pilots into our young weapon." *D III 88* was made just before war broke out in 1939. *Kampfgeschwader* was made two years later, a retrospective of the Polish campaign:

Everybody would want to see this film!

Millions have enthusiastically seen *D III 88*, so they all [should] be interested [in] *Kampfgeschwader Lützow* which is so to speak a sequel of this first great flight film of Tobis. They only need to know that here the fate of the two young pilots and friends [from the first film] leads in a dramatic and thrilling way to a tragic climax. But all who have not seen *D III 88*, might and must be won for *Kampfgeschwader Lützow*, too.

For the plot is self-contained!

The many great scenes of battle engagement are modeled exactly from reality and, connected with a plot, are so lifelike in their natural plainness, as to make a thrilling and moving film on a high level. Daring attacks on Polish airfields and traffic routes and their successful destruction — the emergency landing of a bomber and the rescue of its lost crew out of Polish swamps — the rescue of transported ethnic Germans by low-flying German aircraft — an air attack on English convoys and the heroic action of a pilot in greatest danger build the dramatic highlights. The impact of these thrilling images and atmospheric scenes is enhanced by the score of the film.

Norbert Schultze, the composer of the song "Bombs on England," who

A poster for *Kampfgeschwader Lützow*.

already has supported director Hans Bertram most excellently with the great documentary *Feuertaufe* by his score, has again created something outstanding. Besides many old and new soldier songs, he has integrated his song, well known through broadcasts, *"Wir fliegen gegen Engelland, und mit uns fliegt der Tod"* ("We Are Flying Against Engelland, and Death is Our Co-Pilot") into his overall score for *Kampfgeschwader Lützow*.

We don't say much when we claim:

The sure success of this film
will surpass your expectations if you
adapt your promotion to the greatness of this movie![19]

There is not much dialogue in *Kampfgeschwader Lützow*, but there are many exciting air battles which were outlined carefully in the screenplay by Hans Bertram.[20] One of them is reproduced below.

Scene 22

Air battle

115 *Close:* (aerial shot)
(frontal through windshield on the violent Slavic face
of a Polish fighter pilot)   / engine noise and machine-
                              gun fire according to fighting /
(In the beginning the picture is slightly out of focus
as if fighter aircraft approaches out of the mist.)
116 *Part:* (aerial shot)
(from the side on a line of Polish fighter pilots
flying in close formation,)
The Polish national emblem is visible.
117 *Long Shot:* (aerial shot)
(Reverse Angle: over cockpit into flight direction)
(Camera is mounted in control column of a
fighter aircraft)
The planes tilting forward dive in high speed
onto both German fighter aircraft flying in
equal flight direction several hundred feet
below.
118 *Close:* (Inside 25 A 33)
(snipers of 25 A 33)
Zeisler bends down and roars into the cockpit: Fighters!
119 *Close:* (Inside 25 A 33)
Paulsen flies calmly.
120 *Close:* (Inside 25 A 33)
(over shoulder: Guggi in the nose)
Guggi, his machine-gun at the ready.
121 *Close:* (Inside 25 A 33)
Zeisler has his machine gun at the ready, too.
122 *Long Shot:* (aerial shot)
(out of the rear of 25 A 33)
Two Polish fighters burst out from behind
onto the 25 A 33.
(the control surfaces of the German plane are seen)
123 *Long Shot:*
(P.O.V. Polish fighter aircraft)
(Camera inside cockpit mounted in flight direction.)

(The camera plane flies as second fighter aircraft.)
The two fighter aircraft approach at high speed from behind
and above the 25 A 33. The plane in front fires and banks
up to the right. The second plane (camera plane)
now bursts onto the 25 A 33, firing, then banks
to the left past the German plane.
124 *Long Shot:* (aerial shot)
(cockpit: pilot, over shoulder to outside left)
The second Polish fighter pilot on the pursuit in
a left turn [with] the aircraft [standing on its wing].
Paulsen (double) sees the Polish fighter aircraft flying on
the left side (over shoulder) and tilts his plane in a left turn behind
the Polish fighter.
125 *Long Shot:* (from the ground)
Both German fighter aircraft and three Polish fighters in
dogfight.
The fighter aircraft circling wildly around the German
planes which fly closely together.
(Extensive footage in order to intercut scenes.)
126 *Long Shot:* (aerial shot)
(same as scene 123, P.O.V. Polish fighter pilot)
Two Polish aircraft attack 25 A 33 from the front.
(Again camera plane flies as second fighter aircraft.)
127 *Long Shot:* (aerial shot or rear projection)
Out of the cockpit over shoulder Guggi (double). He fires from
the nose on two Polish fighters which bank shortly one
after the other in front of the 25 A 33 to the right and
left.
(If this aerial shot cannot be accomplished effectively,
a process plate has to be shot in the air focusing without
end piece onto both Polish fighter aircraft banking upward
to the right and left.)
128 *Close-Up:* (inside 25 A 33)
Front of instrument panel 25 A 33.
A burst of fire from the second Polish fighter's machine-
gun hitting the instrument panel.
(Instruments in front. They are destroyed and crack.)
129 *Long Shot:* (aerial shot)
A German fighter aircraft (Me 109) as it flies in low altitude
Over a heavy bank of cloud, approaching the camera plane.
130 *Close-Up:*
(view from front instrument panel on head of German
fighter pilot)
The German fighter pilot, sporting the fresh young face of a
lieutenant, wears a funny Tyrolean hat instead of a cap.
(This lieutenant who will reappear in later dogfights
represents the type of carefree, daring German fighter pilot.)
Approaching the edge of the clouds the lieutenant takes a
quick look beneath the left side and becomes aware of the

situation. He prepares for action without haste and takes a
nose-dive.

130a *Long Shot:* (aerial shot) [handwritten note]

(This shot is intercut in scene 130.)

(P.O.V. German fighter pilot downward over left wing.)

(Shot from a BF 108)

The Poles circling around the closely flying German fighters.

131 *Long Shot:* (aerial shot)

The German fighter aircraft dives on the edge of a heavy cumulus
cloud and bursts (camera pans) downward.

131a *Long Shot:* [handwritten note]

Dogfight.

132 *Long Shot:* (aerial shot)

(P.O.V. fighter pilot in flight direction)

The Me 109 bursts onto the fighting planes in the back of Polish
fighter which immediately makes a dash for freedom.

133 *Long Shot:* (aerial shot)

P.O.V. Guggi (out of cockpit of 25 A 33)

The German fighter aircraft pursues the Polish fighter pilot
who tilts his plane in a wild curve. The German fighter aircraft,
however, is hard on the Pole's heels.

133a [handwritten note]

The fighter aircraft pursues Poles.

134 *Medium Close Shot:* (Inside 25 A 33)

(Reverse Angle: Paulsen at control column and Guggi)

Guggi, pleased, turns to Paulsen. He grins and points to the
fleeing Pole.

Paulsen, who is pleased too, gazes at him. Then both men
look outside the window on the other side in order to
search for the other two Poles.

135 *Long Shot:* (aerial shot)

(P.O.V. Guggi)

136 *Long Shot:* (from the ground)

(frontal on the Polish fighter which is pursued by the
Me 109)

Both planes race closely one after the other above
Camera and fill the screen.

137 *Close-Up:*

(same as scene 130, i.e. from the front on German fighter)

The German pilot as he sits a little bent forward behind his
control column smiling grimly and prepares to fire.

138 *Close-Up:*

The trigger of the machine gun.

The pilot's hand rests calmly on the control column
and (after a while) pushes the trigger.

139 *Long Shot:* (aerial shot)

(same as scene 132, i.e. P.O.V. fighter pilot,
flight direction)

The German fighter closes in on the back of the Pole [and]

hits the Polish fighter aircraft.
139a [handwritten note]
The Pole starts to burn.
140 *Long Shot:* (aerial shot)
(P.O.V. Guggi out of the 25 A 33 on dogfight)
The burning Polish fighter starts to go down in a
spin.
140a [handwritten note]
P.O.V. fighter = 142
141 *Long Shot:* (aerial shot)
The burning Polish fighter going down in a spin in
front of a heavy cloud.
142 *Close-Up:*
(same as scene 130, i.e. front on German pilot)
The German pilot gazes at his victim. His face brightened
by a tiny smile of satisfaction.
Then he looks around searching for a new enemy.
As he doesn't find another Pole he sits more comfortably
and tilts the plane to the left.
143 *Long Shot:* (aerial shot)
(same as scene 132, i.e. P.O.V. pilot, flight direction)
The Me 109 is pulling upward between the German
planes flying side by side.
The gunners (Zeisler and Hasinger) wave.
144 *Long Shot:* (aerial shot)
(out of the cockpit of the 25 A 33 as it flies on the fighter's
right with the 25 B 33 on the left)
The fighter has placed itself between both aircraft fighters
flying closely by his comrades.
The gunner of 25 B 33 (Hasinger) waves back.
145 *Close:*
(from the left to the fighter's cockpit)
The very young lieutenant as he gives a friendly smile
taking off his funny little hat to the comrades of the
fighter aircraft flying on his left.

The première of Bertram's action-filled film was attended by Reich Minister Dr. Goebbels as well as Ministers Darré and Schwerin-Krosigk, and Reichsführer-SS Heinrich Himmler: "Horrido and hussassa *Kampfgeschwader Lützow*!"

Carl Otto Bartning, as editor of *Feuertaufe* and *Kampfgeschwader Lützow* one of Hans Bertram's closest collaborators, and Bertram's production manager Wilhelm Stöppler in 1941 joined forces with effects cameraman Karl Ludwig Ruppel to make another semidocumentary for Tobis that mixes stock footage, studio scenes, and model shots "without second thoughts": *Front am Himmel* (*Front in the Sky*). They even catapulted model airplanes through the sound stages of Tobis Studios in Berlin-Johannisthal. After the war, Ruppel and Bartning teamed with director Alfred Weidenmann in making another war epic, *Der Stern von Afrika* (*The Star of Africa*), starring Joachim Hansen as pilot hero Marseille, this time using British traveling matte techniques for incorporating the model airplanes. *Front am Himmel*, however, was not screened regularly. The Battle of Britain was already lost for the German Luftwaffe when the picture was finished. Scenes of Germany's air raid warning system in operation during an actual aerial attack didn't help the film pass the censors, nor did details of various British attacks on Germany. Only parts of it turned up in German newsreels.

Not released, too, was another production by "Professor Karl Ritter"— also due to the situation on the front —*Besatzung Dora* (*Garrison Dora*). Ritter spent six full weeks

> as a soldier with the reconnaissance aircraft before I went to write the screenplay. Impressed by the experience during this command the plan developed to open up every national comrade for the fresh milieu as real and pure as possible and to shoot no single take on the sound stage but on location with real fliers and their officers. Only the leads should be cast with actors, who fit the real people at the front in a way that one cannot see a difference. Also the scenes of the Berlin complex weren't filmed on the stage or on the backlot. We went with the whole crew to the West, to the men who are flying against England, we were at the Leningrad Front, on the Eastern Front, and we were in the hot South. I think one feels that seeing our film. From the screen there blows a fresh air which I had hoped for. This is the delightful and heart-warming spirit which dominates our front, and nobody who has lived for some time among its men will forget that experience. Everybody at home must take a few breaths from it now and then. There is no better cure in this time.
>
> So our film serves two tasks: to give those staying at home a feeling of the front experience from flight and to entertain by a relaxed plot for an hour of cheerful reflection. Then however behind the play of the protagonists primarily a visible and remaining memorial shall be erected in the hearts of everybody for our splendid reconnaissance planes and their great efforts which they make just wonderfully day after day as a matter of course.
>
> Greetings and a word of thanks to the brave comrades on the Eastern and Western front who have helped with *Besatzung Dora*.[21]

Goebbels found *Besatzung Dora* "very appealing" but thought that it would be more suitable "for the second than the fourth year of the war. And so I am somewhat skeptical when assessing the new Ritter production's chances of success."[22] Too many scenes about fronts, however (i.e., the Russian and North African fronts) made it impossible to show it, and so once more a Nazi film had to be banned by the Nazis themselves in November 1943. As a director Ritter fell out of favor with Hitler and his cohorts, as did his master Hermann Göring, whose *Luftwaffe* had lost the Battle of Britain and seemed helpless against the Allied "air terror." To make matters worse for Göring, there even was talk about the Reich Marshall's morphine addiction. Interestingly, one of the *Dora* stars, Hubert Kiurina, was married to Frau Emmy Göring's niece. For similar reasons of delicate content, other projects had to be stopped before filming, for instance a UFA picture titled *Charkow*. Ritter was upset that *Dora* was canned and felt deeply offended when Goebbels' state secretary Dr. Gutterer told him on April 14, 1943, that the minister considered that his picture did not correspond with National Socialist perception.[23]

Junge Adler (*Young Eagles*), first announced as *Der Schritt ins Leben* (*Step into*

Life—which for many was to become a step into death) or *Jugend von heute* (*Youth of Today*)—boys working in an aircraft factory and dreaming of becoming pilots themselves—continued where the Hitler Youth projects had left off. It was the legacy of Nazi films to post-war German Films. Its writer-director Alfred Weidenmann resumed his career in Federal Republic of Germany, as we have seen, and his associate Herbert Reinecker, another former Hitler Youth journalist who once had been rejected by the glider plane movement because of his glasses, became the most successful writer of old-fashioned t.v. crime series like *Der Kommissar* and *Derrick*. Reinecker wept crocodile tears when he thought about his past.[24] Youthful stars like Dietmar Schönherr, Gunnar Möller, and Eberhard Krüger a.k.a. Hardy Krüger went on to dominate cinema screens and t.v. sets. Hardy Krüger even played supporting roles in several successful foreign language movies like Howard Hawks' *Hatari!* starring John Wayne. In his book *Tadellöser & Wolff*, German author Walter Kempowski, who had seen Weidenmann preparing for location shooting in Warnemünde, described him as a gaunt guy in long leather overcoat, resembling Count Ciano a little bit, Mussolini's unfortunate son-in-law and longtime Italian secretary of state. Ingeborg Lohse wrote about the national "Director of the Youth" in *Film-Kurier*.[25]

> "Alfred Weidenmann is no unknown to us. There is the film *Young Europe* that evoked a remarkable echo with the audience, but which wasn't credited in name to its director. Well, he is Alfred Weidenmann.
>
> *Young Europe*—*Young Eagles*—titles that all lead in a certain direction. And under these conditions of youth we enter the sound stage in Tempelhof to watch Alfred Weidenmann at work. A nice scene is about to unfold. Eight to ten boys, according to the screenplay apprentices in a big airplane factory, are standing in a tent, which is supposed to be somewhere in the Baltic. From the dialogue we learn that during the absence of the boys from the factory a fire destroyed some of the just finished parts of the planes. "Just at the spot where our cockpits are stored," Bäumchen, the youngest, starts to say. "*So eine Sch…* (*Scheisse*—Shit)" The word comes that honest and sincere out of the boy's mouth that all of them burst out laughing. The scene is rehearsed once again and again, but each time when the ominous passage is to be delivered an insolent smirk flits across the faces followed by a friendly ringing laughter. The director stands in front of the boys. His mischievous face gives away how he enjoys them. But first the play comes to a halt. The language that flies around is getting more clear, and the laughter does not end. "Now, Gentlemen, calm down. This scene must be finished." "Hey man, when you are writing such stuff in your screenplay you cannot expect that we will keep a straight face," one of the lads quips and has everybody laughing wildly. Finally every obstacle is negotiated successfully and the play goes on.

The show must go on—up to the bitter end…

CHAPTER 7

Surrounded
by Enemies

Films like the 1940 *Feinde* (*Enemies*) and the 1941 Viennese production *Heimkehr* (*Homecoming*) tell odd stories about the fate of German nationalists abroad after the outbreak of war and try to "explain" why certain countries had to be invaded. The slogan was "*Heim ins Reich*" ("Home into the Reich").

The enemies in the *Enemies*, of course, are the Poles, who start to attack German farms close to the border, killing the owners, plundering the farmhouses and burning them down. Polish hooligans, secretly supported by the Warsaw authorities, become more threatening daily. The Germans are forced to pack all the belongings they can and leave by night in the hope of reaching the German frontier. A young girl, whom all thought a Pole but who is really German, leads them across a dangerous boggy moor to the safety of the Reich.

"This great Bavarian production — masterly directed by V. Tourjansky — deals with the fate of a group of German nationalists expelled from their farms by bestial and instigated soldiers of another state who are chasing them to death in cold blood.

"From this mighty picture the intense atmosphere of a foreign country blows into our face that voluptuously sets his 'men' at defenselessly fleeing Germans.

"Like a magnificent symbol these scenes are penetrated by a tremendous and indestructible love for the native place and faithfulness of a group of German nationalists who have been declared war on by a vindictive government.

"In an area near the German border the atmosphere is tense. Criminal elements are sabotaging the cultural work of the Germans. These 'men' are creeping jealously spotting each single opportunity for dirty work. Persecution and

Paula Wessely in *Heimkehr*.

mockery of the Germans increase in fanatical hatred and brutal blood-thirstiness. Stout-hearted men and a woman's defiance of death help the hunted people escape into territory which is controlled by the German Reich.

"From the lips of these people, like a rousing fanfare of triumph, resounds the song of their distant birthplace to which they have to fight their way through. For the viewer, however, a perception of something great and wonderful takes shape and confirms: the belief in Germany — the love for the native country! And this is the great testimony of this movie which will be understood by everybody feeling for the sufferings."[1]

Enemies was partly filmed in the Polish town Chorzele. This from a shooting review: "Chorzele is a 'town.' At least so the Polish called this nest because a mayor resided here and because the farmers of the surroundings disposed of their products in the marshy market-place. The shop signs around the market-place give the profiteers away: one Polish trader is opposed by nine unmistakably Jewish names. No wonder that of 3,000 inhabitants in Chorzele about 2,000 prayed to a Mosaic god for the good success of their bargains?"[2]

Homecoming is another movie that deals with Polish (and Jewish) "aggressiveness." By the spring of 1939 several Germans living in Volhynia have been killed, and their women have been stoned to death. After beating the remaining Germans up, Polish gendarmes transport them in lorries to the prison of Luzk, where 200 of them vegetate in a cellar consisting of three small cells, with water up to their ankles. Paula

A scene from *Heimkehr*.

Wessely, the star of the film, tries to comfort her fellow countrymen with the following *blood and soil* speech.

> Just think what it will be like, my friends, just think what it will be like when there are just Germans around us, and when you go into a shop it won't be Yiddish or Polish that you hear, but German! And it's not just the whole village that will be German, but everything all around us will be German. And we'll be in the middle of it, in the heart of Germany. Just think, my friends, what it will be like! And why shouldn't it be like that? We'll be living on the good old warm soil of Germany. In our own country and at home. And at night, in our beds, when we wake from our sleep, our hearts will quicken suddenly in the sweet knowledge that we are sleeping in the middle of Germany, in our own country and at home, surrounded by the comforting night and millions of German hearts that beat softly and as one. You are at home, my friend, at home with your own people. There will be a wonderful feeling in our hearts when we know that the soil in the field and our little bit of life, the rock, the waving grass, the swaying branches of the hazelnut and the trees, that all this is German. Just like us, belonging to us, because it has all grown from the millions of German hearts that have been buried in the earth and have become German earth. Because we don't just live a German life, we also die a German death. Even when we're dead, we're still German, we're still a real part of Germany. A handful of soil for our grandchildren to grow corn in.

Attila Hörbiger protects two boys in *Heimkehr*.

These wretched people are about to be liquidated when a German air-raid rescues them and puts an end to the "ignominious, infamous actions of Polish devils."

The same year Tobis director Fritz Peter Buch helmed an anti–Yugoslav propaganda project titled *Menschen im Sturm* (*Men in Struggle*). With the Serbs organizing the Terror against the Volksdeutschen, Vera, the German wife of a Slovene, secretly assists her countrymen to escape across the frontier. One night as she is driving German orphans [!] in a carriage, she is discovered by the Serbs and shot. In *Die goldene Stadt* (*The Golden City*), a 1942 UFA production in Agfacolor, a young peasant girl from a clean Sudeten village, who is visiting vicious Prague, is seduced by her Czech cousin-by-marriage. In the end, returning to her village, she goes to the nearby moor where her mother died and drowns herself. We will hear more of this movie's director and his star: Veit Harlan and Kristina Söderbaum.

But not only in Europe — everywhere in the world a German Diaspora was waiting for its rescue, even in Africa. One of the first violently anti–British films was *Die Reiter von Deutsch-Ostafrika* (*The Riders of German East Africa*), made as early as 1934. It was produced under the patronage of the Reichskolonialbund (Reich Colonial League). Advisor Willibald von Stuermer had served as a lieutenant colonel of the former German Schutztruppe (colonial force). Parts of the movie were illegally filmed on locations in Tanganyika. 1914: Peter Hellhoff, a farmer in Deutsch-Ostafrika, and his bride Gerda are just celebrating marriage at the time general mobilization is ordered. Taking his men, Hellhoff immediately joins the colonial force and faces his former friend, British officer Robert Cresswell, now a sworn enemy, as treacherous as an Englishman can be.

But the "mightiest" anti–British African picture of them all was *Ohm Krüger* (*Uncle Krüger*), "an Emil Jannings Film by Tobis Filmkunst" that was supposed to be on the same level as *Gone With the Wind*, one of Goebbels' personal favorites. It had big production values, costumes, a score by one of Germany's leading composers, Theo ("Bel Ami") Mackeben — it was a period piece on a grand scale, a movie that had absolutely everything, except a novel as large as Margaret Mitchell's, color, Vivien Leigh and Clark Gable. Instead it offered the pompously overacting Emil Jannings in the title role. Nominally it was directed by a Nazi, Hans Steinhoff, who had introduced himself with *Hitlerjunge Quex* and seemed to assume a position second only to that held by Veit Harlan and Karl Ritter, but in fact the picture was Jannings' work. Jannings had been Germany's great silent film star. For the late F. W. Murnau he did *Der letzte Mann* (*The Last Laugh*), *Tartuff* and *Faust*. In 1928, while he was under contract to Paramount in Hollywood, he accepted the first Academy Award given to a male star for two productions, *The Last Command* and *The Way of All Flesh*. Returning to Germany, he involuntarily helped a relatively unknown Marlene Dietrich to stardom by producing *Der Blaue Engel* (*The Blue Angel*). Jannings, not fluent in the English language, decided to stay in Germany where he came to an accommodation with the brown rulers; he was par-ticularly close to Dr. Goebbels, who valued Jannings' international fame highly. Since Jannings despised Steinhoff, he himself took over part of the directing and even hired two other directors, Herbert Maisch (who had done a movie called *Friedrich Schiller* with Horst Cas-par) and Karl Anton, without the knowledge of an infuriated Stein-hoff. For his services Jannings received the "Ring of Honor of the German Cinema," whatever that was.

In flashbacks Ohm (Uncle) Krüger, a Boer war hero, blind and dying in exile in a Swiss hospital after traveling around Europe beseeching help for the Boer cause, tells his life story, drawing a terrible picture of his British enemies dur-ing the Boer war. It all starts when British mine lord Cecil John Rhodes, a veritable picture-book imperialist, finds gold near Johan-

A depiction of Emil Jannings as Uncle Krüger in *Ohm Krüger*.

nesburg. To secure a British mandate he plots riots in the once peaceful Boer country, the Transvaal and Orange Free State. "The English are terrible villains one and
all. They incite the colored natives by handing out guns during a mission service to
the tune of 'Onward Christian Soldiers.' They feed rotten meat to the Boer women
and children in the giant concentration camps they have invented in South Africa,
and bayonet the prisoners without regard to age or sex; the viewer is told that 26,000
women and children were murdered. (The unbelievable gall of blaming the institution of concentration camps on the British — whether true or not — showed Goebbels
at the height of his cynicism.)"[3]

In one sequence Uncle Krüger meets Queen Victoria, who tries to lure "the old
fool" into some kind of peace arrangement. She is of the same kind that the Nazis
accused Winston Churchill of being — a whisky-swilling harridan. "If there's gold to
be found, then of course it's our country. We British are the only ones capable of
carrying the burdens of wealth without becoming ungodly." (Churchill himself
appears in a cameo as the overfed commandant of a concentration camp for Boer
women.) In another sequence, Gustaf Gründgens' Chamberlain ("Providence has
called on England to educate small and backward nations") complains about defeats
and retreats due to the Boer activities led by Krüger: "For this reason the cabinet has
decided to dismiss the former commander-in-chief, Sir Colley, and to entrust General Kitchener with the command in South Africa. May I ask you, General Kitchener, to develop your strategy for us!"

Kitchener answers icily: "The prime mistake of my predecessors was the fact that
they clung to certain military principles, which may be applicable in normal conditions but are misplaced in Africa. This war is a *colonial* war, Gentlemen; therefore it
must be fought by *colonial* means!"

"What does that mean?" Chamberlain wants to know.

"What this means is an end to humanitarian mawkishness!" Kitchener demands.
"We must hit the Boers where they alone are vulnerable! We must burn their farms,
separate wives and children from their menfolk, and place them in concentration
camps! From today all Boers, without exception, are outlaws. No distinction is to be
made between soldiers and civilians!"[4]

One of Krüger's sons, Jan, who was raised in Britain and educated in Oxford
and in the beginning didn't believe that Britain was indulging in a policy of intrigues,
has now followed in his dad's footsteps and joined the free corps of commander de
Witt after his wife was assaulted by a drunken British sergeant. When he secretly
visits his wife in a British concentration camp, he is captured and hanged in a location that resembles the Biblical Golgotha, the site of Jesus's crucifixion. A martyr for
the Boer cause, Jan says, "I die for the Fatherland" as he is executed. Following is the
scene as described in the screenplay[5]:

Scene 99

Free Place in Concentration Camp
   (Under the monkey-bread tree, which stands in the middle of the camp, a rostrum is erected. From a withered branch a rope hangs for execution.)
662.
The execution commando stands ready

in square. — Drum roll —

663.

The commander of the camp reads the verdict:

> "Jan Krüger is to be hanged as a rebel. For a more severe punishment it is herewith ordered that the inmates of the camp, in particular the relatives of the traitor, have to attend the execution…"

He sits up and cynically turns to the women:

> "That will be more likely to keep you from disturbing my night's sleep."

664.

The lined up women — among them Petra and Mrs. Krüger — silently and solemnly stare at the sand.

> — Once again drum roll —

665.

Jan Krüger, the wounded arm in the bandage, is led by six soldiers of the firing squad to the tree which stands hard against the flickering horizon. His posture is upright.

666.

Now he climbs the rostrum. The rope is laid around his neck.

Emil Jannings (right) and Ferdinand Marian in *Ohm Krüger*.

667.
A woman cannot stand it anymore and
shouts:

> "Aren't you ashamed to hang a wounded
> man?!"

668.
The commander roars:

> "Quiet!! Shall we first wait till the doctor has
> him patched up again?"

He laughs at this remark and
expects the physician of the camp,
who stands next to him, to join in.
However, the other doesn't show
more than an insolent smirk.

— Drum roll once again —

669.
The women have all looked
ahead and now partly turn around, partly
shield the eyes with their hands. The
commander shouts to the soldiers who
are supposed to hang Jan Krüger:

> "Stop!"

The women remain in their posture.
670.
The commander [in the foreground],
in the background the offender.
The commander addresses the women:

> "Will you kindly watch?!"

671.
The women don't move. The commander
cannot do without some kind of
entertainment:

> "Get a move on, will you. In theatre one has
> to pay admission for something like that!"

Several soldiers who have lined up behind the
women, tear them apart and try by force to
make them comply with the request of
the commander.
672.
Petra shoves away the soldiers, she pushes her
way to the front. With cutting voice she shouts:

> "I w a n t to see!
> I want to s e e ,
> so that I won't forget it!"
> — Drum roll —

673.
Jan on the rostrum, the rope around his neck.
He shouts with strong voice:

> "A curse on England!"

„OHM KRUGER"
Der Emil Jannings-Film der Tobis

Then the rostrum is pushed away under his
feet.
674.
Jan's call is repeated by the women:

> "A curse on England!"
> The chorus of voices gets unreal, lingers
> through the air, spreading horror like the
> fury call of the Erynis.

The film's final scene, however, has been reserved for the memory of Jan's father, the
uncanny Krüger Sr.:

[Flashback]:
Krüger's room in the Swiss hotel
677.
Krüger's voice [his image superimposed]:

> "Thus England defeated the little Boer
> people…"

Slowly the face of the blind Krüger forms
out of the wavering, just as we saw it
in the beginning of the film.
As the camera moves back…, he speaks
the final lines:

> "And yet I believe: So much bloodshed can-
> not be to no avail,

> so many tears cannot be wept to no avail,
> and so much heroism cannot have been to
> no avail.
> For if the history of the world makes sense
> it can be only thus:
> A new future of peoples which is based upon
> deep yearning of men for the final peace will
> surely come one day after the war which is
> fought for justice!!!"

Fade Out!
THE END.

According to Krüger Sr., "great and powerful nations will arise to reduce the British to pulp."

Noted film historian Erwin Leiser, on the other hand, argues that evil Englishmen are portrayed in even more gaudy colors in Max W. "Axel" Kimmich's *Germanin* (1943): "In this film the German 'Bayer 205' as a remedy for sleeping sickness is superior to all other medicines used against that plague. German Professor Achenbach, whose experimental laboratory in the jungle was destroyed by the beginning of the war in 1914 by the English, developed the specimen during the war and returns in 1923 with an expedition to Africa to fight sleeping sickness once and for all. The English regard his activities as a threat to their position and prevent him from helping the ill Negroes. They order him to leave Africa and destroy his Germanin. Only one ampoule escapes destruction. Although Achenbach himself is seriously ill with sleeping sickness he heals his own deadly enemy, an equally ill English colonel, and in return gets the license that allows a clearing of African forests and with that a more intense fight against the tsetse fly. The contrast between the arrogant and brutal representatives of perfidious Albion and the selfless German researcher, who sacrifices his life for the health of Negroes [!], shall convince even the most stupid viewer who really has the mission to own colonies."

Kimmich, who had worked some time for Universal in America during the silent days, was Dr. Goebbels' brother-in-law and already responsible for two other anti–British (and pro–Irish) films: *Der Fuchs von Glenarvon* (*The Fox of Glenarvon*) and *Mein Leben für Irland* (*My Life for Ireland*). Goebbels was particularly pleased by *Fox*: "*Fuchs von Glenarvon*, a film about the Irish struggle for freedom by Axel Kimmich. It is wonderful now, and will come in very useful for our propaganda."[6]

A drawing of Max W. Kimmich who directed *Mein Leben für Irland.*

A similar anti–British Hans Albers production was the Bavaria project *Carl*

An ad for *Mein Leben für Irland*.

Peters (1941) filmed in Barrandor Studios in Prague. This from the Bavaria press-book:

It was an auspicious start

when Bavaria-Filmkunst announced in its 1940-41 program the Hans Albers *Gross-film* [spectacular] **Carl Peters**.

Hans Albers,
the ideal impersonator of fearless men full of fighting spirit starring as a resolute German man, who had his own way against arbitrary use of power, faint-heartedness and intrigues in order to achieve his aim in life: to acquire colonial possessions for the German nation.

Carl Peters,
the pioneer and founder of Deutsch-Ostafrika!

This promise is fulfilled now

With it one of the biggest German films of this year has originated. A movie that is meaningful and always topical not only for the present day but as a memorial for an undying Germany in all future time, too!

A German fate
is told by this movie in impressive scenes. A German fate means a fighting fate; it means a life full of sacrifices, privations and dangers—for Germany! Shaped in a grand outline, portrayed in a plot of almost confusing plenty, and full of excitement and adventurousness, this life becomes visible. Impossible to describe all the thrilling scenes in a short synopsis; impossible to emphasize one or another highlight of the story! This movie can be felt only as a whole, viewed and felt as a strong experience carrying all away with its enthusiasm![7]

"In the case of Dr. Carl Peters pre-war Germany has blamed herself decisively. Authorities, Reichstag, Jewish press, and a public of *Spiesser* (petit bourgeois) united in a many-voiced chorus of atrocities against the conqueror of East Africa, whom each other country would have used as a battering-ram into the world. We Germans then didn't possess the political instinct which prevented us from flogging to death the minor defects of this genius personality in public discussion instead of ignoring them in silence. Peters was the strongest and politically most pronounced of our colonial pioneers— difficult as geniuses usually are but, nevertheless, an enthusiastic German, who even after his 'fall' bravely refused all British offers to have himself praised in the services of England....

"Hans Albers in the title role convincingly portrays the flaming activity and Lower Saxonian tenacity of this great African explorer. Albers has what is most important: the expression of energy. He impersonates 'a strolling, charged battery of willpower.' Again he holds his audience in firm hands, and often suspense explodes in

Hans Albers featured in his title role in *Carl Peters*.

frenetical applause."[8] Not to forget that in this one Hans Albers is opposed not only by the British but by Jews, who combine in a plot to have him murdered.

Carl Peters was premiered under the patronage of *Reichsstatthalter* and *Reichsleiter* (Reich Governor/Reich Leader) Ritter von Epp in Munich. Present were Adolf Wagner, *Gauleiter* and Minister of State, and former fighters from Deutsch-Ostafrika.

The premiere was opened by a military band that played in the uniforms of the old East-African *Schutztruppe* (peace-keeping force) and with a speech by Josef Viera from the Reichskolonialbund. Munich's Ufa Palace was decorated with the colors of the *Bewegung* (the movement) (i.e., swastikas) and the colonial flag.

After successfully wrapping *Carl Peters*, director Herbert Selpin got the assignment for another anti–British film, *Titanic*, a fatal assignment indeed that cost him his life. "The maiden journey of the giant liner serves only the speculative interests of the president of the White Star Line, which owns the ship. In order to save the company, which is on the verge of financial collapse as the result of the cost of building the liner, and in order to insure for themselves gigantic profits, President Ismay (Ernst Fürbringer) bribes the captain (Otto Wernicke), to sail to New York at full speed along the northern route which is endangered by ice floes. The 'Blue Ribbon' must be won, which will supposedly raise the stock of the company to its former level. At first, however, the shares fall and Ismay plans to buy them at a low price just before the ship arrives in New York."[9]

British plutocrats responsible for the death of 1,600 passengers!

A film about the *Titanic* was first announced by Tobis Filmkunst in 1940. Curt J. Braun and Pelz von Felinau, himself a survivor of the catastrophe, were commissioned to write a screenplay. Karl Ludwig Diehl was going to play the lead. When the project appeared again in the 1941-42 release prospectus Hilde Weissner and Michael Bohnen had been added to the cast, and Herbert Maisch was scheduled to direct from a screenplay by Harald Bratt. Shooting finally started on February 23, 1942, in Jofa Studios in Berlin-Johannisthal with Herbert Selpin as directorial helmsman.

> "*Titanic* was intended as one of the prestige spectaculars of the Nazi film industry. The dramatic possibilities of the sinking of the great ship (recreated or reflected in many previous movies [the first produced in Berlin in 1912]) were obvious, and for Goebbels the propaganda aspect was present in the theme of British pig-headedness. It would be easy to show the German passengers on board as more heroic than the British, even to add characters like a German first officer who warns the captain of the perils of undertaking such a fast run. Director Herbert Selpin, a capable director (and a man not sympathetic to the Nazis), was given a big production budget and a first-class cast, featuring above all the "German Garbo," Sybille Schmitz…. Despite the often confusing intrigues of the plot line, it is hard to fault the acting, particularly of Sybille Schmitz as the enigmatic Sigrid, perhaps her best performance. Attired in a rather odd vampish black wig, she slithers through the picture with remarkable style and dominates every scene in which she appears. The sinking of the ship, a combination of model-shots and truly spectacular footage photographed by Friedl Behn-Grund in Gdynia and Berlin, can hardly be bettered.[10]

Apparently shooting proceeded smoothly in Berlin but problems arose during location shooting. To reconstruct this maritime catastrophe of epic proportions, Selpin sent Nazi writer (and co-author of *Carl Peters*) Walter Zerlett-Olfenius (who was responsible for distorting the facts to emphasize the anti–British line) with a second unit crew and extras to the harbor of Gdynia (Gotenhafen) for exteriors. Zerlett-Olfenius, however, didn't achieve anything worthwhile. Several weeks later, Selpin took the train to Gdynia.

> The two men went to the nearby *Kurhaus* [spa hotel] at Zoppot, where Selpin demanded to know why his instructions had been ignored. Zerlett-Olfenius told him that the local naval officers, who were under orders from the Propaganda Ministry to cooperate on the production, were interested only in romancing the girls from Berlin.
>
> Selpin then asked why Zerlett-Olfenius did not put his foot down, since he had the necessary authority to do so. He answered that those who wore the *Ritterkreuz* [the Knights' Cross, a German military decoration] were supermen, crusaders who could allow themselves what they wanted, and could spend the night with the whole crew of [female] extras if they felt like it. Selpin, who had managed to keep his temper under control during the interview, if not his drinking, snapped back that, as far as he could see, the decoration must certainly be awarded for the number of actresses seduced. When Zerlett-Olfenius continued to defend his "supermen," Selpin shouted at the top of his voice (according to witnesses at the postwar trial): "*Ach du! Mit deinen Scheissoldaten, du Scheissleutnant überhaupt mit deiner Scheisswehrmacht!*"[11]

Blaming Germany's "fucking soldiers and fucking army in front of a fucking lieutenant," Zerlett-Olfenius, the upset screenwriter had nothing better to do than to run to his friend, SS *Obergruppenführer* Hans Hinkel, to denounce Selpin. Selpin was immediately ordered to Goebbels' offices at Wilhelmstrasse in Berlin.

"Goebbels came from behind his desk," wrote David Stewart Hull — "an unusual procedure as he preferred to hide his deformed foot — and told Selpin that he had a report that the director had made some remarks about the German navy at Gdynia, but that he was certain the whole incident had been misunderstood. Selpin told him that everything Goebbels had heard was true. Goebbels, making an attempt to control his temper, tried to give Selpin another chance to avoid a charge of treason. Selpin refused to take the bait.

"Finally the propaganda minister shouted: 'Do you really stand by those statements?' Selpin turned white and said, 'Yes, I do.' Goebbels turned to the SS guards and screamed, 'Then arrest this man and take him where he belongs!'...

"Sometime near midnight of Friday, July 31, 1942..., two guards went to Selpin's cell and proceeded to tie his suspenders to the bars of a window high in the ceiling. They brought in a bench, told Selpin to stand on it and grasp the bars, then tied the suspenders around his neck and took the bench away. When the unfortunate man no longer held on, he was strangled to death."[12] His widow was informed that her husband had committed suicide as often was done in such cases. The informer was sentenced to a working camp after the war until 1951.

The *Titanic* project was finished by another director, Werner Klingler, and Selpin's name was removed from the credits. The disaster scenes, however, were too crude to be shown to a German audience in 1942; then the première print was destroyed during an air raid. Eventually, the screening in Germany was forbidden, the negative seized. So the movie was only screened in France, to great success. In Germany it was distributed after the war in a limited release — limited because the

Allied High Commission feared the propaganda impact even in 1950. "Seven years after completion it had been passed in the American zone, premiered in Stuttgart. Though the Stuttgart papers recognized the technical perfection of the movie, they called the story Nazi activism. The audience, however, was waiting in front of the cinemas in long lines. Great Britain's high commissioner protested against the screening to the high commissioner of the United States. In Britain's House of Commons a member demanded that the movie be forbidden. Bevin explained according to the 'Daily Telegraph' that *Titanic* in its present form didn't contain any anti–English tendency but Churchill said such films should be better avoided in the contemporary situation." On the other side, *Titanic* was passed at the same time by the Soviet Film Control section and cleared for showing throughout East Berlin and East Germany. Finally, "on May 5, 1955, the day of German sovereignty, the *Titanic* film for which Germany had to wait long years was finally free, too," we read in a West-German pressbook[13]. It was released under the effective slogan "Forbidden! Forbidden! Forbidden!" Parts of the disaster scenes were used in a 1958 British movie, *A Night to Remember*, directed by Roy Ward Baker, written by Eric Ambler, and starring Kenneth More and David McCallum.

Finally come the Russians. In Gustav Ucicky's 1933 action film *Flüchtlinge*, Hans Albers leads a group of 40 German refugees out of the hell of the Chinese Civil War in 1928. Their most pertinacious pursuer is a Soviet commissar who, for the first time, is played by Andrews Engelmann, the villain par excellence.

Friesennot (*Frisians in Trouble*), made in 1935, depicted "*Ein Schicksal Deutscher auf russischer Erde*" ("Germans' fate on Russian soil") as it was conceived by *Reichsfilmdramaturg* Willi Krause, who co-wrote the screenplay under the nom de plume Peter Hagen. "German peasants were living in seclusion somewhere in Russia in the Volga area, in a village in the middle of the jungle, literally isolated from the outside world," we read in this shooting review which praises the authentic atmosphere of the project. "Soviet authorities didn't know anything in the beginning about this village in the forest until it accidentally was discovered by a military pilot. Now a time of suffering begins for the farmers who have conserved their *Deutschtum* [Germanness] although their families have lived in Russia for generations. Their cattle is confiscated by Red Guards, and when they grumble a number of them are shot.... These Red Guards are real Russians, although not Soviet people but Russian emigrants living in Berlin. Their leader is V. Inkijinoff whose extraordinarily distinctive Asian face has remained in good memory from the Russian film *Storm over Asia*.

"In the past one would have cast in such a film without any fuss German extras and German actors as Russians. Today this is impossible. For one thing it is out of the question in a sound film; it never would sound right if German extras would curse in a smattering of Russian; especially in the last years we have adopted an outspoken feeling for the Russian. German extras trimmed by the make-up artist won't transform into Slavonic types. In the past nobody would have noticed that but in the meantime we have sharpened our awareness of Russian stereotypes."[14]

This is the synopsis:

> ...a Soviet commissar is sent with Red Guards to systematically raid the village.
> The farmers have to deliver their supplies and their cattle; since they trust in

V. Inkijinoff (left) and Friedrich Kayssler in *Friesennot*.

authorities prescribed by God, they do it without a murmur till the unbridled soldiers indecently assault women and girls and desecrate the house of God; in this moment the religious leader of the community, a man, who had preached up to now fear of God and obedience, arms himself and shoots the villains. With the little that was left to them the Germans march on in the search for a new homeland.

Under the direction of Werner Kortwig [*sic*] and Peter Hagen the Germanness on Russian soil is impressively portrayed. These peasants have built their houses due to the building material in Russian blockhouse fashion but otherwise just the same as their ancestors did on German soil; these are old Lower Saxonian houses, and the language is the one their fathers spoke. The same is true for the clothing. Typically German are the characteristic heads and the unshakeable belief of the fathers, in particular the strongly developed public spirit. They contrast sharply with the Communists whose leaders bear outspoken Mongolian features; one feels immediately: here actually ends Europe; however, even this half–Mongolian is not a true Communist, he feels himself only as the executive agency of Soviet authorities, a professional soldier who obeyed the Czarist regime equally blindly; personally he has long since come to the conclusion that one cannot live happily in Russia, he has his own ideas about the official abolition of religion, too, but as he is firmly joined with the Communist world he doesn't manage to get away from it.

In one wonderful episode the Red guards are devastating the village church; one has covered himself in an altar cloth, just like a Russian pope. He steps to

Horseriders in the woods in *Friesennot*.

the pulpit obviously wanting to scornfully commit a blasphemy when another soldier in a low voice intones an old Russian church hymn. Originally he wanted to
satirize but now the old melody casts its spell over him as the others join in quietly. Suddenly out of the Red guards' mouths sound one of those beautifully old
church choruses—until the Russian commissar comes dashing in and ends the
ghostly manifestation.[15]

Chernov, the Commissar, declares to one of the Germans that there certainly is
no God in all of Russia.

> THE GERMAN (Wagner). So there's no God in Russia. Who says so? Who
>   can suddenly abolish him?
> CHERNOV. The authorities.
> THE GERMAN (Wagner). But don't you see that all authority comes from
>   God. How can you abolish God?
> CHERNOV. It's easy if you can capture the souls of the masses.

Karl Anton's 1936 *Weisse Sklaven* (*White Slaves*) shows scenes of "Bolshevist"
cruelty during the Russian Revolution in Sebastopol: plunder, murder and unrestrained festivities become the order of the day. The former servants now have become
the masters. But such scenes were not to the liking of the Propaganda Minister:
"Goebbels was able to reverse a ban on the film by Hitler in October 1936 ('realisti-
cally based on Bolshevism. Close to the limit. A break at the end,' 14.10.1936) by pro-

A scene from *Weisse Sklaven* (later rereleased as *Panzerkreuzer Sebastopol*).

ducing a heavily modified new version. Though it seems to have been very popular with the public, this was not yet the Nazi settling of accounts with Communism that Hitler and Goebbels had in mind."[16]

White Slaves was eventually re-released in West Germany as *Panzerkreuzer Sebastopol* (*Battleship Sebastopol*) to rave reviews:

> A work made at a time when they still worked fanatically in the movies.[17]

> The reunion with one of the big-budget movies which was produced at the peak of German filmmaking ... once again we bow to the German filmmakers' craftsmanship in those days and regret to notice today's impediment to reaching these heights again.[18]

In accordance with that attitude, satisfied exhibitors' telegrams piled up on the distributor's desk:

> despite pre-christmas week battleship Sebastopol in the first 3 days 7,000 patrons enthusiastic reception by the audience characterized as one of the best German films congratulations
> scalacinema lang frankfurtmain

WERNER HINZ   **PANZERKREUZER SEBASTOPOL**   KARL JOHN
CAMILLA HORN   (WEISSE SKLAVEN)   AGNES STRAUB
THEODOR LOOS   FRITZ KAMPERS

The mob is armed in *Weisse Sklaven* (later rereleased as *Panzerkreuzer Sebastopol*).

battleship sebastopol in 6 days made 10,000 patrons at a seating of 350 stop congratulations to this audience success we'll prolong
   apollotheater wiesbaden

despite carnival big business as expected with battleship sebastopol stop we'll prolong
   centraltheater hanau

despite carnival time in mainz the stronghold of carnival and against strongest competition battleship sebastopol sold out for the first three days at three screenings daily
   capitol mainz.[19]

Starke Herzen (*Strong Hearts*) directed by Herbert Maisch was similar anti–Soviet propaganda, but it was not distributed during Nazi times. It was finally released during the Cold War in West Germany as *Starke Herzen im Sturm* (*Strong Hearts in the Storm*). In UFA's program for 1937-38 it was announced: "…the fate of a city drawn into the witches' cauldron of revolution in 1919. The struggle of a conspiracy against the messengers of Bolshevism. In this chaos, two human beings find their way to each other — bound by duty and a willingness to make sacrifices, these two hearts resonate in a stirring witness to the triumphant power of love over hatred and death." The subject had been accepted by the new Reich film dramaturge, Ewald von Demandowsky, by Ufa production chief Ernst Hugo Correll, and by the Propaganda Min-

WERNER HINZ **PANZERKREUZER SEBASTOPOL** KARL JOHN
CAMILLA HORN AGNES STRAUB
THEODOR LOOS (WEISSE SKLAVEN) FRITZ KAMPERS

A scene from *Weisse Sklaven* (rereleased as *Panzerkreuzer Sebastopol*).

istry. The production history is a rather odd one. The picture, originally planned as a showcase for Hungarian-born singer Martha Eggert, was first considered under the opera title *Tosca* (or *Eine Tosca*) in 1936, but negotiations with Ms. Eggert failed. Then Wilhelm Meydam, head of UFA distribution, spotted the less expensive Bessarabia-born singer Maria Cebatori who was under contract to the Dresden opera house. The story, as envisioned by its authors, Walter Wassermann and C. H. Diller, i.e. Lotte Neumann, was to take place in 1919 in a Hungarian town where Béla Kun Communists raid an opera house during a performance of Puccini's *Tosca*. But when the Hungarian embassy asked that Hungary not be used as the scene of the plot the story was shifted from Magyar settings to the time of the Munich *Räterepublik* (soviet republic), then to Finland which had been introduced into the "witches' cauldron" of the Russian revolution. After some costly retakes the movie (starring Gustav Diessl and Walther Franck) was mysteriously banned in November 1937 after several submissions to the censors. Friedrich Kahlenberg[20] found a clue to the banning "in the substantially more cogent presentation of the position of the revolutionaries as compared with the portrayal of the national cause." According to Goebbels it was "utterly middle-class and simplistic, without sharp lines or contrast"[21]: "How the *Stahlhelm* sees Bolshevism. Typical of Ufa."[22] Another UFA project, *Der rote Tod* (*The Red Death*), had already been called off tacitly when authorities appeared not willing to invest in such a picture.

After the German-Soviet Nonaggression Pact of 23 August 1939, all anti–Soviet films produced up to that point were banned, too, at least for some time, and all current anti–Bolshevik projects were canceled. Like most other Germans, the producers, too, were taken completely by surprise by this change of policy. The old program was re-started in 1941 with Germany's sudden attack on the Soviet Union in Operation Barbarossa. *Friesennot*, for instance, was re-released under the title *Dorf im Roten Sturm* (*Red Storm Over the Village*).

Karl Ritter also released a new propaganda piece for UFA, *GPU*, a big-budget film that cost the exorbitant sum of almost RM 1.6 million. (Another anti–Russian film, *Anschlag auf Baku*, the story of a former German officer who defeats Soviet and British sabotage on gushers at the Caspian Sea, turned out even more expensive, at the then unheard of sum of RM 2.6 million. Its production manager, Hans Weidemann, was temporarily suspended.) "Revealing, warning and charging this film rips off the mask of the face of the most dangerous, because underground and secret institution of the Moscow central of revolution and shows it in all its criminal force. Never solved murders, world-shaking assassins, mysterious bomb attacks are to be blamed to GPU which as depicted by this movie in intrepid reality pursues its subversion in secrecy throughout the world in order to spoil and destroy people."[23]

Will Quadflieg in *GPU*.

"Bolshevism," we read in the opening titles, "tries to spread anarchy and chaos over all countries of the earth." The initials GPU are spelled:

G   *Grauen* [horror]
P   *Panik* [panic]
U   *Untergang* [destruction]

In 1919 Commissar Boksha, with his own hand, has shot the parents, brothers and sisters of the later violinist Olga Feodorovna. She only lives to avenge the murderer, and to hit him for sure she joins GPU, the instigator of numerous assassinations, where Boksha has made a career for himself since, although, as someone remarks, "he is neither Jew nor proletarian. That is rare with us. Headquarters thinks highly of him." After a long and secret pursuit of Boksha she succeeds in winning his confidence and spots a weakness in his life: some private financial resources and a refuge in lovely Brittany, which is sufficient to have him liquidated by his comrades. (*En passant*, Nikolai Boksha is played by Andrews Engelmann who had had a similar part as early as 1933 in Ucicky's *Flüchtlinge*.)

Finally Olga returns to Moscow and the GPU headquarters (the atmosphere clearly suggests that Ritter has seen Ernst Lubitsch's *Ninotchka*). We see a GPU official giving fatal orders to his underlings preparing the Fifth Column for world-wide riots and strikes: "Strikes in France? Section 4. Sabotage on cruiser *Birmingham*—chief! New list of agents from London —chief, immediately have it decoded. Shanghai. The Nanking minister murdered. Summary over Nanking and Hankau. Section 4. Australia ... Dockers on strike ... strike in the Australian coal mines ... 23,000 workers on strike ... respectable, respectable. Section 4. Ah ... anti–Nazi demonstration in Johannesburg. Police powerless in the face of the mob. Chief ... chief ... chief ... chief ... chief. The stainless steel process from Sweden. Report from Stockholm legation. Ah ... by comrade Kollanty (*a woman*)—love and steel! Section 3. Göteborg and Helsinki, at last, we were waiting for that!"

The chief himself is introduced as a truly sinister character: "Surrounding the Axis Powers ... in this web we have to suppress them."[24]

For a moment it looks as if Olga, who refuses the decoration offered to her, is going to shoot him but then she kills herself: "I do not want a reward from murderers, robbers, and criminals."

A contributing factor in the movie's main plot is the destiny of the student Peter Assmus and the secretary Irina, who are both mixed up in the intrigues of GPU and are saved in Holland from sure death by invading German troops. "The film leads us through half of Europe, from Riga to Göteborg, from Helsinki to Paris and finally to Rotterdam. Everywhere Moscow has organized its subhuman specimens, everywhere a wave of murder and destruction pours from the trade unions over the country. Many a scene reflects great suspense. Once a package is delivered to an Armenian by an unsuspecting intermediary; we have a premonition of the contents, and during a loving dialogue we concentratedly listen to the detonation. In many and skillfully varied examples it is shown how GPU every time succeeds in deceiving and checkmating each respective country's police organs."[25]

Goebbels, however, was dissatisfied with *GPU*, calling it a "shoddy, dilettante

Laura Solari and Andrews Engelmann in *GPU*.

effort." Ritter "treats political and military themes merely superficially, and so they do not actually succeed any more in these realistic times."[26] As a consequence Ritter was given less directorial work in the future. For aforementioned reasons, there was also no further need for Göring propaganda.

Quite rare in feature films, however, was anti–American propaganda as the

United States entered the European stage late. So in *Sensationsprozess Casilla*, an UFA production from 1939, the American way of life was ridiculed in a more "sophisticated" manner: Heinrich George as a famous American lawyer is convinced that the (German) defendant is not guilty. He is accused of having kidnapped a child, but this child is his own daughter who was brought up by foster parents. The girl has become a film star, and the foster parents, not wishing to lose this income, regularly inject a serum into her which prevents growth. In one instance, more or less subliminal anti–American propaganda was financed by American distributors themselves. In 1934 actor-director Luis Trenker, whose career had started with Arnold Fanck and Leni Riefenstahl, and who was affiliated with Universal for some time, played on the Biblical theme in *Der verlorene Sohn* (*The Prodigal Son*): Tonio Feuersinger, a woodcutter from the Dolomites, rescues an American millionaire and his daughter in the mountains. Both invite him to New York, but on his arriving there he finds that Mr. Williams and Lilian have left on a world tour. So starving Tonio is stranded during the Depression among the unknown millions and the mountainous skyscrapers. He is terribly homesick. Landing a job as boxing second in Madison Square Garden he meets Williams and his daughter. Lilian is still in love with him, but Tonio has learned his lesson. He turns her down, and his soul is saved by returning to his homeland and the girl he left behind.

Universal president Carl Laemmle, whose company had released *All Quiet on the Western Front*, made this consolation piece especially for the German nation and its cinemas. In 1935, at the Biennale in Venice, the film was awarded the Prize of the Italian Ministry for Education as the ethically best foreign film. But this didn't help Laemmle for long. He had to close his German branch.

CHAPTER 8

The Eternal Jew: Anti-Semitic Films

In his almost prophetic book *Die Stadt ohne Juden* (Town Without Jews) in 1922, Hugo Bettauer developed a community that expels all Jews. The result is: Culturally, everything starts to get boring. On the streets people walk wearing lederhosen and dirndls. Nobody goes to the theatre anymore, because on the stage the only dramatics being offered are of the most conservative kind, Anzengruber and Ganghofer. The operetta is suffering from consumption as it becomes evident that the most successful composers and librettists were Jews. In the end, the circumstances are turned back again. The Exiled return. At least in the novel. Not so in Nazi Germany and Austria.

In his book *La Pureté Dangereuse*, which is based on a conversation with Salman Rushdie, French philosopher Bernard-Henri Lévy clearly defined Nazism as anti–Semitism. The Holocaust (the term derived from Greek "holokautein," a ritual sacrifice of offering to be burned profoundly) is no by-product but constitutive to Nazism, as Lévy sees it.

On January 30, 1939, in a speech addressed to the members of the Reichstag at Kroll-Oper, Hitler announced, "Today I will once more be a prophet: if the international Jewish financiers in and outside Europe should succeed in plunging the nations once more into a world war, then the result will not be Bolshevizing of the earth, and thus the victory of Jewry, but the annihilation of the Jewish race in Europe!" At that time, Hitler considered European Jews as hostages if the Western allies turned against his policy of annexation. In September 1939, after the outbreak of war, the NS regime first intended to install a *Judenreservat* (Jews' reservation) in the Eastern part of occupied Poland, then in summer 1940 on the African island of Madagascar.

In 1940–41, Heinrich Himmler and his aid SS *Gruppenführer* Reinhard Heydrich changed their minds and decided to deport European Jews to the Soviet Union. In his book *Hitler's Willing Executioners*, Daniel Jonah Goldhagen takes it a step further by pointing out that the Nazis were no isolated case in German history but that German history itself was always a breeding ground for anti–Semitism, in medieval, intolerant Christianity as well as in the racist approach of the nineteenth century. Jews were transformed into the symbol of all that was awry in the world. Goldhagen writes:

> The German anti–Semites' evil and malevolent image of Jews was sufficient to cast the Jews as this secular worldview's Devil, no less, if not as explicitly articulated, than medieval Christian minds had identified Jews with the Devil, sorcery, and witchcraft. Race-based anti–Semitism appropriated and reproduced the *form* of Christian anti–Semitism's cognitive model while injecting it with new *content*. Because of this, the transformation was performed and accepted by Germany's enormous anti–Semitic constituency with remarkable ease. The new anti–Semitism was a "natural" modern successor to the age-old, enduring animus, the Christian cognitive elaboration of which resonated in the emerging, ever more secular era with but diminished power. This new, politically different era required contemporary justifications that mapped the changing social conditions if the animus against the Jews was to remain central.... The language and accusations of racist anti–Semitism leave no doubt that the Jew was the source of, and was more or less identified with, everything awry in society. As it had in medieval times, the anti–Semitic litany included virtually every social, political, and economic ill in Germany. Yet in its modern form, German anti–Semitism attributed to Jews a new and still greater cosmological centrality. In medieval times, to be sure, the Jews were seen to be responsible for many ills, but they remained always somewhat peripheral, on the fringes, spatially and theologically, of the Christian world, not central to its understanding of the world's troubles. Because modern anti–Semites believed that the Jews were the prime source of disorder and decay, they could assert that until the Jews were vanquished, the world would never see peace. Medieval Christians could not say this, for even if the Jews were to disappear, the Devil, the ultimate source of evil, would remain. Because modern German anti–Semites had transformed the Jew from being an agent of the Devil into being the Devil himself, the descriptions and depictions of the Jews and the harm that they putatively wrought in Germany were fearsome. From the descriptions of the Jews, abounding in organic metaphors of decomposition, it would be hard to recognize that human beings were at issue. Simply put, Jews were poison.[1]

Jews were accused of having masterminded World War I (for example by General Ludendorff who feared danger equally from the Freemasons) and being the inventors and agitators of Bolshevism. These sentiments culminated in the Weimar Republic, and the Nazi Party profited from that kind of superstition and from the fictitious racial clash of civilizations.

"Purity of essence," as General Jack D. Ripper in Stanley Kubrick's *Dr. Strangelove* termed it, is the plain objective of all religiously twisted, maniacal "*Weltverbesserer*" (people who think they can set the world to rights) striving for a return to the roots, to absolute *Reinheit* (purity).

With war in the wings, Hitler decided that propaganda had to become more determined. Why weren't there any anti–Semitic films? Of course, there had been an odd but relatively harmless love story between Richard Hellwerth, the son of a patrician, and Lissy Eickhoff, daughter of a Jewish speculator: *Am seidenen Faden* (*Hanging Upon a Thread*), directed by Robert Adolf Stemmle in 1938. And there was a film version of Gustav Baeder's popular *Singspiel* (musical play) farce from 1856 (successfully performed with Jewish actors in the theatre), *Robert und Bertram*. In the musical, a nouveau riche banker of the Biedermeier period appeared; in the movie he was transformed into the "parasitic" Jewish money-lender Nathan Ipelmeyer: "May I trust you with a big secret?: I am an Israelite." ("Ipel," by the way, is a South German variation of *übel*, meaning "evil.") For the audience of the day, it was quite right that two vagabonds, Robert and Bertram, who introduce themselves as the Count of Monte Cristo and a famous music professor named Müller and therefore are being invited to a Jewish wedding and a rather grotesque fancy-dress ball, rob this depressing character and all the decadent guests present of their jewels and give them to the poor; specifically to an indebted restaurant owner and his daughter Lenchen. Finally they escape in a balloon up into the sky and are rewarded by the heavenly hosts. But films like these were exceptions.

On December 12, 1939, Goebbels complained: "The Führer is being very critical about films, and particularly about newsreels. I do not think this is quite justified. He behaves like this in front of all his officers and aides. But he has the right to do so, he is a genius." According to Goebbels' old adversary Alfred Rosenberg (December 11, 1939) Hitler called the newsreels "shallow and put together without any sense of a more profound interest": "Enormous things are happening in G.(ermany) in terms of popular mobilization, but film takes no notice of this. He cuts his footage to size without giving the nation what it wants through consistently interesting management ... established, that we have had a N.(ational)S.(ocialist) revolution. There is no sense of this kind of subject matter at all. Dr. G.(oebbels): But we do have good nationalist films (Ritter). Führer: Yes, a few generally patriotic ones, but nothing N.S. Many things had been criticized, but our films hadn't dared to attack the Jewish Bolsheviks."[2]

To placate Hitler Goebbels immediately ordered production companies to go ahead and deliver more. One of the first films of this kind was *Die Rothschilds*, not to be confused with the 1934 American movie *The House of Rothschild* starring George Arliss and Boris Karloff. This one was to have the subtitle *Aktien auf Waterloo* (*Stocks in Waterloo*). In the pressbook we read that it was not intended as a

portrayal of the problem of "Jewry" as a whole but depicts a striking episode of Jewish ambition for power in the environment of Capitalist England. It was the aim of this film to not restrain historical facts in the cinematic rendering. And the result was: The Jews and the representatives of English Plutocracy are worthy of one another.

In the beginning of the work for this film there was a war unleashed against National Socialist Germany by the machinations of English Plutocracy. The interaction of the ruling classes of Great Britain with Jewry should be traced back in this movie to its roots. But the beginning of *Verjudung* in England [Britain becoming Jewish] was introduced by the House of Rothschild, that corrupting supra-

Carl Kuhlmann (left) and Klaus Pohl in *Die Rothschilds*.

national force of the 19th century that had a hand in almost every major political event.

In the center of the film plot there is the historically authenticated occurrence of that stock-market maneuver surrounding the Battle of Waterloo which was used by Nathan Rothschild for the money interests of his house.[3]

Yet *The Rothschilds* directed by Erich Waschneck wasn't received favorably at all. In fact, due to differences with the "Führer's deputy" Rudolf Hess and others it was withdrawn two months after its première (the premiere was on July 17, 1940) although it had already taken 1.3 million Reichsmarks at the box office.

Another film project in this line was *Jud Süss*, but it wasn't just one more movie version of Lion Feuchtwanger's famous novel, originally filmed in 1934 by producer Michael Balcon and Gaumont-British. They had had marvelous Conrad Veidt and even wanted to cast Emil Jannings, but he was committed to various other engagements.

Lothar Mendes strove to make the film in the same spirit in which Lion Feuchtwanger wrote the book — with depth of feeling and leisure of movement. The movement, perhaps, is too leisurely. Mr. Mendes has preserved the accents of the book — its tone of fervor, racial pride, and religious piety. He gives a fine descriptive account of the extravagances and treachery of the times, of the privilege and oppression, of the luxury overlapping poverty, the life and color of the Ghetto; but all this, I think, is done at some cost of the central character, the Jew himself. Conrad Veidt's performance is sensitive, moving, full of sinister grandeur, but the real power and passion of the man has to yield, now and then, to the com-

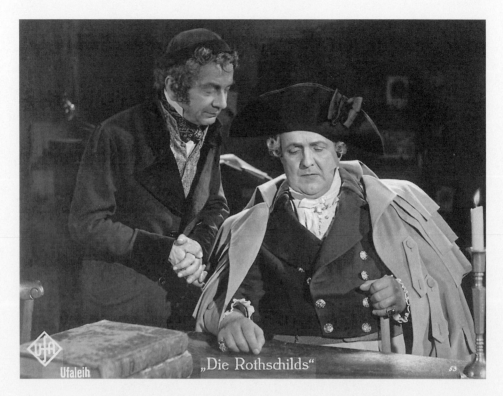

Erich Ponto (left) and Carl Kuhlmann in *Die Rothschilds*.

plex relations of all the persons concerned — dukes, duchesses, lords, rabbis, mistresses, officials, flunkeys. Is not Süss described as a man "parted out into a thousand interests"? These interests "part out" the film, too. The author had time to linger over them in the book; the screen has no time.

Nevertheless, to all interested in an intelligent screen, this picture is a genuine achievement. Its climax, with the hanging of the Jew in his cage, is one of the great scenes in pictures, intensely moving and dramatic, and beyond comparison one of the finest closes to a picture achieved in this country.[4]

The British *Jew Süss* was a success with the reviewers, not with the audiences. It is out of the question that Goebbels had seen this film (he even thought for some time of dubbing it to his taste and releasing it in Germany) and that he knew Feuchtwanger's bestselling novel very well. The book was written between July 1921 and September 1922 but published years later, in 1925, because no publisher wanted to touch it. It seemed to be too risky, too explosive, since it dealt with a severe case of anti–Semitism and a Jew who, nevertheless, was a doubtful character. When it was finally published, an American editor, Ben Huebsch from Viking Press, read it during a trip through Europe and made Feuchtwanger an enthusiastic offer. In October 1926, it was offered under another title, *Power*, for the first time in the United States. Up to 1933, in Germany alone 300,000 copies were sold. In 1930 when Sergej M. Eisenstein came to Hollywood it was offered to him as one possible film project. In an "Open Letter to Seven Berlin Actors," among them Ferdinand Marian, Eugen Klöpfer and

Heinrich George, Feuchtwanger vehemently dissociated himself from the later Nazi version of *Jew Süss*: "…when I translate the pompous waffle modeled on the Führer's bombast into German, it means: You, Gentlemen, have transformed my novel 'Jew Süss' by addition of a little bit of Tosca into a wildly anti–Semitic smear-film in the manner of Streicher and of his 'Stürmer.' You all know my novel 'Jew Süss.' Five of you, … perhaps all seven, have played in stage adaptations of this my novel [the first written by Feuchtwanger himself in 1916; the second, in 1930, adapted by Paul Korn-feld]. When you then discussed details with me, you showed that you understood the book. You certainly have spoken about it in terms of admiration."[5]

While the British film should have been a contribution to understanding, the German version was an appeal to *Endlösung*, the final solution of the so-called Jew-ish question. In fact, and to Feuchtwanger's relief (although his widow Martha after the war took action against the later movie), *Jew Suss* wasn't based on the novel, as some claim, but on Wilhelm Hauff's serialization of 1827. But in Hauff's novel, which focuses on a love story between secretary Gustav Lanbek and Süss' sister Lea, Jew Süss is only a supporting character, and the Duke of Württemberg doesn't appear at all. Amazingly, the earlier novel isn't even that anti–Semitic.

The German *Jud Süss* film was the brainchild of Eberhard Ludwig Metzger. It is said that he had already written a similar treatment for the silents in 1921 which never got before the cameras. In 1933, there had been a stage play about Süss by Eugen Ort-ner and in 1937 a radio opera by Karl Otto Schilling. Finally, in 1939, Metzger got Terra's story editor, Alf Teichs, interested enough to announce the project in the release program of 1939-40. Dr. Peter Paul Brauer himself, who replaced Alfred Greven as Terra's production chief in February 1939, was extremely keen on this directorial assignment. To help him write the screenplay Metzger got the support of Eberhard Wolfgang Moeller, a prominent court writer of the Nazis. Moeller was responsible for *thing* plays like *Anruf und Verkündung der Toten* (1932–34), *Die Inster-burger Osterfeier, ein Heroldspiel von der Überwindung des Todes* (1934), *Das Südender Weihnachtsspiel, ein Laienspiel für die SA aus der Kampfzeit 1934* and *Die Verpflich-tung* (both 1935), and *Das Frankenberger Würfelspiel* (1936). Written for broadcast were *Arminius, Schlageter oder der Ruhrkampf* and a radio version of his play *Roth-schild siegt bei Waterloo*, adapted for "The Hour of the Nation." The Metzger-Moeller screenplay was revised between November 1939 and March 1940.

Moeller clearly dissociated himself from Wilhelm Hauff in an October 1939 interview: "Hauff was living in a time which sang of the Jews as well as of the Poles and wanted to 'liberate' them, and something of this tendency has flown into his novel." The screenwriter called it his intention to prove "the abyss between Jewish and Aryan posture."

In a typical scene from the movie version an organ-grinding *Bänkelsänger* (singer of street ballads) appears on the market place of old Stuttgart:

> *Liebe Freunde und Gevattern,*
> *hört das Lied vom grossen Vampyr,*
> *schlimm sind Wölfe, Ratten, Nattern,*
> *doch das allerschlimmste Raubtier:*
> *Ist der Jud, der Jud, der Jud;*
> *führt im Land das Regiment,*

Shooting *Jud Süss*, with actors Werner Krauss (left) and Ferdinand Marian in the title role.

saugt uns aus bis auf das Blut,
nimmt uns Haus und Hof und Hemd.
Jagt den Jud zum Teufel!
Steuer, Brand und Pest sind schimpflich,
schändlich auch sind Krieg und Unfried;
gegen den sind sie noch glimpflich,
der aus allem den Gewinn zieht:
Wie der Jud, der Jud, der Jud;
führt im Land das Regiment,
saugt uns aus bis auf das Blut,
nimmt uns Haus und Hof und Hemd.
Jagt den Jud zum Teufel!

Translation:
Dear friends and godfathers,
listen to the song of the great vampire,
wolves, rats, vipers are bad,
but the worst of all predators is:
the Jew, the Jew, the Jew;
he reigns in the country,
sucking our blood,
takes away house and farm and shirt.
To the Devil with the Jew!
Taxes, fire and plague are shameful,
war and discord are dreadful, too;
these things are nothing yet against

the beneficiary of it all:
the Jew, the Jew, the Jew;
he reigns in the country,
sucking our blood,
takes away house and farm and shirt.
To the Devil with the Jew!

This *Jew Süss* clearly paraded the Jewish molester and pornographer, in search of *Erotica Judaica*. The original Joseph Süss Oppenheimer was born in Heidelberg in 1698. His business career began in Mannheim. In 1733 he assumed the coining prerogative in Darmstadt, moved to Frankfurt and from there to Stuttgart. Finally, Duke Carl Alexander of Württemberg, a pleasure-hungry monarch who lived in great style, made him his private banker and *Geheimer Finanzrat* (secretary of the treasury). Due to Süss' accomplishments the Jewish ban was at least partially canceled in Wurttemberg. After the duke's death from a stroke in 1737, Süss, although an innocent man who had often acted scrupulously, was handed over to be dealt with by the courts and sentenced to death, as the scapegoat for the deeds of the duke, one of the most hated persons in the region. A victim of malicious gossip, Süss died on February 4, 1738.

In the title role, that of Duke Karl Alexander's financial advisor, Goebbels first saw "Bel Ami" Willi Forst, then changed his mind and turned to Germany's most prominent actor, Emil Jannings; but when Veit Harlan reclaimed the director's chair, plans changed again. By the way, every book claims that Harlan was "ordered" to do *Jew Süss*, but it is most likely that he made himself available. Harlan convinced the propaganda minister that there were already two heavyweights cast, Heinrich George as the duke and Eugen Klöpfer as Councilor Sturm, and that Jew Süss himself should be slim and suave and seductive, like a devil. For it had not been Feuchtwanger's idea that Jew Süss was going to seduce a German woman, Sturm's daughter Dorothea, and then brutally rape her while her lover, who was planning a revolt against Süss, was tortured in a cellar. (In Feuchtwanger's novel, Süss' daughter Naemi is driven to despair and death by the duke.)

This from the screenplay[6]:

490. ...
Dorothea is leaning at the mullion and transom
praying: Father in Heavens—
She goes on praying quietly, folds her
hands and looks heavenwards.
491. *Close-up:*
The Jew.
His hatred is increased to the extreme.
Suddenly he shouts at her:

                              Yes, pray to your God!
                              But not only the Christians have a God. We Jews
                              have a God, too. And this God
                              is the God of Revenge!

He jumps up.
With wild fanaticism he says: An eye for an eye —
                                                      a tooth for a tooth!

492. Close-up:
Dorothea.
She quietly stammers: Let me out.
493. Close-up:
The Jew.
He approaches Dorothea.
The camera pans with him —
Then Dorothea comes into the picture.
Meanwhile he says in a friendly way: Do you want me to make
                                                      it so that high traitors
                                                      won't be hanged?

Dorothea says: Don't touch me!
The Jew grabs her.
He takes her and embraces her firmly.
He says: Don't make such a fuss!
                                                      Then you will get back
                                                      your secretary.

Dorothea manages to escape and drown herself.

Scene 84
On the banks of Neckar River
(Night)
506. Long Shot:
Torches reflecting in the midst of the black river.
The silhouettes of a boat are recognized
slowly rowing towards the bank.
— The camera pans with it —
507. Medium Shot:
Now the boat heads for the bank.
The boat arrives.
Faber and his two friends
leave the boat.
With a face of stone Faber carries the dead Dorothea
to the bank.
Dismayed and pale with fright,
the old maid and other citizens surround
Faber and the dead body on the bank.
Faber lifts the dead body.
The shots of the procession with the dead body are
always superimposed upon Faber with the dead
body.

                                                      — A choral begins —

Scene 85
Street in front of Palais Süss
(Night)
508. Long Shot:

Torchlight illuminates the street.
Faber arrives with Dorothea's dead body
in his arms, followed by his friends, the old maid
and many people.
They sing: —The choral increases—
509. *Long Shot:*
Windows and doors are being opened,
shocked and terrified faces everywhere.
510. *Full Shot:*
In front of Palais Süss Faber arises
the dead body in accusation,
singing.   —singing—
Then the procession moves on.
511. *Medium Close Shot:*
Röder pushes through the crowd.
He sees the dead body in Faber's arms.
Faber raises the dead body a little bit.
Röder stands petrified.
After a while Faber only utters quietly: Drowned. The Jew has
                                                            her on his conscience.

Röder is unable to say anything.
Suddenly pulling himself together he goes—
the Camera pans with him —
to the higher stairs of Palais Süss.
Röder on the half-landing.
The people approach him.
512. *Close:*
Röder murmurs with quiet voice: I wouldn't have believed
                                                            it.

His eyes sparkle wickedly, and he
begins to exert his increasing will-power to
address the people: That unholy regiment
                                                            which allows such an evil
                                                            deed to happen and cele-
                                                            brates its parties abuses
                                                            us and our life.
One hears voices out of the crowd: Let's knock him off!
                                                            Down with the slave-
                                                            driver!

That woman, the dead body, was played by Harlan's own wife, actress Kristina Söderbaum, who after that formidable scene was nicknamed *"Reichswasserleiche"* (Reich Water Corpse), a fate she faced again in *Die goldene Stadt*. Finally, after the duke's death, Süss is sentenced to death. He whimpers,

> Mercy, Gentlemen!
> I want to reimburse all damage
> I did double!
> Naked I will leave the country!
> But only spare my life!

A scene from *Jud Süss.*

Originally, as Harlan claims to remember in his memoirs, he gave Süss a final speech before his execution (which is not in the different versions of screenplays resting in the files of Filmmuseum Berlin but may have been filmed). In Harlan's version the Jew, bound in an iron cage, cursed his judges:

"You madmen, servants of Baal, judges of Sodom! May your limbs wither as the willows of dry Kidron! May your bodies rot during your lifetime, may the bones of your children and grandchildren be filled with pus. Every day shall bring you wretchedness, misery and pain. No sleep shall soothe your eyes; wicked neighbors shall destroy your peace. May your first-born son bring you shame, may your memory be cursed, and may your cities be destroyed by fires from heavens..."

Apparently, Goebbels was terrified when he heard these words. If we are going to believe Harlan, the minister simply took out these lines. Instead, the Jew, whimpering, is agonized by the fear of death. In the original screenplay it was just a short lament: "I am innocent! I am only a poor Jew! Let me live! I want to live! I want to live! Live!" In the film itself his last words are lengthened a little bit: "I was only a loyal servant of my master! What can I do if your duke was a traitor? I'll make up for everything—I swear it to you. Take my property, take my money, but spare my life—I am innocent! I am only a poor Jew! Let me live! I want to live, want to live, li—."

The film ends with Dorothea's father pronouncing that all Jews have to leave Württemberg in three days: "Herewith, the Jew ban is in force for all of Wurttemberg!"[7]

Several actors had been tested for the part, still with Brauer helming the project — all of the suave villains of German-language movies: René Deltgen, Paul Dahlke, and Siegfried Breuer (who already had played a Jewish Bel Ami in Vienna Film's *Leinen aus Irland* and after the war turned up in a meaty part in *The Third Man*). The casting people thought as well of Gustaf Gründgens, Rudolf Fernau, and Richard Häussler. After the war, most of them maintained that their opposition to the Nazi regime was the reason they were not selected for the part. (At least one actor really refused and therefore was put on ice: Albrecht Schoenhals.) Tested also was Ferdinand Marian. Nobody seemed to have been happy with the prospect of getting the part. Marian thought his portrayal of a caftaned Jew made him a doubtful choice for the part. But with Veit Harlan assuming the director's chair, there was a rethinking of the matter. Required was no caftaned Jew. However, after making a new test, Ferdinand Marian suddenly seemed to be a perfect choice for the part. In the beginning, though, Marian had his doubts about taking the part as he feared for his screen image as lover and womanizer. But Goebbels was sure he could convince him for he had his "methods." On December 5, 1939, the minister recorded in his diary: "Discussed *Jew Süss* film with Harlan and Müller [*sic*]. Harlan who shall direct now has a lot of new ideas." Goebbels seemed to be very satisfied, resuming on December 15 that the screenplay had been magnificently revised by Harlan.

In a newspaper, *Ostdeutscher Beobachter*,[8] the actor was strongly portrayed as an ideal villain.

"At the time, Ferdinand Marian played the title role in Veit Harlan's Terra film *Jud Süss*, the actor was often asked how it was possible for him to put himself in the Jew Süss Oppenheimer's position. Ferdinand Marian had this answer:

"Sure, the Jew Süss of this film is a truly unscrupulous criminal man. In the beginning he lives withdrawn, but when the emissary of the Duke of Wurttemberg approaches him and the financial embarrassment of the pleasure-seeking monarch opens up golden horizons for him we recognize in this Jew, who in fact is a little *Jiddchen*, the eternally great enemy who within himself bears the satanic bacillus in a truly demonic manner. When his secretary Levi, played by Werner Krauss, blames him for retiring from the management to get into Stuttgart easier, Süss answers him, 'I open the door for all of you!' This elegant Jew who is able to look like a cavalier desires the daughter of *Landschaftskonsulent* [district consultant] Sturm, the beautiful Dorothea, played by Kristina Söderbaum, and when he is rejected and affronted by Sturm (Klöpfer), Süss, who was given in the meantime a license by the somewhat morbid duke (Heinrich George) for all his exploitative and criminal deeds, lures the girl to himself and rapes she who had rejected him. This Süss sports a captivating kindness and the next moment an irresistible impertinence, then again a smart indulgence. He doesn't have the mark of Cain on his forehead. When the duke dies the outraged Wurttemberg citizens sentence the Jew to the gallows. But even in the hour of death, the Jew curses the city, the country, the people, everybody, and he does so in a mixture of fear of death and an innate despising (this confirms Harlan's version of Süss' last soliloquy).

"If an actor would say: I won't play a villain again then it would almost sound like: from now on I won't move my left arm. In the portrayal of criminals there lies deep sense, too. It serves the beauty, the good by setting off the difference between evil and good. So it is not only the pleasure in a part shimmering with many colors which might stimulate the actor to enthusiastically accept such a role. On the contrary, it is so that 'one isn't only an actor but also forty years of age' and that one must feel what one achieves.

"For myself," Ferdinand Marian resumes, "it was a pleasant moment when Veit Harlan one day said: Nobody else should play the Jew Süss. The more as I had never acted under Harlan's direction before. Perhaps he had seen me on the stage and in a couple of movies. Working with Harlan, the pleasure deepened. I have met in him a very great director."

But, in fact, it was not Harlan but Brauer who first thought of Marian and put his name on the list. Later, in a statutory declaration, the actor presented a view slightly different from that which he had told Nazi reviewers: "I knew the plot by Hauff and Feuchtwanger and could imagine in what way it was intended this time. For this reason, I rejected the part by letter. In the course of the next week, I heard that Herr Brauer corresponded with several other colleagues about this role. All refused." In September 1939, Brauer offered the part a second time. In the screenplay the Jew is presented as robber chief and leader of the caftaned Jews.

> Again I refused and returned the script. Again weeks went by, and I already hoped to have shot of the thing once and for all. Approximately in November Brauer approached me a third time, now by phone. After I had explained to him verbally and unmistakably that the part would be the last thing I wanted to do and that I couldn't accept it under any circumstances, Herr Brauer nevertheless asked me to attend a personal meeting by claiming it would be in my own best interests and that he didn't want to say more on the phone. This meeting took place in an office at Terra and lasted for almost three hours. Brauer had taken care to include "witnesses." Present were alternately a typist, then a story editor. First Brauer tried to lure me into a political trap, for instance by explaining to me with an amicable glance that he could imagine that I wouldn't accept the part for political reasons. He wouldn't like to direct, too. But now everybody would be obliged to do so etc. But I substantiated my refusal to take over the role again and again with artistic reasons and wouldn't fall into his trap. Suddenly he "confidentially" advised me to become a *P.G.* [*Parteigenosse*, or party member] as soon as possible because it would be known that my wife had been married to [the Jew] Julius Gellner in her first marriage and had a daughter with him. He answered my question about what that could mean by saying, "it could have awkward consequences for myself." I refused to talk about any private matters and wanted to finish the conversation. Now Herr Brauer told me he couldn't accept my refusal because it was the explicit wish of Minister Goebbels that I should take over the part. I responded that I couldn't believe that and expected that the Minister would tell me himself.[9]

Instead of getting an answer from the minister, Marian was issued a friendly invitation to a screen test on November 17, 1939. Fellow actors were waiting in line, too. "These were the gentlemen René Deltgen, Richard Häussler, Rudolf Fernau, Paul Dahlke, Siegfried Breuer and I myself. The tests took place and were sabotaged outstandingly by all of us. Brauer ... wasn't a match for our tricks, and so everybody succeeded to make clear by make-up (we all chose plait wigs) and style of acting their non-suitability for this part. For these six artists it was solely a competition of being the worst. Our success didn't fail to materialize for Herr Goebbels was deceived. He didn't like the tests at all." Then, during one Sunday in Advent, the charismatic Harlan stood in front of Marian's door and presented his concept of an assimilated Jew. Marian was flattered. It is true: He actually considered Harlan a great director who was offering him the challenge of a lifetime. Once actors are condemned to hell, they would even play in front of the devil. The matter was concluded by the minister himself. "I need that movie. At once," he told Marian. "From now on, such films will be produced continually. But I do not want to breed within my German film ensemble specialists for Jewish portrayals. From now on everybody must get [a turn]. You are first. Heil Hitler!"[10] Marian, according to his statement, asked for a second screen test because he had never worked with Harlan before and because the part was alien to his nature. "With the second screen test," Marian said, "the sabotage didn't succeed. It started with make-up. This time I wasn't allowed to freely select but was dictated to by Harlan. I wasn't allowed the plait wig but Jewish temple curls, and the typical chin-beard was stuck on, too. I got a skullcap and had to wear a caftan. Just visually, regarding my type, that make-up was convincing. All of the screen test was for the optical impression because I had only one line of dialogue: I thought Wurttemberg is rich? So I had no chance whatsoever for sabotage by an actor's means."

On January 17, 1940, *Film-Kurier* announced: "The title role of Jud Süss hasn't been cast yet — the selection isn't simple for Harlan because, as he says, he doesn't want to make it too easy for himself and doesn't want to use just a type, who in make-up and acting would equal one of the usual business Jews. Instead, a personality should portray him whom one would accept in the part of the financial adviser of a prince and who nevertheless is able to present coldly and objectively the alien race." Goebbels echoed such sentiments in an issue of *Angriff* on January 18, 1940. "For *Jud Süss* we are still looking for an actor. He must combine the worldly elegance of the assimilated Jew with the underhand demoniac power and coldness of a greedy, sensual Hebrew. Jud Süss is a Jew who denies his race in order to act for them behind the curtain. He is the 'disguised' Jew with civilized manners and noble living style. The typically Jewish individual is turned inside within this multiple millionaire, who commands the torture of a secretary and rapes his bride." The *Neue Wiener Tagblatt* reported on January 24, 1940: "Süss behaves like an Aryan as much as possible. This makes casting so enormously complicated, and for this reason the casting has not yet been done."

However, Harlan also used a group of "real" Jews in the synagogue scenes and went to Poland to recruit them. "In order to portray the synagogue scenes as authentically as possible, I first drove with my collaborator Alfred Braun and my location manager Conny Carstennsen to Lublin in Poland. There I explained in the presence of a rabbi very exactly what I was going to shoot, the subject of the movie, and that everybody should be aware that Goebbels didn't want to make a philo–Semitic film. A big number of Jewish citizens from Lublin volunteered, who were very interested in leaving Lublin as they believed it would be safer in Berlin."[11]

Conny Carstennsen (a.k.a. Friedrich Wirth) later reported as follows: "When we arrived in Lublin we went to the senior rabbi of the community and expressed to him our needs. We were invited to coffee by the senior rabbi. When Harlan asked

Albert Florath (rotund man, center), and Malte Jaeger carrying Kristina Söderbaum in *Jud Süss.*

him if he could be helpful somehow to the Jews in Lublin the rabbi told us that all books had been confiscated. Harlan promised the rabbi immediately to find a remedy and succeeded with the German commander of Lublin in returning the library to the Jews. In grateful recognition for his services the senior rabbi presented him in the name of the community with a Torah."[12]

But when suddenly typhus broke out in Lublin Harlan preferred to disappear and to shoot the "proper" synagogue scenes in the Barrandov Studios in Prague.

Jud Süss was premiered in Venice. Ovations hail Harlan's and Goebbels' final selection, Marian. The reviewers applauded him enthusiastically. Later film director Michelangelo Antonioni reviewing the film for *Corriere Padano* wrote: "The play of his hands, of his glances, modulations of his voice, movements of his body — everything is perfect." The opening in Berlin's Ufa Palast am Zoo was a social event, too. First a short was shown: *Baumeister Chemie* (*Master Builder Chemistry*). Then the orchestra of the Staatsoper conducted by Johannes Schüler played *Les Préludes* by Franz Liszt. Ferdinand Marian thawed considerably. After that he was sent to bow in front of audiences in Hamburg, Dresden, Posen, and Munich.

In his book about Ferdinand Marian, Friedrich Knilli quotes audiences' reactions to the movie. A Hamburg boy, then a member of the Hitler Youth, remembered: "I was 13 years old then. I saw the movie together with my comrades. We all regarded the plot of the film as historical truth, and I myself as well as my comrades were deeply impressed by the wickedness of the Jews."

A 29 year old supported such sentiments. "After the screening it was generally said that one could see accurately how Jews really are ... what a depraved race the Jews are... The comrades were people of my age, mostly workers and peasants."

Somebody who had attended the movie in Budapest said: "I saw a Jew who was torn at the beard by people who had apparently left the cinema."

A former prisoner of the concentration camp at Sachsenhausen recalled the reactions of SS guard detachments to seeing Harlan's film. "One day, it might have been in spring or summer of 1941, all the bearers of the Star of David were called back from the punishment battalion by their commandos and had to gather in front of block 10. There *Scharführer* Knippler and Vickert declared that the evening before they had seen the movie *Jud Süss* and recognized now that the Jews were even worse than they had thought up to that time. This remark they made together with the usual dirty insulting that was reserved for Jews quite regularly. They explained to us that we must receive a *Denkzettel* [warning] because of that movie. All of us, almost 25 men, had to enter the barrack, man by man, and were mistreated separately by Knippler in Vickert's presence. I myself had to lay down on the table and got 10 lashes by Knippler with the *Ochsenziemer* (strong whip). Others got considerably more lashes."[13]

On the other hand, perversely enough, Marian himself got laundry baskets of love letters.

Jud Süss had been "successfully" screened in all parts of Europe. It was re-released in 1944-45, in France and Hungary. It was even intended to screen *Jud Süss* on the occasion of an "All-European Anti-Semitic Congress" in Cracow during summer 1944, but the project failed.

At the end of the war, Marian, a hopeless alcoholic, who once had dreamed of getting to Hollywood, sought refuge amongst Nazis in Allgäu (Bavaria). Americans prevented him from continuing in his profession as an actor through a *Spielverbot* (acting prohibition). He met a violent death on a road leading to Freising on August 9, 1946. His colleagues believed it was suicide. Anti-Semites smelled conspiracy and claimed that Marian was murdered by vengeful Jews. And, ironically, some anti-fascists are convinced that he was a victim of the Werewolf, Nazi partisans, raised by the *Jew Süss* movie, who considered him the perfect image of a real Jew: a mistake, so to speak. Even jealousy could have been a motive since the actor's Czech mistress also had a liaison with a G.I., who eventually married her after Marian's death. And, to make matters worse, there was an argument between Marian and his stepmother of the same age.

Tragic incidents doomed the fate of other participants in this fatal production. In July 1944, one of the actors, Hans Meyer-Hanno, was accused of plotting high treason and of fraternization with the enemy, sentenced to three years prison and murdered in Dresden on April 22, 1945. Harlan's chief electrician, Fritz Kühne, and his wife committed suicide at the end of 1944. Murdered, too, were 50 Jewish extras, who involuntarily became involved in the shooting of the dancing in the synagogue.

"The efforts of the actors overall are excellent," French writers Francis Courtade and Pierre Cadars acknowledge in their book *Histoire du cinéma nazi*. "However, *Jud Süss* shows that principal lack that one has to hold against all Nazi films, especially those directed by Veit Harlan: they are perfectly carried out handiworks without any genius. The technical quality is impeccable, the expense colossal, but

A scene from *Jud Süss*.

missing is an artist's genius."[14] In books like *Histoire du cinéma nazi*, everything is reduced to cineast genius and artistry; not given are the objective reasons of those within the film industry and the Nazi state for making this movie.

Jew Süss ends with the Jews leaving town, as a bystander comments, "May the citizens of other states never forget this lesson." And they didn't forget. Ralph Giordano, a well-known Jewish author who survived the Third Reich, remembers that as a youth he attended a screening of *Jew Süss* accompanied by his "Aryan" friend. After the screening, the friend didn't talk to him until he sputtered, "There will be some truth in it."

Already in November 1940, *Das schwarze Korps* (*The Black Corps*), the organ of the SS, reported that 700,000 had seen *Jud Süss*. By the fifteenth month of its run, Harlan's film had made RM 5,970,000, and with that had covered three times its budget (which had been about RM 2 million).

Of course, after the war Veit Harlan claimed to have been forced into making this movie. In an interview with Charlotte Koehn-Behrens (who later dissociated herself from the pathetic concoction) of *Völkischer Beobachter*,[15] however, he claimed an early affinity for National Socialists in order to construct his own legend in front of the then reigning government, all this in theatrically pathetic words.

"I like it," Harlan tells us quickly answering my question about how he found *us*, "I like that I eventually have the opportunity to speak about it... A lot comes together here. Basically it had to do with the single, great, terrible and deeply moving experience of my life. You see, I have been raised in a severe tradition of national, even most national, *Gesinnung* [fundamental beliefs]. My father, the poet Walter Harlan, was an officer in his youth, my uncle is the well-known *Flieger-Hauptmann* [air-force officer] Harlan; right and left in the family we served the three big terms: God, King, Fatherland. The love for my homeland, too, for a long time has been in my blood and is by no means a merit... But how did I come to my confession to National Socialism? When you have heard my story, you will grasp it fast.

"I loved my father adoringly, he was so fine, so quiet, so good ... much, much softer than I myself... Then, in those dreadful years which we finally have left behind us, he was president of the *Verband Deutscher Bühnenschriftsteller* [Association of German Stage Writers]. Because of his severe national convictions he was not on the good list, and the people of that (bygone) Marxist era were looking for ways to oust him. When the ministry allocated him (in his function as president at that time) a benefit fund for impoverished colleagues, my father expanded the circle to the Association of German Narrators, too, which was a Wildenbruch foundation that equally consisted of struggling and penniless artists. He then examined everything exactly and acted to the best of his knowledge and belief when he allotted benefits out of this fund to the penniless poets of Germanness. That was too much for the predominant people in those days. The ruling, Jewish and Marxist gentlemen called my father to account, — ach — what do I say ... account!" — Veit Harlan's passionate voice darkens in excitement and a self-willed strand falls into his face. — "account. My father was able to settle for himself, — but they pounced on him! Herr Rehfisch, the poetic hero of those 14 years, was the leader! My father couldn't make use enough of his elbows, he was not able to pay them in the same coin, — because the gold of true conviction had long declined in value! So he resigned from his post. Before that he wanted to take responsibility.

"In a big gathering held at the Eden Hotel he confronted his opponents. He held a great, wonderful speech in which his German heart was illuminated and bled, — he once again resumed his life. In this hour he concluded his fundamental beliefs and fought for the spiritual, artistic Germany.

"Malicious remarks by Herr Rehfisch and comrades hit him. They hit him better and deeper than was good for him. My father rejected the accusations and closed his big speech with the words, 'Of these last ten seconds, gentlemen, I will think for the rest of my life!!'

"After he had said that he collapsed and was dead!!"

Silence.

Neither of us can find the right word for a whole minute.

Eventually, Harlan continues:

"Even today I see my father lying in front of me, see myself picking up my mother with whom I had to keep quiet about the truth, and feel myself acting the same evening in [a stage play titled] *Blauer Boll*, with all this insanity in my brain: Father is dead ... dead!!...

It was terrible."

"Yes," I want to say — but in this moment I feel too strongly the inadequacy of all words that might express understanding.

"And now comes the best! Herr Rehfisch, my father's outspoken enemy, was commissioned by Wenzel Goldbaum to eulogize at my father's grave!"

"But how did one dare to?..." I asked horrified.

"How did one dare?—yes, how did one dare?! ... The answer to such things was national revolution! And with that you have Alpha and Omega of my way!

"And then," said Harlan after a thoughtful pause, "there was another event which divided myself clearly from the world 'beyond.' You know of my quarrel with [Jewish actor Fritz] Kortner. When he made very nasty remarks about my wife, I beat him up. I was very young then and almost ruined my career. Herr Alfred Kerr [a leading critic of the 1920s] tried to bring me to heel by threatening me. Then, in this memorable night, I answered Kerr, 'As father of a family, my career must mean a lot to me but not as much as the honor of my wife!'

"I paid a high price. As a 'non-soothed Goth'—by the way Herr Jessner's favorite term—I had to moderate my needs to nothing parts or to the crumbs that fell from the table of the State Theatre. However, I proved faithful to myself, and I have no regrets!! Our time, Germany's great time has come! And so bright and clear like this tender April day the future lies in front of us who love our Fatherland!...

"That is my confession to National Socialism! Nevertheless, I will stress that in spite of all bitter experiences it is love for the German movement that leads me and my life, not hatred. For it is my firm insight into the way of the world that hatred destroys. And, eternally building, only love remains!"

That Harlan's father died presiding at a meeting is true. But other remarks are invented by his son. Not Rehfisch but Julius Bab gave the eulogy. And it is not true that critic Alfred Kerr tore Harlan Jr. to pieces. So we could go on and on. As for the Kortner "affair": Harlan was an extremely jealous and impulsive man. He accused Kortner of having molested his first wife, Hilde Körber, in September 1929. He boxed Kortner's ears and beat him up with a riding whip. The right-wing press ran down "Cohn who calls himself Kortner" (*Der Angriff*) as having dishonored German womanhood. It was speculated that Kortner had not only molested Hilde Körber but also chained her up and raped her. Kortner doesn't mention Harlan in his autobiography *Aller Tage Abend*, published in 1959, by name but calls him Kunz. This Kunz is characterized by Kortner as left-wing, philo–Semitic and very amusing. But there had been a rivalry between the two friends, typical of actors. In his view, Hilde Körber deliberately aroused Harlan's jealousy and invented an obscure wine bar in Martin Luther Street where Kortner allegedly had chained her up. Harlan, finally, realized that he had been taken advantage of. He apologized but the friendship between the two actors was destroyed for all time.

An "expert" in anti–Semitic films, Harlan worked on another project from September to October 1944, writing a screenplay based on Shakespeare's *The Merchant of Venice*. Werner Krauss was asked to repeat the part he had played on the stage of the Burgtheater Vienna under the direction of Lothar Müthel. For the rest of the cast the following actors were considered: Gustaf Gründgens (Antonio), Horst Caspar (Bassanio), Kristina Söderbaum (Portia), Bettina Moissi (Jessica) and Ulrich Haupt, Paul Wegener, Joachim Brennecke, Gustav Diessl, Otto Tressler, Hans Brausewetter, Käthe Dyckhoff, Heinz Lausch, Erich Ponto, and Paul Bildt. There might even have been other anti–Semitic projects in the wings for Harlan. He personally considered *The Merchant* the "most tenable."

From early October to November 1939—immediately after German occupation troops had marched into Poland — Dr. Fritz Hippler, head of the German newsreel service *Deutsche Wochenschau*, took camera crews to film poverty-stricken Jews driven into degradation in the ghettos of Lodz, Warsaw, Lublin, and Cracow. In the Nazi press, Hippler stressed a so-called documentary quality: "No Jew was forced into any kind of action or position during the shooting (of *The Eternal Jew*). Moreover, we let the filmed Jews be on their own and tried to shoot in moments when they were unaware of the camera's presence. Consequently, we have rendered the ghetto Jews in an unprejudiced manner, real to life as they react in their own surroundings. All who are going to see this film will be convinced that there is never a forced or scared expression in the faces of the Jews who are filmed passing by, trading or attending ritual services."[16] But could they possibly be "their own surroundings" when those surroundings were created by the Nazi occupation forces? *The Eternal Jew* is an obscene propaganda compilation that manipulates and reinterprets an alternative reality. It was written by Dr. Eberhard Taubert who, at Goebbels' ministry, was in charge of active propaganda against Jews and of the Antikomintern. As early as 1937, Taubert wrote:

"As well as the (Moscow) wire-pullers of this extermination campaign deliberately and systematically attacking peace, today the big mob of little Jews and Bolshevists does the same everywhere in the world, undermining and semi-undermining. Bolshevist and semi–Bolshevist intellectuals working as a secret vanguard of Moscow..."

The Eternal Jew, a "cinematic contribution to the problem of world Jewry," was loosely based on a 1937 exhibition of the same title that was devoted to "degenerate art" and even contained a short "documentary" denouncing Jewish film actors of the Weimar Republic. The 1937 short, however, was rejected by Goebbels: "A bad propaganda film about Jews in films. Made despite my ban. I shall not pass it. Too pushy."[17] The 1940 *Eternal Jew* mixes fresh footage with Hollywood and other film clips, newsreels, and further so-called documentaries made by the Ministry of Propaganda, as well as still photographs and photomontages. "By recycling newsreel and documentary footage and incorporating it with footage shot in the Polish ghettos and excerpts taken from fictional feature films, director Fritz Hippler and his staff heightened the perceived documentary character of the film and hence strengthened the illusion of the images' accuracy. This heightened sense of authenticity bolstered the audience's predisposition to believe that the film tells nothing [other] than the truth. More importantly, by intersplicing newsreel, documentary and fictional film footage within a framework that purports to be a documentary itself, the boundaries between fact and fiction, between ideology and reality, collapse."[18]

The Eternal Jew opens with a lengthy sequence of images of the newly created Jewish ghettos in occupied Poland. "The war in Poland has given us the opportunity to get to know Jewry at its heart. Nearly four million Jews live here in Poland, although you would seek them in vain among the rural population. Nor have they suffered from the chaos of the war, as has the native population. They squatted indifferently, as non-participants, in the dark street of the Polish ghetto — and within an hour of the German occupation they had resumed their money dealings." After the opening credits, animated text informs the audience that the film uses documentary footage in order to show Jews in their original state, or as the narrator explains, before "they put on the mask of civilized Europeans." According to Goebbels[19] "Jews are not human beings": "Predators equipped with cold intellect that have to be rendered harmless."

"These physiognomies refute conclusively the liberal theories of the equality of all men," the film continues. "Jews change their outward appearance when they leave their Polish haunts for the wider world. Hair, beard, skullcap, and caftan make the Eastern Jew recognizable to all. If he appears without his trademarks, only the sharp-eyed can recognize his racial origins. It is an intrinsic trait of the Jew that he always tries to hide his origin when he is among non–Jews."

Hippler then shows a "bunch of Polish Jews—now wearing caftans—ready to steal into Western civilization." As these "assimilated" Jews look a little bit awkward in front of the camera, the commentary has to concede that "these Ghetto Jews do not yet know how to look at ease in fine European suits." But "Berlin Jews are more adept. Their fathers and forefathers lived in ghettos, but that's not apparent now. Here in the second and third generation, Aryanization has reached its zenith. Outwardly they try to imitate their hosts. People lacking in intuition let themselves be deceived by this mimicry and think of Jews as just the same as they are. Therein lies the dreadful danger. These assimilated Jews remain forever foreign bodies in the organism of their hosts, no matter how they seem to appear outwardly." This story sounds like the *Invasion of the Body Snatchers*, like *Alien* or other incredible science fiction horror. "We recognize the *pestherd* (center of pestilence) which threatens the Aryan race." "These Jews only want to haggle." Hagging is their "natural desire," and it is based on "unscrupulous egotism," which represents a Godly law to each Jew: "They need other people because they need the goods with which to carry on business. The things that are valued by the creative Aryan peoples have been reduced by the Jew to the level of a mere piece of merchandise, which he buys and sells but cannot produce himself. He leaves production to the laborers and peasants of the people upon whom he has imposed his presence. The Jews are a race without farmers and without natural laborers, a race of parasites." They spread like an epidemic. Hippler shows what lurks behind the mask, according to Nazi propaganda: animals, monsters, and beastlike freaks: "Comparable with the Jewish wanderings through history are the mass migrations of an equally restless animal, the rat.... Wherever rats appear they bring ruin, they ravage human property and foodstuffs. In this way they spread disease: plague, leprosy, typhoid, cholera, dysentery, etc. They are cunning, cowardly, and cruel and are found mostly in packs. In the animal world they represent the element of craftiness and subterranean destruction—no different from the Jews among mankind!"

Jews are what the Nazis called *Untermenschen*, undermen or subhuman specimens. In a 1935 publication edited by the head office of the SS, we read:

> ...As Night rises against Day, as Light and Shadow are eternally hostile towards each other—the biggest enemy of the Earth-conquering man is man himself.
>
> The subhuman creature—this biologically absolutely similar nature's creation with hands, feet, and some kind of brain, with eyes and mouth, in reality is a totally different, dreadful creature. It only resembles man, with humanoid features—but mentally, emotionally is on a level deeper than the animals. Inwardly, in this man rages a cruel chaos of wild, unbridled passions; nameless destructive will, the most primitive obsession, most unconcealed meanness.

Subhuman specimen — nothing else!

For they are not equal to those which display human features. Woe betides you if you will forget this!

What this Earth possesses in great works, thoughts and arts — man has devised, created and perfected. It was he who made up and invented it. For him there was only one goal: to work his way up to a higher existence, to rectify insufficiency, to replace inadequacies with things that were better.

So culture grew.

Thus came the plough, the tool, the house.

Thus man became sociable, thus family was created, the people, the state. Thus man became good and great. Thus he rose above all other creatures.

Thus he became next to God!

But the subhuman creature was living, too. It hated the work of the other. It raged against it, secretly as a thief, publicly as a blasphemer — as murderer. It joined its own kind.

Beast called upon beast.

Never did the subhuman creature keep peace, never did it behave orderly. For it needed the semi-darkness, the chaos.

It shunned the light of cultural progress.

For self-preservation it needed swamp, hell, not sun.

And this underworld of subhuman creatures finally found their leader in — the eternal Jew!...

The Jew as disease-causing agent, louse, germ, poison, abscess, ulcer, parasite, and flagellum. The Jew as incarnation of an apocalyptic plague. The Nazis were going to "cure" an ill society, which was a pure Garden of Eden in the beginning, from Jewish plague.

The movie introduces different types of Jews:

The Jew as criminal: according to Herr Hippler and Herr Taubert 98 percent of white-slave traffic is in the hands of Jews.

The Jew as politician: guilty of the catastrophe of the Versailles Treaty.

The Jew as capitalist: superimposed we see the capitals of the world under the Star of David. "Today New York is the centre of Jewish power, and the New York stock exchange, the financial center of the world, is ruled by Jewish banking houses — Kahn, Loew, Warburg, Hanauer, Wertheim, Lewisohn, Seligmann, Guggenheim, Wolf, Schiff, Kraus, Stern, etc. These kings of finance love to keep themselves in the background and let their power dramas take place behind the scenes. In appearance they have adapted themselves to their host nation. They look almost like genuine Americans."

The Jew as radical revolutionary (but secretly collaborating with Jewish plutocrats): "1918. Let us remember those vile days, when Germans lay defenseless. It was then that the Jews seized their chance... Masquerading as selfless public benefactors, they promised great things, and incited the masses to break the bonds of civil order. Unchecked personal freedom and enjoyment of life to the full for the individual, rejection of all obligations to an ideal and denial of all higher values. Recognition of the lowest material form of pleasure, unrestrained criticism of the most sacred things, revolt, in fact, against everything that had existed, incitement of youth, stirring people up to class war and terror acts. It is no accident that this false doctrine, which disrupts whole nations, sprang from the brain of a Jew. Karl Marx, son of the rabbi and lawyer Margochei in Trèves. The founder and first organizer of the German Social Democratic Party was the Jew Ferdinand Lassalle-Wolfson. The Jewess Rosa Luxemburg — whose real name was Emma Goldmann, one of the most notorious Communist agitators."

The Jew as excessive creative artist: "The Northerner's concept of beauty is by nature completely incomprehensible to the Jew and will always remain so. The rootless Jew has no feeling for the purity and neatness of the German idea of art. What he calls art must titillate his degenerate nerves. A smell of fungus and disease must pervade it; it must be unnaturally grotesque, perverted or pathological." "Instinctively, Jews are interested in all things morbid and depraved" (émigré actor Curt Bois as transvestite, Peter Lorre as child murderer in a scene from Fritz Lang's *M*).

For hundreds of years German artists had glorified figures from the Old Testament, the movie asserted, knowing full well the real face of Jewry.

> In the meantime we have learnt to use our eyes and now we know that the Hebrews of biblical history could not have looked like this. We must correct our historical picture. This is what genuine Hebrews look like. The following scenes show a Jewish Purim festival, taken by Warsaw Jews themselves for their own use as a "cultural film." This harmless-looking family celebration commemorates the slaughter of 75,000 anti–Semitic Persians by Biblical ancestors of our present-day Jews. The Bible says that on the next day, the Jews rested, feasting and exchanging gifts. They agreed to name the two days Purim, insisting it be remembered by their children's children, from one generation unto another.
>
> Educated Germans, objective and tolerant as they are, regarded such tales as folklore or an example of some strange custom. But that is the tribe of Israel rubbing its hands and celebrating the feast of vengeance, even if the bowdlerized West European clothing conceals the Eastern origins of present-day Israelites.

What we get to see are scenes from that Jewish festival primarily intended for children, and Jews eating with bad table manners. However, the commentary does not reveal that these clips are not from a documentary but from a Yiddish comedy, produced in pre-war Poland, by the title of *Der Purimshspiler*.

At its première *The Eternal Jew* was shown in two different versions. One contained "original shots of a kosher butchering." This from an announcement of the NSDAP Reichspropagandaleitung (Reich Propaganda Directorate):

> "Because in the screening at 6:30 p.m. additional original footage of animal slaughter according to Jewish rites is shown it is recommended that sensitive souls will attend the shortened version at 4:00 p.m.
>
> Women as well are allowed only to the screenings at 4:00 p.m."

Germans don't like rats but they like pastoral lambs, and these peace-loving animals are falling victim to the knives of Jewish butchers without anesthesia. It was announced that the slaughter sequence contained the most cruel scenes ever depicted. "The following pictures are genuine. They are among the most horrifying that a camera has ever recorded. We are showing them even though we anticipate objections on the grounds of taste. Because more important than all objections is the fact that our people should know the truth about Judaism." "Things shown that are so cruel and brutal in detail that your blood runs cold. Such brutishness makes you recoil with horror. The Jewish race must be annihilated."[20] These scenes appeal to the "Germanic respect and love for animals": "When the film ends by showing German people and images of German nature, the spectator breathes a sigh of relief. From deepest lowly spheres he rises to light again. And he feels the distance between Past and Now never that deep, the enormous change since the upheaval scarcely so clear anywhere as in the face of these images that speak for themselves without many words."

In *Mein Kampf* Hitler, in his Social Darwinism influenced by terms like "struggle for existence" and "survival of the fittest," wrote:

> The black-haired Jewish boy lurks for hours, in his face satanic pleasure, for the innocent girl in order to rape her, with his blood taking her, the girl, alienating her from her people. By all means, he tries to spoil the racial foundation of the people he is going to subjugate. As he is methodically spoiling women and girls he doesn't shrink from tearing the limits of blood for others to an even bigger extent. Jews were and are responsible for bringing Negroes to the Rhine, as ever with the same ulterior motive and clear perspective, to destroy the hated white race through inevitable hybridizing, to throw it from its cultural and political heights and rise as masters themselves.
>
> "A pure-bred people however, which is aware of its own blood, will never be subjugated by the Jew. On this Earth, he eternally will be only a master of bastards.
>
> "Therefore he deliberately tries to sink the level of race through permanent poisoning of the individual.
>
> Then, suddenly, he begins to replace the thought of democracy by dictatorship of proletarians.
>
> In the organized masses of Marxism he has found the weapon which allows him to spare democracy, and instead to subjugate and rule people dictatorially with a brutal fist.

(Hitler's anti–Semitism was influenced in his youth by Richard Wagner, of course, and by some Austrian idols, but only one of these others was mentioned by him: Vienna's legendary nationalist mayor Dr. Karl Lueger, a so-called *Judenfresser* [Jew eater]. In a little known film of 1942, *Wien 1910* [*Vienna 1910*], directed by E. W. Emo, Lueger [in a grandfatherly way played by Rudolf Forster, the submarine commander of *Dawn* fame], who in March 1910 is nearly blind and dying, is shown uncovering a Jewish-inspired financial speculation that is ruining the city's economy. He summons his last energies in order to combat Kommerzialrat Josef Lechner who, backed by Dr. Adler, a Socialist, and the Viennese Jewry, has been endangering the city loans by his highly speculative maneuvers. Heinrich George plays another famous

anti–Semite of those days, Georg von Schönerer, and so is the only actor to have
starred in two films of this "genre." Schönerer accuses Lueger in a short but pivotal
sequence of not caring for a future Pan-Germany but for decadent Austria Hungary.)

The Eternal Jew was released in October 1941, and that same year the deporta-
tion of the Jewish citizens of the German capital began. Trains took them to the East.
Foreign correspondents were told that "these Jews will be in no camp, neither concentration camp nor jail. They will be treated individually. Where they will be cannot be said for reasons of warfare economics." In the public transport system, signs
appeared such as: "Jews are our misfortune. They have longed for war in order to
destroy Germany. National comrades of Germany, don't ever forget!"

Hitler clearly used the war to realize his worst racist aims.

"Regarding the *Judenfrage* [Jewish question] the Führer is determined to sort
things out. He has told the Jews that if they provoked another world war they would
face annihilation. That was [not just a] phrase. Now that we have world war, the annihilation of Judaism must be the consequence. This question has to be regarded without any sentiment. We are not here to pity the Jews but to feel compassion for our
German people. When the German people now in the Eastern campaign have
sacrificed about 160,000 fatalities, the originators of this bloody conflict will pay with
their own lives."[21]

The idea that death and death alone was the only fitting punishment for Jews
was publicly articulated by Hitler for the first time on August 13, 1920, in a speech
entirely devoted to anti–Semitism: "In the middle of that speech, the still politically
obscure Hitler suddenly digressed to the subject of the death sentence and why it
ought to be applied to the Jews. Healthy elements of a nation, he declared, know that
'criminals guilty of crimes against the nation, i.e., parasites on the national community,' cannot be tolerated, that under certain circumstances they must be punished only with death, since imprisonment lacks the quality of irrevocableness. 'The
heaviest bolt is not heavy enough and the securest prison is not secure enough that
a *few million* could not in the end open them. Only one bolt cannot be opened —*and
that is death.*' That was not a casual utterance, but reflected an idea and resolve that
had already ripened and taken root in Hitler's mind."[22]

CHAPTER 9

The Great King

A satisfied Goebbels, in a speech in front of filmmakers on February 28, 1942, declared that never before had German films had such a strong basis for amortization as then. German films, as far as they were controlled by the Reich, were yearly making between RM 50 and 80 million net. That was almost the sum it cost the Reich to acquire most of the German film industry. (In his diary[1] Goebbels added: "It would have been wonderful if the high surpluses we are now making in the film industry stood the private sector in good stead.") However, Goebbels had to concede that the market they had won outside the Reich was not created by the films themselves but by military successes which made the biggest part of Europe a sales territory for German "culture." So-called genius films were trumps: nationalist biographies of Teutonic personalities, fighting artists, physicians etc., who superseded the "out-of-date" by their vision, like *Paracelsus* (starring Werner Krauss), *Friedrich Schiller* (Horst Caspar), *Friedemann Bach* (Gustaf Gründgens, who was bisexual, in a soft, feminized portrayal of Johann Sebastian Bach's son), *Andreas Schlüter* (Heinrich George), *Robert Koch* (Emil Jannings), and of politicians like *Bismarck* (Paul Hartmann), about the political unifier of the Second Reich. Likewise, the internationally undisputed reputation of German films was forced by the conquest of European cinemas and audiences. But the satisfaction was short-lived.

Now that bombs were already falling upon the German capital and the countryside, and now that the Russian campaign had come to a standstill not far from Moscow, the only chance of political escapism was a recollection of the historical *Vorbilder*: monumental personalities, heroic idols from the past. Goebbels himself up to the last reminded Hitler of Friedrich II whom he called once the first National Socialist.

So Veit Harlan's next film after *Jew Süss* was allowed the then unheard budget for a German movie of RM 4,779,000 in order to tackle the biography of Frederick the Great, Prussia's Great King and an early example of the Great Dictator! Such a project had first been suggested by Emil Jannings in November 1939. National Fridericus Rex films had been popular since the silents, since *Der alte Fritz* (*Old Fritz*) in 1922. Harlan himself had played in one of those films: 1933's *Der Choral von Leuthen*, directed by Carl Froelich. But as Goebbels prophetically envisioned, the new *Der grosse König* (*The Great King*) shouldn't star the *Gartenlaube* (garden arbor) Frederick of former movie versions, but the one who had been defeated at Kunersdorf, the one who had wrenched the command of the army out of the hands of his recalcitrant generals, the one who had thus won the final victory in the teeth of defeat. Hitler, too, considered the generals leading the Russian campaign incompetent and himself unfailing: "Goebbels and Hitler had both read Frederick the Great's writings several times, and both quoted them at critical moments of the war. Goebbels, who was not slow to use analogies with the Prussian King in his speeches either, ultimately wanted a film about Frederick that precisely fitted in with his image and ideas of the king. Goebbels also seems to have preferred a film that was more powerfully military and propaganda-orientated, with the Prussian army's major defeat at Kunersdorf in 1759 as the starting point of the plot. This would make it easier to stage the 'miracle of the House of Brandenburg' and the end of the Seven Years War in 1762 with the victories at Schweidnitz and Freiberg all the more effectively."[2]

Nobody is able to defeat the Great King. This from the screenplay:

Scene 87
Hill
877 *Close:*
The King.
He breathes heavily.
His eyes are sparkling.
He says:
Have you ever heard such a fire?
— Camera pulls back slowly —
The King continues: This almost sounds like the
                                                    Last Judgment.

878 *Close-up:*
The King.   /Noises of battle./
He profoundly remarks: Like Trombones of Death!
Suddenly he is hit.
He sinks forward onto the horse.
879 *Close:*
An aide-de-camp observes it.
He jumps from his horse and says,
paralyzed with horror: For God's sake — Majesty!
880 *Close:*
The King on his horse.
He lies fallen forwards.
The adjutant pulls him from the horse.
881 *Close-up:*
The fur coat is pulled off the uniform.
On the uniform, right beneath the Order of the

Otto Gebühr looks up at Kristina Söderbaum in *Der grosse König*.

Star, there is a bullet-hole.
882 *Close-up:*
The adjutant
as he puts the King on the ground and says: Right beneath the heart!
Trembling he shouts: My King!

883 *Close-up:*	
The King	
as he opens the eyes:	What does He do to me? Can't He make himself useful?
— Camera pulls backward —	
The adjutant says:	Majesty are you wounded?
The King rises and shouts:	No!
The adjutant says:	But your Majesty is bleeding!
884 *Close:*	
The King:	By cashiering him I will tell him: The King is not wounded!
885 *Close:*	
The adjutant and another officer.	
The adjutant says softly:	The fur coat! The fur coat has saved him!
886 *Close-up:*	
The King — victorious:	The bullet which will kill me —
points upward —	will come from up there.
887 *Full Shot:*	
The King as he mounts his horse.	
Doing this he says:	Forward! To victory!

Harlan was excited: "For the film *Der grosse König* I got everything which I considered necessary. I got five thousand horses when I needed them and I was allowed to film battles of every extent with real soldiers. Money didn't matter. General Daluege put almost the entire [!] Berlin police at my disposal."[3] (Remarks like these are the proof that Harlan didn't speak the truth too often.)

As ever Harlan this time, too, made the most of the opportunity to cast his wife Kristina. She appears as a young miller's daughter who confronts, unbeknownst to her, the King while he is billeted in a bombed out mill, one of the main locations of the movie. To achieve a love story (the King was obviously too old at this juncture), Harlan invented a corporal, Treskow, who is caring for the miller's daughter, Luise.

After Harlan's collaborator (and former chauffeur) Friedrich Karl von Puttkamer had finished the editing, Harlan screened the film for Emil Jannings and other delighted bigwigs of Tobis Film, the production company. Goebbels, though, was not that convinced by Harlan's colossal picture. A diary entry of June 1, 1941, reads: "Just the opposite of what I wanted and expected. This is a Frederick the Great from Ackerstrasse. I am very disappointed. Discussed extensively with [Fritz] Hippler and [Ewald von] Demandowsky." On June 6 he found Harlan not open to reason: "Possibly I have to assign an entirely new director." On June 15: "Jannings wants to revise somewhat Harlan's *Great King*. He, too, finds it unworthy of discussion."

Part of Goebbels' criticism originated from the fact that in the movie a Russian general named Chernichev helped the King to victory. However, on June 22, 1941, Germany had invaded the Soviet Union. For this reason Harlan's version had to be corrected, and Paul Wegener, who had played the character, was invited to expen-

Seated, left to right: Hans Hermann Schaufuss, Paul Wegener (as Russian general), and Otto Gebühr in *Der grosse König.*

sive re-takes written by Gerhard Menzel and Hans Rehberg, who had qualified himself for the job by writing a play about the Seven Year's War. (Other actors' footage was deleted entirely and landed on the cutting room floor: Lola Müthel as Madame Pompadour, Hilde von Stolz as Dauphine, Auguste Pünkösdy as Maria Theresia, and Ernst Fritz Fürbringer as Louis XV. But in the end Harlan didn't lose the minister's confidence.) The altered version let the Russians become Frederick's allies only in order to stab him in the back.

At the première of *The Great King* on March 3, 1942, Harlan issued a pathetic article, "History and Film."

> There are many who demand of artists that they serve easygoing plays to an audience in difficult times, something entertaining, something that makes them laugh and lets them forget the difficult weekday. Certainly there is much legitimacy in such a demand. However, I think that the German people even in these fateful days, in hours of artistic pleasure will feel an elation more noble because it remains in an intellectual world that addresses their worries, hope, and pride. Works of art that will conquer the hearts of man must not aim at distraction. Distraction is escapism, escaping thoughts that capture our heart and brain. But today we do not want to flee from our thoughts. Our time and our thoughts are not only tough but rather awe-inspiring, and it is a more awe-inspiring world into which I want to lead my movie *Der grosse König.* It is the song of songs of a great man, who led his people through most dreadful set-backs and disappointments, in

spite of the biggest lack of understanding of his family and of many of his generals, through his own painful doubts and fights without deviating from glorious victory and a big aim. I was aware that I wouldn't have served the German people if I had constructed, in times of inexorable reality, a pure fabrication about Friedrich II. Therefore, writing the screenplay, I strictly stuck to history. But the true facts of the Seven Years War result often in an astonishing parallel to the events of our days so that I regard it necessary to emphasize: The King's most important remarks come out of his own mouth, and the story's events, with the exception of temporal reductions which are necessary in order to create a work of art as unity, correspond with the real events. The only fabrication is the story of a miller's daughter and a corporal. In the miller's daughter speaks the simple girl, who initially finds nothing in the strokes of fate, and in the corporal speaks the brave, simple soldier, who is racked with guilt because he doesn't comprehend the loving kindness of his King. But both feel the greatness of the King, and they come back to their belief in the justice of his good cause for which they are willing to die. These popular characters are not heroically idolized but they have to fight for their heroism, they acquire it in order to possess it. They are, of course, Prussians—they are Germans. With their weaknesses and their extraordinary power of sacrifice and love.

The historian has the task of telling people the truth, the artist has the task to arise man and give him strength and belief. The creator of a historic work of art has to fulfill both tasks. For the stage drama this principle does not apply as exclusively as it does in the movies. Confined to its sets the stage is that far away from reality that one possibly might apply the law of an inner truth rather than the serious rules of historical truth. Its art form is striving more for stylization rather than portrayal of reality. The film, however, is much nearer to reality. Therefore, screenwriter and director hold a different kind of responsibility toward history than the stage writer. The art form of movies doesn't bear that centuries-old tradition and experience of the theater. Therefore we cannot apply final laws to it. I get the impression that movies through all artistic revolutions, which they still have to stride through, have to protect the face of reality. It does not matter if they create comedies or fairy tales or historical events. In this knowledge I have tried to bestow on the character of the King the features of reality. I have omitted every heroic pose. Instead, I wanted to look into the agonized countenance of a man, who after a lost battle completely collapses under the burden of responsibility he has taken upon himself. Gouty fingers and a gouty back portray his character, but when he stands upright or rides a horse he overcomes his pain, because of the posture, and sets an example. His eyes reflect love, not hatred. Often his face is distorted by indignation, sometimes overpowered by weakness, but every time it is strengthened and rejuvenated by the belief in victory. In my film you won't find any of those famous anecdotes and no affable stories that in the past were used to bring their greatest King to life again for the German people. Instead, one will see the King, I believe, as he really was—as he must have been.

Never would a ruler like Friedrich capitulate (and the same was true of Hitler). That was the very essence of *The Great King*.

> FRIEDRICH. Capitulate? I take over the supreme command. We shall fight
> again! Whoever is afraid to accompany me may go home.
> COMMENTATOR. Friedrich wages his wars not for the sake of war but from

a historical necessity. Everyone knows that this great statesman would prefer to serve his people in peaceful work, that this great artist on the throne would prefer to stay with his beloved art than to carry out the cruel handicraft of murderous war.

Usually, the King had been played on the screen by actor Otto Gebühr. To his from previous screen adaptations, Harlan was going to cast the part with Werner Krauss, but Hitler himself ordered him to stay faithful to Gebühr, who had been a supporter of the National idea since long before 1933. In the movie Otto Gebühr, unfortunately, speaks in a somewhat lower Berlin street idiom, which of course was impossible for a King such as the educated and distinguished Friedrich. So he had to be dubbed over in several takes in order not to be ridiculed. That notwithstanding, Hitler made Gebühr a *Staatsschauspieler* (state's actor), and *Der grosse König* was hailed as and rated Film of the Nation. Harlan received the German film ring that was connected with that rating. Günther Schwark in his review in *Film-Kurier* applauded: "With films like this the cinema outgrows the character of sheer entertainment, it becomes a 'morals institution' in the highest sense of artistic and national political meaning. Colossal battle scenes of never before seen power and vehemence have been staged. What impressions when the Prussian musketeers in endless phalanx (in effective sloping perspective to the viewer) line up for a fight with lowered bayonet, when enormous cavalry regiments attack, when an army of many thousands on the march fills the whole plain in full width and depth."

Otto Gebühr (center), with assistance from man and animal, shooting a scene for *Der grosse König*.

Linda Schulte-Sasse[4] concluded her analysis of that Harlan movie by looking at a scene that shows the "fascist" potential of the Frederick legend: the montage sequence ending *The Great King*.

> It is a coda that is "tacked on" to the rest of the film after the story is definitively over, after a spectacular (and specular) battle has at once destroyed and saved the social body. It stands out from the rest of the movie and from the rest of the Frederick genre by dispensing altogether with cinematic realism in favor of a style that recalls the work of Leni Riefenstahl as well as Hollywood's religious epics. It is, moreover, an attempt to *show* Frederick's omnipotent gaze in cinematic terms. Multiple exposures superimpose Frederick's giant eyes over the windmill that throughout the film stands metaphorically for *Heimat*, over a plow cutting the earth, and over peasants plowing and sowing fields. Finally, the Prussian flag flaps in the wind and a poem appears on the screen whose text is sung by a (nondiegetic) chorus: "You black eagle/ of Frederick the Great/ Like the Sun/ Cover/ The abandoned and/ Homeless/ With/ Your golden/ Wing." (Du schwarzer Adler/ Friedrich des Grossen/ Gleich der Sonne/ Decke du/ die Verlassenen und/ Heimatlosen/ Mit/ Deiner goldenen/ Schwinge zu.)
>
> By superimposing Frederick's eyes over privileged icons of romantic anticapitalism, nation, and *Volk*, the sequence amalgamates Mother and Father, nurturance and discipline, the bodily and the abstract, icon and verbal text.

Hitler's generals, of course, didn't like what they heard about *The Great King*. Goebbels: "There were many gentlemen from the OKW there who were somewhat benumbed by the film. They were fully aware of the sharp criticism made in the film of the generals' defeatism. They obviously notice this aim — and are annoyed by it!"[5] "I came to know of the hard fight which has broken out in the Führer HQ over the Frederick the Great film. In the end the Führer resolved the matter. Although he had not seen the film, he had so many details explained to him that he was able to make quite a graphic image of it. How benevolent this characterization of the Great King has been to him. He asks me to place a copy of the film at his disposal. He intends sending it with an accompanying letter to the Duce. Of course, in such an atmosphere, my suggestion for radicalizing our efforts has a very positive effect on the Führer."[6]

The Russian campaign was to become the beginning of the end for the Nazi regime. Hitler, almost voluntarily, was repeating his idol Napoleon's mistake and allowing himself to be caught in the Russian winter. The image of the Great King didn't help Hitler, as Caesar's image didn't help Benito Mussolini. Around the time Hitler suggested sending him a print of *Der grosse König*, the Duce, a film buff himself, who a few years before had suggested a joint venture between his son Vittorio and American producer Hal Roach, planned to write his own screenplay on the subject of Julius Caesar in earnest and make the movie in association with German technicians. Finally, the once so proud Duce became a marionette of the German Führer. Hitler, after surviving an attempt upon his life in 1944 (and constantly fogged by the drugs of his dubious physician, Professor Theodor Morell), regarded himself more and more a savior, selected by Providence, and wouldn't listen to any advice. Thus disaster was assured.

CHAPTER 10

Black-Out:
The Home Front,
or, "That's Not the
End of the World"

On the home front brides and fiancées were stranded waiting for their brave, faithful soldiers to return triumphantly, at least on leave. In *Ein schöner Tag* made in 1943 (the title, *A Beautiful Day*, could have satisfied only those with a firm belief in what they used to call "final victory") a soldier named Friedrich Schröder, who is married and the father of a child, has been corresponding with a girl from Berlin, Barbara, in order to continue receiving the packets of cigarettes which she sends him at the front. He and his friend Fritz Schröder (Schröder is a common name in Germany) have a few hours leave to spend in the capital of the Reich. Friedrich naturally wants to spend it with his wife, and therefore sends the friend to Barbara who promptly falls in love with Fritz. When repairing his uniform Barbara finds a photo of Friedrich's wife and child. Assuming that Fritz is married she leaves him without a word. In the end the unfortunate matter is cleared up, and two happy couples look forward to final victory.

Most of Germany's leading female stars of the war, apart from Ilse Werner, however came from foreign countries and were totally different from the Nazi vision of the blonde *Fräulein* or the ugly hag proudly producing the Mutterkreuz on their bosom, a medal awarded to prolific mothers (who gave birth to a race of future warriors), the equivalent of the soldiers' Iron Cross. Marika Rökk was Hungarian, Kristina Söderbaum and Zarah Leander were Swedish. In Rolf Hansen's melodrama *Die grosse Liebe* (*The Great Love*), seen by more Germans during and after the war than any other German film, No. 1 vamp star Zarah Leander in the role of Hanna Holberg, a singer at Berlin's Scala revue who commands flocks of admirers, is finally engaged on the home front to Paul Wendlandt, a first lieutenant of the *Luftwaffe*, who is constantly forced to the front until their relationship breaks down for her lack of patience.

In the original screenplay by Peter Groll, Alexander Lernet-Holenia and Hansen titled *Das silberne Netz* (*The Silver Net*) Hanna is called Ingrid and doesn't want Wendlandt to return to the Russian front.

Scene 104
Ingrid's Room in Hotel Città in Rome [where both are on vacation]
300.
Wendlandt, upset, speaks with the firm voice of a soldier:

Ingrid!—Each hour I am not with my squadron a comrade must stand in applying all his energies. Especially now—

301.
Ingrid, upset too and tormented:

But after all you don't know if they *really* need you!

302. Close-up:
Wendlandt abruptly says:

Yes, this I know. And I want to leave! I must get back to my comrades. I can't stand it any longer here! I ask you, don't torment me!

He hears Ingrid's desperate, calm answer:

I can't stand it, too! *This* I can't stand!

Two-shot:
Her eyes are fixed on Wendlandt. She hears him say:

What is it that you have to bear? Is it that I have less time for you? That we have had to postpone our wedding?

304.
Once again, urgently:

This is war, Ingrid! Millions of women have to make sacrifices worse than that, they have to... I thought you knew what it means to become an officer's wife.

Ingrid, pleading:	Just wait until they call you to duty.
Wendlandt remains firm:	I ask you to no longer make me give up my decision, my duty!
Ingrid, quiet, ruled by her feelings:	I ask you to stay here at least until you get orders.
There is a pause. Wendlandt who went back and forth in the room stops in front of Ingrid:	Is there nothing else you have to tell me?
Ingrid, firmly: Wendlandt leaves the room. Ingrid buries her head in her hands.	No!

But when Paul is taken to a military hospital, Ingrid-Hanna begins to understand the needs of the front. Eventually she accepts the role of a German war bride and agrees to marry Wendlandt during his recovery.

Scene 123
In Germany, terrace of a reserve military hospital
368.
Ingrid stands in front of Wendlandt, closely.
The dog jumps at her.
She strokes the dog's back, unable to say
anything.
Wendlandt helps Ingrid with unshattered
lust for life:

> What do you say? …
> Three shots they have fired
> into the brat; for that we
> finally will have three
> weeks time for each other.
> Three bullets … for each
> week respectively! Haven't I
> told you that I have a
> proverbial luck?

Ingrid grasps his hand, smiling:

> Three weeks…! And what
> will happen then?

O.S. engines of planes getting louder and louder.
Wendlandt looks up.
Ingrid, too.
369.
They see a squadron which thunderingly roars
over their heads.
370.
Ingrid as she smilingly nods to Wendlandt.
He gently takes her hand and both see
371.
— the squadron vanishing over the horizon.

Bruno Balz, a homosexual, had written Zarah Leander's hit songs for that film in a Gestapo prison (his release was brought about by the intervention of composer Michael Jary): "That's Not the End of the World" and "I Know Someday a Miracle Will Happen." This was clearly what Hitler's Germany was in need of military-wise — a miracle. (In 1943, when Zarah Leander returned to Sweden and into safety, Heinrich Himmler sighed relieved, "At last German women can breathe again.")

Wartime Germans tried to keep each other's spirits up by singing lustily. Goebbels agreed with it. The situation at the front was becoming precarious. The "Wunschkonzert (Request Concert)" show hosted by Heinz Goedecke was Germany's favorite radio broadcast uniting combat front and home front.

This from the screenplay of *Wunschkonzert* the movie:

Scene 142
Grosser Sendesaal [broadcasting studio]
424.
Goedecke in front of the
microphone:

Here is *Grossdeutscher Rundfunk* [Pan-German Radio]. We begin the 10th Request Concert for German *Wehrmacht*. We summon the soldiers: (follows a list of names)

425.
While the reading out of the names goes on the camera depicts — over the shoulder of Goedecke — the big studio which is crammed to the last seat. In the audience there are mostly wounded persons accompanied by their relatives.
426.
Shot from the gallery: the whole studio up to the stage where orchestra and chorus are placed.
Goedecke:

We greet you by playing the march: "Volk ans Gewehr" ["People to the Arms"] (or another march)

427.
The military orchestra instantaneously joins in.

— march music —

Scene 143
Shelter in the apron of the Western Front
428.
Gathered around Kramer's portable radio are the men of von Zülkow's platoon.
They listen to the music.

— march music —

Suddenly the phone rings.
One of the soldiers picks up the receiver

— buzzing —

and places it in front of the loudspeaker;
he gestures towards Friedrich:
'*Du hast das vergessen —*
die wollen hören!—'
Scene 144
Hangar at military airfield
429.

Group of mechanics led by Zimmermann working on a plane. They work in a lively manner in rhythm and — whistle —	— march music —

Scene 145
Stable of a battery near the front
430.

Gunners cleaning and grooming their horses.	— march music through loudspeaker —

Scene 146
Cockpit of a fighter aircraft
431.

Commander and pilot of a fighter aircraft sitting side by side. They are on their way back. The radio operator has tuned in to Request Concert.	— march music —

Scene 147
Grosser Sendesaal
432.

Reverse angle with sound technician at mixing desk through window in front onto stage.	— march music —

Some of Germany's most popular actors appear in the movie in cameos: Marika Rökk singing "Eine Nacht im Mai" ("A Night in May"), Heinz Rühmann, Hans Brausewetter, and Josef Sieber "*Das kann doch einen Seemann nicht erschüttern*" (greeting U boat lieutenant commander Prien: *Ahoy!*), Willy Fritsch "Tausendmal war ich im Traum bei Dir" ("A Thousand Times I Was with You in Your Dreams"), Wilhelm Strienz "Gute Nacht, Mutter" ("Good Night, Mother"), and from *Heurigen* (new wine drinking) Vienna Paul Hörbiger with "*Apolonerl, Apolonerl, Apolonerl ist gut*" ("Apolonerl, Apolonerl, Apolonerl Is Good").

In between we see Ilse Werner as Inge Wagner, who (thanks to footage from Leni Riefenstahl's *Olympia* films) is able to go to the 1936 Berlin Olympics, but her aunt has forgotten the tickets. Lieutenant Herbert Koch comes to her rescue and offers her an extra ticket left him by a soldier called to duty. Only when Hitler arrives does reluctant Inge abandon caution and enter the stadium with Koch. They fall in love and decide to marry, but as a pilot of Hermann Göring's *Luftwaffe* Koch has to join *Legion Condor* and aid Franco's fascists in Spain. For three years they don't meet again. Inge picks up with him once more when Koch calls into Request Concert asking for the music of the 1936 Olympics; in this way, he signals that he has not forgotten her. Unfortunately Herbert wrongly assumes that Helmut, an infatuated young lieutenant from Inge's hometown, is engaged to her, but the confusion is resolved

Ilse Werner starring in *Wunschkonzert*.

when Helmut is injured and all three meet in a hospital. (Approximately 26.5 million people had seen this movie by the end of the war.)

In the meantime, with the men fighting abroad and the females either singing or working in factories replacing male workers, the enemy has already established his fifth column in the country. This from a review of 1940's *Achtung! Feind hört mit!* (*Attention! The Enemy Is Listening!*):

The reality of recent days is filled by great dramatic events. For the artist the contemporary subject presents itself with the biggest effect in the great vital matters of the nation, in the events which lead to the great moving matters of our life. The film *Achtung! Feind hört mit!* is taken from the life of the time. The title already suggests the essential contents: it is a spy movie, a movie that shows in its thrilling, suspenseful plot the great responsibility that everybody put in an important position in the nation's struggle for life has to bear. In the course of events the film shows with great conviction how everybody should be aware of this responsibility and how he should prepare for it. A factory, for example, that plays a vital role in the life of the nation in reality is far more than just a factory: Its members share a common fate and stand every minute of their work as well as in their private life in the first line of the national front.[1]

The screenplay was written by Kurt Heuser from an idea by Georg C. Klaren.

After the critical days of September 1938 foreign agents get increasingly interested in the important armament factories of Germany. The *Kettwig-Werke*, located near the border and having almost doubled their staff in the last year, comes under fire on all sides from espionage.

Old man Kettwig and his chief engineer, Dr. Hellmers, are well aware of the dangers for the factory and each *Gefolgsschaftsmitglied* [employee]. Hellmers, who is called the "Edison of Kettwig," is especially prepared to do everything necessary regarding counter-intelligence.

But whom could he trust? Inge Neuhaus, his assistant? Bernd Kettwig, the assistant chief? They both know about the secret of an alloy invented by Hellmers, from which a wire can be created that makes balloon barriers even more effective than before.

Inge and Bernd are friendly with each other. Their relationship is cordial but hasn't gone beyond the borderline of a nice comradeship. At that point, for the first time in her life, Inge meets a man, who means more to her. He calls himself Faerber; the secret of an adventurous life surrounds him. Inge accompanies him to Baden-Baden. There Bernd bumps into her and makes the acquaintance of Lilly, who owns a fashion shop in Baden-Baden and is a friend of Faerber. Bernd is a little troubled by Inge, who after visiting a casino goes for a nightly stroll with Faerber, but Lilly's affection makes him forget everything.

A short time later exciting things are happening. Nolte, a waiter in the canteen of *Kettwig-Werke*, has been gotten rid of by his foreign client, who considers him troublesome and incompetent, and is extradited to German authorities. Grelling, a draftsman, is convicted of similar criminal acts. When he tries to push his camera, which he had used to photograph important documents, to Inge, he causes her great difficulties. She became suspicious already a few days before when Faerber gave himself away by a rash remark, but the affection to the man has prevented her from gasping things with all the sharpness of her otherwise lively intellect. Now she recognizes the brutal expediency of all of Faerber's deeds. The man, in whose love she had believed, has followed her with the notion to use her for his personal plans.

Bernd, too, identifies Lilly's true intentions. The second he understands the motives for her action, Bernd, the big playful boy, becomes a man, who is aware of his responsibility. He delivers Faerber's accomplice to the authorities.

Now the crunch has come! When Bernd wants to enter his car to return to the factory as fast as possible he discovers that all four tires are punctured. Eventually he gets to the factory. There is a full-scale alarm!

Faerber, who had been warned, forced an entry into the shed which housed Bernd's sports plane. He achieved the almost impossible, and succeeded in pulling out the plane and taking off. But in the meantime the balloon barrier has risen, and a squadron brought into action for an exercise barricades the last way out.

Bernd pulls the agent out of the flames and debris of the crashed plane. Into the night of his death the dying man takes the knowledge that Germany is on alert, on alert and strong and confident of victory.

In an interview[2] director Arthur Maria Rabenalt spoke about this movie that was made on the sound stages in Berlin-Tempelhof.

The plan for this film is perhaps one and a half years old but had to be put aside for several reasons. You, too, can imagine that Kurt Heuser as screenwriter was faced with a not so easy task of a difficult and plot-wise extremely complicated subject of a "spy movie." Not least maybe because he stuck to *reality* in the basics of story construction and characters.

The film is mainly a *Tatsachenbericht* [factual report]. And for that reason no usual "spy movie." Everything "romantic," everything ballad-like and painted-over vanishes. The film doesn't play in that illusionist world which often served as background for spy movies and in which, for the effect on the public, adventure, sensation and "soft" spine-chilling are intertwined. Our film has the full, unshakeable objectivity of the world that surrounds *us*, in which we all live and work. There is no trashy writing at all, there is only report by facts. The viewers will feel this in the inevitable consequences and dynamic fates and characters, which are all realized in breathtaking toughness. In cinematography, too, this "reality style" should express itself.

What can I tell you in detail about the story of the movie? In a case like this, that is not easily done, — the story exhibits an almost confusing wealth of thrills, involvements, heightenings. We show the subject of espionage and counter-intelligence not in a particular case but in the most different variations. It deals not only with industrial but also military espionage.

Spies and agents make great efforts to lie in wait for and beguile a team of employees of a factory and draw them into their machinations: the young son of the owner, who is an energetic man, not at all an arrogant factory heir, Inge, the secretary, Nolte, the waiter of the casino, Böttcher, the foreman, and a draftsman. All these figures are portrayed in their fates and characters in a real-life way: for instance the secretary whom an agent wants to lure in a roundabout way through love faked as real passion, the waiter of the casino, who gets involved, via a credit institution that had loaned him a few hundred Marks, in a currency offense till he is forced by cunning brutality from offence to crime. Or the draftsman, who is the type of a man of weak character, entirely asocial, and forfeits his life out of sheer gambling and greed.

Opponents are the spy and his girlfriend, who has disguised herself as the owner of a fashion shop. The female agent is played by Kirsten Heiberg. René Deltgen lends his distinctive face and his rich art of great subtlety of nuance to the agent. Lotte Koch — who had appeared for the first time as partner of Zarah Leander in

Prof. Carl Froelich's Maria Stuart film — plays Inge, the secretary. She got her teeth into her part with the ambition of a real human portrayal. With Ernst Waldow as the waiter of the casino, Rolf Weih as Kettwig, Jr., Rudolf Schündler as the draftsman these parts are in well-tried hands.

(Mr. Schündler should be known to American audiences, too, from his having played the German butler who is accused of being a Nazi by Jack MacGowran in *The Exorcist*.)

Die goldene Spinne (*The Golden Spider*) was made in 1943 by Terra Filmkunst. This from a preliminary synopsis:

Rosa Sykora, the manager of the "Red Mill," a variety theater, one day is found dead in her office. Commissary Freise with a handkerchief carefully takes away a glass from the hands of the dead woman and smells hydrocyanic acid. Obviously Sykora knew too much...

Recently there were two suspects observed in the "Red Mill": Agnes Jordan, a cabaret singer, who was also seen as Klara Asmus in the assembly department of the Kattenbeck factory, and a certain Petersen, who likewise appeared as a canteen supplier at the Kattenbeck.

Both have suddenly disappeared off the face of the earth. In the quarters where they were living until then it looks like there was a hurried escape. Who may have warned them?

At the same time Axel Rüdiger, engineer at the Kattenbeck and good friends with Christa Fischer, daughter of the chief, has left under suspicious circumstances. Rüdiger is known as careless. One believes him capable of more or less stupid affairs with women, but — high treason?

Kneisler, a member of the Kattenbeck works security, admits to have engaged in a little criminal investigation after he had noticed Klara Asmus. Through his activities Asmus began to wonder and was warned in time. But how did she get through inspections? With a pass of the factory's physician. Christa Fischer deputized for the physician and issued the permit to Asmus. The same Christa Fischer is being arrested by the *Geheime Staatspolizei* [the Gestapo] in Axel Rüdiger's apartment. Seeing the open drawers the officer asks her, "Did you search something? No? But you have spoken to him? Phoned him? You have warned him, haven't you?" The small package which the "nurse" wanted to push aside inconspicuously with her foot contains a handful of splinters in a cotton wrapping.

Could there be any use in these few fragments? One can analyze the new steel alloy and from the traces of combustion on the grenade splinters deduce the new explosive force... But Petersen wants more, he wants to do the whole work. During a concert of the Philharmonists in the break he steals into the assembly hall. Captain Hartung, who called him to account, sorted out another matter, too. But that already reveals too much.

The inspection in the trains and on the train stations has been intensified. An inspector stops a nurse, who travels in the nurses' compartment of a hospital train: "Would you please take off your glasses and your cap? ... Well, you see, you are looking much better so, Miss—Jordan!"

After publishing this preliminary text something seems to have been changed, at least several characters' names. Miss Jordan turns out to be not a British (or American) spy but a Russian one, Lisaveta, who is highly interested in a new German tank weapon prepared by the Kattenbeck factory. She tries to leave the country with a package she got from Petersen (who is now renamed Smirnoff) disguised as a Red Cross nurse but is caught by the SS near the border. One of those betrayed by her at the home front wants to strangle her immediately: "Mendacious spy riff-raff!" "And the new tank?" Otto Gebühr playing Privy Councilor Fischer, Christa's father, the factory owner, is being asked.—"It is ready for action," Gebühr assures the audience. This from a contemporary review[3]:

> For years countless posters in big letters have been warning of enemy spies. Countless people have seen these posters and grasp the warning. Others, however, tend to recognize in these warning signs only a monitory finger which points at the beloved fellow man. Himself? Please no! Such things cannot happen to myself! I myself will recognize the swindle immediately if somebody should try "something like that" on me… Such is, alas, the thinking and talking of many. This is fine if one believes in his inner and exterior steadfastness. And because almost everybody is convinced of his smartness, both of these insights might lead one to pay no heed to written or spoken warnings of this kind and to say to oneself: I won't let myself sound off and I won't tell anything…
>
> The Terra film *Die goldene Spinne* has undertaken once again (as other movies have before) the educational task, by the most vivid perception of hammering everybody about the cunning proceeding of enemy agents and how easily even the smartest is caught in a net out of which there is no escape. Woven around the plot are a few piercing improbabilities—but in this case it doesn't matter at all! In such a film there is more at stake. And I think that everybody in Germany will understand this today.

Besides the spies there are *Falschmünzer* (*Counterfeiters*) who distribute false 50 Mark notes: "How do the police really work? That's the question which is answered by this picture. It was written and directed [by people] conscious of the serious responsibility of enlightening the audience on exact methods of police investigation of bogus money."[4] This money finds its way into Germany through the Swiss border, and so there is a nice cooperation between Nazi and Swiss authorities.

There were family sagas to nurture the hope that war could not destroy the tradition of the German community, such as the sentimental *Annelie* (1941). Its star, Luise Ullrich as a woman who is always late, was awarded the Coppa Volpi (the Volpi Cup) for best actress at the Film Festival of Venice. Annelie's *Love Story* (according to the subtitle) begins with her birth in 1871. Her husband dies a noble soldier's death: "In a tear-jerking sequence, the heroine (again too late) has reached her husband on the battlefield of World War I, only to have him die in her arms. She is unable to express her grief and is abruptly brought back to reality when a wounded soldier, unaware of the situation, asks her to light his cigarette for him. She does this in a moment worthy of Wyler at his best, and it still can bring an audience to instant tears."[5] Her own life comes to an end in 1941 when her sons enter the battlefields of World War II. Or there was Helmut Käutner's *Auf Wiedersehen, Franziska*, produced in the same year as *Annelie*. Marianne Hoppe, in private life married to Gustaf Gründgens, falls in love with a man (Hans Söhnker), who serves as a passionate newsreel

Die Degenhardts: a family saga.

cameraman on the exotic front in China. According to Käutner there was an injunction by the Propaganda Ministry that an additional sequence had to be shot: "This man should become aware of his duty to serve the fatherland, he should realize that his former life had been wrong and foolish, that he was a German and that he had to fulfill his duty in his fatherland and had to stay with the woman and eventually — in order to kill two birds with one stone — to go to war for Hitler as a consciously German man."[6] Films like these usually ended with farewell scenes and images of women waiting for their menfolk to return (a promise which numerous men were not able to keep): "The constant presentation of farewells, renunciation, self-denial and fidelity was intended to reassure men at the front and at the same time remind women of their duty to be faithful given the many married couples separated by the war."[7]

In *Die Degenhardts* (1944), the story of a Lübeck family (and the German answer to MGM's highly acclaimed *Mrs. Miniver*), Heinrich George played a longtime civil servant who is unjustly forced to retire but then voluntarily returns to his old post after the city's centuries-old cultural heritage is damaged by Allied bombing; he freely sacrifices his soldier sons to the Führer. (In those days of "greatest realism" it might be that one had to leave the cinema due to an air raid!) "With its film *Die Degenhardts* Tobis leads into an area into which all of us are involved in reality, into the area of the life at home during the war. On the basis of the fate of a family, which is living in a town in northern Germany, director Werner Klingler produced a generally apposite picture of the colorful joy and sorrows of the individual. Somehow

Heinrich George in *Die Degenhardts*.

everybody experiences the great fate of war from his own personal experience. So this film placed special emphasis on the private."[8] Goebbels readily agreed: "The war in the air is included as a subject here for the first time, and it is done in a very tactful and psychologically ingenious way. [Ewald von] Demandowsky is the only production chief who will touch political material and usually brings it off."[9]

At that time Germany's cities were bombed to piles of rubble with a national community living in air-raid shelters. Even old stars didn't mean anything anymore. For his last Nazi project titled *Mann im Sattel* (*Man in the Saddle*) aging veteran actor-director Harry Piel, who had been a faithful party member, was ordered to accept the support of Klingler of *Degenhardts* fame. But although Piel hoped to get the film finished and feverishly worked until April 22, 1945, he had to flee the project when Russian troops occupied the first Berlin suburbs. The popular actor escaped in German tanks that took him safely to Hamburg. But the loss of *Mann im Sattel* hit him hard as not only had his private film collection been destroyed in the flames of an air-raid, but his previous film, *Panik*, on which he had worked for years, had not been passed by the censors in 1943 for it showed a Zoological Gardens that was bombed, with braveheart Piel starring as big game hunter Peter Völker rescuing all the animals. Fortunately for the desperate Piel, who wasn't seen on the screen for more than ten years, the *Panik* footage was finally returned to him by the Russians in 1952 so that he could release it as a testimony in 1953.

CHAPTER 11

Götterdämmerung:
Kolberg and the
Fall of the Third Reich

For General Erich Ludendorff, wire puller and éminence grise in Germany's High Command during the period of 1914–1918, a future war would place even bigger burdens on the people's shoulders than World War I. The relationship between army and people, the psychical unity of the whole, would be more crucial to warfare than ever before. So he wrote in a publication titled *Total War*.

We may assume that Joseph Goebbels did know Ludendorff's main theses (at least he met Ludendorff once and was very impressed by him) when he entered Berlin Sportpalast on February 18, 1943, at 5:00 P.M. to indoctrinate a selected group of 14,000 German *Volksgenossen* (national comrades) with an "openness" that was rare for Nazis. He officially admitted the end of the *Blitzkrieg* strategy. However, he could afford to avoid the usual deliberate deception of the public as even the dumbest German by that time did know that victories of the swastika had become scarce. Two weeks before, on February 2, the Sixth German Army under General Friedrich Paulus had had to surrender to the Red Army in Stalingrad. All of Hitler's fantastic, arrogant aims in the East: to conquer Baku and make a thrust to Mesopotamia, had been broken into pieces. Now the Minister for National Education and Propaganda was forced to depict the situation and resulting consequences in an unvarnished way that was unheard of. But his "openness" was only the seed of a more subtle propaganda. One might imagine that a big claque had carefully been instructed by the organizers to applaud and hail total war which Goebbels seductively praised as the only way out of the dilemma.

The Sportpalast had been Goebbels' private auditorium and always was. "In the East we experience a hard military load," he exclaimed there. The steppe's assault against "our venerable continent" this winter has broken off with a force that runs counter to all human and historical conception. "The Huns are at the gate!" Goebbels talked in length about the Bolshevist danger to the Reich and all of Europe. Only the armed forces of the German *Wehrmacht*, and the German people and their allies had the necessary combat effectiveness to save Europe, the occident and even the whole world from this eerie Jewish world revolution. "In Judaism we have recognized an immediate danger for every country." Listeners fanatically applauded, some shouted to hang the Jews. In Goebbels' anti–Semitic *Weltanschauung* (world-view), Judaism was an infectious symptom. "Terrorist Judaism has made 200 million people in Russia serve its purpose." The minister concluded that the war of mechanized robots against Germany and Europe had reached its peak. "In the East a war is raging without any mercy. The Führer has characterized it correctly in his proclamation of January 30 telling us that in the end there would be no victors and defeated but only survivors and annihilated. So total war is fitting in with the needs of the present. There must be an end to bourgeois primness." He postulated that total warfare should become a matter involving all people. "We have closed all nightclubs [loud interruption, "That's only for idlers"], because they began to injure our morale and dim the impression of war. German people can no more tolerate things like that. All luxury will be cut down: restaurants, shops et al. We prefer to wear patchwork for a few years than to stumble in rags for the next centuries." Dr. Goebbels also criticized young couples riding through the forest of Tiergarten at 9:00 A.M. which of course would leave an irritating impression on a working-class woman returning from a ten-hour night shift with the prospect of having to care for three, four or five kids. "And the soldier — how should he describe what he has seen at the home front? War isn't for the amusement-greedy mob." He promised to take drastic action. The minister, well known for his sexual escapades, summoned German women to replace men who had had to leave for the front. He seemed to anticipate that that front and the so-called home front would unite very soon. To overcome the crisis, he cited the one and only Prussian prototype, the aforementioned idolized Fridericus Rex, the Great King, who had stolidly defied the superior forces of enemies. At the end, in the climax of his speech, Goebbels asked ten rhetorical questions.

> GOEBBELS. The English claim that the German people are resisting government measures for total war.
> CROWD. Lies! Lies!
> GOEBBELS. It doesn't want total war, say the English, but capitulation.
> CROWD. Never! Sieg Heil! Sieg Heil!
> GOEBBELS. Do you want total war?
> CROWD. Yes! [People shouting and applauding frenetically.]
> GOEBBELS. Do you want it more total, more radical, than we could ever have imagined?
> CROWD. Yes! Yes! [Loud applause.]
> GOEBBELS. Are you ready to stand with the Führer as the phalanx of the homeland behind the fighting *Wehrmacht*? Are you ready to continue

the struggle unshaken and with savage determination, through all the vicissitudes of fate until victory is in our hands?

CROWD. Yes!

GOEBBELS. I ask you then: Are you determined to follow the Führer through thick and thin in the struggle for victory and to accept even the harshest personal sacrifices?

CROWD. Yes! Sieg Heil! [*A chant of "Führer, befiehl, wir folgen!"* ("*The Führer commands, we follow!*")]

GOEBBELS. You have shown our enemies what they need to know, so that they will no longer indulge in illusions. The mightiest ally in the world — the people themselves — have shown that they stand behind us in our determined fight for victory, regardless of the costs.

CROWD. Yes! Yes! [Loud applause.]

GOEBBELS. Therefore let the slogan be from now on: "People arise, and storm, break loose!" [Extended applause.]

Goebbels was satisfied. He let his audience renew the oath to the Führer and asserted that through the mouths of thousands, the German people had manifested their mind in front of the world. Afterwards, he cynically wondered if his listeners would have jumped from a high-rise building if ordered to. (Perhaps he remembered a similar scene from Ernst Lubitsch's Hollywood satire *To Be or Not to Be*.)

From now on, all propaganda efforts had to serve the formula of total war. On June 1, 1943, Dr. Goebbels issued a written order to Professor Harlan at Ufastadt Babelsberg:

> I hereby commission you to make a major film titled *Kolberg*. The purpose of this film will be to demonstrate through the example of the Prussian city that gives the film its title, that a policy supported both at home and on the front can overcome every opponent... I authorize you to request whatever help and support you deem necessary from all agencies of the army, state and party and to point out that the film I have commissioned here is being made in the service of our intellectual war effort.

According to Goebbels, the *Kolberg* project was backed by Hitler himself. First ideas for that movie went back to the year 1941. "It must have been a most unusual exorcism — a mad notion that one could ban reality from history and put illusion in its place," Klaus Kreimeier observed in his book *The UFA Story*. He defined what Goebbels called intellectual warfare as "war conducted in the mind alone, war as a scenario concocted by a delirious imagination cut off from reality."[1] Goebbels bashfully christened it "poetic truth." UFA proudly announced the project of a "colossal painting" (Goebbels' term) and launched a press conference with production chief Wolfgang Liebeneiner and director Veit Harlan. Liebeneiner enthused about the greatest challenge: to have a picture influence the present day by sheer profundity of thought (*Gedankentiefe*). Harlan explained that they didn't want to produce an academic history lesson; rather, they wanted to make a movie that reminded the German people of what they always had been. The project should strive upwards as a monument to the citizens of the Prussian city Kolberg (which 140 years before had resisted Napoleonic troops) and to the German people of today (that strained every nerve to put a stop to the Red Army).

Shooting Veit Harlan's *Kolberg* in 1944. (*From the personal files of the late cinematographer Gerhard Huttula.*)

This movie of epic proportions was framed by a flashback personally written (or at least masterminded) by Goebbels. In 1813, in the name of all Prussian generals, August Graf Neidhard von Gneisenau (played by a too youthful Horst Caspar) appeals to his hesitant King, Friedrich Wilhelm III, to issue a proclamation to the people, who are eager to take up arms against Napoleon and the French, "War shall be a matter no more just for the army." The King in true Prussian tradition remains doubtful and calls Gneisenau a starry-eyed idealist, a poet, a German dreamer. "Proclamation to the people? War is still and will be a matter for the army! People only suffer from war. People are opposed to war." But Gneisenau does not give up easily and suggests a militia, a folk's storm, a people of soldiers. "A king has to lead his people. That is a natural duty willed by God. Otherwise he must resign." Outside, to emphasize Gneisenau's emotional words, the tramping masses of Breslau citizens echo their fighting spirit with lyrics by Theodor Körner — "*The people rise up; the storm breaks loose!*" To further motivate the King and tune him to his people, Gneisenau recounts the story of the fight for Baltic Kolberg, an action that he was actively involved in. In 1807, during the Franco-Prussian war and after Napoleon's victorious battles of Jena and Austerlitz, Kolberg, located in East Prussia, was severely attacked and besieged by superior forces of French troops. German audiences of course would recognize a strong similarity between that steadfast fortress city of history and the desperate post–Stalingrad situation of the struggling Third Reich.

Goebbels and his comrades were heavily inspired by the Teutonic *cult of death* myth of the legendary *Nibelungen* that in the highly acknowledged silent film *Die Nibelungen* by Fritz Lang had so impressed them. Hagen von Tronje, one of the Burgundians, had betrayed and killed Christlike Siegfried, the noblest of heroes. This

Hagen was a true native of the north and did not have much in common with Christianity. Kriemhild, Siegfried's widow, brooded on the subject of vengeance. She accepted the proposal of Etzel-Attila, mighty chief of the Huns, and invited her Burgundian brothers to join her (and find their death in Etzel's castle). Realizing what her sister had in mind, the Burgundians managed to secure Etzel's big hall and lock themselves in. As they bravely refused to exchange their wartime comrade Hagen, Kriemhild ordered her (in Goebbels' terms) "subhuman" Huns to set the hall on fire, and one by one her brothers inside died. When Hagen staggered out from the ruined, burned hall, Kriemhild killed him herself. In turn, she was killed by one of Etzel's vassals who hated to see the devastation that cruel female (!) mind had wrought. That was exactly what the chief propagandist of the Third Reich envisioned for his own people: to stay faithful to their oath to the Führer, as the Burgundians did in face of the hordes from the steppe, and die in the ruins of their bombed cities. The German language created the idea of "*Nibelungentreue*" which describes an unquestioning loyalty unto death. Nazi leaders and the German High Command by that time knew that the war was lost. That meant a heroic fight to the last man. The defeat was an integral part of a stylized heroic epic, at least in German minds. Like a religious sect, Germans should sacrifice their lives for Adolf Hitler so that the memory of their agony could live forever and bear new Nazis in a better (or worse) future. (Among the uncredited *Kolberg* writers was Thea von Harbou who in the early 1920s scripted *Die Nibelungen* for her former husband, Fritz Lang. Among the supporting players was Margarete Schön, Lang's original Kriemhild, now playing the bit part of a housekeeper.)

Again, as in *Jud Süss* (*Jew Suss*), Heinrich George was chosen for the leading part. He and his wife, Berta Drews, had been present at Goebbels' Sportpalast speech. According to a rumor, George raved enthusiastically while newsreel footage only showed him in solemn agreement. George was commissioned to play Kolberg's patriotic council member Joachim Nettelbeck (1738–1824). The historical Nettelbeck was a brewer's son (in the movie the French ridicule the "distiller" whom Napoleon arrogantly wants to give a kick up the backside). He spent an adventurous life as a steersman, ship's captain and slave-trader. Later he became a Prussian reformer in the spirit of Stein, Hardenberg and Scharnhorst. He organized the civilian resistance (to be levied as last line of resistance, the "folk's storm," by the Nazis) against the obvious defeatism of Colonel Von Loucadou, the city's military commander played by Paul Wegener, who had decided to surrender immediately to Napoleon's generals.

A shipowner named Goldow, one of the wealthiest men in town, agrees with Loucadou's sentiments simply in order to save his business. "Of course, one needs to rule — but why should we rule ourselves?" He suggests bowing to the French Emperor and accepting public reorganization. Disgustedly, Nettelbeck shakes his head, "No, we do not want to become servants in our own home." But the dozen or so cannons of the city have rusted since, and citizens are not trained for war. Months pass by. It is winter now. Nettelbeck heads the town council and translates a letter by Napoleon's appointed Governor of Pomerania, who ultimately orders them to surrender. "So we are simply conquered by mail," Nettelbeck remarks bitterly. His great, convincing eloquence is the motive power for the majority of the council to resist the humiliating nature of the letter. Consequently, an irritated Napoleon decides to demoralize

"that dump Kolberg" by the force of his engine of war. Nettelbeck in the meantime
has been imprisoned by Loucadou for reasons of insubordination. Through the grat-
ing of his prison cell he slips a letter into his niece Maria's hand and asks her to
smuggle it to Königsberg where the King has retreated. But she isn't passed in front
of the monarch from whom Nettelbeck expects Loucadou's replacement. Instead,
promoted by a well-meaning adjutant, she is welcomed by the divine Queen of Prussia who sentimentally declares that only a few gemstones are left in the crown of Prussia, "Kolberg is one of those," and delegates one of her best officers to support
Nettelbeck. (Frank Noack, author of a Veit Harlan biography, reads unintended les-
bian undertones in the play of the two actresses.) Eventually, Loucadou is replaced
by the flashback's narrator, Gneisenau. On his arrival in Kolberg, Gneisenau finds a
more than willing partner in the released Nettelbeck, aided by Maria's war-experi-
enced boyfriend, Lt. Ferdinand Von Schill (Gustav Diessl who seemed wooden in this
part since he had suffered from a stroke), a person in his own words "married to war."
Together they succeed in transforming the citizenship into a local militia, some only
armed with pitchforks, similar to what we saw some years later in Akira Kurosawa's
The Seven Samurai. In desperate straits, while the French bombard the city, Gneisenau is deeply moved by the older Nettelbeck's credo, "Better to be buried under the
ruins than to capitulate. I have never gone to my knees to anyone before. Now I'm
doing it. Gneisenau, Kolberg must not be surrendered!" "That is what I wanted to
hear from you, Nettelbeck! Now — we can die together." Both men, willing to stick
through thick and thin, embrace each other. The German soul, plagued by so many
defeats, seems to be fascinated with such a Dance of Death. According to Veit Harlan's memoirs, Goebbels recognized himself in the figure of the idealistic Nettelbeck
who is prepared to suffer the greatest fatigue. The minister even dictated some of the
dialogue: "They might burn our houses but our earth they cannot burn. So let's
become moles." In fact, Hitler and Goebbels died molelike in the bunker under the
Reichskanzlei. Harlan strongly denied the theory that Goebbels foresaw the political
and military developments at the time he contrived the project. Allegedly, he just
wanted to describe that the main burden of the resistance against Napoleon was
placed on the shoulders of the common people and not on those of the military (the
democratic army, however, is a French and American idea, not a Prussian one). As
Goebbels saw it, he was the man of the people, he represented the common feeling,
because he didn't belong to the unholy inner military circle of the Third Reich where
narrow-minded generals the likes of Keitel and Jodl dominated. He himself, as he
pointed out, came from humble beginnings.

"Hitler as well as Goebbels must have been obsessed by the idea that such a
movie could be more useful than a battle won in Russia," decided Veit Harlan.[2] In
her diary, his wife Kristina Söderbaum called it "a terrible notice that Veit should do
Kolberg." For Veit Harlan, however, it was not so much a terrible but a *terrific* thing
to have been appointed director of such a megalomaniacal venture. Before shooting
began, he told his crew that they were working by personal order of the Führer. No
opposition was allowed, neither to the Führer nor to his proxy, the "Spielleiter" (i.e.,
director) of this movie. Finally, Harlan had become his own general commanding a
small army without any danger to his own life or that of his wife Kristina (and with
the prospect of the couple earning a double fee). Frau Söderbaum, as usual, played

Filming a crowd scene for *Kolberg*. (*From the personal files of the late cinematographer Gerhard Huttula.*)

the love interest, in this case the fictitious farmer's daughter Maria who urges her two brothers and boyfriend to die for the glory of Prussia. One brother, Friedrich, obeys and dies bravely, but the other, Claus, a cosmopolitan who, without hesitation, fraternizes with the enemy, sports no fighting spirit at all. He has attended the conservatory in Strasborg and prefers to play the violin instead of joining the battle. Nevertheless, he is damned to lose his life during the French siege of Kolberg (beginning March 1807) in an attempt to save the beloved instrument. In the final scene, Nettelbeck comforts his heartbroken niece standing in front of the smoking ruins while the inhabitants sing the Thanksgiving Hymn "We Gather Together" under the blasted roof of the cathedral. "Greatness is only born in pain... You're great, Maria, it is your victory too." Goebbels and Harlan deliberately overlooked one tiny detail: It was not the Kolberg citizens' resistance or a disagreement of French officers ("The Prussians are fighting like lions!" "You want to surrender to a stubborn Pomeranian farming community?!") that stopped hostilities on July 2, 1807, but the armistice of Tilsit that was no page of glory in German history either. French General Loison couldn't ignore the message a courier had brought from Tilsit. On the other hand, the screenplay by Veit Harlan and associate Alfred Braun ignores the fact that Prussia as a result lost half of its territory, and that the French marched into Kolberg. By the way, the Kolberg citizens then were supported from sea by the gunfire of a Swedish frigate and a British brig. The screenwriters also concealed British arms delivery for the besieged city.

Harlan claimed a remarkable total of 6,000 horses and 187,000 *Wehrmacht* troops as extras, and every writer since seems to have believed in this propaganda trick.

There was an enormous number of Napoleonic troops to be seen in some long shots, but it was "only" several thousands. Even for Goebbels, it would have been impossible to recruit almost 200,000 soldiers, i.e. 19 divisions, from the declining fronts in the East. For comparison, at Stalingrad almost 150,000 German soldiers died in the Soviet offensive, and another 90,000 became prisoners of war. Harlan stated that he was allowed to recruit any number of soldiers out of service, even raiding the barracks. Although he regarded himself No. 2 in the Nazi hierarchy, Harlan's mentor Goebbels wasn't as powerful as Hitler's other paladins. In the final years of the Third Reich, everything was filtered by the Führer's almighty secretary Martin Bormann. Goebbels' secret ambition, to actively participate in the bleeding Reich's fight to the death, was fulfilled only in the last months of his life, when Hitler put him in charge of total warfare (July 26, 1944) and made him defender of Berlin.

Nevertheless, the number that marched towards the cinematic Kolberg was still enormous, but it was by no means three times the combined number of French and Prussian soldiers fighting during the historical battle for the city. Harlan proudly noted that Goebbels intended to create "the biggest movie of all time" that should dwarf even the most expensive U. S. productions. "For one scene, I even got the original crown of Karl der Grosse including scepter and orb. Twenty detectives watched over the priceless goods." Norbert Schultze, composer of the famed wartime ballad "Lili Marlene," was responsible for the main choral theme of that film, "The people rise up," which reminds us of Goebbels' infamous Sportpalast speech.

"I have high hopes for this movie," Goebbels confided to his diary. "It exactly fits the military-political landscape of the time when the picture will be released." (Contrary to Harlan's statement of above, he actually seemed to foresee German defeat but didn't want it to be inglorious. If their star was on the wane, the ultimate fight was supposed to be apocalyptic in its dimensions and unforgettable in history.) The same time *Kolberg* was released, Hitler issued his fortress order. Every East German town attacked by Russian troops should hold out and resist as a fort following the example of the Kolberg citizens. By showing the sentiment and heroism of their Prussian ancestors, Goebbels declared to the German cinema buffs that "this is the core of which you were born, and it is with this strength that you will today rise to victory." In his book *Film in the Third Reich* David Stewart Hull rightly describes *Kolberg* as the apotheosis of the Nazi film. By incorporating the 1813 Breslau flashback and the King's proclamation to the people (incidentally, not Gneisenau's idea), Goebbels linked Napoleon's defeat in the Battle of the Nations near Leipzig (October 16–19, 1813) to the Kolberg example. Therefore, in Goebbels' propaganda, disgrace transformed into victory. The method is questionable, of course; questionable also is whether Harlan actually shot parts of that Leipzig battle so that the end of the movie itself came out like a glorious victory for the imperturbable Kolberg citizens. (In propaganda terms, this proceeding was called "ultimate victory," and every German, even more so after Stalingrad, was invited to religiously believe in that absurd formula.)

Ironically, Heinrich George's acting career had begun in Kolberg's municipal theater in 1912, in a play written by Paul Heyse: *Colberg 1807*. His interpretation of the Clausewitz creed was broadcast regularly at the turn of the years 1941–1943. In this lecture the Germans were summoned to submit to the service of the fatherland.

Months before the shooting of his scenes, George was at Harlan's disposal. However, he was well paid for his participation in *Kolberg*. Originally, for his part as Nettelbeck, a monthly fee of RM 25,000 was agreed upon, RM 150,000 for six months, instead of what George usually would have asked for (which was RM 45,000 less for that amount of time). Goebbels was annoyed by the actor's demand and didn't agree. He suggested a compromise of RM 120,000. In a 3-page letter dated May 13, 1944, Heinrich George opposed this decision. (He generally did not oppose acting in such a movie.) He claimed that he had to cancel all starring tours and public appearances and therefore suffered severe financial damage. Due to the long shooting schedule, he persisted in his claim for RM 150,000. Cleverly, he compromised a little by assuring the authorities that he was perfectly aware of the circumstances and agreed with the intention of waging intellectual warfare as the main reason for the movie. He signed "Heil Hitler!" On September 12, 1944, German *Filmkurier*[3] announced that George had to face a great challenge impersonating Nettelbeck in the *Kolberg* movie but implied that he could meet it: "The character demands a male calmness as well as sensitiveness, qualities that both combine so well in Heinrich George's art." Five days later a fee of RM 150,000 was granted. With a total cost of RM 8.8 million *Kolberg* was by far the most expensive German movie up to that time. Napoleon, at least in one of his short scenes, was played with some dignity by Charles Schauten. It is a well-known fact that Hitler was an admirer of Bonaparte, and so Harlan filmed Schauten in front of the sarcophagus of Friedrich II in Potsdam. The Emperor murmured that he wouldn't have stayed there as conqueror if the Great King had still been alive. In some way, Hitler regarded himself as Bonaparte's heir.

There were several delays due to script changes and unavailability of certain actors who were committed to other projects. Finally on October 10, 1943, Harlan started shooting at the actual site of Kolberg. Hundreds of roofers and craftsmen reconstructed the buildings and created an impressive set. For the winter scenes a hundred railcars brought salt to the shooting locale to transform the mole of the Baltic Sea harbor into a snowy landscape. (We don't get to see much of it in the final film.) Harlan never got tired of remarking that money didn't count. According to his autobiography, the battle scenes had to be photographed before all the costumes [10,000, not 187,000] had arrived, and the troops in the rear were forced to dye their military uniforms overnight and wear sashes improvised from toilet paper. There was a shortage of ammunition in the East, but factories were put on overtime to make the necessary blank bullets for this movie. Millions of feet of color negative film [a total of 90 hours!] had to be especially prepared and developed at a staggering cost.[4] Harlan and his director of photography, Bruno Mondi, fixed interesting camera perspectives: "Six cameras, one of them on a boat and one in a tethered balloon, simultaneously recorded the destruction of the city. Thirty pyrotechnicians were in charge of the innumerable explosions, and to stage a flood a small stream [*Persante*] was redirected into canals dug specially for the purpose. Remote controls set off charges of underwater explosives." Not all of the thirty explosives experts had film experience, with obviously fatal results. In the spring of 1944, Gerhard Huttula had been invited by his colleague Mondi to serve as the film's second cameraman. "*Kolberg* was the most embarrassing experience of my whole professional career," Huttula said. "It was sheer torture. I do not want to talk about it. This man Harlan was a fanatic, really. Didn't care for any of the employees." Harlan communicated with the different units by wireless. He later had to admit that during the shooting of some of the most crucial scenes soldiers were "in short supply": another hint that there never were 187,000 troops involved. He tried to get 4,000 sailors on a U-boat course in the harbor of Kolberg. A high-ranking marine officer told him that this would be utterly impossible. Harlan produced the proxy signed by Goebbels. An hour later the officer had to give in: "You won, Professor!" Admiral Karl Dönitz' protest came too late. But even here numbers differ. Curt Riess (who after the war authored the film book *Das gab's nur einmal*[5]) knew of only 2,000 sailors. However, Riess himself is no reliable source. But he was correct in stating that five of the extras rounded up by Harlan (*Sieg Heil!*) to storm a hill died during the shooting. At least most of the servicemen were relieved to have a break from the cruelties of the front. For the stunt-riding scenes involving the character of cavalry lieutenant Von Schill, Harlan recruited some of General Vlassov's Cossacks who had deserted (in her autobiography, Kristina Söderbaum spoke of acrobats). Wrapping location shooting in Pomerania in April 1944, Harlan's team moved back to exteriors not that far away from Babelsberg Studios (Gross-Glienicke, Staaken) where parts of Kolberg had been reconstructed. Here filming went on more smoothly for another three weeks, although there were lots of technical problems throughout as assistant cameraman Heinz Pehlke remembers. "Every day something got broken, cables were tearing, something was missing and so on." Pehlke estimates that they used 5,000 extras. While *Kolberg* was edited and re-edited to Goebbels's specifications, war's arm finally reached the Harlan family. Their house in Berlin-Grunewald's Tannenbergallee 28 (designed by Hans Poelzig, a famous architect) was destroyed by bombs on December 12, 1944. While working on another anti–Semitic project, *The Merchant of Venice*, Harlan interfered on behalf of his chief electrician, Fritz Kühne, who was supposed to join *Volkssturm*, which would have meant sure death for his Jewish wife, Loni. In spite of Harlan's protection, on November 5, 1944, the couple, terrified to death, committed suicide. They left a farewell letter: "Dear Professor and dear Mrs. Harlan! All your great kindness and love unfortunately was in vain. We don't have any strength to bear our fate. Too often our hearts were torn apart for an undeserved fate. Please accept our sincerest thanks. God will reward what you have done for us. In faithful gratitude Yours, Loni and Fritz Kühne."[6] Kristina Söderbaum, accompanied by fellow actor Kurt Meisel, went to the funeral; Harlan didn't, apparently because of *Kolberg*.

To protect himself from critics, Harlan later claimed that Goebbels, who saw the rushes repeatedly, over and over again, had the finished movie "butchered" and ordered production head Wolfgang Liebeneiner to remove all the bloodshed, RM 2 million worth of footage that he considered demoralizing. In fact, there had been cuts of the effects of "total war" and "horrors of the battle" but not as many as Harlan would have wished:

All "monstrous battle scenes" and some takes in the city had to be trimmed in favor of expanding the narrative starring famous personalities.

Scenes with a pregnant woman were deleted.

The hysterics of Maria's brother Claus were shortened.

Extras marching in a scene being shot for *Kolberg*. (*From the personal files of the late cine-matographer Gerhard Huttula.*)

In the sequence with Maria and the Queen of Prussia, two close-ups are missing.

During the first meeting of Gneisenau and Nettelbeck, Gneisenau's remark that he solely would be in charge is cut. Censors felt that this statement would have diminished Nettelbeck's merits.

Strangely enough, one little incident is missing from the prologue. In Braunau am Inn in 1806, Johann Philipp Palm, a bookseller who had printed and distributed a paper "Deutschland in seiner tiefsten Erniedrigung" (Germany in its deepest humiliation), is sentenced to death and executed by the French. (Every Nazi of course knew that Braunau later became the Führer's birthplace.)

There is at least one editorial mistake, too: In an interior scene, Kristina Söderbaum is singing a nursery rhyme to a little child, and in the next one, an exterior, she is assisting a one-legged citizen with a fire hose.

In a last meeting on December 25, 1944, further cuts were discussed by the decision-makers. By that time, Harlan and some editing tables had been evacuated to the city of Guben. The released movie is extraordinarily tedious and pathetic when you compare it with the model prototype, the highly acclaimed Selznick production of Margaret Mitchell's *Gone With the Wind*, which ran over a hundred minutes longer. Nevertheless, Germany's ninth Agfacolor feature film was sort of impressive. In addition, it was awarded Film of the Nation. "It would seem that cameraman Bruno Mondi at last solved most of the problems of the tricky Agfacolor film," David Stewart Hull observed in his book. "Flesh tones are remarkably real, and the exteriors have a vivid quality quite unlike previous attempts with the new stock. Only the interiors tend to be unpleasant, with a predominance of pink hues."

When Goebbels told Hitler about the new *Kolberg* film and described a few scenes from it, the Führer was moved almost to tears: "He asks me to bring the film out as quickly as possible, calling it a battle won in the political conduct of war, on the basis of what I have told him."[7] But when postproduction was completed in January 1945, most German cinemas had been bombed, and with the prints hastily struck at the Afifa laboratory, no new cinemas could be delivered to play them. According to UFA files, some of the prints found their way to leading party and SS members: to Reich Marshal Hermann Göring, to Walter Funk, minister of economic affairs, to "worthy party comrade" and head of the film division, *Gruppenführer* Hans Hinkel, to General Heinz Guderian, even to Heinrich Himmler and General Otto Ernst Rehmer, the self-proclaimed political soldier who had helped to wipe out the last resistance of Prussian officers against the regime in 1944. All in all, there were about 40 prints.

We have to consider that at that time there were enormous shortages in the film industry, too. A letter addressed by Ufa-Film G.m.b.H. (Ufi) to its subcompanies[8] regarding use of negative film stock said: "Our main suppliers of negative film confidentially draw our attention to the fact that because of arms expenditure a bottle-neck in the supply of iodine has occurred, especially the day-to-day supply of iodine is not secure. Iodine is a vital ingredient in the production of negative film stock." In order to save film stock, the letter called clause 3b of *Leistungssteigerungserlass* (decree of improvement in output) to mind: "For interior shooting, takes should be repeated no more than twice." For a usual black and white movie, that meant a maximum of between 45,000 and 60,000 feet, but 88,500 feet was usually registered for film negatives.

Because it would mean a far-reaching intervention "in the work of our creative film artists, we want to avoid limiting the consumption of negative per film by quotas, but for that newly occurring and compelling reason we have to ask you within the bounds of your own responsibility to give your greatest attention to the observance of the decree of improvement in output and especially put it to the directors that they should execute rehearsals in a way that comparatively less negative film stock is used." Of course that didn't apply to a director like Veit Harlan.

Kolberg premiered in Berlin on January 30, 1945 (the 12th and final anniversary of the Nazi's seizure of power and the day the KdF ship *Wilhelm Gustloff* was torpedoed by a Russian submarine, with 9,000 people dying, among them 4,000 kids). Eventually, one print (#24) was provided for a simultaneous premiere in the Atlantic fortress of the still occupied French city of La Rochelle. Goebbels wrote, "May this film document for you and your brave troops the unshakable steadfastness of a people who, in these days of world conflict, are at one with our men at the front and who are prepared to follow the great examples in our glorious past." In La Rochelle at that time 60,000 French inhabitants and 18,000 German occupying forces were besieged. Once La Rochelle was the most important U-boat base, but now no operating submarine was left in the huge concrete bunkers. We cannot confirm that there is truth to the story that the Propaganda Minister had ordered the *Luftwaffe* to fly a daring mission behind enemy lines and drop the recently completed film by parachute. We can't even say for sure if the movie was shown at all in front of the German garrison. The only evidence we have is an enthusiastic telegram by Vice Admiral

30. Januar 1945

Uraufführung in La Rochelle und Berlin

Kolberg

ein zeitgeschichtliches Dokument

Doppelheft Nr. 61   DM 1,–/öS 10,–/sfrs. 1,50

A program for the 1965–66 reissue of *Kolberg*.

Ernst-Wilhelm Schirlitz (misspelled in the press as Schirwitz), commandant of La Rochelle/La Pallice from August 20, 1944, congratulating Dr. Goebbels on his cinematographic deed: "Opening performance of color film *Kolberg* took place today in La Rochelle Theater (Théâtre de la Ville) for soldiers of all units of defense zone. Profoundly moved by the courageous action and heroic stand of the Kolberg fortress and by this artistically unsurpassable rendering of it, I convey to you along with my thanks for the dispatch of this film for January 30 a renewed vow to emulate the heroic struggle of those on the home front and not to lag behind them in endurance and commitment. Long live Germany, long live our Führer!"[9]

That sounded dashing, but although *Kolberg's* second premiere city, the German capital, became a scene of a fight to death, there was no struggle at all in La Rochelle. According to the amusing *The Hollywood Hall of Shame*, compiled by the brothers Harry & Michael Medved of *Golden Turkey Awards* fame, La Rochelle surrendered to the Americans two weeks after the memorable premiere. But if a print was dispatched to La Rochelle, it would have been almost impossible to fly it in or ship it by other means without the knowledge of the Allies. And there were not prints enough to repeat the allegedly daring flight mission. And, by the way, La Rochelle did not surrender two weeks after the premiere. What really happened? We asked

Horst Bredow, in charge of "*Stiftung Traditionsarchiv Unterseeboote/U-Boot-Archiv*" (Tradition Archives Submarine Foundation) in Cuxhaven. He proved extremely monosyllabic. In a letter dated April 10, 1997, he responded, "Did you ever hear about the 'Morgenthau Plan' according to which our generation was threatened with being castrated, our women sterilized and Germany degenerated to a desolate region? That is one of the reasons why our generation of war participants didn't surrender that easily although one could anticipate that the war was lost. Would you have wanted to survive as a castrate?"

However, in the case of La Rochelle Herr Bredow was wrong. La Rochelle finally surrendered *without* any serious battle action registered during the last months. From research we know that there was a secret agreement between Schirlitz and the Resistance represented by Capitaine de Frégatte Hubert Meyer who acted as peace negotiator. Therefore, Meyer was even suspected of collaboration with the *boches* by some French fundamentalists. Wasn't he sort of a *boche* himself? He was born in Lothringen (Lorraine) which is in the frontier country between France and Germany. To negotiate from a strong position, Schirlitz played a trump. He had mined the harbor of La Rochelle and La Pallice (which was one of the most important on the Atlantic coast) and made it crystal clear that he would be willing to blow it up. For the Allies it was a priority to get the harbor undestroyed. So a big air raid was out of the question. Anyhow, the French commander-in-chief was convinced that the fortress would capitulate without blood shed. He believed in Schirlitz' guarantee that he wouldn't start a counter-attack (how could he?) or blow up the harbor. What they did was to play war and wait. So, by tacit permission of the Allies, La Rochelle was supported from sea and by train. Not even the electricity was cut off. German Field Marshal Von Rundstedt had left it to his commandants to act in their own estimation as long as they held the fortresses. He raised no objection to negotiations provided they took long enough. To avoid any misunderstanding, Schirlitz's conduct of negotiations was explained in a message (*Geheime Kommandosache* [military secret]) to the German Admiralty: "Most important aspect for commandant of fortress is to gain time. He has to register that training of his troop is [important requirement]. Troop not qualified for sallies and too weak. So the offer of French negotiator just suits him. His only duty is to prevent enemy from using the harbor." The message states that the impeccable reputation of Admiral Schirlitz excludes any danger of a disastrous involvement in a diplomatic entanglement.

Now for the Berlin premiere. The Medved Brothers[10] claim that since most of Berlin's film theaters had burned to the ground, "Goebbels' staff at last located a small theatre that was still in working order and opened the film there with as much fanfare as they could muster." In fact, UFA Palast am Zoo, flagship of the company, had been destroyed, but Tauentzien Palace and U. T. Alexanderplatz were still operating and could by no means be called small cinemas. Nevertheless, it was a poor premiere. Only some of the Hitler Youth saw *Kolberg* with a growing, glowing admiration. Despite all the national kitsch, German film critic Peter W. Jansen who saw it when he was 14 was overwhelmed. Indoctrinated boys sacrificed their lives uselessly to save their Führer's life. For all the others, it was a bitter mockery. With some difficulty, UFA officials had arranged the shadow of a cold buffet (some tuna and sardines in oil) after the screening to be consumed in great haste by a worried public eager to get home before the next air raid. "J. Sch." who reviewed the movie for *Völkischer Beobachter*[11] considered it

> a great film otherwise we wouldn't have been allowed to see it on January 30 in such a significant year. To appreciate its artistic qualities, the modest interplay of the greatest of actors under the supervision of a master craftsman, to copy the wild decency of the moving masses of citizens and soldiers, to re-create the harmony of color, image and plot—all this could be alluring. But these means of sympathy demanding excitement recede into the political background…. You have to see that movie not from the viewpoint of a smaller past, you have to experience it in the realm of greater present days…. Of course, we know that there are bigger dangers than 35,000 enemy soldiers and 500 enemy cannons—but the citizens of Kolberg didn't know that. To admire what they achieved, one cannot judge their heroism in light of the trials we have had to face.

The reviewer thinks it worthwhile to model our heroes after Nettelbeck or Gneisenau or even "Maria" Söderbaum.

> Technique and warfare, war aims and dangers have changed and become enormous in proportions since the battle of Kolberg, but what made people valuable hasn't changed in the last 150 years. You are supposed to recognize in French squadrons the herds of tanks that reign in our modern battlefields, in the licentiousness of a foreign soldateska the arbitrariness of Bolshevist force, in the burning of old patrician buildings the flaming ocean of our pained cities, you'll hear in the march of foreign battalions that shook the earth of our East-German provinces the boots of Soviet armies. Therefore, one leaves the cinema in the knowledge that a grim belief in the good righteousness of the issue will finally overcome any superior forces…. Kolberg surely wasn't Germany, France wasn't Bolshevism, but what the citizens under the command of Nettelbeck and what Prussian soldiers under Gneisenau were able to do, we can do too.

Meanwhile, the commandant of real-life Kolberg that was crowded with fugitives from the East asked the Führer to surrender. Goebbels was outraged. He compared the officer with defeatist Loucadou and called the generals irresponsible and without any emotion towards history. He was only soothed when Hitler replaced the man with a young officer. Instead of active help, this officer only got a print of the movie to show in the city of the same name. Nevertheless, Kolberg was lost. When the city finally fell on March 18, an already suicidal Goebbels sadly noted a day later, "Despite heroic struggle the city could no longer be defended. I will take care that evacuation is not mentioned in the report of OKW [German High Command]. We should not mention it because of psychological damage [it would possibly do vis-à-vis] *Kolberg* movie." A few weeks later, the newly wed Hitler and Eva Braun, as well as Dr. Goebbels, his wife Magda and their six children, were dead. Hitler and Goebbels shot themselves, their wives took poison, and the kids were poisoned, too. Exactly two weeks before his death, on April 17, 1945, Goebbels recalled the *Kolberg* movie and asked his listeners and employees to imagine themselves in a future Hollywood movie. "Gentlemen, in a hundred years someone will show a beautiful color film about these dreadful days that we are living through. Don't you want to play a role

Shooting a horseriding scene for *Kolberg*. (*From the personal files of the late cinematographer Gerhard Huttula*.)

in this film? I can assure you it will be a fine and devastating picture, and for the sake of this prospect it is worth standing fast. Hold out now, so that a hundred years hence the audience does not hoot and whistle when you appear on the screen." In this regard, *Kolberg* was more a political legacy, a summary of a weary-of-life Nazi's historical belief, than effective propaganda. Finally, the Nazis fell for their own propaganda tricks. In his essay "War and Cinema," Paul Virilio wrote that "the population perceived the war as a show that became increasingly spectacular all the time and that could not be outdone even by Hollywood superproductions with their biblical cataclysms." While that statement certainly is untrue for most of Germany's war-weary population, it is true at least for Goebbels who saw himself as one of the heroes in what he considered the current sequel of the *Nibelungen* epic. In fact, they did make some movies of those miserable days in the *Führerbunker*. In the British-Italian *Hitler: The Last Ten Days*, Alec Guinness starred in the title role and John Bennett as Joseph Goebbels while *100 Jahre Adolf Hitler—Die letzte Stunde im Führerbunker* by Christof Schlingensief was a low-budget underground movie. Both films are certainly not what Goebbels might have envisioned as his "beautiful color film." The final battle of Berlin did little but claim hundreds of thousands of lives more. On the other hand, La Rochelle surrendered on May 9, 1945, without any battle at all, one week later than Berlin (which surrendered on May 2).

In Babelsberg Studios they worked all the time up to the end. According to director Oscar Fritz Schuh,[12] "there was an air-raid almost each day. So we were able to work only in the morning for one or two hours, then the siren howled. Usually it lasted for several hours. Because UFA didn't have any real air-raid shelters, only splinter trenches, we were driven outside into the greens where it was less dangerous. At 3:00 P.M. we used to return and to do some more takes. Often these were a waste because the actresses looked overstressed after the fatigues of an alarm." Cameraman Gerhard Huttula in the meantime worked extensively on the process shots for UFA's last but unfinished wartime movie with the almost prophetic title *Das Leben geht weiter* (*Life Goes On*), directed by the submissive Liebeneiner and produced by Karl Ritter. It literally was a bombastic project that was supposed to issue a general proclamation to hold out and unite in difficult times. They all worked with the grim humor typical in such situations. It was the first *Trümmerfilm* (productions that were filmed in the ruins of destroyed cities), a genre that naturally spread after the war. Goebbels, who pushed the project considerably, wanted "to show a Berlin air raid night in a block of flats in the Hansaviertel (a Berlin district). It will involve the whole building, with all its individual floors and families."[13] Ironically, much of the footage was lost during location shooting in the Lüneburg Heath, where it was deposited in two zinc caskets. Huttula was present when the Red Army conquered Babelsberg Studios April 24, 1945. "They occupied a screening room, and we let them see the harmless, entertaining Agfacolor piece *Frau meiner Träume* (*Woman of My Dreams*) starring Marika Rökk. The Russian officers were enthusiastic and everybody who had worked on that movie got an extra ration of butter. Fortunately, we didn't show them *Kolberg* at that time. [They were eventually shown it at the Agfa factory in Wolfen.] I was able to smuggle a camera and my showreels outside before they raided the costume department and the film bunker and cleaned out all the equipment including my background projectors." (Years later, the studio lot became East Germany's nationally owned Defa while the rest of UFA was dismantled in West Germany.)

Veit Harlan met Goebbels for the last time on February 17, 1945, a few days after the massive air raid against Dresden. Goebbels by this time was determined to depart this life. His protégé Harlan wasn't. The "devil's director," who later described Goebbels as sort of a charming devil, almost immediately settled for denazification, as so many supporters of the system did, and therefore was able to make more movies. Later, he successfully left the courtroom after two trials: the first by a jury in 1949–50; the second in 1958 that resulted in a verdict by the highest German court, the Bundesverfassungsgericht (Federal Constitutional Court). It all began when Harlan needed a license from the Western allies, a political *Unbedenklichkeitsbescheinigung* (a certificate that there was no objection) in order to successfully enter Germany's post-war film industry. The commission was all too willing to register him as *unbelastet* (having a clean record), but in that moment opposition arose from the press. *Tägliche Rundschau*, a Berlin newspaper, called the case of this former Nazi, made *Reichskultursenator* and professor by Hitler and Goebbels, a scandal. At the beginning of 1948, Harlan and his wife attended the première of Kurt Maetzig's Defa movie *Ehe im Schatten*, which portrayed the tragic suicide of the actor couple Gottschalk during the Third Reich (she was half–Jewish). Although the movie itself was made with the participation of several artists, who were involved in the shooting of *Jud Süss* (composer Wolfgang Zeller and actress Hilde von Stolz), it was only the Harlans whose attendance was regarded as annoying. As a reaction the commission hesitated, and Harlan applied for new proceedings. Then, Vereinigung der Verfolgten des Nazi-Regimes (VVN, Association of Victims of Nazi Regime Persecution) and Notgemeinschaft der durch die Nürnberger Gesetze Betroffenen (Emergency Action Organization of Persons Affected by the Nuremberg Laws) entered a petition accusing Harlan of crimes against humanity. This petition was supported by the Jewish community in Hamburg and the executive committee of the Social Democratic Party in Hamburg. The trial was opened on March 3, 1949, in the Land Court of Hamburg, with 35 witnesses called upon. Among them were former top executives of Terra Filmkunst, Dr. Peter Paul Brauer, who called Harlan the most talented director who had abused his own talent, and Alf Teichs, who claimed that it was Harlan who had saved the *Jud Süss* project (while Alfred Greven accused Teichs of having pushed the project since 1937); Harlan's co-writer Alfred Braun, who was and would become again a famous radio reporter; Harlan's location manager, Conny Carstennsen; director Erich Engel; actors Gustav Fröhlich and wife; Malte Jaeger (who assured the court that none of the actors was aware that they were participating in a propaganda film), Eugen Klöpfer, Hans-Herrmann Schaufuss, Maria Byk (the widow of Ferdinand Marian), and even a stepson of Wilhelm II, Prince Ferdinand zu Schönaich-Carolath. Members of the now East German controlled Babelsberg Studios (Defa) gave evidence in favor of Harlan: Wolfgang von Gordon, then story editor at Terra, now with Defa, emphasized that Harlan wasn't enthusiastic when he got the assignment but then handled it correctly and engaged himself. "My party is art. I am a patriot," the director resumed almost pathetically, regarding his involvement with National Socialist politics. "I love my homeland. I have received fantastic film offers from South America. I have refused all of them. I want to stay here and work here. I am no politician. I am a director." The jury seemed to agree with what Harlan told them: that politics shouldn't be confused with art and vice versa. Since he wasn't a member of the NSDAP, the jury gave way to pure expediency. Incidentally, Harlan, like many Germans, didn't find everything the Nazis did horrible — their hatred of the Jews, yes, the persecution of Catholics and a few other things, but not everything. Harlan even went so far as to quote several Jewish colleagues from the stage of the Weimar Republic as involuntary witnesses: Max Reinhardt, Guido Herzfeld, Leopold Jessner, and Fritz Kortner (who had no reason at all to side him). And, of course, it was stressed that one shouldn't forget that Goebbels was vindictive. So reasons were cited for Harlan's having feared his former mentor Goebbels. (During the trial, Harlan almost had a heart attack when Goebbels' former press officer and stenographer, Otto Jacobs, reported that Kristina Söderbaum bathed nude in Venice to entertain the minister).

After the first trial, which ended on April 23, 1949, the chairman of the Council of the Jewish Community in the British Zone, Norbert Wollheim, wrote:

> Veit Harlan, director of the anti–Semitic smear-film *Jud Süss*, is exonerated of crimes against humanity in Hamburg. With ovations, which started in the courtroom and were not reprimanded by the judge, the former movie hero of the "Thousand-Year Reich" is lifted on the shoulders by his fellow men, and with triumphant cheering is carried to his vehicle.... The legally necessary causal connection between the crimes of the Nazi regime and this shoddy anti–Semitic effort, so the judges have decided, has not been proved. To judge the moral responsibility of the comedian in the dock in front of them of actively participating in the incitement of the masses in the Third Reich against us Jews didn't come within their authority they argued. And since Harlan today is as impertinent, as characterless as during Goebbels' lifetime, in his summing up he cunningly parried the charge that accused him of being "the devil's director," and by adding a scorn-

ful remark that the judges from yesterday had participated as devil's actors, too, they appeared exactly in the black shadow into which Harlan had accurately cast them.

With Harlan's acquittal, anti–Semitism again got a *Persilschein* (certificate of blamelessness).

Harlan was allowed to return to his profession, to filmmaking. But there was another obstacle in the person of Erich Lüth, then in charge of the Hamburg State Press Office, who picked an argument with German film distributors over Harlan (and therefore was seriously attacked by old and new Nazis). In an open letter, Lüth demanded that Germany's reputation in the world shouldn't be ruined by robust money makers: "For Harlan's turning up again must tear up scarcely healed wounds and in a terrible way renew subsiding distrust to the disadvantage of German *Wiederaufbau* [rebuilding]. For all these reasons it is not only the right of honorable Germans but their duty to be ever ready to fight against this unworthy representative of the German film including through a boycott, too." Producers and distributors successfully won a temporary injunction against the boycott at the Land Court of Hamburg, which decreed such an action illegal. "We should ourselves be happy that in our state art is relieved of the political sphere," the commentator of *Münchener Allgemeine Wochenzeitung für Politik, Wirtschaft und Kultur* rejoiced,[14] "that art is only judged by artist's standards." Together with Harlan some of the other star directors of the Third Reich resumed their chairs, too, for example Arthur Maria Rabenalt, Wolfgang Liebeneiner, Franz Seitz, and Hans Deppe. And with them the old stars returned and were welcomed with open arms: Willy Birgel, Paul Dahlke, Heinz Rühmann, Carl Raddatz and René Deltgen. The defeated Erich Lüth made a profound statement broadcast by Nord-West-Deutscher Rundfunk (NWDR) on November 22, 1951. "The Jews came to Auschwitz and Theresienstadt. Nothing happened to Veit Harlan. All that was expected from him was—silence. There was no need for him to become a director again, there would have been other professions open to him. He could have become a film editor, prop master, cabinet-maker or usher in a cinema, door-keeper or 'last man' in the strict sense of Jannings' films (i.e., toilet man) if he would have been reasonable enough to moderate himself." Golda Meir, on the other hand, commented in a more conciliatory tone. "Harlan was one of the many shadow figures in the Nazi Reich. We don't need to pursue the many figures but to search for the men in charge, who put the figures into movement."[15] Carl Raddatz, who had appeared in films by Karl Ritter as well as by Veit Harlan, characterized Harlan as dangerous, though. "Even in February 1945, he trumpeted: the Führer will be victorious! The secret weapons! He never did believe in such things. Harlan was a highly intelligent man but very dangerous, as a director. He confused power with brutality—and feeling emotion with sentimentality. That was a great danger. And the biggest danger was his mania to enact everything himself. With that attitude he could destroy much of the actor's work. By all means, he was obsessed, obsessed by the movies."

Kristina Söderbaum re-saw *Kolberg* shortly after the war. Officers of the U.S. Army got hold of a print and invited her to join them while she was playing on the stage in Erlangen. When they watched one impressive long shot of the approaching

French army — green grass, blue sky, blue uniforms — it looked to them like a painting. "How bad for Harlan that he didn't have three or four little clouds in the scene," one of the officers remarked. "That would have made his composition perfect." Söderbaum claimed that just at that moment, five little clouds of shrapnel exploded and the American sat in awe.[16] After the war, UFA got quite a few offers to re-release *Kolberg*. To the delight of some exiled Nazis, the movie turned up in Argentina under the title of *Burning Hearts*. In Sweden it was *Brinnande Hjärtan*. In Zurich they still played it in the early 1950s as *Entsagung — Die letzten Tage von Kolberg* (*Abdication: The Final Days of Kolberg*), but the Swiss distributor had removed Veit Harlan's name from the credits. However, an early attempt of Ilse Kubaschewski's distribution company Gloria Film to present the epic in Federal Chancellor Konrad Adenauer's Germany failed.

A decade later, Hanns Eckelkamp, a struggling classic and art movie distributor and cinema owner in Duisburg, became obsessed with the idea of acquiring a package of Nazi movies and release it with added commentary in order to save his Atlas Film company. Nazis were still a good subject in post-war Germany, East and West; pretended Anti-Fascism or even Nazi nostalgia was a good business. Eckelkamp remembers that he heard of Germany's most expensive war-time movie still lying on the shelves unreleased, possibly except for a single contested screening in the Akademie der Künste in West Berlin, organized by Gero Gandert and Ulrich Gregor in 1964. "We were going to start our series with *Kolberg*," Eckelkamp said. "We had high hopes as we were told that it easily could attract 4 million customers. That was what we desperately needed. After all, we were on the verge of bankruptcy." *Kolberg* was released uncut, together with a documentary by Erwin Leiser, Raimond Ruehl, Dr. Gerd Albrecht, Gert Berghoff, and Lothar Kompatzki and with the added attraction of a wartime newsreel with the German army armed to the teeth [*Deutsche Wochenschau* No. 3, 1945]. Four clips of Goebbels' appeal to hold out had been optically inserted into the newsreel and there was an epilogue of three minutes' length summarizing what else happened on January 30. Eckelkamp hadn't seen *Kolberg* yet and was astonished when he realized that he had bought the rights to a pathetic, boring movie that in no way equaled *Gone with the Wind* in scope and grandeur, as film historian David Stewart Hull firmly believed it did. But even Hull had to concede that the script was far too talky, and that it took an interminable amount of time to get the action going. In spite of their long film experience, most of the cast tend to be theatrical and hammy, as if acting to the last row. Kristina Söderbaum is even worse. Her naive, amateurish performance ruins part of the movie. Without wavering, Eckelkamp had the film screen-tested by Professors Udo Undeutsch (who had already done a similar *sozialwissenschaftlichen* [social science-like] test together with his colleague Wilhelm Salber), Josef Hitpass and Georges Schmitz. In November 1965, previews were organized in Bonn, Duisburg, Kassel and Kiel. Precisely 2,205 of those who attended were interviewed. According to a press release by Atlas Film, the audience wasn't subliminally affected by seeing the movie. On the contrary, it was stated that they became more critical about fascist tendencies. In West German cinemas *January 30, 1945: Kolberg* only sold 400,000 tickets, and a year later Atlas went bankrupt in the traditional way (with a pile of debts that amounted to DM 20 million), just before they could release other Nazi entries such as *Hitlerjunge Quex*

(*Hitler Youth Quex*, with a commentary by later Hitler biographer Joachim C. Fest) and *Der grosse König* (*The Great King*, with the help of renowned *Spiegel* journalist Morlock). Eckelkamp was accused of spitting Nazi venom over all of Europe. East German *Junge Welt* gleefully cited West German cinema-goers: "I served as an officer for Adolf Hitler, in the Third Reich. I must tell you that I admire the courage of this political system (Federal Republic of Germany) to show a movie like this;" "I think that we might face the same situation they did. Maybe we need some exhortation to hold out, too;" "I have seen it three times in two days." With simplistic remarks like these, it was clear to East Berlin that the release could be only a revanchist act by a government that still was yearning for the German borders of 1937. "One shouldn't say there isn't any similarity between Nazi ideology as in the *Kolberg* movie and Bonn's government practice." (East German Defa, however, which was founded by the Russians just after the war, made its first money by finishing left-overs from Dr. Goebbels' film heritage of the last year, such as Geza von Bolvary's *Die Fledermaus*, Paul Verhoeven's *Das kleine Hofkonzert*, Roger von Norman's *Moselfahrt mit Hindernissen*, Peter Voss der Millionendieb, and *Träum' nicht, Annette* starring Jenny Jugo.) Dr. van Dam, a member of Germany's Jewish Council, more likely saw the real reason for the re-issue of *Kolberg*—commercial considerations.

Harlan didn't live to watch the rerelease. He died April 13, 1964, on the Isle of Capri after having converted from Protestantism to Catholicism. In the 1950s he had made several movies for Ilse Kubaschewski's Divina-Film and Berlin's Arca-Film-produktion. Arca producer Gero Wecker also put up the money for *Anders als du und ich* (U.S.: *The Third Sex*) that Harlan's biographer Frank Noack[17] called "a homosexual remake of *Jew Suss*," in some way a forerunner to Wecker's 1960s *Teutonic Enlightenment* series written for the screen by Oswalt Kolle. In 1959, Harlan angrily rejected an offer to do a horror film for producer Wolf C. Hartwig (*Die Nackte und der Satan*, released in the United States as *The Head*). Instead, he badly wanted to do a movie about Philip II, Spain's *Catholic King*. But *Kolberg*'s infamy fame proved irrepressible. Over the years, it still circulated in 16mm prints. Finally, it was shown on TV (ARTE channel, 1998), with an epilogue feature by director Hans-Christoph Blumenberg who documented the pitiful death of *Kolberg* star Heinrich George (played by Vadim Glowna). On September 25, 1946, at 3:00 P.M., the great actor, born in 1893, passed away in a Soviet prison camp in Oranienburg.

During the 1990s, two well-known filmmakers, director Franz Oz and Allen Daviau, cinematographer on Steven Spielberg's *E. T. The Extra-Terrestrial*, prepared a movie about the shooting of *Kolberg*, but nothing came of it. Even Stanley Kubrick showed interest in the life story of Veit Harlan. (Kubrick was married to Harlan's niece, Susanne Christiane.)

War films were not forgotten in German post-war history and went on to play an important role. Now they were called anti-war films: Stalingrad epics *Hunde, wollt ihr ewig leben?* by Frank Wysbar, who had returned from Hollywood, *Stalingrad* by Joseph Vilsmaier, *Enemy at the Gates* by Jean-Jacques Annaud (largely financed by German funds), *Steiner — das Eiserne Kreuz* by American director Sam Peckinpah, who went to Germany accompanied by actor James Coburn (Richard Burton came for the sequel, *Steiner 2*), Alfred Weidenmann's air force film, *Der Stern von Afrika*, and Wolfgang Petersen's internationally successful *Das Boot* (*The Boat*). Returning to (West) Germany, émigré director Robert Siodmak was amazed at how little had changed on the whole. There was even a UFA although it was not the same as it had been. In 1964, almost reduced to the living dead, it had been acquired by the mighty Bertelsmann Group of Gütersloh. In 1981 a new Ufa-Filmproduktion G.m.b.H. was established which in 1996 merged with CLT Luxembourg to become Europe's biggest t.v. producing company.

Kurt Schumacher, a well-known German politician, who had to suffer under the NS regime, once remarked that the Nazis succeeded in completely mobilizing human stupidity. Could it be repeated…? No, Germany has changed since due to its great and long-term economic success. But what will happen in a new depression? There are still lots of old ideas.

Just imagine Hitler had survived. I don't mean to invoke one of those idiotic survival legends that spread in the early post-war years: Hitler seen in South America, having escaped the fall of the Third Reich in a submarine, and in Tibet, fired off by a manned V-rocket out of the ruins of Berlin, rescued by a U.F.O. and flown to a sanctuary at the South Pole, and planning the Cold War with Stalin. No such irrational legend seemed too absurd. No, I mean the Hitler we see almost daily in the papers and on t.v. The Hitler whose portrait decorates numerous book covers and the rooms of baldheaded neo–Nazis, the Hitler who has become an icon of the World-WideWeb. The legend lives on, in the minds of antagonists and inconvincible worshippers.

In the churchyard in Berlin-Dahlem, there are two small gravestones not far away from each other. These belong to persons who couldn't have been more different. One marks the grave of Horst Joachim Arthur Caspar (1913–1952), *Kolberg*'s arrogantly eloquent Gneisenau; the other, that of Dr. Rudi Dutschke (1940–1979), leader of the '68 Berlin student movement whose members opposed their Nazi fathers and the whole *Kolberg* spirit. Now they turn to dust in the same soil.

Filmography

Achtung! Feind hört mit! (Attention! The Enemy Is Listening)

1940. *Director:* Arthur Maria Rabenalt. *Producer:* E. G. Techow. *Location Manager:* Willi Hermann-Balz. *Assistant Director:* Hans Müller. *Screenplay:* Kurt Heuser from an idea conceived by Dr. Georg C. Klaren. *Cinematography:* Willy Winterstein, Gustav Weiss. *Stills Photographer:* Erich Tannigel. *Music:* Franz Grothe. *Art Directors:* Erich Czerwonski, Carl Böhm. *Sound:* Werner Mass. *Fashion Adviser:* Reingard Voigt. *Editor:* Alice Ludwig.

Cast: Michael Bohnen (Kettwig, *Betriebsführer* [leader of a factory]), Rolf Weih (Bernd Kettwig, engineer, his son), Christian Kayssler (Dr. Hellmers, chief designer), Lotte Koch (Inge Neuhaus), Josef Sieber (Böttcher, master craftsman), Karl Dannemann (Portloff), Armin Münch (Brändle), Rudolf Schündler (Grelling, draftsman), Adolf Fischer (Hermann), Ernst Waldow (Nolte), René Deltgen (Karl Ludwig Faerber), Kirsten Heiberg (Lilly, owner of a fashion boutique), Lola Müthel (Phillis), Ruth Lommel (Margot), Theo Shall (Sir Reginald), Gertrud Schirmacher (Miss Reginald), Erich Ponto (Monsieur Bock), Kate Kühl (Madame Bock), Peter Elsholtz (man in trenchcoat), Karl Artel (artist), Peter Voss (General from the Army's Technical Office), Fritz Böttger (Captain Burger from the Army's Technical Office), Elsa Wagner (Mrs. Neuhaus), Cläre (Claire) Reigbert (Mrs. Böttcher), Klaus Pohl (book-seller), Hans Herrmann-Schaufuss (chemist).

Produced and distributed by Terra-Filmkunst G.m.b.H., Berlin. *Production Group:* E. G. Techow. *Staatsauftragsfilm.* 35mm. *Premiere:* September 3, 1940.

Die Affäre Rödern (The Rödern Affair)

1944. *Director:* Erich Waschneck. *Screenplay:* Gerta Ital, Toni Huppertz. *Cinematography:* Walter Findter. *Music:* Norbert Schultze.

Cast: Paul Hartmann, Annelies Reinhold, Clementia Egies, Rudolf Fernau, Karl Dannemann, Franz Schafheitlin, Herbert Hübner, Hans Leibelt, Inge Drexel, Hugo Werner-Kahle, Ursula Herking, Carl Günther, Werner Schott, Otz Tollen, Elfriede Dugal, Otto Hüsch.

Produced by Berlin-Film G.m.b.H., Berlin. *Production Group:* Mülleneisen and Tapper. *Premiere:* July 14, 1944, Breslau; November 7, 1944, Berlin. *Distributed by* DFV, Berlin. *Subject:* Plans for novel underground fortification at Fort Schweidnitz prepared by Frederick the Great's General Dietrich von Rödern.

Das Alte Recht (The Ancient Law)

1933–34. *Director:* Igo Martin-Andersen. *Screenplay:* Igo Martin Andersen, Armin Petersen. *Cinematography:* Georg Krause. *Music:* Wolfgang Zeller.

Cast: Edit Linn, Bernhard Goetzke, Hans Kettler, Fritz Hoopts, Hans Rastede, Agnes Diers.

Produced by Andersen-Film-Produktion, Berlin. *Staatsauftragsfilm. Premiere:* January 27, 1934, Oldenburg, Wall-Lichtspiele; April 10, 1934, Berlin, Capitol. *Distributed by* Deutsche Universal-Film A.-G. (subsequently Rota-Filmverleih G.m.b.H.), Berlin. *Subject:* Reintroduction of "Erbhofgesetz" by the nazis (not all sons but only the eldest one will inherit a farm).

Am seidenen Faden (Hanging Upon a Thread)

1938. *Director:* Robert A. Stemmle. *Producer:* Bruno Duday. *Production Manager:* Erich Holder. *Location Manager:* Fritz Schwarz. *Assistant Director:* Fritz Andelfinger. *Screenplay:* Robert A. Stemmle, Eberhard Frowein, based on the theme of the novel *Mein eigenes properes Geld* (*My Own Proper Money*). *Cinematography:* Franz Weihmayr. *Assistant Cameramen:* Kurt Hasse, Bruno Stephan. *Stills Photographer:* Josef Höfer. *Music:* Herbert Windt. *Art Directors:* Otto Hunte, Karl Vollbrecht. *Wardrobe:* Wilhelmine Spindler, Max König, Walter Salemann. *Make-Up:* Atelier Jabs, Waldemar Jabs. *Sound:* Max Langguth. *Editor:* Axel von Werner.

Cast: Willy Fritsch (Richard Hellwerth), Käthe von Nagy (Lissy Eickhoff), Carl Kuhlmann (Wilhelm Eickhoff), Bernhard Minetti (Dr. Heinrich Breuer), Erich Ponto (Theodor Kalbach, authorized signatory), Paul Bildt (Brögelmann, banker), Stella David (Frida Mann, housekeeper), Willi Schur (Schwafels, master craftsman), Hildegard Barko (Anna, maid), Eduard Wandrey (Bellert, court official), Ina Albrecht, Erich Bartels, Eduard Bornträger, Johanna Blum, Inge Conradi, Peter Elsholtz, Adolf Fischer, Kurt Fisser, Robert Forsch, Hildegard Friebel, Brunhilde Födisch, Hermann Mayer-Falkow, Otto Hennig, Clemens Hasse, Kurt Klotz-Oberland, Helmuth Lang, Erik von Loewis, Kurt Morvilius, Hermann Pfeiffer, Albert Pussert, Werner Pledath, Ethel Reschke, Georg Heinrich Schnell, Rudolf Schündler, Vera Schultz, Walter Schramm-Duncker, Wilfried Seyferth, Wolfgang Staudte, Hans Sobierayski, Hildegard Unger, Albert Venohr, Kurt Waitzmann, Kurt Weisse, Ursula Zeitz.

Produced by Universum-Film A.-G. (Ufa), Berlin. *Production Group:* Bruno Duday. 35mm. *Laboratory:* Afifa. *Shooting:* beginning of April–end of May, 1938. *Interiors:* Ufastadt Babelsberg. *Exteriors:* Berlin. *Running time:* 92 minutes. *Premiere:* September 23, 1938, Wuppertal-Elberfeld, Modernes Theater and Ufa-Palast; September 23, 1938, Berlin, Tauentzien-Palast. *Distributed by* Universum Filmverleih G.m.b.H. (Ufaleih), Berlin.

Annelie (Die Geschichte einer Liebe) (Annelie: A Love Story)

1941. *Director:* Josef von Baky. *Assistant Director:* Walter Wischniewsky. *Dialogue Director:* Werner Bergold. *Producer:* Eberhard Schmidt. *Production Assistant:* Horst Kyrath. *Location Manager:* Herbert Junghanns. *Screenplay:* Thea von Harbou, from the stage play *Annelie* by Walter Lieck. *Cinematography:* Werner Krien. *Operator:* Hanns König (?). *Special Photographic Effects:* Ernst Kunstmann. *Music:* Georg Haentzschel. *Lyrics:* Werner Kleine. *Art Director:* Emil Hasler. *Assistant Art Director:* Otto Gülstorff. *Costumes:* Manon Hahn. *Choreography:* Maria Sommer. *Sound:* Erich Schmidt. *Editor:* Walter Wischniewsky.

Cast: Luise Ullrich (Annelie), Werner Krauss (Dörensen, land registry councilor, her father), Käthe Haack (Mrs. Dörensen, her mother), Karl Ludwig Diehl (Dr. Laborius), Albert Hehn (Reinhold), Axel von Ambesser (Georg), Ilse Fürstenberg (Ida, maid), John Pauls-Harding (Gerhard), Johannes Schütz (Rudi), Eduard von Winterstein (Heberlein, medical officer), Josefine Dora (midwife), Hansi Arnstaedt, Roma Bahn, Erich Dunskus, Ursula Herking, Helga Hesse, Melanie Horeschowski, Käthe Jöken-König, Paulette Koller, Eva Lissa, Juan Martinez-Peres, Margarethe Schön, Marianne Schulze, Agnes Windeck, Gertrud Wolle.

Produced by Universum-Film A.-G. (UFA), Berlin. *Production Group:* Eberhard Schmidt. 35mm. *Laboratory:* Afifa. *Interiors:* Ufastadt Babelsberg, Ufa Studios Berlin-Tempelhof. *Shooting:* January 13–April 1941. *Running time:* 99 minutes. *Premiere:* September 4, 1941, Venice (IFF); September 9, 1941, Berlin, Gloria-Palast. *Distributed by* Universum Filmverleih G.m.b.H. (Ufaleih), Berlin.

Anschlag auf Baku *(Attack on Babu)*

1940–41. *Director:* Fritz Kirchhoff. *Assistant Director:* Erich Kobler. *Producer:* Hans Weidemann. *Location Manager:* Heinz Karchow. *Screenplay:* Hans Weidemann, Hans Wolfgang Hillers, from an idea conceived by Hans Weidemann. *Cinematography:* Robert Baberske. *Camera Operators:* Herbert Körner, Klaus von Rautenfeld, H[ugo] O[tto] Schulze. *Music:* Alois Melichar. *Art Directors:* Otto Hunte, Karl Vollbrecht. *Costumes:* Carl Heinz Grohnwald. *Sound:* Alfred Zunft, Georg Gutschmidt. *Editor:* Erich Kobler.

Cast: Willy Fritsch (Hans Romberg), René Deltgen (Percy Forbes), Lotte Koch (Sylvia Camps), Fritz Kampers (Mathias Ertl), Hans Zesch-Ballot (Barakoff, minister of police), Paul Bildt (Campers, American oil magnate), Erich Ponto (Jenssen, Danish oil magnate), Aribert Wäscher (Mamulian, American oil magnate), Joachim Brennecke (Ali Baba, security officer), Alexander Engel (Steffens, British Agent), Walter Janssen (Hanson, Swedish oil magnate), Heinrich Marlow (Lord Seymour, British officer), Hellmuth Helsig (Twinning, British agent), Walter Holetzko (Richartz, British agent), Reginald Pasch, Arthur Reinhardt, Fred [Selva-] Goebel, Nico Turoff (British agents), Josef Kamper (Zolak, security officer), Wilhelm König (Thatul, security officer), Herbert Gernot (Achmed Bey, Turkish oberst [colonel]), Boris Alekin, Angelo Ferrari (Turkish officers), Günther Ballier (Jenssen's secretary), Erik Radolf (Forbes' servant), Willy Maertens (Jenssen's notary), Werner Völger, Herbert Scholz (two assassins), Aruth Wartan (GPU officer), Nikolai Kolin (Russian waiter).

Produced by Ufa-Filmkunst G.m.b.H., Berlin. *Production Group:* Hans Weidemann. *Staatsauftragsfilm.* 35mm. *Laboratory:* Afifa. *Interiors:* Ufastadt Babelsberg. *Exteriors:* Oilfields in Romania, Chorzele (Poland), Trebbin/Baltic. *Shooting:* November 4, 1940–end of August 1941. *Budget:* RM 2.6 million. *Running time:* 93 minutes. *Premiere:* August 25, 1942, Berlin, Tauentzien-Palast, Atrium, U.T. Friedrichstrasse, and Stella-Palast. *Distributed by* DFV (Deutsche Filmvertriebs G.m.b.H.), Berlin. For political reasons the movie had to be changed to some extent.

Auf Wiedersehen, Franziska *(Good-bye, Franziska)*

1940–41. *Director:* Helmut Käutner. *Producer:* Hans Tost. *Location Managers:* Werner Drake, Willi Rother. *Assistant Director:* Rudolf Jugert. *Screenplay:* Helmut Käutner, Curt Johannes Braun. *Cinematography:* Jan Roth. *Stills Photographer:* Kurt Schlawe. *Music:* Michael Jary. *Songs:* "Wir geh'n so leicht am grossen Glück vorbei"; "Mein Leben und Dein Leben"; "Sing, Nachtigall, sing." *Lyrics:* Bruno Balz. *Art Director:* Willi A. Herrmann. *Costumes:* Margot Hielscher. *Sound:* Erich Kroschke. *Editor:* Helmuth Schönnenbeck.

Cast: Marianne Hoppe (Franziska Tiemann), Hans Söhnker (Michael Reisiger), Fritz Odemar (Professor Tiemann), Rudolf Fernau (Dr. Christoph Leitner), Hermann Speelmans (Buck Standing), Margot Hielscher (Helen Philips), Herbert Hübner (Ted Simmons), Josefina Dora (Mrs. Schöpf), Frida Richard (Kathrin), Klaus Pohl (Pröckl, postman), Erich Ziegel (physician), Rudolf Kalvius (lawyer), Traute [Trude] Baumbach, Marianne Beckmann, Ursula Herking, Edith Hildebrand, Gustl Kreusch, Ruth Kruse, Vera Mayr, Ernö René, Annemarie Schäfer, Marianne Stanior, Hans Wallner, Beryl Roberts, Louis [Lovis] Brody, Aribert Wäscher, Evelyn Künneke.

Produced and distributed by Terra-Filmkunst G.m.b.H., Berlin. *Production Group:* Hans Tost. 35mm. *Interiors:* Ufastadt Studios Berlin-Tempelhof. *Exteriors:* Burghausen/Salzach. *Shooting:* October 30, 1940–mid–February, 1941. *Running time:* 100 minutes. *Premiere:* April 24, 1941, Munich, Atlantik-Palast; May 6, 1941, Berlin, Capitol am Zoo.

Aufruhr in Damaskus (Riot in Damaskus)

1938–39. *Director:* Gustav Ucicky. *Screenplay:* Philipp Lothar Mayring, Jacob Geis, from a treatment by Herbert Tjadens. *Cinematography:* Oskar Schnirch, Paul Rischke. *Music:* Willy Schmidt-Gentner.

Cast: Brigitte Horney, Joachim Gottschalk, Hans Nielsen, Ernst von Klipstein, Paul Westermeier, Paul Otto, Gerhard Bienert, Friedrich Gnass, Willi Rose, Ingolf Kuntze, Adolf Fischer, Ludwig Schmid-Wildy, Hellmut Passarge, Gustav Püttjer, Jac Diehl, Erich Dunskus, Hansjacob Gröblinghoff, Peter Leska, Serag Monier, Claire Reigbert, Erika Streithorst, Heinz Welzel.

Produced by Terra-Filmkunst G.m.b.H., Berlin. *Staatsauftragsfilm. Premiere:* February 24, 1939, Leipzig; March 8, 1939, Berlin. *Distributed by* Terra-Filmverleih G.m.b.H., Berlin. *Subject:* The Arabian-Syrian Front in 1918.

Besatzung Dora (Garrison Dora/Crew of the Dora)

1942–43. *Producer-Director:* Karl Ritter. *Production Manager:* Gustav Rathje. *Location Managers:* Herbert Junghanns, Willi Rother. *Screenplay:* Fred Hildenbrand, Karl Ritter.

Cinematography: Heinz Ritter. *Aerial Cinematography and Optical Effects:* Theodor Nischwitz. *Music:* Herbert Windt. *Costumes:* Gertrud Steckler. *Sound:* Werner Maass. *Editor:* Gottfried Ritter.

Cast: Hannes Stelzer (Lieutenant Joachim Krane, chief pilot), Hubert Kiurina (Lieutenant Franz von Borcke, navigator), Josef Dahmen (Sergeant Otto Roggenkamp, radio operator), Georg Thomalla (Fritz Mott, noncommissioned officer, gunner), Ernst von Klipstein (Captain Kurt Gillhausen, staff commander), Clemens Hasse (First Lieutenant Erich Krumbhaar, pilot), Helmut Schabrich (First Lieutenant Semmler), Wolfgang Preiss (Dr. Wagner, medical officer of reserves), Suse Graf (Dr. med. Marianne Güldner), Charlott Daudert (Mathilde Kruschke, called Cora Corona), Carsta Löck (Betty Schütte, tram conductor), Roma Bahn (laboratory assistant in military hospital of reserves), Otz Tollen (lieutenant colonel).

Produced by Ufa-Filmkunst G.m.b.H., Berlin. *Production Group:* Karl Ritter. 35mm. *Exteriors:* Western Front, Eastern Front, Ostia, Ufastadt Babelsberg (back lot), surroundings of Berlin. *Shooting:* August 4, 1942–January 1943. *Running time:* 91 minutes. *Distributed by* DFV (Deutsche Filmvertriebs G.m. b.H.), Berlin. The film, about a reconnaissance plane squadron on the Western, Eastern and African fronts, was banned in November 1943 by Filmprüfstelle.

Bismarck

1940. *Director:* Wolfgang Liebeneiner. *Screenplay:* Rolf Lauckner, Wolfgang Liebeneiner. *Cinematography:* Bruno Mondi. *Music:* Norbert Schultze.

Cast: Paul Hartmann, Friedrich Kayssler, Maria Koppenhöfer, Werner Hinz, Ruth Hellberg, Walter Franck, Lil Dagover, Käthe Haack, Margret Militzer, Karl Schönböck, Günther Hadank, Helmuth Bergmann, Karl Haubenreisser, Karl Meixner, Hans Junkermann, Jaspar von Oertzen, Franz Schafheitlin, Paul Hoffmann, Karl Fochler, Harald Paulsen, Bruno Hübner, Eduard von Winterstein, Otto Graf, Otto Gebühr, Otto Stoeckel, Erich Ziegel, Werner Pledath, Walter Werner, Bernhard Goetzke, Theodor Thony, Otto Below, Carl Heinz Peters, Ingolf Kuntze, Albert Venohr, Robert Forsch, Franz W. Schröder-Schrom, Wilhelm P. Krüger.

Produced by Tobis Filmkunst, Berlin. *Staatsauftragsfilm. Premiere:* December 6, 1940. *Distributed by* Tobis, Berlin. *Subject:* Highlights of Otto von Bismarck's political career.

Blutsbrüderschaft (Blood Brotherhood)

1940. *Director:* Philipp Lothar Mayring. *Producer:* Walter Tost. *Location Manager:* Hans Naundorf. *Assistant Director:* Boleslaw Barlog. *Screenplay:* Harald G. Petersson, Philipp Lothar Mayring. *Cinematography:* Ekkehard Kyrath. *Stills Photographer:* Curt Schlawe. *Music:* Michael Jary. *Art Director:* Hans Naundorf. *Costumes:* Gerda Leopold. *Sound:* Frantisek Pilat. *Ballet:* Fritz Böttger. *Editor:* Gertrud Hinz.

Cast: Hans Söhnker (Olden), Ernst von Klipstein (Wendler), Anneliese Uhlig (Barbara), Paul Westermeier (Blunck), Rudolf Platte (Stoldte), Walter Pose (Schultz), Axel Monje (Markwitz), Gerda Maria Terno (Lilly), Fritz Odemar (Mr. Cunnings), Max Gülstorff (captain), Erich Ponto (Gösch), Wolfgang Staudte (speaker), Dr. Ernst Stimmel (physician), Friedrich Schütze (innkeeper), Gustav Püttjer (Jürgensen), Karl Dannemann (Berger), Eduard Bornträger (Kinzel), Ernst Waldow (Mr. Nickel), Otto Below (Diersche), Wilhelm H. König (Wolter), Eric Radolf (Link), Peter Elsholtz (Bertram), Herbert Gernot (commissary), Franz Loskarn (Communist leader), Fritz Böttger (police lieutenant), Reinhold Bernt (worker), Wolf Kersten (1st draftsman), Oskar Sabo (functionary at registration office), Armin Schweizer (prison guard), Carl Iban (waiter in waiting-room), Josef Eichheim (policeman at main guard), Lothar Glathe (official), Ludwig Schmid-Wildy (official at police-station), Theo Shall (French officer), Paul Hoffmann (Count Trollberg), Gerhard Haselbach (Lieutenant Schwendt), Wilhelm Althaus (Lieutenant von Winterfeldt), Franz Arzdorf (officer), Karlheinz Reichel (Englishman), Klaus Pohl (newsdealer), Wolf Dietrich (officer), Fritz Hube (2nd functionary at registration office), Erich Dunskus (foreman), Oskar Höcker (worker), Josef Kamper (worker), Siegfried Drost (young worker), Wilhelm P. Krüger (Kaluweit, farmer), Jeanette Bethge (old farmer's wife), Otto Klopsch (policeman), Josefine Dora (flower-girl), Alfred Stratmann (turner), Willi Rose (Braun, noncommissioned officer), Fritz Claudius (driver), Adolf Fischer (driver), Wilhelm Grothe (driver), Hans Meyer-Hanno (overman), Lucie Becker, Gerti Kammerzell, E. G. Schiffner, dancers Annette & Tagunoff.

Produced and distributed by Terra-Filmkunst G.m.b.H., Berlin. *Production Group:* Walter Tost. *Staatsauftragsfilm.* 35mm. *Sound System:* Tobis-Klangfilm. *Premiere:* January 3, 1941.

Carl Peters

1941. *Director:* Herbert Selpin. *Production Manager:* E. W. Tetting. *Location Managers:* August Lautenbacher, Rudolf Kley, Alfred Tscheuschner, Joe Rive, Anton Höhn. *Assistant Director:* Erich Frisch. *Screenplay:* Ernst von Salomon, Walter Zerlett-Olfenius, Herbert Selpin. *Cinematography:* Franz Koch. *Stills Photographer:* Rudolf Reissner. *Music:* Franz Doelle. *Production Designer:* Fritz Maurischat. *Art Directors:* Fritz Lück, Peter Adam, Heinrich Gödert. *Sound:* Hans Wunschel. *Costumes Consultant:* Bert Hoppmann. *Costumes Assistant:* Hans Dupke. *Editor:* Friedel Buckow.

Cast: Hans Albers (Dr. Carl Peters), Karl Dannemann (Dr. Karl Jühlke), Fritz Odemar (Count Pfeil), Toni von Bukovics (Frau Pastor Peters), Hans Leibelt (Professor Engel), Dr. Rolf Prasch (Kaiser Wilhelm I), Friedrich Otto Fischer (Bismarck), Herbert Hübner (Leo Kayser, counsellor), Erika von Thellmann (his wife), Hans Mierendorff (German consul in Zanzibar), Ernst Fritz Fürbringer (Count Behr-Bandelin, chamberlain), Friedrich Ulmer (Prince Hohenlohe-Langenburg), Justus Paris (Julius Kayser), Jack

Trevor (British consul in Zanzibar), Richard Ludwig (British ambassador in Berlin), Dr. Philipp Manning (Sir Anthony Terry), Theo Shall (Robert Mitchell), Georg Heinrich Schnell (Stacy), Walter Neusel (Jonny), Andrews Engelmann (Captain Mathew), Reginald Pasch (Captain Behrends-Greenwood), Theodor Thony (Dr. Nicolo), André Saint-Germain (Captain Bekker), Mohammed Husen (Ramasan), Lea Niako (dancer in Piccadilly Club), Reinhold Bernt, Louis Brody, Ali Ghito, Fred Goebel, Egon Herwig, Albert Johannes, Wilhelm P. Krüger, Gertrud de Lalsky, Karl Meixner, Arthur Reinhardt, Aruth Wartan, Hauptmusikzugführer Herms Riel and *Reichsmusikzug des Reichsarbeitsdienstes* (Reich Music Corps of Reich Labour Service).

Produced by Bavaria-Filmkunst G.m.b.H., Munich. *Staatsauftragsfilm*. 35mm. *Interiors:* Barrandov Studios, Prague. *Budget:* RM 3,190,000. *Premiere:* March 21, 1941, Hamburg; May 29, 1941, Berlin. *Distributed by* Bavaria-Filmkunst Verleih G.m.b.H., Munich.

D III 88

1939. *Director:* Herbert Maisch. *Aerial Supervisor:* Hans Bertram. *Production Manager:* Fred Lyssa. *Location Managers:* Körner, Dettmann, Walkenbach. *Assistant Director:* Wolf-Dietrich Friese. *Screenplay:* Hans Bertram, Wolf Neumeister. *Cinematography:* Georg Krause. *Aerial Cinematography:* Heinz von Jaworsky. *Special Photographic Effects:* Ernst Kunstmann. *Sound:* Erich Lange. *Military Adviser:* General z. V. Wilberg. *Naval Adviser:* Oberleutnant z. S. a. D. Voigt. *Editor:* Carl Otto Bartning.

Cast: Christian Kayssler (Lieutenant Colonel Mithoff), Otto Wernicke (Bonicke, first foreman), Heinz Welzel (Fritz Paulsen, lance corporal), Hermann Braun (Robert Eckhard, lance corporal), Horst Birr (Pilot Hasinger, mechanic), Adolf Fischer (Private Zeissler, mechanic), Fritz Eberth (Lindner, radio operator), Karl Martell (Lieutenant Ludwig Becker, fighter pilot, 1918), Paul Otto (general), Carsta Löck (Lina, maid), Paul Bildt, Hans Bernuth, Ernst Diernburg, Erich Dunskus, Heinz Engelmann, Ilse Fürstenberg,

Malte Jaeger, Josef Kamper, Hilde Land, Günter Markert, Hans Meyer-Hanno, Ferry Reich, Egon Vogel, Eduard von Winterstein.

Produced by Tobis Filmkunst G.m.b.H., Berlin. *Staatsauftragsfilm*. 35mm. *Laboratory:* Geyer. *Sound System:* Tobis Klangfilm. *Interiors:* Jofa Studios, Berlin-Johannisthal. *Budget:* RM 1,268,000. *Premiere:* October 20, 1939, Stralsund; October 27, 1939, Berlin. *Distributed by* Tobis Filmverleih G.m.b.H., Berlin.

Die Degenhardts

1944. *Director:* Werner Klingler. *Producer:* Heinrich George. *Production Manager:* Conrad Fleckner. *Location Managers:* Fritz Schwarz, Willi Strenger. *Assistant Director:* Rudolf Hilberg. *Screenplay:* Wilhelm Krug, Georg Zoch, from an idea conceived by Hans Gustl Kernmayr. *Dialogue:* Kai Möller. *Cinematography:* Georg Bruckbauer. *Music:* Herbert Windt. *Art Directors:* Fritz Maurischat, Fritz Lück. *Costumes:* Gertraud Radke. *Sound:* Hans Rütten. *Editor:* Ella Ensink.

Cast: Heinrich George (Karl Degenhardt), Renée Stobrawa (his wife), Wolfgang Lukschy (Robert), Ernst Schröder (Jochen), Ilse Petri, Gunnar Möller, Hilde Jansen, Erich Ziegel, Heinz Klingenberg, Herwart Grosse, Walter Bechmann, Ernst Legal, Werner Pledath, Knut Hartwig, Alfred Maack, Robert Forsch, Trude Tandar, Günther Körner, Karl Kemper, Werner Kepich, Georg Koch.

Produced by Tobis Filmkunst G.m.b.H., Berlin. *Staatsauftragsfilm*. 35mm. *Laboratory:* Geyer. *Interiors:* Jofa Studios, Berlin-Johannisthal. *Premiere:* July 6, 1944, Lübeck; August 11, 1944, Berlin. *Running time:* 89 minutes. *Distributed by* DFV (Deutsche Filmvertriebs G.m.b.H.), Berlin.

Drei blaue Jungs—Ein blondes Mädel (Three Sailors and a Blonde)

1933. *Director:* Carl Boese. *Screenplay:* Marie Luise Droop. *Cinematography:* Franz Koch. *Music:* Eduard Künneke.

Cast: Charlotte Ander, Hans Richter, Heinz Rühmann, Friedrich Benfer, Fritz Kampers, Sophie Pagay, Hans Albin, Gerhard

Dammann, Adolf Fischer, Karl Hannemann, Hans Hermes, Karl Klöckner.

Produced by Carl Boese-Film G.m.b.H., Berlin. *Staatsauftragsfilm. Premiere:* October 2, 1933, Berlin, Atrium and Titania-Palast. *Distributed by* Metropol-Filmverleih A.-G., Berlin; Rheinische Film G.m.b.H., Cologne; Fritz Stein Film-Verleih G.m.b.H., Berlin. *Subject:* Three sailors on shore leave at Warnemünde.

Drei Käserjäger (Three Soldiers in the Kaiserjäger)

1933. *Directors:* Robert Land, Franz Hofer. *Screenplay:* Fred Angermayer from his play. *Cinematography:* Bruno Mondi. *Music:* Richard Ralf.

Cast: Heinz Salfner, Erna Morena, Paul Richter, Fritz Alberti, Else Elster, Carl Wery, Grit Haid, Fritz Kampers, Heinrich Heilinger, Ludwig Auer, Albert Hörrmann, Oskar Marion, Albert von Kersten, Robert Thiem, Michael von Newlinski, Fritz Greiner, Otto Braml, Paula Klär, Jeanette Bethge.

Produced by Sirius-Farben-Film G.m.b.H./ ABC-Film G.m.b.H., Berlin. *Staatsauftragsfilm. Premiere:* November 15, 1933, Berlin, Primus-Palast and Titania-Palast. *Distributed by* Vereinigte Star-Film G.m.b.H., Berlin; Filmhaus Nietzsche A.-G., Leipzig. *Subject:* Assassination of the Archduke at Sarajevo and the start of World War in a story about an Austrian Kaiserjäger regiment.

Drei Unteroffiziere (Three Non-Commissioned Officers/Three NCOs/Three Warrant Officers)

1938–39. *Director:* Werner Hochbaum. *Producers:* Ernst Martin, Hans Herbert Ulrich. *Location Manager:* Herbert Junghanns. *Assistant Director:* Bruno Koch. *Screenplay:* Jacob Geis, Fred Hildenbrandt, from an idea conceived by Werner Schoknecht. *Cinematography:* Werner Krien. *Stills Photographer:* Ernst Baumann. *Music:* Hansom Milde-Meissner. *Lyrics:* Klaus S. Richter. *Art*

Directors: Willy Schiller, Carl Haacker. *Sound:* Alfred Zunft. *Editor:* Else Baum.

Cast: Fritz Genschow (Kohlhammer, non-commissioned officer), Albert Hehn (Rauscher, non-commissioned officer), Wilhelm H. König (Struve, non-commissioned officer), Christian Kayssler (Dr. Lautenbach, band-leader), Heinz Engelmann (Lieutenant Strehl), Ruth Hellberg (Gerda), Hilde Schneider (Käthe, teacher of physical exercises), Claire Winter (Lotte), Ingeborg von Kusserow (Lisbeth), Wilhelm Althaus (Captain Gruber), Wolfgang Staudte (Staff Sergeant Kern), Louise Morland (Frau Werner), Hermann Pfeiffer (Lohmann, assistant director), Ferdinand Reich (actor playing Preying), Elisabeth Schwarzkopf (actress playing Carmen), Günther Treptow (actor playing Don José), Sepp Rederer, Günther Ballier, Josef Gindorf, Malte Jäger, Erwin Laurenz, Günther Mackert, Paul Mehler, Hermann Mayer-Falkow, Waldemar Pottier, Herbert Reichelt, Herbert Scholz, members of army and air force: Wachregiment Berlin, Infanterie-Lehr-Regiment, Panzer-Lehr-Abteilung, Jagdgeschwader Richthofen.

Produced by Universum-Film A.-G. (Ufa), Berlin. *Production Group:* Ernst Martin — Hans Herbert Ulrich. 35mm. *Laboratory:* Afifa. *Shooting:* beginning of October 1938– beginning of January 1939. *Interiors:* Ufastadt Babelsberg; Ufa Studios Berlin-Tempelhof. *Exteriors:* military training area of Döberitz, Wünsdorf. *Running time:* 94 minutes. *Premiere:* March 31, 1939, Berlin, Ufa-Palast am Zoo. *Distributed by* Universum Filmverleih G.m.b.H. (Ufaleih), Berlin.

Dreizehn Mann und eine Kanone (Thirteen Men and a Cannon)

1938. *Director:* Johannes Meyer. *Production Manager:* Karl Schulz. *Location Managers:* Walter Zeiske, Anton Höhn. *Assistant Director:* Viktor Becker. *Screenplay:* Fred Andreas, Georg Hurdaleck, Peter Francke, based on an idea conceived by Pizarro Forzano. *Cinematography:* Kurt Hasselmann, Hans Georg Fehdmer. *Music:* Peter Kreuder. *Art Directors:* Max Seefelder, Franz Berner. *Costumes*

Advisor: Max Eugen Baron von Engelhardt. *Sound:* K. A. Keller. *Editor:* Max Michel.

   Cast: Friedrich Kayssler (General), Otto Wernicke (Fischer, commissary), Herbert Hübner (General Lobanov), Erich Ponto (Colonel Worochin), Edwin Jürgensen (Russian artillery officer), Paul Wagner (Captain Grothe), Hans Kettler (Lindemann, vice sergeant), Alexander Golling (Ruland, private), Fritz Genschow (Keller, private), Ernst Fritz Fürbringer (von Hessler, gunner), Hans Pössenbacher (Matzke, gunner), Karl Dannemann (Geissler, gunner), Anton Pointner (Kranz, gunner), H. J. Schaufuss (Seiffert, gunner), Walter Hillbring (Mrachatsch, gunner), Erwin van Roy (Spollo, gunner), Ludwig Schmitz (Küppers, gunner), Lutz Götz (Lübbs, gunner), Beppo Brem (Rainlechner, gunner), Werner Pledath, Rudolf Schündler, Otz Tollen, Fritz Reiff, Carl Graumann, Ernst Schiffner, Otto Kronburger, Toni Färber, Karl Schaidler, Werner Scharf, Erich Haussmann, Heinz Burkard, Willi Gronauer, Franz Schönemann.

   Produced by Bavaria-Filmkunst G.m.b.H., Munich. *Staatsauftragsfilm.* 35mm. *Sound System:* Tobis Klangfilm. *Interiors:* Bavaria Studios, Geiselgasteig. *Distributed by* Bavaria-Filmkunst Verleih G.m.b.H., Munich.

Die Entlassung (The Dismissal)

1942. *Director:* Wolfgang Liebeneiner. *Screenplay:* Curt Johannes Braun, Felix von Eckardt. *Cinematography:* Fritz Arno Wagner. *Music:* Herbert Windt.

   Cast: Emil Jannings, Werner Krauss, Theodor Loos, Werner Hinz, Karl Ludwig Diehl, Otto Graf, Christian Kayssler, Paul Bildt, Paul Hoffmann, Franz Schafheitlin, Hildegard Grethe, Margarete Schön, Walther Süssenguth, Herbert Hübner, Fritz Kampers, Rudolf Blümner, Werner Pledath, Heinrich Schroth, Otto Ernst Hasse, Friedrich Maurer, Eduard Wandrey.

   Produced by Tobis Filmkunst, Berlin. *Staatsauftragsfilm. Premiere:* October 6, 1942. *Distributed by* DFV, Berlin. *Subject:* Sequel to Liebeneiner's first BISMARCK film.

Der Ewige Jude (Ein Dokumentarfilm über das Weltjudentum) (The Eternal Jew: A Documentary About World Jewry)

1939–40. *Director:* Dr. Fritz Hippler. *Screenplay:* Dr. Eberhard Taubert. *Cinematography:* A. Endrejat, A. Hafner, R. Hartmann, F. C. Heere, H. Kluth, E. Stoll, H. Winterfeld. *Animation:* Studio Svend Noldan. *Music:* Franz R. Friedl. *Editors:* Hans-Dieter Schiller, Albert Baumeister.

   Produced by Deutsche Filmherstellungs- und Verwertungs-G.m.b.H. *Premiere:* November 28, 1940, Berlin. *Distributed by* Reichspropagandaleitung, Hauptamt Film.

Ewiger Wald

1935–36. *Directors:* Hans Springer, Rolf von Sonjewski-Jamrowski. *Producer:* Albert Graf von Pestalozza. *Screenplay:* Albert Graf von Pestalozza, Carl Maria Holzapfel. *Cinematography:* Sepp Allgeier, Werner Bohne, Otto Ewald, Wolf Hart, Guido Seeber, Wilhelm Siem, Adolf-Otto Weitzenberg, Bernhard Wentzel. *Special Photography:* Ernst Kunstmann, Heinrich Weidemann. *Music:* Wolfgang Zeller. *Singer:* Wilhelm Strienz. *Chorus:* Waldo Favre, Berliner Solistenvereinigung, Lehrergesangverein Berlin.

   Narrated by Günther Hadank, Heinz Herkommer, Paul Klinger, Lothar Körner, Kurt Wieschala.

   Cast: Aribert Mog and men and women from different parts of Germany.

   Produced by Lex-Film, Albert Graf von Pestalozza, Berlin (for N.S. Kulturgemeinde). *Premiere:* August 28, 1936, Oldenburg. *Distributed by* Carl Cürten-Film Verleih (Munich/Berlin); from September 1937: Degeto-Kulturfilm G.m.b.H. (Berlin).

Fahrt ins Leben (Journey to Life)

1939–40. *Director:* Bernd Hofmann. *Screenplay:* Bernd Hofmann. *Cinematography:* Erich Claunigk. *Music:* Bernd Scholz.

   Cast: Ruth Hellberg, Ursula Herking, Karl Ludwig Schreiber, Herbert Hübner, Hedwig Bleibtreu, Karl John, Walter Werner, Ernst

Schröder, Hans Joachim Schaufuss, Siegfried Schürenberg, Werner Pledath, Paul Westermeier, Oscar Sabo, Alfred Maack, Claire Reigbert, Albert Venohr, Auguste Prasch-Grevenberg, Karl Platen, H. J. Schölermann, Ferdinand Reich, Viktor Carter, Helene Westphal, Rudolf Vones, Christa Dilthey, Eduard Bornträger, Willy Meyer-Santen, Paula Lena, Fred Goebel, Hildegard Fränzel.

Produced by Bavaria, Munich. *Staatsauftragsfilm. Premiere:* February 29, 1940, Sonneberg; April 29, 1940, Berlin. *Distributed by* Bavaria, Munich. *Subject:* Sailing cadets in 1901.

Falschmünzer (Counterfeiters)

1940. *Director:* Hermann Pfeiffer. *Assistant Director:* Max Diekhaut. *Producer:* Eduard Kubat. *Location Managers:* Günther Regenberg, Georg Kroschel. *Screenplay:* Per Schwenzen, Walter Maisch. *Cinematography:* Walter Pindter. *Stills Photographer:* Otto Krahnert. *Music:* Michael Jary. *Art Director:* Max Mellin. *Assistant Art Director:* Gerhard Ladner. *Costumes:* Elfriede Gampe. *Sound:* Ernst Walter. *Editor:* Alexandra Anatra.

Cast: Kirsten Heiberg (Juliette Balouet), Rudolf Fernau (Gaston de Frossard), Hermann Speelmans (Harry Gernreich), Theodor Loos (Professor Bassi), Karin Himboldt (Hanna Weidling), Hermann Brix (Herbert Engelke), Leo Peukert (Johann Weidling), Lutz Götz (Poppinger, livestock dealer), Axel Monjé (*Obersturmführer* Dr. Brack, detective superintendent), Max Gülstorff (Zeltlin, detective), Oskar Sabo (Oskar), Bruno Hübner (Hubert Bonifatius), Ingeborg von Kusserow (Else Bornemann), Jacob Tiedtke (Father Schmidt), Peter Elsholtz (Gert), Hans Stiebner (Nico), Olga Engl, Julia Serda, Christa Dilthey, Franz Arzdorf, Walther Bechmann, Friedrich Beug, Heinz Berghaus, Eduard Bornträger, Erich Dunskus, Fritz Eckert, Wilhelm Egger-Sell, Benno Gellenbeck, Fred Goebel, Knut Hartwig, Oscar Höcker, Fred Köster, Hermann Mayer-Falkow, Paul Mederow, Michael von Newlinski, Georg Profe, Klaus Pohl, Walter Pose, Alfred Pussert, Max Vierlinger, Ewald Wenck, Willy Witte.

Produced and distributed by Terra-Filmkunst G.m.b.H., Berlin. *Production Group:* Eduard Kubat. 35mm. *Interiors:* Ufastadt Babelsberg.

Feinde (Enemies)

1940. *Director:* Viktor Tourjanski. *Production Manager:* C. W. Tetting. *Location Managers:* August Lautenbacher, Rudolf Kley. *Assistant Director:* Auguste Barth. *Screenplay:* Emil Burri, Arthur Luethy, Viktor Tourjanski. *Cinematography:* Fritz Arno Wagner. *Stills Photographer:* Rudolf Reissner. *Music:* Lothar Brühne. *Art Directors:* Julius von Borsody, Herbert Hochreiter, Alfred Metscher. *Costume Advisor:* Ruth Wagner. *Sound:* Ludwig Heiss. *Editor:* Walter Fredersdorf.

Cast: Brigitte Horney (Anna), Willy Birgel (Keith), Ivan Petrovich (Jan), Carl Wery (Martin), Reinhold Lütjohann (Wegner), Gerd Höst (Marianne, Wegner's daughter), Fritz Eugens (Paul, Wegner's son), Nikolas Kolin (Andreas), Hedwig Wangel (Liska), Karl Heinz Peters (Antek), Arnulf Schröder (Wladek), Hannes Keppler (Hans Martin), Beppo Brem (Wegereit), José Held (Stach), Friedrich Ettel (Keller, German settler), Ludwig Schmid-Wildy (Lessing, German settler), Walter Holten (Böhme, German settler), Katharina Berger, Hans Benedikt, Heinz Burkardt, Peter Busse, Willy Cronauer, Anita Düvell, Walter Ebert-Grassow, Franz Froehlich, Carl Gelfius, Fred Goebel, Karl Hanft, Maria Heil, Walter Hilbring, Charles Willy Kayser, Walter Kindler, Otto Kuhlmann, Helmut Kutzner, Emanuel Matousek, Justus Paris, Artur Reinhardt, Kurt Uhlig, Werner Völger, Dolf Zenzen.

Produced by Bavaria-Filmkunst G.m.b.H., Munich. *Staatsauftragsfilm.* 35mm. *Interiors:* Bavaria Studios, Geiselgasteig. *Distributed by* Bavaria-Filmkunst Verleih G.m.b.H., Munich.

Feuertaufe (Baptism of Fire)

1939–40. *Director:* Hans Bertram. *Production Manager:* Wilhelm Stöppler. *Music:* Norbert Schulze. *Lyrics:* Wilhelm Stöppler. *Editor:* Carl Otto Bartning.

Produced by Tobis Filmkunst G.m.b.H.,

Berlin. By order of Reichsluftfahrt-Ministerium. 35mm. *Laboratory:* Geyer. *Distributed by* Tobis Filmverleih G.m.b.H., Berlin.

Flüchtlinge (Refugees)

1933. *Director:* Gustav Ucicky. *Producer:* Günther Stapenhorst. *Production Manager:* Erich von Neusser. *Location Manager:* Otto Lehmann. *Screenplay:* Gerhard Menzel, from his novel *Deutsche wollen heim* (*Germans Want Home*). *Cinematography:* Fritz Arno Wagner. *Music:* Herbert Windt, Ernst Erich Buder. *Song:* "Marschlied der Kameraden." *Lyrics:* Franz Baumann. *Art Directors:* Robert Herlth, Walter Röhrig. *Sound:* Hermann Fritzsching. *Editor:* Eduard von Borsody.

Cast: Hans Albers (Arneth), Käthe von Nagy (Kristja), Eugen Klöpfer (Laudy), Ida Wüst (Megele), Walter Hermann (German deputy), Karl Rainer (Peter), Franziska Kinz (pregnant woman), Veit Harlan (Mannlinger), Hans Adalbert Schlettow (Sibirian), Friedrich Gnass (hussar), Karl Meixner (Pappel), Fritz Genschow (Hermann), Hans Herrmann-Schaufuss (dwarf), Josef Rahmen (red-haired), Rudolf Biebrach (watchmaker), Carsta Löck (Hellerle), Maria Koppenhöfer (Volga German), Andrews Engelmann (Russian commissar).

Produced by Universum-Film A.-G. (Ufa), Berlin. *Production Group:* Günther Stapenhorst. 35mm. *Laboratory:* Afifa, Berlin. *Shooting:* end of July–October 1933. *Interiors:* Ufa-Atelier Neubabelsberg. *Exteriors:* Seddin near Potsdam, backlot of Babelsberg Studios. *Running time:* 88 minutes. *Premiere:* December 8, 1933, Berlin, Ufa-Palast am Zoo. *Distributed by* Universum Filmverleih (Ufaleih), Berlin.

(From this film a French version *A Bout Du Monde* was produced, directed by Gustav Ucicky and Henri Chornette, starring Pierre Blanchar, Käthe von Nagy, Charles Vanel, Line Noro, Raymond Cordy, Pierre-Louis.)

Fridericus

1936. *Director:* Johannes Meyer. *Screenplay:* Erich Kröhnke, Walter von Molo, from the novel by Walter von Molo. *Cinematography:* Bruno Mondi. *Music:* Marc Roland.

Cast: Otto Gebühr, Hilde Körber, Lil Dagover, Agnes Straub, Käthe Haack, Bernhard Minetti, Paul Klinger, Carola Höhn, Paul Dahlke, Lucie Höflich, Wilhelm König, Will Dohm, Paul Westermeier, Heinrich Schroth, Alfred Kerasch, Ernst Karchow, Hans Mierendorff, Bruno Zioner, Hermann Frick, Karl Platen, Paul Bildt, Rudolf Biebrach, Hugo Flink, Angelo Ferrari, Fred Goebel, Bernhard Goetzke, Harry Hardt, Walter Janssen, Harry Frank, Oskar Marion, Anton Pointner, Gustav Püttjer, Luis Ralph, Franz W. Schröder-Schrom, Otto Sauter-Sarto, E. G. Schiffner, Arthur Reinhardt, Franz Klebusch, Rio Nobile, Otto Kronburger, Kurt Keller-Nebri.

Produced by Diana-Tonfilm G.m.b.H., Berlin. *Premiere:* February 8, 1937. *Distributed by* Syndikat-Film G.m.b.H. (Tobis Syndicate), Berlin. *Subject:* Another example of the Frederick the Great series.

Friesennot—Ein Film vom deutschen Schicksal (rerelease title 1941: Dorf im roten Sturm) (Frisians in Peril/Red Storm Over the Village)

1935. *Director:* Peter Hagen. *Producer:* Hermann Schmidt. *Creative supervisor:* Willy Krause, Reich Film Dramaturge. *Screenplay:* Werner Kortwich, Peter Hagen [i.e., Willy Krause], based on a novel by Werner Kortwich. *Cinematography:* Sepp Allgeier. *Music:* Walter Gronostay. *Art Director:* Dietrich.

Cast: Friedrich Kayssler (Jürgen Wagner), Helene Fehdmer (Katrin Wagner), V. Inkijinoff (Commissioner Tchernoff), Jessie Vibrog (Mette Kröger), Hermann Schomberg (Klaus Niegebüll), Ilse Fürstenberg (Dörte Niegebüll), Gertrud Boll (Telse Detlevsen), Martha Ziegler (Wiebke Detlevsen), Kai Möller (Hanke Peters), Marianne Simson (Hilde Winkler), Maria Koppenhöfer (Widow Winkler), Franz Stein (Christian Kröger), Fritz Hoopts (Ontje Ibs), Aribert

Grimmer (Commissioner Krappin), Jacob Sinn (Jan Wittmaak).

Produced by Delta-Filmproduktion G.m.b.H., Hermann Schmidt. 35mm. *Exteriors* filmed in Schamanovo near Potsdam. *Premiere:* November 19, 1935. *Distributed by* Reichspropagandaleitung der NSDAP, Hauptamt Film. On September 7, 1939, this film was forbidden, but in 1941 it was re-released.

Front am Himmel
(Front in the Skyfront)

1940–42. *Directors:* Carl Otto Bartning, Karl Ludwig Ruppel. *Production Manager:* Wilhelm Stöppler. *Special Photographic Effects:* Karl Ludwig Ruppel. *Editor:* Carl Otto Bartning.

Produced by Tobis Filmkunst G.m.b.H., Berlin. *Interiors:* Jofa Studios, Berlin-Johannisthal.

Fronttheater (Front Theatre)

1941. *Director:* Arthur Maria Rabenalt. *Screenplay:* Georg Hurdalek, H. P. Köllner, Werner Plücker, from an idea conceived by Werner Scharf. *Cinematography:* Oskar Schnirch. *Music:* Werner Bochmann, Hans-Martin Majewski.

Cast: Heli Finkenzeller, René Deltgen, Lothar Firmans, Hedi and Margot Höpfner, Wilhelm Strienz, Willi Rose, Rudolf Schündler, Bruni Löbel, Hilde von Stolz, Gerhard Dammann, Adolf Fischer, Arnim Münch, Alice Treff, Peter Elsholtz, Elsa Wagner, Franz Zimmermann, Ernö René, Ernst Bader, Elmer Bantz, Günther Ballier, Fredy Barten, Albert Bessler, Bill Bocketts, Ilse Buhl, Fritz Gerlach, Hellmuth Heyne, Oskar Höcker, Kurt Holhart-Hunger, Käthe Jöken-König, Josef Kamper, Ernst Karchow, Melitta Klefer, Kurt Kramer, Fred Krüger, Fritz Lafontaine, Arthur Malkowski, Monika Möbius, Hermann Pfeiffer, Klaus Pohl, Gustav Püttjer, Willi Puhlmann, Erik Radolf, Arthur Reinhardt, Walter Ringelwald, Maria Sigg, Elisabeth Scherer, Anita Schulz, Wera Schultz, Eckart Schulz-Ewart, Walter Stein-

weg, Hans Hermann Strömer, Leo Vieten, Theodor Vogeler, Egon Vogel, Rudolf-Günther Wagner, Helga Warnecke, Eduard Wenck, Willi Witte.

Produced by Terra-Filmkunst G.m.b.H., Berlin. *Staatsauftragsfilm.* 35mm. *Interiors:* Ufastadt Babelsberg; Cineton Studios Amsterdam and Den Haag. *Premiere:* November 24, 1942. *Distributed by* DFV (Deutsche Filmvertriebs G.m.b.H.), Berlin.

Der Fuchs von Glenarvon
(The Fox of Glenarvon)

1939–40. *Director:* Max Wilhelm Kimmich. *Producer:* Herbert Engelsing. *Production Manager:* Hans Lehmann. *Screenplay:* Wolf Neumeister, Hans Bertram, from a novel by Nicola Rohn. *Cinematography:* Fritz Arno Wagner. *Music:* Otto Konradt. *Art Directors:* Otto Erdmann, Willy Depenau.

Cast: Ferdinand Marian (Grandison, justice of peace), Olga Tschechowa (Gloria, his wife), Joachim Pfaff (Patrick, his son), Karl Ludwig Diehl (Baron John Ennis of Loweland), Traudl Stark (Kit, his daughter), Albert Florath (Baron O'Connor, Ennis' uncle), Lucie Höflich (Baroness Margit, O'Connor's wife), Else von Möllendorff (Mary-Ann, O'Connor's daughter), Richard Häussler (Major McKenney, British officer), Ellen Bang (Lady McKenney, his wife), Elisabeth Flickenschildt (Brigit Erskynne), Kurt Lucas (Beverly, banker), Paul Otto (Colonel Stewart, British officer), Werner Hinz (Sir Tetbury, commander of a special force), Hans Mierendorff (O'Morrow), Hermann Braun (Desmond O'Morrow, his son), Hans Richter (Robin Cavendish, student from Eton), Horst Birr (Rory, student), Peter Elsholtz (Tim Malory, Grandison's gamekeeper), Bruno Hübner (Mildon, Grandison's secretary), Friedrich Kayssler (O'Riorden), Karl Dannemann (Pat Moore), Aribert Mog (Thomas Dealy), Bernhard Goetzke (Duff O'Mally, lighthouse keeper), Karl Hannemann (Thripp), Hilde Körber (Maureen, Irish nurse), Franz Weber (Donelly, janitor), Ferdinand Terpe (Koph, country constabulary), Albert Venohr (Beardsley, country constabulary), Hannes Waschatko (Morrison, servant), Lilly Schönborn, Wilhelm Grosse, Günther Langenbeck, Hellmuth Passarge, Edmund Pouch, Gustav Püttjer, Isolde Laux, Elli Löffler, Kurt Dremel, Max Grosse-Linden, Kurt Polter.

Produced by Tobis Filmkunst G.m.b.H., Berlin. *Production Group:* Herbert Engelsing. *Staatsauftragsfilm.* 35mm. *Laboratory:* Geyer. *Sound System:* Tobis Klangfilm. *Interiors:* Jofa Studios, Berlin-Johannisthal. *Premiere:* April 24, 1940. *Distributed by* Tobis Filmverleih G.m.b.H., Berlin.

Geheimakte W. B. 1 (Secret File W. B. 1)

1941–42. *Director:* Herbert Selpin. *Screenplay:* Walter Zerlett-Olfenius, Herbert Selpin from the novel "Der eiserne Seehund" by Hans Arthur Thies. Adapted by Curt Johannes Braun and Franz Weichenmayr. *Cinematography:* Franz Koch. *Music:* Franz Doelle.

Cast: Alexander Golling, Eva Immermann, Richard Häussler, Günther Lüders, Herbert Hübner, Gustav Waldau, Willi Rose, Wilhelm P. Krüger, Walter Holten, Viktor Afritsch, Andrews Engelmann, Philipp Manning, Karl Meixner, Theo Shall, Jack Trevor, Friedrich Ulmer, Paul Wagner, Albert Arid, Karl Hanft, Michl Lang, Richard Ludwig, Justus Paris, Heinz Thiele, Aruth Wartan, Dolf Zenzen.

Produced by Bavaria, Munich. *Staatsauftragsfilm.* *Premiere:* January 26, 1942, Munich; February 3, 1942, Berlin. *Distributed by* Bavaria, Munich (subsequently DFV, Berlin). *Subject:* Adventure story about Wilhelm Bauer, inventor of the submarine.

Germanin (Die Geschichte einer kolonialen Tat/The Story of a Colonial Deed)

1942–43. *Producer-Director:* Max Wilhelm Kimmich. *Assistant Director:* Erich Kobler. *Production Manager:* Hans Lehmann. *Location Managers:* Gustav Lorenz, Karl Sander, Victor Eisenbach. *Screenplay:* Hans Wolfgang Hillers, Max Wilhelm Kimmich, based on the novels *Germanin* by Hellmuth Unger and *Tsetse* by Norbert Jacques (uncredited). *Cinematography:* Jan Stallich, Jaroslav Tuzar. *Stills Photographer:* Otto Krahnert. *Music:* Theo Mackeben. *Art Director:* Anton Weber. *Sound:* Gustav Bellers. *Editor:* Erich Kobler.

Cast: Peter Petersen (Prof. Dr. Achenbach), Luis Trenker (Dr. Hans Hofer), Lotte Koch (Anna Meinhardt, assistant), Albert Lippert (Colonel Crosby), Rudolf Blümner (Privy Councilor Wissberg), Carl Günther (Dr. Bode), Ernst Stimmel (Director Claassen), Henry Stuart (Sir Edward Craigh), Joe Münch-Harris (Captain Evans), Hans Bergmann (British sergeant), Helmuth Helsig (Dr. Gordon), Louis Brody (King Wapunga), Valy Arnheim, Erich Kestin, Gerda von der Osten, Herbert Weissbach.

Produced by Ufa-Filmkunst G.m.b.H., Berlin. *Production Group:* Max W. Kimmich. *Staatsauftragsfilm.* 35mm. *Interiors:* Ufastadt Babelsberg, Cinecittà, Rome. *Exteriors:* surroundings of Rome. *Shooting:* March 11, 1942–March 1943. *Running time:* 94 minutes. *Premiere:* May 15, 1943, Hamburg, Ufa-Palast; May 17, 1943, Berlin, Ufa-Palast am Zoo, and Odeum Spandau. *Distributed by* DFV (Deutsche Filmvertriebs G.m.b.H.), Berlin.

Das Gewehr über (Shoulder Arms)

1939. *Director:* Jürgen von Alten. *Production Manager:* Emil Unfried. *Location Manager:* Gustav Lorenz. *Screenplay:* Kurt E. Walter, from a treatment by Marc Roland, Fred Hildenbrandt, Karl Bunje, F. B. Cortan, Captain Hesse, freely based on the book *Kompagnie Olympia* by Wolfgang Marken. *Cinematography:* Phil Jutzi. *Music:* Hanson Milde Meissner. *Art Directors:* Bruno Lutz, Carl Roys. *Sound:* H. Opitz. *Military Adviser:* Major Findeisen. *Editor:* Willi Zeunert.

Cast: Rudi Godden (Charlie), Rolf Möbius (Paul), Carsta Löck (Lotte), Hilde Schneider (Trude), Charlott Daudert (Evelyne), Franz

W. Schröder-Schrom (Hartwig, Sr.), Georg Heinrich Schnell (Thomson), Alfred Maack (Father Bornemann), Walter Bechmann (Schmitz, secretary), Leopold von Ledebur (Henning, General, retd.), Wilhelm Althaus (Captain Wehnert), Ernst Bader (Lieutenant Stolle), Franz Kossak (Grosse, staff sergeant), Wolfgang Staudte (Schmidt, non-commissioned officer), Adolf Fischer (non-commissioned officer), H. R. Knitsch (Private Hellermann), Horst Birr (Soldier Derksen), H. Asmis (Soldier Hambacher), Hans Jöckel (Soldier Lutz), W. Teuscher (Soldier Kagelmann), Bernhard Kaspar (Soldier Heinz), Lucy Millowitsch, Eva Jöken-König, Gerti Gerth, Georg Völckel, Heinz Berghaus, Victor Carter, Erwin Laurenz, Martin Baumann.

Produced by Germania Film G.m.b.H., Munich. *Staatsauftragsfilm.* 35mm. *Sound System:* Tobis Klangfilm. *Distributed by* Forum-Film.

Die goldene Spinne
(The Golden Spider)

1943. *Director:* Erich Engels. *Assistant Director:* Edmund Firsbach. *Producer:* Eduard Kubat. *Location Managers:* Willi Herrmann, Curt Bierbaum, Alfons Powollik-Ronay. *Screenplay:* Wolf Neumeister in cooperation with Dr. Ulrich Vogel. *Cinematography:* E. W. Fiedler. *Stills Photographer:* Georg Kügler. *Music:* Werner Eisbrenner. *Art Directors:* Franz Bi, Bruno Lutz, Eugen Schmidt. *Costumes:* Gerda Leopold-Pindter. *Sound:* G. Olierhoek, Albert Krämer. *Editor:* René Métain.

Cast: Kirsten Heiberg (Lisaweta), Jutta Freybe (Dr. Christa Fischer), Harald Paulsen (Smirnoff), Otto Gebühr (Private Councilor Fischer), Rolf Weih (Axel Rüdiger), Jaspar von Oertzen (Captain Hartung), Maly Delschaft (Rosa Sykora), Josef Sieber (Berger), Hermann Brix (Freise, commissary), Karl Dannemann (Bumm), Ernst Schlott (Zähringer, criminal assistant), Ewald Wenck (Kneisler), Werner Pledath (Heinsius), Robert Bürkner (Dr. Eberding), Lieselotte Schaack (Miss von Holleben), Lutz

Götz (Vonhoff, detective superintendent), H. Fuchs, Paul Mederow, Eduard Wenck, Georg Kröning, Knut Hartwig, Cläre Reigbert, Conrad Cappi, Edith Wolff, Luise Bethke-Zitzmann.

Produced by Terra-Filmkunst G.m.b.H., Berlin. *Production Group:* Eduard Kubat. 35mm. *Shooting:* March 22–July 23, 1943. *Exteriors:* Amsterdam, The Hague, and Berlin and surroundings. *Premiere:* December 23, 1943, Berlin, U.T. Kurfürstendamm, and Germania-Palast. *Distributed by* DFV (Deutsche Filmvertriebs G.m.b.H.), Berlin.

Die goldene Stadt
(The Golden City)

1942. *Producer-Director:* Veit Harlan. *Production Manager:* Hans Conradi. *Location Managers:* Conny Carstennsen, Rudolf Liebermann, Friedrich Link. *Assistant Director:* Wolfgang Schleif. *Screenplay:* Veit Harlan, Alfred Braun (i.e., Werner Eplinius), based on the play *Der Gigant* (*The Giant*) by Richard Billinger. *Cinematography:* Bruno Mondi. *Stills Photographer:* Otto Krahnert. *Music:* Hans-Otto Borgmann (and melodies by Bedřich Smetana). *Art Directors:* Erich Zander, Kurt Machus. *Sound:* Gustav Bellers (i.e., Bruno Suckau). *Editor:* Friedrich Karl von Puttkamer.

Cast: Kristina Söderbaum (Anna Jobst), Eugen Klöpfer (Melchior Jobst), Annie Rosar (Mrs. Opferkuch), Liselotte Schreiner (Maruschka, housekeeper), Dagny Servaes (Mrs. Tandler), Paul Klinger (Christian Leidwein, engineer), Kurt Meisel (Toni Opferkuch), Rudolf Prack (Thomas, first farm-hand), Ernst Legal (Pelikan), Hans-Herrmann Schaufuss (Nemerek), Inge Drexel (Julie), Walter Lieck (Ringl), Frida Richard (Mrs. Amend), Valy Arnheim, Conrad Cappi, Josef Dahmen, Else Ehser, Hugo Fink, Robert Forsch, Karl Harbacher, Emmerich Hanus, Maria Hofen, Josef Holzer, William Huch, Jaromir Krejci, Maria Loja, Josef Reithofer, Max Rosenhauer, Ernst Rotmund, Franz Schöber, Hans Sternberg, Rudolf Vones, Harry Hardt, Walter Schramm-Duncker, Josef Hustolis, Louis Ralph, Fritz Eysenhardt.

Produced by Ufa-Filmkunst G.m.b.H.,
Berlin. *Production Group:* Veit Harlan.
35mm. *Laboratories:* Afifa; Agfa, Wolfen.
Color by Agfacolor. *Running time:* 110 minutes. *Premiere:* September 3, 1942, Venice
(IFF); November 24, 1942, Berlin, Ufa-Palast
am Zoo, and Germania-Palast. *Distributed
by* DFV (Deutsche Filmvertriebs G.m.b.H.),
Berlin.

GPU (G.P.U./The Red Terror)

1941–42. *Producer-Director:* Karl Ritter.
Production Manager: Gustav Rathje. *Location
Manager:* Ernst Mattner. *Screenplay:* Karl
Ritter, Felix Lützendorf, Andrews Engel-
mann, from an original idea by Andrews En-
gelmann. *Cinematography:* Igor Oberberg.
Music: Herbert Windt. *Limehouse Blues:*
Freddie Brocksieper and Band. *Art Directors:*
Heinrich Weidemann, Johannes Massias.
Sound: Ernst-Otto Hoppe. *Editor:* Conrad
von Molo.

Cast: Laura Solari (Olga Feodorovna), An-
drews Engelmann (Nikolai Bokscha), Ma-
rina von Dittmar (Irina), Will Quadflieg
(Peter Assmus), Karl Haubenreisser (Jakob
Frunse), Helene von Schmithberg (Aunt
Ljuba), Albert Lippert (hotel manager),
Wladimir Majer (GPU chief), Lale Ander-
sen (singer), Hans Stiebner (judge), Maria
Bard (president of Women's League), Karl
Klüssner (Aramian), Ernst-Albert Schah, Ivo
Veit (two Soviet diplomats in Helsinki), Nico
Turoff, Walter Holetzko, Arthur Reinhardt,
Carl Hannemann, Ferdinand Classen, Wal-
ter Brückner, Hans Bergmann (Frunse's
seven helpers), Ernst Grohnert, Siegfried
Niemann, Gerda von der Osten, Hans
Meyer-Hanno, Heinz Wemper, Heinrich
Troxbömker, Willy Keil, Lili Schoenborn,
Theo Shall, Gösta Richter, Viggo Larsen,
Julius Eckhoff, Walter Lieck, Karl Wagner,
Bill-Bocketts.

Produced by Ufa-Filmkunst G.m.b.H.,
Berlin. *Production Group:* Karl Ritter. *Staatsauftragsfilm.* 35mm. *Laboratory:* Afifa. *Interiors:* Ufastadt Babelsberg. *Exteriors:* Berlin
and surroundings, Paris, Potsdam, Stettin.
Shooting: December 11, 1941–mid–May 1942.
Running time: 99 minutes. *Budget:* RM

1,556,000. *Premiere:* August 14, 1942, Berlin,
Capitol am Zoo, and Lichtburg Gesund-
brunnen. *Distributed by* DFV (Deutsche
Filmvertriebs G.m.b.H.), Berlin.

Der grosse König (The Great King)

1940–42. *Director:* Veit Harlan. *Production
Manager:* Willi Wiesner. *Location Managers:*
Conny Carstennsen (a.k.a. Friedrich Wirth),
Harry Dettmann, Kay Dietrich Voss. *Assis-
tant Directors:* Wolfgang Schleif, Herbert
Kiehne. *Screenplay:* Veit Harlan; uncredited:
Gerhard Menzel, Hans Rehberg. *Cinematog-
raphy:* Bruno Mondi. *Stills Photographer:*
Eugen Klagemann. *Music:* Hans-Otto Borg-
mann. *Art Directors:* Erich Zander, Karl
Malchus. *Costumes:* Ludwig Hornsteiner.
Wardrobe Master: Johannes Krämer. *Make-
Up:* Atelier Jabs. *Sound:* Hans Rütten. *Mili-
tary Adviser:* M. W. von Eberhardt. *Editor:*
Friedrich Karl von Puttkamer.

Cast: Otto Gebühr (Friedrich II), Kristina
Söderbaum (Luise, a miller's daughter),
Gustav Fröhlich (Corporal Treskow), Hans
Nielsen (Niehoff, cadet), Hilde Körber
(Queen Elisabeth), Paul Wegener (General
Chernichev), Otto Wernicke (Colonel Ro-
chow), Harry Hardt (first adjutant from
Dessau), Hans-Herrmann Schaufuss (Gen-
eral Zieten), Claus Clausen (Prince Heinrich
the Elder), Claus Detlef Sierck (Prince Hein-
rich the Younger), Paul Henckels (Spiller, in-
fantryman), Elisabeth Flickenschildt (Mrs.
Spiller), Franz Schafheitlin (Colonel Bern-
burg), Kurt Meisel (Alfons), Karl Günther
(Count Kaunitz), Otto Graf (General Sey-
dlitz), Hans Stiebner (Fourmentier, cook),
Erik Radolf (second adjutant), Franz Nick-
lisch (cornet), Herbert Hübner (Count
Finkenstein), Otto Henning (General von
Finck), Reginald Pasch (General Manteuf-
fel), Josef Peterhans (General Tempelhof),
Heinrich Schroth (General von Schenk-
endorff), Jaspar von Oertzen (von Prittwitz,
cavalry captain), Jakob Tiedtke (mayor of
Berlin), Bernhard Goetzke (General von
Hülsen), Otz Tollen (General Tauentzien),
Ernst Dernburg (General Ramin), Leopold

von Ledebur (General von Retzow), Alexander Kökert (General von Platen), Günter Markert (adjutant), Auguste Pünkösdy* (Maria Theresa), Heinz Salfner (councilor), Anton Pointner (General Daun), Walter Franck (General Laudon), Ernst Fritz Fürbringer* (Louis XV), Lola Müthel* (Madame Pompadour), Hilde von Stolz* (Dauphine), Herbert Gernot (Russian officer), Karl Hellmer (Russian sergeant), Paul Westermeier (Prussian sergeant), Armin Schweizer (Franz, servant), Hans Sternberg (the miller), Maria Krahn (the miller's wife), Wolf Trutz (servant), Heinrich Marlow (old general), Kristian Veit Harlan (Luise's son), Ferdinand Asper, Fanny Cotta, Hans Eysenhardt, Leonore Ehn, Arthur Eugens, Franz Fiedler, Hugo Flink, Erich Gast, Knut Hartwig, Clemens Hasse, Jürgen Hollmers, Käte Jöken-König, Herbert Kiurina, Maria Loja, Hermann Meyer-Falko, Hans Mayer-Hanno, Michael von Newlinski, Luis Rainer, Louis Ralph, Hans Reiners, Just Scheu, Werner Schott, Walter Steinweg, Ernst Stimmel, Willi Witte.

Produced by Tobis Filmkunst G.m.b.H., Berlin. *Staatsauftragsfilm.* 35mm. *Interiors:* Jofa Studios, Berlin-Johannisthal. *Exteriors:* Döberitz-Seegrund; Prague; military training area Jüterborg. *Running time:* 118 minutes. *Premiere:* March 3, 1942, Berlin, Ufa-Palast am Zoo. *Distributed by* DFV (Deutsche Filmvertriebs G.m.b.H.), Berlin.

Die grosse Liebe (The Great Love)

1941–42. *Director:* Rolf Hansen. *Producer:* Walter Bolz. *Screenplay:* Peter Groll, Rolf Hansen, from an idea conceived by Alexander Lernet-Holenia. *Cinematography:* Franz Weihmayr. *Music:* Michael Jary. *Lyrics:* Bruno Balz. *Art Director:* Walter Haag. *Miniatures and Process Photography:* Gerhard Huttula. *Process Technician:* Willi Körner. *Sound:* Werner Pohl. *Choreography:* Jens Keith. *Editor:* Anna Höllering.

Cast: Zarah Leander (Hanna Holberg),

Viktor Staal (First Lieutenant Paul Wendlandt), Paul Hörbiger (Alexander Rudnitzky, composer), Grete Weiser (Käthe, Hanna Holberg's maid), Wolfgang Preiss (First lieutenant von Etzdorf), Hans Schwarz, Jr. (Alfred Vanloo), Leopold von Ledebur (Mr. Westphal), Julia Serda (Mrs. Westphal), Viktor Janson (Mocelli), Dr. Wilhelm Althaus, Paul Bildt, Erich Dunskus, Olga Engl, Karl Etlinger, Hugo Froelich, Ilse Fürstenberg, Wilhelm P. Krüger, Walter Lieck, Henry Lorenzen, Hermann Pfeiffer, Gothart Portloff, Grete Reinwald, Just Scheu, Erna Sellmer, Arnim Schweizer, Ewald Wenck, Agnes Windeck.

Produced by Ufa-Filmkunst G.m.b.H., Berlin. *Production Group:* Walter Bolz. *Staatsauftragsfilm.* 35mm. *Laboratory:* Afifa. *Interiors:* Tonfilm-Studio Froelich (UFA), Berlin; Vienna Rosenhügel (starting in October 13, 1941). *Exteriors:* Citta Hotel, Rome. *Budget:* RM 2.7 million. *Premiere:* June 12, 1942, Berlin, Ufa-Palast am Zoo and Germania-Palast. *Distributed by* DFV (Deutsche Filmvertriebs G.m.b.H.), Berlin.

Hände Hoch (Hands Up)

1942. *Director:* Alfred Weidenmann. *Screenplay:* Alfred Weidenmann. *Cinematography:* Emil Schünemann. *Music:* Horst Hanns Sieber.

Cast: Erich Dunskus (landowner), Willi Witte (teacher), Johannes Schütz (Hitler Youth leader), Maria L. Fodorowa, Pimpfe (Hitler Boys) in a camp of *Kinderlandverschickung* at the border of Hohe Tatra in Slovakia.

Produced by Deutsche Filmherstellungs- und Verwertungs-G.m.b.H. (DFG). *Exteriors:* HJ camp in Hohe Tatra. *Premiere:* October 25, 1942. *Distributed by* Reichspropagandaleitung NSDAP, Hauptamt Film.

In June 1942 in Florenz, *Hände hoch* was awarded the Prize of Reich Minister for People's Education and Propaganda in the category *Jugendspielfilme* (Youth Feature Films).

These actors were removed from the release version.

Hans Westmar—einer von Vielen (Ein deutsches Schicksal aus dem Jahre 1929) (Hans Westmar, One of Many)

1933. *Director:* Franz Wenzler. *Producer:* Robert Ernst. *Location Manager:* Conrad Flockner. *Assistant Director:* Werner Bruder. *Screenplay:* Hans Heinz Ewers from his book *Horst Wessel. Cinematography:* Franz Weihmayr. *Stills Photographer:* Fritz Vopel. *Music:* Ernst Hanfstengel, Dr. Giuseppe Becce. *Musical Director:* Dr. Giuseppe Becce. *Songs:* "Bei uns gibt es kein Hindernis"; "Die Internationale"; "Die Wacht am Rhein"; "Horst Wessel Song: Die Fahne hoch"; "SA marschiert." *Art Directors:* Hans Sohnle, Otto Erdmann. *Make-Up Artists:* Frieda Lehmann, Maria Arnold. *Wardrobe:* Jenny Pieper. *Sound:* Eugen Hrich. *SA Advisor:* Richard Fiedler. *Editor:* Alice Ludwig.

Cast: Emil Lohkamp (Hans Westmar), Gertrud de Lalsky (Mrs. Westmar, his mother), Irmgard Willers (Agnes), Carla Bartheel (Maud, a young American woman), Heinz Salfner (Maud's father), Paul Wegener (Kuprikoff), Heinrich Heilinger (Camillo Ross), Rudolf Thiem (Georg Beyer), Wilhelm Diegelmann (landlord), Arthur Schröder (Menart, student of Law), Grete Reinwald (Klara), Otti Dietze (Mrs. Salm), Hanns Heinz Ewers (an elderly gentleman from Corps Normannia, a student duelling society), Carl Auen, Hugo Gau-Hamm, Richard Fiedler and members of SA Berlin-Brandenburg, Unit 4, Unit 5 (Horst Wessel), Unit 6, Landespolizeigruppe Wecke zur besonderen Verwendung (a special police contingent), Berlin Corps Kösener S.C.

Produced by Volksdeutsche Film G.m.b.H., Berlin. *Staatsauftragsfilm.* 35mm. *Sound System:* Tobis Klangfilm. *Shooting:* July 1933. *Interiors:* Jofa Studios, Berlin-Johannisthal. *Exteriors:* Berlin. *Premiere:* October 3, 1933, Berlin Capitol—I; December 13, 1933, Berlin Capitol. *Distributed by* Siegel Monopolfilm, Dresden and Berlin.

Heimkehr (Homecoming)

1941. *Director:* Gustav Ucicky. *Producer:* Erich von Neusser. *Production Manager:* Ernst Garden. *Location Managers:* Heinz Fiebig, Felix Fohn. *Assistant Director:* Wolfgang Schubert. *Screenplay:* Gerhard Menzel. *Cinematography:* Günther Anders. *Music:* Willy Schmidt-Gentner. *Art Directors:* Walter Röhrig, Hermann Asmus. *Costumes:* Albert Bei, Max Frey. *Sound:* Alfred Norkus. *Editor:* Rudolf Schaad.

Cast: Paula Wessely (Maria Thomas), Peter Petersen (Dr. Thomas), Attila Hörbiger (Ludwig Launhardt), Ruth Hellberg (Martha Launhardt), Carl Raddatz (Dr. Fritz Mutius), Otto Wernicke (Father Manz), Elsa Wagner (*Wehmutter* Schmid), Eduard Köck (Father Schmid), Gerhild Weber (Josepha Manz), Werner Fütterer (Oskar Friml), Franz Pfaudler (Balthasar Manz), Berta Drews (Elfriede), Hermann Erhardt (Karl Michalek), Gottlieb Sambor (i.e., Boguslaw Samborski).

Produced by Wien-Film G.m.b.H., Vienna. *Production Group:* Erich von Neusser. 35mm. *Laboratory:* Afifa. *Sound System:* Tobis Klangfilm. *Interior:* Studio Rosenhügel Vienna, Studio Vienna Sievering, Studio Vienna Schönbrunn. *Exteriors:* Chorzele (Poland), Ortelsburg (East Prussia). *Budget:* RM 4,020,000. *Running time:* 96 minutes. *Premiere:* August 31, 1941, Venice/Italy Cinema San Marco; October 10, Vienna Scala; October 24, Berlin, Ufa-Palast am Zoo.

Heldentum und Todeskampf Unserer Emden (Heroism and Death Struggle of the Cruiser "Emden")

1934. *Director:* Louis Ralph. *Screenplay:* Louis Ralph. *Cinematography:* Franz Koch. *Music:* Fritz Wenneis.

Cast: Louis Ralph, Willi Kaiser-Heyl, Fritz Greiner, Werner Fuetterer, Charles Willy Kaiser, surviving officers and crew of the cruiser "Emden."

Produced by Richard Herzog & Co., Berlin

in association with Tobis-Melofilm G.m.b.H., Berlin (new Version). *Staatsauftragsfilm.* *Premiere:* November 13, 1934, Berlin, Titania-Palast. *Distributed by* Richard Herzog & Co., Berlin; Nord-Film G.m.b.H., Hamburg; Siegel Monopolfilm, Dresden/Berlin; Filmverleih Seidel Vortragsdienst, Erfurt; local distributors. *Subject:* Exploits on board of the doomed German cruiser "Emden" in World War I.

Henker, Frauen und Soldaten (Hangmen, Women and Soldiers)

1935. *Director:* Johannes Meyer. *Screenplay:* Max W. Kimmich, Jacob Geis, from the novel "Ein Mannsbild namens Prack" von Fritz Reck-Malleczewen. *Cinematography:* Franz Koch. *Music:* Peter Kreuder.

Cast: Hans Albers, Charlotte Susa, Jack Trevor, Ernst Dumcke, Annie Markart, Aribert Wäscher, Hubert von Meyerinck, Otto Wernicke, Fritz Genschow, Max Weydner, Bernhard Minetti, Oskar Marion, Fita Benkhoff, Gerhard Bienert, Charlotte Radspieler, Gustav Püttjer, Zerah Achmed, Paul Rehkopf, Wera Schwarz.

Produced by Bavaria-Film A.G., Munich. *Premiere:* December 19, 1935. *Distributed by* Bayerische Film G.m.b.H., Munich. *Subject:* The unfortunate love story of a German World War I Air Ace and a female Bolshevik spy.

Der Herrscher (The Ruler)

1936–37. *Director:* Veit Harlan. *Screenplay:* Veit Harlan, Curt Johannes Braun, freely adapted from "Vor Sonnenuntergang" bei Gerhard Hauptmann. *Cinematography:* Günther Anders, Werner Brandes. *Music:* Wolfgang Zeller.

Cast: Emil Jannings, Marianne Hoppe, Harald Paulsen, Hilde Körber, Paul Wagner, Maria Koppenhöfer, Hannes Stelzer, Käthe Haack, Herbert Hübner, Helene Fehdmer, Max Gülstorff, Theodor Loos, Paul Bildt, Walter Werner, Heinrich Schroth, Rudolf

Klein-Rogge, Hans Stiebner, Peter Elsholtz, Ursula Kurtz, Heinz Wemper.

Produced by Tobis-Magna-Filmproduktion G.m.b.H., Berlin. *Staatsauftragsfilm.* *Premiere:* March 17, 1937. *Distributed by* Syndikat-Film G.m.b.H. (Tobis Syndicate), Berlin. *Subject:* Emil Jannings as industrial magnate of Germany's Ruhr area.

Himmelhunde (Bloody Dogs/ Sky Hounds)

1942. *Director:* Roger von Norman. *Production Manager:* Eduard Kubat. *Dialogue Director:* Ulrich Erfurth. *Screenplay:* Philipp Lothar Mayring, from an idea conceived by Hanns Fischer-Gerhold and Hans Heise. *Cinematography:* Herbert Körner. *Music:* Werner Bochmann. *Art Director:* Hermann Asmus. *Miniatures and Process Photography:* Gerhard Huttula. *Process Technician:* Willi Körner.

Cast: Erik Schumann (Werner Grundler), Malte Jäger, Waldemar Leitgeb, Lutz Götz, Albert Florath, Josef Kamper, Toni von Bukovics, Klaus Pohl, Erna Heidersdorf, Edgar Hollot, Siegmar Schneider, Rudolf Vones, boy members of a Hitler Youth glider pilot group.

Produced by Terra-Filmkunst G.m.b.H., Berlin. *Production Group:* Eduard Kubat. *Staatsauftragsfilm.* 35mm. *Premiere:* February 20, 1942, Stuttgart; April 1, 1942, Berlin. *Distributed by* Terra and subsequently by DFV (Deutsche Filmvertriebs G.m.b.H.), Berlin.

Hitlerjunge Quex. Ein Film vom Opfergeist der deutschen Jugend (Hitler Youth Quex/ Hitlerboy Quex)

1933. *Director:* Hans Steinhoff. *Producer:* Karl Ritter. *Location Manager:* Fritz Koch. *Screenplay:* Karl Aloys Schenzinger, Bobby E. Lüthge, based on the novel by K. A. Schenzinger. *Cinematographer:* Konstantin Irmen-Tschet. *Assistant Cameramen:* Fred Fernau, Erich Rudolf Schmidke. *Stills Photographer:*

Otto Schulz. *Music:* Hans-Otto Borgmann. *Lyrics and Patronage:* Baldur von Schirach, Reichsjugendführer. *Songs:* "Lied der Hitlerjugend: Unsere Fahne flattert uns voran"; "Die Internationale"; "Manchmal gelang die Sache" (street ballad); "Das ist die Liebe der Matrosen" (by Werner Richard Heymann). *Music Publisher:* Ufaton-Verlags G.m.b.H., Berlin. *Art Directors:* Benno von Arent, Artur Günther. *Make-Up Artist:* Waldemar Jabs. *Wardrobe:* Berta Grützmacher, Paul Haupt. *Sound:* Walter Tjaden, Erich Leistner. *Editor:* Milo Harbich.

Cast: Hitlerjunge Jürgen Ohlsen (Heini Völker, nicknamed Quex), Heinrich George (Father Völker), Berta Drews (Mother Völker), Hermann Speelmanns (Stoppel, functionary of the Communist Party), Rotraud Richter (Gerda), Claus Clausen (Kass, District Leader), Karl Meixner (Wilde), Hans Richter (Franz), Ernst Behmer (Kowalski, printer), Hans Joachim Büttner (physician), Franziska Kinz (Hospital Sister), Karl Hannemann (owner of food shop), Ernst Rotmund (police sergeant), Rudolf Platte (street ballad singer), Reinhold Bernt (announcer), Hans Deppe (second-hand dealer), Anna Müller-Lincke (a neighbor of Völkers'), Hans Otto Stern (landlord), Hitlermädchen Helga Bodemer (Ulla Doerries), Hitlerjunge Franz Ramspott (Fritz Doerries, *Kameradschaftsführer*), Hermann Braun, Heinz Trumper, boys and girls of the Berlin Hitler Youth.

Produced by Universum-Film A.-G., Berlin. *Production Group:* Karl Ritter. *Staatsauftragsfilm.* 35mm. *Laboratory:* Afifa. *Sound System:* Tobis Klangfilm. *Shooting:* July–August 1933. *Interiors:* Ufa Studios, Neubabelsberg. *Exteriors:* Berlin (Anhalter Bahnhof etc.) and Seddinsee near Berlin. *Premiere:* September 11, 1933, Munich (Phoebus-Palast); September 19, 1933, Berlin (Ufa-Palast am Zoo). *Budget:* RM 225,000. *Running time:* 95 minutes. *Distributed by* Universum-Filmverleih G.m.b.H. (Ufaleih), Berlin.

Der Höhere Befehl
(The Higher Command)

1935. *Director:* Gerhard Lamprecht. *Screenplay:* Philipp Lothar Mayring, Kurt Kluge, Karl Lerbs. *Cinematography:* Robert Baberske. *Music:* Werner Eisbrenner.

Cast: Lil Dagover, Karl Ludwig Diehl, Heli Finkenzeller, Friedrich Kayssler, Eduard von Winterstein, Aribert Wäscher, Hans Leibelt, Hans Mierendorff, Gertrud de Lalsky, Karl Dannemann, Siegfried Schürenberg, Günther Ballier, Gertrud Wolle, Walter Schramm-Duncker, Heinz Köneke, Friedrichfranz Stampe, Ernst Rückert, Armin Süssenguth, Otti Dietze, Ernst Behmer, Rudolf Biebrach, Volker von Collande, Gerhard Dammann, Robert Forsch, Karl Hannemann, Heinz Klockow, Leopold von Ledebur, Theodor Loos, Werner Pledath, Claire Reigbert, Berthold Reissig.

Produced by Universum-Film A.-G., Berlin. *Staatsauftragsfilm. Premiere:* December 30, 1935. *Distributed by* Universum-Filmverleih G.m.b.H. (Ufaleih), Berlin. *Subject:* Germany occupied by Napoleon's troops.

Ich für dich—Du für mich
(I for You—You for Me)

1934. *Director:* Carl Froelich. *Screenplay:* Hans G. Kernmayr. *Cinematography:* Emil Schünemann. *Music:* Hanson Milde-Meissner.

Cast: Maria Wanck, Inge Kick, Ruth Eweler, Ruth Claus, Karl Dannemann, Carl de Vogt, Knut Hartwig, Eleonore Stadie, Liselotte Wahl, Heinz Rippert, Paul W. Krüger, Katja Bennefeld, Hugo Froelich, Ernst Gronau, Emilie Unda, Toni Tetzlaff, Edna Greyff, Gisela Breiderhoff, Dolly Raphael, Inge Kadon.

Produced by Carl Froelich Filmproduktion G.m.b.H., Berlin *Premiere:* November 30, 1934, Berlin; Ufa-Theater Universum, Germania Palast, Picadilly, Alhambra. *Distributed by* Reichspropagandaleitung der NSDAP, Abteilung Film, Berlin. *Subject:* A women's Labour Corps camp.

Ich Klage An! (I Accuse!)

1940–41. *Producer-Director:* Wolfgang Liebeneiner. *Production Executive:* Ewald von Demandowsky. *Production Manager:* Dr. Heinrich Jonen. *Production Assistant:* Cay-Dietrich Voss. *Location Manager:* Kurt Moss. *Assistant Directors:* Peter Pewas, Hilde Vissering. *Screenplay:* Eberhard Frowein, Harald Bratt, inspired by the novel *Sendung und Gewissen* by Hellmuth Unger and an idea conceived by Harald Bratt. *Cinematography:* Friedl Behn-Grund. *Assistant Cameraman:* Franz von Klepacki. *Stills Photographer:* Eugen Klagemann. *Music:* Norbert Schultze. *Art Directors:* Fritz Maurischat, Fritz Lück. *Sound:* Herrmann Storr, Hans Grimm. *Medical Consultant:* Dr. Hellmuth Unger. *Legal Adviser:* Horstmann, prosecutor. *Editor:* Walter von Bonhorst.

Cast: Paul Hartmann (Prof. Thomas Heyt), Heidemarie Hatheyer (Hanna, his wife), Mathias Wiemann (Dr. Bernhard Lang), Margarethe Haagen (Berta), Harald Paulsen (Eduard Stretter), Charlotte Thiele (Dr. Barbara Burckhardt), Hans Nielsen (Dr. Höfer), Albert Florath (Prof. Schlüter), Curt Lukas (Klapper, medical officer), Hansi Arnstaedt (Mrs. Klapper), Werner Pledath (Görner, parson), Franz Schafheitlin (Stranten, lawyer), Karin Evans (Erna Balg), Christian Kayssler (Kriebelmeyer), Just Scheu (Dr. Scheu), Leopold von Ledebur (Knevels, judge at regional court), Otto Graf (Engel, attorney at law), Franz Weber (Rehefeld, forester), Ernst Sattler (Major retd. Döring), Helmut Bergmann (Rohlfs, locksmith), Bernhard Goetzke (Zienecke, ancestral estate farmer), Karl Haubenreisser (Schönbrunn, Studienrat/high school teacher), Wilhelm P. Krüger (Rummel, drugist), Erich Ponto (Professor), Wolfgang Osterholz, Dr. Peters, Harry Hardt, Hintz Fabricius, Willi Rose, Helmut Kollek, Werner Siegert, Hans Ulrich Bach, Ernst Legal, Erich Ziegel, Hans Meyer-Hanno, Gertrud Roloff, Eva Blut, Carla Werner, Barbara Clemen, Else Mentel, Karl Dannemann, Lisl Eckhardt, Rudolf Vones, Crosse, Frau von Rüths, Else Gründling, Jürgen Gründling, Grete Greef, Käthe Kamossa, Gertrud Maria Kai, Ilse Fürstenberg, Kurt Dremel, Roswitha Koennecke, Paul Rehkopf, Kurt Mikulski, Keller-Nebri, Gisela Morgen, Frau Hauff, Walter Janssen.

Produced by Tobis Filmkunst G.m.b.H., Berlin. *Staatsauftragsfilm.* 35mm. *Laboratoy:* Geyer. *Sound System:* Tobis Klangfilm. *Interiors:* Jofa Studios, Berlin-Johannisthal. *Running time:* 125 minutes. *Budget:* RM 960,000. *Premiere:* August 29, 1941. *Distributed by* Tobis Filmverleih G.m.b.H., Berlin.

Im Kampf gegen den Weltfeind (At War with the World's Enemy)

1939. *Producer-Director:* Karl Ritter. *Screenplay:* Werner Beumelburg. *Cinematography:* Heinz Ritter, Eberhard von der Heyden, Walter Hrich, Herbert Lander. *Assistant Cameraman:* Conrad Fischer. *Music:* Herbert Windt. *Military Advisers:* Major Graf Fugger, Lt. Philipps. *Editor:* Berndt von Tyszka. *Editorial Assistant:* Lore Seitz. *Narrators:* Paul Hartmann, Rolf Wernicke.

Produced by Universum-Film A.-G., Berlin. 35mm. *Laboratory:* Afifa. *Running time:* 94 minutes. *Premiere:* June 15, 1939, Berlin, Ufa-Palast am Zoo. *Distributed by* Universum Filmverleih G.m.b.H. (Ufaleih), Berlin.

Im Trommelfeuer der Westfront (Constant Barrage of the Western Front)

1935–36. *Director:* Charles Willy Kayser. *Screenplay:* E. H. Raven, Lille Raven-Kraatz (prologue). *Cinematography:* Günther Anders. *Music:* Karl Buchholz.

Cast: Ernst Rückert, Viggo Larsen, Paul Rehkopf, Kurt Felden, Valy Arnheim, Max Hochstetter, R. Vincenti-Lieffertz, Hellmuth Passarge, Hermann Mayer-Falkow, W. Tholen, Emmerich Hanus, Josef Peterhans, Otz Tollen, G. Schmidt-Rudow, Max Vierlinger, Ernst Rückert, Max Moll, Erwin van Roy.

Produced and distributed by Filmverleih Richard Herzog & Co. 35mm. *Premiere:* March 6, 1936. Mainly compiled from authentic footage from World War I.

Jakko

1941. *Director:* Fritz Peter Buch. *Assistant Director:* Alfons von Plessen. *Producer:* Herbert Engelsing. *Location Manager:* Heinz Landsmann. *Screenplay:* Fritz Peter Buch, based on the novel *Jakko* by Alfred Weidenmann. *Cinematography:* Paul Rischke. *Music:* Hans-Otto Borgmann. *Lyrics:* Hans Fritz Beckmann, Hein Meiswinkel. *Art Directors:* Robert Dietrich, Karl Böhm. *Costume Consultant:* Eva Lemke. *Sound:* Martin Müller, Gerhard Froboes. *Consulting Official of Navy Hitler Youth:* Hans Loewer. *Shooting crew members:* Paul Görgens, Joe Rive. *Editors:* Lisbeth Neumann, Waldemar Goede.

Cast: Norbert Rohringer (Jakko), Eugen Klöpfer (Anton), Aribert Wäscher (Zaballo), Albert Florath (Schröder, ship's owner), Ali Ghito (Mrs. Schröder), Rüdiger Trantow (Jochen Schröder), Inge Cupei (Sybille Schröder), Carsta Löck (Rosa, maid), Hilde Körber (Aunt Klinkhardt), Armin Schweizer (Buske, administrator), Gerhard Hüfner (Kurt Buske), Heddo Schulenburg (Albert, Jochen's friend), Hans Meyer-Hanno (chauffeur at Schröder's), Paul Verhoeven (Kohler, teacher), Walter Werner (janitor at school), Ewald Wenck (glazier), Paul Westermeier (Stupat), Bettina Hambach (Petja), Trude Hesterberg (soubrette), Ernst Legal (detective superintendent), Lutz Götz (police officer), Gerhard Kreisler (crane-operator), Manfred Leber (captain), Rolf Storch (leader of Navy Hitler Youth), Erich Dunskus, Eduard Wenck, Paul Rehkopf, Harry Hardt, Hans Mierendorff, Eva-Maria Meier, Ilse Scheffels, Inge Schlenker, Ursula Zell, Wilhelm Grosse, Hans-Heinz Wunderlich, Käthe Jöken-König, Franz Berghaus, Günther Clemm, Horst Rittberger, Martin Affelt, Berlin pupils of elementary school, Navy Hitler Youth, Danzig.

Produced by Tobis Filmkunst G.m.b.H., Berlin. *Production Group:* Herbert Engelsing. *Staatsauftragsfilm.* 35mm. *Laboratory:* Geyer. *Sound System:* Tobis Klangfilm. *Interiors:* Jofa Studios, Berlin-Johannisthal. *Premiere:* October 12, 1941. *Distributed by* Tobis Filmverleih G.m.b.H., Berlin.

Jud Süss (Jew Süss)

1939–40. *Director:* Veit Harlan. *Production Supervisors:* Dr. Peter Paul Brauer, Alf Teichs. *Production Manager:* Otto Lehmann. *Location Managers:* Conny Carstennsen (a.k.a. Friedrich Wirth), Herbert Sennewald, Kurt Moos. *Screenplay:* Veit Harlan, Eberhard Wolfgang Möller, Ludwig Metzger. *Scenario Editor:* Wolfgang von Gordon. *Assistant Directors:* Wolfgang Schleif, Alfred Braun. *Cinematography:* Bruno Mondi. *Stills Photographers:* Erich Kilian, Karl Ewald. *Music:* Wolfgang Zeller. *Art Directors:* Otto Hunte, Karl Vollbrecht. *Costume Designer:* Ludwig Hornsteiner (Grosses Schauspielhaus Berlin). *Costumes supplied by* Theaterkunst G.m.b.H. Berlin and Kostümhaus Verch Berlin. *Lighting:* Fritz Kühne. *Sound:* Gustav Bellers. *Choreography:* Sabine Ress. *Art Titles:* Trickatelier Radius. *Editors:* Friedrich Karl von Puttkammer, Wolfgang Schleif.

Cast: Ferdinand Marian (Jud Süss Oppenheimer), Heinrich George (Duke Karl Alexander), Hilde von Stolz (his wife), Werner Krauss (Rabbi Loew/Levy, Süss' secretary), Eugen Klöpfer (Sturm), Kristina Söderbaum (Dorothea Sturm, his daughter), Malte Jaeger (Aktuarius Faber, Dorothea's fiancé), Albert Florath (Röder), Theodor Loss (von Remchingen), Walter Werner (Fiebelkorn), Charlotte Schulz (Mrs. Fiebelkorn), Anny Seitz (Minchen Fiebelkorn), Ilse Buhl (Friederike Fiebelkorn), Jacob Tiedtke (consistory councilor), Erna Morena (his wife), Else Elster (Luziana, Süss' mistress), Emil Hess (Hans Bogner, blacksmith), Käte Jöken-König (his wife), Ursula Deinert (prima ballerina), Erich Dunskus (master of blacksmith guild), Otto Henning (chairman of the jury), Heinrich Schroth (von Neuffer), Hannelore Benzinger (Sturm's maid), Ingeborg Albert, Annette Bach, Irmgard Völker, Valy Arnheim, Franz Arzdorf, Walter Bechmann, Fred Becker, Reinhold Bernt, Louis Brody, Wilhelm Egger-Sell, Franz Eschle, Hans Eysenhardt, Bernhard Goetzke, Georg Gürtler, Oskar Höcker, Karl Iban, Willi Kayser-Heil, Franz Klebusch, Otto Klopsch,

Erich Lange, Horst Lommer, Richard Ludwig, Paul Mederow, Hans Meyer-Hanno, Arnim Münch, Edgar Nollert, Helmuth Passarge, Josef Peterhans, Friedrich Petermann, Edmund Pouch, Arthur Reinhardt, Wolfgang Staudte, Ernst Stimmel, Walter Tarrach, Otz Tollen, Max Vierlinger, Hans Waschatko, Eduard Wenk, Otto Wollmann.

Produced and distributed by Terra-Filmkunst G.m.b.H., Berlin. *Production Group:* Otto Lehmann. *Staatsauftragsfilm.* 35mm. *Interiors:* Ufastadt Babelsberg; Barrandov, Prague, March 15, 1940–end of June 1940. *Budget:* RM 2,081,000. *Running time:* 97 minutes. *Premiere:* September 9, 1940, Venice; September 24, 1940, Berlin, Ufa-Palast am Zoo.

Junge Adler (Young Eagles)

1943–44. *Director:* Alfred Weidenmann. *Assistant Directors:* Carl von Merznicht, Zlata Mehlers. *Producer:* Hans Schönmetzler. *Location Managers:* Victor Eisenbach, Arndt Liebster, Kurt Paetz. *Screenplay:* Herbert Reinecker, Alfred Weidenmann, from an idea conceived by Herbert Reinecker. *Cinematography:* Klaus von Rautenfeld. *Music:* Hans-Otto Borgmann. *Art Directors:* Wilhelm Vorwerg, Rudolf Linnekogel. *Costumes:* Vera Mügge. *Sound:* Ernst Walter. *Editor:* Walter Wischniewsky.

Cast: Willy Fritsch (Roth, chief instructor), Herbert Hübner (Director Brakke), Dietmar Schönherr (Theo Brakke), Gerta Böttcher (Annemie Brakke), Albert Florath (Father Stahl), Karl Dannemann (Bachus, master craftsman), Aribert Wäscher (Zacharias, coffee-house owner), Paul Henckels (Dr. Voss), Josef Sieber (Martin, pilot), Fritz Hoopts (Fischer), Alfred Maack (store-room administrator), Karl Hellmer (Kalubbe, music shop owner), Wolfgang Keppler (physical education teacher), Peter Schäfer (fat person), Gunnar Möller (Spatz, apprentice), Eberhard [Hardy] Krüger (Bäumchen, apprentice), Manfred Schrott (Otto, apprentice), Robert Filippowitz (Wolfgang Kalubbe, apprentice), Klaus Stahl (Friedel, apprentice), Harald Behrend (Rolf, apprentice), Joachim Möbus (Borst, apprentice), Arnfried Gomm (swot), Heinrich Schmidt (apprentice), apprentices of an aircraft factory.

Produced by Ufa-Filmkunst G.m.b.H., Berlin. *Staatsauftragsfilm.* 35mm. *Laboratory:* Afifa. *Interiors:* Ufa-Atelier Berlin-Tempelhof, Froelich-Studio Berlin-Tempelhof, Ufastadt Babelsberg. *Exteriors:* Warnemünde. *Shooting:* September 8, 1943–beginning of April 1944 (?). *Budget:* RM 1,779,600. *Running time:* 107 minutes. *Premiere:* May 24, 1944, Berlin, Titania-Palast, Tauentzien-Palast, and U.T. Weissensee. *Distributed by* DFV (Deutsche Filmvertriebs G.m.b.H.), Berlin.

Jungens (Boys)

1940–41. *Director:* Robert A. Stemmle. *Producer:* Eberhard Schmidt. *Location Manager:* Herbert Junghanns. *Assistant Director:* Fritz Andelfinger. *Screenplay:* Otto Bernhard Wendler, Horst Kerutt, Robert A. Stemmle, from the novel *Die dreizehn Jungens von Dünendorf* by Horst Kerutt. *Cinematography:* Robert Baberske. *Music:* Werner Egk. *Assisted by* Ludwig Preiss. *Lyrics:* Hans Fritz Beckmann. *Art Directors:* Emil Hasler, Otto Gülstorff. *Sound:* Erich Schmidt. *Editor:* Walter Wischniewsky.

Cast: Albert Hehn (Hellmut Gründel), Hilde Sessak (Lene), Eduard Wandrey (Ottokar Waschke, landlord), Kurt Fischer-Fehling (Krüger, youth leader), Eduard Wenck (Albert Faustmann, dune guard), Maria Hofen (Frau Faustmann), Bruni Löbel (Anne-Liese Gründel), Botho Kayser (Hartmann, Bannführer), Rudolf Koch-Riehl (Franz, driver), Georg Thomalla (Jochen Krafft), Franz Bochum, Conrad Cappi, Wilhelm Grosse, Hugo Gau-Hamm, Gerhard Jeschke, Karl Junge-Swinburne, Wilhelm König, Philipp Manning, Maria Michael, Lili Schoenborn, Erhart Stettner, Ulrich Strelow, Wolfgang Staudte, Eva Steffen, Gisela Scholz, Reinhold Weiglin, Sepp Rederer, Hitler Youth of Adolf Hitler Schools in Sonthofen (Heini Faustmann and other boys).

Produced by Universum-Film A-.G., Berlin. *Production Group:* Eberhard Schmidt.

Staatsauftragsfilm. 35mm. *Laboratory:* Afifa. *Interiors:* Ufastadt Babelsberg. *Exteriors:* Kurische Nehrung [Kurland sand-bar]. *Shooting:* September–December 1940. *Running time:* 87 minutes. *Premiere:* May 2, 1941, Berlin, Tauentzien-Palast, U.T. Friedrich-strasse, Atrium. *Distributed by* Universum Filmverleih G.m.b.H. (Ufaleih), Berlin.

Kadetten (Cadets)

1939–41. *Producer-Director:* Karl Ritter. *Location Manager:* Ludwig Kühr. *Assistant Director:* Gottfried Ritter. *Screenplay:* Felix Lützkendorf, Karl Ritter, based on historical facts suggested by Alfons Menne. *Cinematography:* Günther Anders. *Stills Photographer:* Ferdinand Rotzinger. *Music:* Herbert Windt. *Art Director:* Walter Röhrig. *Wardrobe:* Gisela Bornkessel, Paul Haupt. *Make-Up Artists:* Adolf Arnold, Wilhelm Weber. *Sound:* Heinz Martin, Günther Bellers. *Editor:* Gottfried Ritter.

Cast: Mathias Wiemann (Rittmeister von Tzülow), Carsta Löck (Sophie, kitchen help), Andrews Engelmann (Colonel Goroschew, Cossack leader), Theo Shall (Captain Jupow), Josef Keim (Sergeant Schönbrunn), Erich Walter (General Count Tschernitschew), Willi Kayser-Heyl (General von Buddenbrock), Wilhelm Krüger (engineer major), Lydia Li (Russian singer), Bernd Russbült (Bork, cadet), Klaus Detlef Sierck (Hohenhausen, cadet), Martin Brendel (Schack, cadet), Jürgen Mohrbutter (Potron, cadet), Rolf Ullmann-Schienle (Jordan, cadet), Hans-Otto Gauglitz (Lampe, cadet), Gert Witt (Tiesenhausen, cadet), Klaus Storch (Raden, cadet), boys from Nationalpolitische Erziehungsanstalt Potsdam, Nico Turoff, Dieckmann, Marschneck, Corvin, Franz Jan Korssak, Kurt Hagen.

Produced by Universum-Film A.-G., Berlin. *Production Group:* Karl Ritter. *Staatsauftragsfilm.* 35mm. *Laboratory:* Afifa. *Shooting:* April 3–beginninig of June, 1939. *Interiors:* Ufastadt Babelsberg. *Exteriors:* surroundings of Berlin, backlot Babelsberg. *Running time:* 94 minutes. *Premiere:* December 2, 1941, Danzig, Ufa-Palast; December 18, 1941,

Berlin, Ufa-Palast am Zoo. Original premiere was scheduled in August 1939, but release was stopped for reasons of Hitler-Stalin pact.

Kameraden auf See (Comrades at Sea)

1938. *Director:* Heinz Paul. *Screenplay:* Peter Francke, J. A. Zerbe, from an idea conceived by Toni Huppertz and J. A. Zerbe. *Cinematography:* Hans Schneeberger. *Music:* Robert Küssel.

Cast: Paul Wagner, Fred Döderlein, Rolf Weih, Carola Höhn, Ingeborg Hertel, Theodor Loss, Jaspar von Oertzen, Julius Brandt, Josef Sieber, Heinrich Schroth, Angelo Ferrari, Reinhold Bernt, Hans Kettler, Albert Hahn, Günther Vogdt, Theo Brandt, Ferry Reich, Ernst Behmer, Maria Seidler, Gustav Püttjer, Kurt Iller, Hans Huber, Josef Peterhans.

Produced by Wölffer-Film/Terra-Filmkunst G.m.b.H., Berlin. *Staatsauftragsfilm.* *Premiere:* March 12, 1938. *Distributed by* Terra-Filmverleih G.m.b.H., Berlin. *Subject:* Another torpedo boat love story. Background: Spanish Civil War.

Kampfgeschwader Lützow (Fighting Squadron Lützow)

1940–41. *Producer-Director:* Hans Bertram. *Production Manager:* Robert Wuellner. *Location Managers:* Karl Buchholz, Karl Gillmore. *Assistant Directors:* Rudolf Hilborg, Fritz Wendel. *Screenplay:* Hans Bertram, Wolf Neumeister. *Collaboration Treatment:* Heinz Orlovius. *Cinematography:* Georg Krause. *Aerial Cinematography:* Heinz von Jaworsky, Walter Rosskopf. *Stills Photographer:* Josef Höfer. *Music:* Norbert Schultze. *Art Directors:* Otto Moldenhauer, Franz Bi. *Special Photographic Effects:* Ernst Kunstmann. *Sound:* Erich Lange. *Military Advisers for Luftwaffe:* General der Flieger Schweickhard and Major Lüpke; *for Waffen-SS:* Standartenführer Bittrich; *for Inspektion der Schnellen Truppen:* Captain Neubeck; *for Navy:* Korvetten-Kapitän Hashagen. *Editor:* Ella Ensink.

Cast: Christian Kayssler (Lieutenant Colonel Mithoff), Hermann Braun (Eckard, non-commissioned officer), Heinz Welzel (non-commissioned officer Paulsen), Hannes Keppler (Guggemos, non-commissioned officer), Marietheres Angerpointner (Grete Kubath), Carsta Löck (Lina Zeisler), Adolf Fischer (Zeisler, non-commissioned officer), Horst Birr (Hasinger, lance corporal), Kurt vom Hofe (Private Hellweg), Peter Voss (Major Hagen), Dr. Ernst Stimmel (Lehwald, teacher), O. K. Kinne (first lieutenant Körner, adjutant), Rudolf Vones (Captain Pebal), Hans Bergmann (Richards, non-commissioned officer), Curt Pflug (Private Christoff), Horst Rossius (Hans Kubath).

Produced by Tobis Filmkunst G.m.b.H., Berlin (supported by the German Wehrmacht, Luftwaffe and Navy). *Production Group:* Hans Bertram. *Staatsauftragsfilm.* 35mm. *Laboratory:* Geyer. *Sound System:* Tobis Klangfilm. *Interiors:* Jofa Studios, Berlin-Johannisthal. *Premiere:* February 28, 1941. *Distributed by* Tobis Filmverleih G.m.b.H., Berlin.

Kolberg

1943–44. *Director:* Veit Harlan. *Screenplay:* Veit Harlan and Alfred Braun (with uncredited input by Thea von Harbou and Dr. Paul Joseph Goebbels). *Executive Producer:* Wolfgang Liebeneiner. *Line Producer:* Wilhelm Sperber. *Location Managers:* Conny Carstennsen (a.k.a. Friedrich Wirth) and Rudolf Fichtner. *Assistant Director:* Wolfgang Schleif. *Cinematography:* Bruno Mondi. *Second Camera:* Gerhard Huttula. *Assistant Cameraman:* Heinz Pehlke. *Lighting:* Fritz Kühne. *Agfacolor Consultant:* Kurt Exner. *Music:* Norbert Schultze. *Art Directors:* Erich Zander, Karl Machus. *Sound:* Hermann Storr. *Explosives:* Erwin Lange. *Editor:* Wolfgang Schleif.

Cast: Heinrich George (Joachim Nettelbeck), Kristina Söderbaum (Maria), Horst Caspar (Gneisenau), Paul Wegener (von Loucadou), Gustav Diessl (Ferdinand von Schill), Otto Wernicke (Farmer Werner), Claus Clausen (Friedrich Wilhelm III), Irene von Meyendorff (Luise, Queen of Prussia), Kurt Meisel (Claus), Jaspar von Oertzen (Prince Louis Ferdinand), Jakob Tiedtke (Goldow, shipowner), Hans-Herrmann Schaufuss (Zaufke), Paul Bildt (Headmaster), Franz Schafheitlin (Fanselow), Charles Schauten (Emperor Napoleon I), Heinz Lausch (Friedrich), Paul Henckels (major in Königsberg), Franz Herterich (Emperor Franz II), Greta Schröder-Wegener (Mrs. von Voss), Fritz Hoopts (Timm), Werner Scharf (General Teulié), Theo Schall (General Loison), Josef Dahmen (Franz), Margarete Schön (housekeeper), Herbert A. E. Böhme (Walkow), Hermann Stetza (stunt rider), Herbert Klatt, André Saint-Germain, Inge Drexel, Betty Wald.

Produced by Ufa-Filmkunst G.m.b.H., Berlin. *Production Group* "Veit Harlan." *Staatsauftragsfilm.* 35mm. *Shooting:* October 22, 1943–August 1944. *Interiors:* Ufa-Stadt Babelsberg. *Exteriors:* Kolberg, Königsberg, Neustettin and Berlin (Gross-Glienicke, Staaken). *Laboratory:* Afifa. *Color by* Agfacolor. *Budget:* RM 8,800,000. *Running time:* 111 minutes. *Premiere:* January 30, 1945, La Rochelle; Berlin, Tauentzien Palast. *Distributed by* DFV (Deutsche Filmvertriebs G.m.b.H.), Berlin.

Kopf Hoch, Johannes (Chin Up, Johannes)

1940–41. *Director:* Victor de Kowa. *Production Manager:* Conrad Flockner. *Assistant Director:* Praefke. *Screenplay:* Toni Huppertz, Wilhelm Krug, Felix von Eckardt, from an idea conceived by Toni Huppertz. *Cinematography:* Friedl Behn-Grund. *Assistant Cameraman:* Franz von Klepacki. *Music:* Harald Böhmelt. *Art Directors:* Emil Hasler, Arthur Schwarz. *Sound:* Rütten. *NPEA consultant:* Skroblin. *Editor:* Lena Neumann.

Cast: Albrecht Schoenhals (Von Redel), Dorothea Wieck (Julietta), Claus Detlef Sierck (Johannes), Leo Peukert (Don Pedro), Karl Dammann (Father Panse), Renée Stobrawa (Mother Panse), Hans Zesch-Ballott (superintendent), Volker von Collande (Dr. Angermann), Rudolf Vones (Kröger, youth leader), Karl Fochler (physician), Wilfried Behrens (leader of a group of hundred), Werner Drohsin (educator), Karl Heitmann (postman), Otto Gebühr (Perlow, servant), Eduard von Winterstein (inspector), Franz Weber (secretary), Gabi [Gabriele] Hoffmann (nurse), Gunnar Möller (Panse), Jürgen Jacob [NPEA. Spandau] (Vorwerk), Günther Leckebusch [NPEA. Spandau] (Dähnke), Harald Föhr-Waldeck (Stadtler), Horst Rittberger (Stolk), von Wechmer [NPEA. Spandau] (Casner) as *Jungmannen* (young men), Christa Grunwald (Panse's first sister), Dagmar Sörensen (Panse's second sister), Eva Zipfel (Panse's third sister), Hans Joachim Zell.

Produced by Majestic-Film, Mülleneisen & Tapper, Berlin. *Staatsauftragsfilm.* 35mm. *Premiere:* March 11, 1941. D*istributed by* Tobis Filmverleih G.m.b.H., Berlin. [Originally announced and pre-released in the season 1939-40.]

Das Leben Geht Weiter (Life Goes On)

1945. *Director:* Wolfgang Liebeneiner. *Producer:* Karl Ritter. *Location Manager:* Heinz Fiebig. *Second Location Manager:* Harry Grünwald. *Assistant Location Manager:* Karl-Franz Roell. *Production Secretary:* Hilde Sonntag. *Assistant Director:* Rudolf Steinboeck. *Director Volontary:* Robert Mischler. *Screenplay:* Gerhard Menzel, Thea von Harbou, Wolfgang Liebeneiner, Karl Ritter. *Treatment:* Kurt Frowein, Hans Heinrich Henne, Gerhard Weise, from an idea conceived by Dr. Joseph Goebbels. *Cinematography:* Günther Anders. *Assistant Cameraman:* Karl Heinz Leiter. *Second Camera:* Hans Fehdmer. *Stills Photography:* Lars Looschen. *Lighting:* Wilhelm Levy, Otto Rösecke, Ludwig Bachmann, Heinrich Hövermann, Karl Lehmann. *Music:* Norbert Schultze. *Lyrics:* Kurt E. Walther. *Sung by* Peter Igelhoff. *Art Director:* Toni Weber. *Second Art Director:* Hans Ender. *Prop Master* (*Exteriors*): Emil Freude. *Prop Masters* (*Interiors*): Erich Schulze, Kurt Leux. *Process Cinematography:* Gerhard Huttula. *Special Photography:* Heinz von Ja-

worsky. *Assistant Special Cameraman:* Heinz Pehlke. *Explosives:* Erwin Lange. *Costumes:* Reingart Voigt. *Wardrobe:* Fritz Schilling, Hugo Kruse, Luise Leder. *Make-Up Artists* (*Gentlemen*): Arnold Jensen, Adolf Arnold. *Make-Up Artists* (*Ladies*): Lotte Kersten, Cilly Didzoneit. *Sound:* Gustav Bellers. *Sound Assistants:* Werner Krubsack, Christian Bender. *Script Girl:* Charlotte Kalinke. *Editor:* Wolfgang Wehrum. *Assistant Editor:* Dr. Eva Kalthoff.

Cast: Gustav Knuth (Ewald Martens), Hilde Krahl (Christl/Gundel Martens), Marianne Hoppe (Renate/Leonore Carius), Viktor de Kowa (Walter Hoesslin), Heinrich George (director of an armament factory), Friedrich Kayssler (Professor Hübner), Will Dohm (Rudi Winkler), Ursula Grabley (Ursel Winkler), Lina Lossen (Mrs. Carius), Gustav Bertram (Butzke, caretaker), Hans Neie (Heinz Butzke), Karl Schönböck (Axel Aressen), Gisa Wurm (Anna, maid), Viktoria von Ballasko (Mrs. Kolling), Oskar Sabo (Appel, driver), Carsta Löck (Mrs. Mielke), Paul Henckels (privy councilor), Hilde Körber (wounded woman), Franz Schafheitlin (Professor Brenkemann), Erich Fiedler (Dr. Fischer), Jaspar von Oertzen (Dr. Steuck), Karl Mathias (Dr. Sedlmayer), Otto Stöckl (Falk, personnel manager), Kurt Mikulski (Kniesche, master craftsman), Wolf Harro (assistant), Ernst Karchow (*general*), Jürgen Peter Jacoby (Werner Martens), Karin Korth (Moni Martens), Else Ehser (woman in stairwell), Otto Mathies (impudent Berlin citizen), Maria Rubach (Mrs. Brenkemann), Maria von Hoesslin (Mrs. Sedlmayer), Waltraud Kogel (Edith, girlfriend), Harald Holberg (Edith's dancer), Kurt Lucas (first lieutenant), Wolf Trutz (engineer), Franz Weber (station master), Wilhelm Grosse (snap switch), Maria Zidek-Meck (snap switch), Wera Schultz (assistant), Lilly Schönborn (1st ticket office clerk), Liesel [Luise] Bethge-Zitzmann (2nd ticket office clerk), Heinrich Troxbömker (worker at switch-tower), Siegfried Niemann (railroad worker), Knuth Hartwig (policeman), Ludwig Schröder (policeman), Käthe Jöken-König, W. Erich Parge, Herbert Hübner, Walter Pech, Ernst

Legal, Gisela Breiderhoff, Walter Werner, Nina Raven-Zoch.

Produced by Ufa-Filmkunst G.m.b.H., Berlin. 35mm. *Shooting:* November 20, 1944–April 16, 1945. *Interiors:* Ufastadt Babelsberg. *Exteriors:* Lüneburg Heath. Film was not finished.

Legion Condor

1939. *Producer-Director:* Karl Ritter avec la collaboration de General der Flieger Wilberg. *Location Manager:* Ludwig Kühr. *Assistant Director:* Gottfried Ritter. *Screenplay:* Felix Lützkendorf, Karl Ritter. *Cinematography:* Günther Anders. *Aerial Cinematography:* Heinz von Jaworsky. *Stills Photographer:* Josef Klietsch. *Music:* Herbert Windt. *Art Director:* Walter Röhrig. *Wardrobe:* Gisela Bornkessel, Paul Haupt. *Make-Up Artists:* Wilhelm Weber, Adolf Arnold. *Sound:* Heinz Martin. *Editor:* Gottfried Ritter.

Cast: Paul Hartmann, Albert Hehn, Heinz Welzel, Herbert A. E. Böhme, Otto Graf, Karl John, Wolfgang Staudte, Fritz Kampers, Josef Dahmen, Willi Rose, Carsta Löck, Marina von Ditmar, Lili Schoenborn, Karl Klüsner, Friedrich Gnass, Andrews Engelmann, Malte Jäger, Franz Jan Kossak, Lutz Götz, Lothar Körner, Lea Niako, Ernst von Klipstein, Ernst Bader, Ursula Ulrich, Ruth Nimbach, Irene Fischer.

Produced by Universum-Film A.-G., Berlin. *Production Group:* Karl Ritter. 35mm. *Laboratory:* Afifa. *Interiors:* Ufastadt Babelsberg. *Production started* on August 7, 1939. Production was shelved on September 1, 1939.

Leinen aus Irland (Linen from Ireland)

1939. *Director:* Heinz Herbig. *Production Manager:* Heinrich Haas. *Screenplay:* Harald Bratt, adapted from a comedy by Stephan von Kamare. *Cinematography:* Hans Schneeberger. *Music:* Anton Profes. *Editor:* Margarethe Steinberg.

Cast: Otto Tressler (Kommerzialrat Kettner, president, Libussa A.-G.), Irene von Meyendorff (Lilly, his daughter), Friedl Haerlin (Mrs. von Gebhardt), Oskar Sima (minister), Hans Olden (von Kalinski, ministerial official), Maria Olszewska (Mrs. von Kalinski), Anny Kupfner (Wanda von Kalinski), Tibor von Halmay (Count Horvath von Genyesfalva), Georg Alexander (Baron von Falk-Prennwiel), Rolf Wanka (Dr. Goll, ministerial secretary), Siegfried Breuer (Dr. Kuhn, secretary general, Libussa A.-G.), Fritz Imhoff (Sigi Pollack), Ernst Arnold (Dr. Seligmann, corporation lawyer, Libussa A.-G.), Karl Skraup (Alois Hubermaier), Oskar Wegrostek (Wenzel, weaver), Karl Kneidinger (Bieringer, Hubermaier's accountant).

Produced by Styria-Film, Vienna. *Staatsauftragsfilm.* 35mm. *Budget:* RM 744,000. *Premiere:* October 16, 1939, Berlin. *Distributed by* Bavaria-Filmkunst G.m.b.H., Munich.

Liebesgeschichten (Love Stories)

1942–43. *Director:* Viktor Tourjansky. *Screenplay:* Gustav Kampendonk freely adapted from the novel by Walter Lieck. *Cinematography:* Igor Oberberg. *Music:* Peter Kreuder.

Cast: Willy Fritsch, Hannelore Schroth, Hertha Mayen, Elisabeth Flickenschildt, Paul Henckels, Käthe Dyckhoff, Joachim Brennecke, Walter Franck, Norbert Rohringer, Eduard Wenck, Erna Sellmer, Franz Schafheitlin, Rolf Prasch, Käthe Jöken-König, Willi Rose, Oscar Sabo, Ursula Voss, Hellmuth Helsig, Willi Puhlmann, Hans Joachim Funk, Paul Esser, Helga Meinel, Josef Lerch, Meta Weber, Maria Zidek, Hans Waschatko, Hans Meyer-Hanno, Fredy Rolf.

Produced by Ufa-Filmkunst G.m.b.H., Berlin. *Staatsauftragsfilm. Premiere:* March 3, 1943, Leipzig; May 27, 1943, Berlin. *Distributed by* DFV, Berlin. *Subject:* Berlin family saga, 1890–1930.

Mann für Mann
(Man by Man)

1938. *Director:* Robert Adolf Stemmle. *Assistant Director:* Boleslaw Barlog. *Producer:* Eberhard Schmidt. *Location Manager:* Horst Kyrath. *Screenplay:* Robert Adolf Stemmle, Hans Schmodde, O. B. Wendler. *Cinematography:* Robert Baberske. *Music:* Friedrich Schröder. *Art Directors:* Otto Hunte, Karl Vollbrecht. *Sound:* Ernst Otto Hoppe. *Editor:* Milo Harbich.

Cast: Josef Sieber (Richard Gauter), Gustav Knuth (Walter Zügel), Carl Kuhlmann (Hans Riemann), Heinz Welzel (Werner Handrup), Hermann Speelmans (Peter Klune), Toni Sepp Stohr (Alois Wille), Walter Lieck (Karl Biermann), Peter Elsholtz (Otto Sens), Erich Oswald Peters (Willi Haeckelt), Viktoria von Ballasko (Else Zügel, Walter Zügel's wife), Gisela Uhlen (Erika Bartels), Eduard Wenck (Father Bartels), Annemarie Holtz (Mother Bartels), Ellen Bang (Anna Jasgulka, barmaid), Lina Carstens (Werner Handrup's mother), Paul Schwed (camp commander), Oskar Höcker (foreman), Johannes Barthel (caisson technician), Fritz Hube (lock-keeper), Dr. Gerhard Jeschke (engineer), Fritz Claudius (cook), Arnim Schweizer (first-aid man), Kurt Waitzmann (physician).

Produced by Universum-Film A.-G., Berlin. *Production Group:* Eberhard Schmidt. *Staatsauftragsfilm.* 35mm. *Laboratory:* Afifa. *Sound System:* Tobis Klangfilm. *Distributed by* Universum Filmverleih G.m.b.H. (Ufaleih), Berlin.

Ein Mann Will nach Deutschland (A Man Wants to Reach Germany)

1934. *Director:* Paul Wegener. *Screenplay:* Philipp Lothar Mayring, Fred Andreas, from the novel by Fred Andreas. *Cinematography:* Fritz Arno Wagner. *Music:* Hans-Otto Borgmann.

Cast: Karl Ludwig Diehl, Brigitte Horney, Siegfried Schürenberg, Ernst Rotmund, Hermann Speelmans, Charlotte Schultz, Hans Leibelt, Willy Birgel, Hans Zesch-Ballot, Willi Schur, Ludwig Trautmann, Günther Hadank, Gerhard Bienert, Gustav Püttjer, Else Reval, Ernst Behmer, Aribert Mog, Harry Hardt, Richard Glahn, Paul Hildebrand, Max Hiller, Erich Harden, Werner Schott, Hans Spielberg.

Produced by Universum-Film A.-G., Berlin. *Production Group:* Bruno Duday. *Staatsauftragsfilm. Premiere:* July 26, 1934, Berlin, Ufa-Palast am Zoo. *Distributed by* Universum Filmverleih G.m.b.H. (Ufaleih), Berlin. *Subject:* Escape drama of two Germans, interned in a prison camp on Jamaica during World War I.

Mein Leben für Irland
(My Life for Ireland)

1941. *Director:* Max Wilhelm Kimmich. *Producer:* Dr. Engelsing. *Screenplay:* Toni Huppertz, Max Wilhelm Kimmich. *Cinematography:* Richard Angst. *Stills Photographer:* Karl Ewald. *Music:* Alois Melichar. *Art Directors:* Otto Erdmann, Willy Depenau. *Sound:* Dr. Claus Jungk.

Cast: Anna Dammann (Maeve Fleming), Werner Hinz (Michael O'Brien the older), Will Quadflieg (Michael O'Brien the younger), René Deltgen (Robert Devoy), Eugen Klöpfer (Duffy), Lucie Millowitsch (Duffy's wife), Paul Wegener (Sir George Beverley), Karl Dannemann (Richard Sullivan), Heinz Ohlsen (Patrick O'Connor), Friedrich Maurer (Thomas Byrne), Claus Clausen (Patrick Pallock), Karl John (Raymond David), Siegfried Drost (Emmet Doyle), Walter Werner (parson), Ernst Wilhelm Borchert (Thomas O'Neill), Odo Krohmann (Liam O'Toole), Axel Monjè (Colman Barry), Peter Elsholtz (Fred Dalton), Franz Schafheitlin (Harrison), Karl Heinz Peters (headmaster of college), Will Dohm (Mr. Barrington, teacher), Walter Lieck (Mr. Croke a.k.a. Brubbel), Hans Stiebner (Sheriff), Jack Trevor (chairman of court-martial), Karl Haubenreisser (Major General Butler, commander of Dublin Castle), Eric Radolf (Spencer, adjutant), Ferdinant Terpe (sergeant of police squadron), Hans Bergmann (captain of Black and Tans), Albert Venohr (Pat Mullins, farmer), Elisabeth Wendt (Nora, Mullins' wife), Josef Renner (sergeant of Secret Service), Hans Quest (Henry Beverley), Norbert Rohringer (Rory Kennedy), Claus Petzold (Billy Hogan), John Pauls-Harding (Mac Bride), Alfred Stein, Maria Krahn, Margarete Kupfer.

Produced by Tobis Filmkunst G.m.b.H., Berlin. *Production Group:* Dr. Engelsing. *Staatsauftragsfilm.* 35mm. *Laboratory:* Geyer. *Sound System:* Tobis Klangfilm. *Interiors:* Jofa Studios, Berlin-Johannisthal. *Premiere:* February 17, 1941. *Distributed by* Tobis Filmverleih G.m.b.H., Berlin.

Mein Leben für Maria Isabell
(My Life for Maria Isabell)

1934–35. *Director:* Erich Waschneck. *Screenplay:* F. D. Andam, Ernst Hasselbach from the novel "Die Standarte" von A. Lernet-Holenia. *Cinematography:* Herbert Körner. *Music:* Herbert Windt.

Cast: Viktor de Kowa, Maria Andergast, Peter Voss, Franz Pfaudler, Hansjoachim Büttner, Hermann Frick, Julia Serda, Karin Evans, Bernhard Minetti, Ernst Karchow, Harry Hardt, Ekkehard Arendt, Hans Junkermann, Hans Zesch-Ballot, Veit Harlan, Anton Pointner, Hugo Flink, Albert Kersten, Gerhard Haselbach, Albert Hugelmann, Erich Fiedler.

Produced by Lloyd-Film G.m.b.H. *Staatsauftragsfilm. Premiere:* February 7, 1935. *Distributed by* Rota-Filmverleih G.m.b.H. (Tobis Syndicate), Berlin. *Subject:* The chaotic final days of World War I around Belgrad.

Menschen im Sturm
(Men in Storm)

1941. *Director:* Dr. Fritz Peter Buch. *Production Manager:* Fritz Klotzsch. *Screenplay:* Georg Zoch, from an idea conceived by Karl Anton and Felix von Eckardt. *Cinematography:* Eduard Hoesch. *Stills Photographer:* Karl Ewald. *Music:* Wolfgang Zeller. *Art Directors:* Hanns H. Kuhnert, Artur Nortmann. *Sound:* Gerhard Froboes.

Cast: Olga Tschechowa (Vera Oswatics), Gustav Diessl (Alexander Oswatics), Hannelore Schroth (Marie-Luise Kronberg, Vera's daughter from first marriage), Siegfried Breuer (Captain Rakic), Kurt Meisel (First Lieutenant Duschan), Franz Schafheitlin (Subotic, commissioner), Heinz Welzel (Hans Neubert), Josef Sieber (Anton), Rudolf Blümner (Paulic, chemist), Walther Süssenguth (commander), Katja Pahl, Reinhold Bernt, Walter Brückner, Werner Pledath, Ernö Renée, Heinrich Troxbömker, Josef Zeilbeck.

Produced by Tobis Filmkunst G.m.b.H., Berlin. 35mm. *Laboratory:* Geyer. *Interiors:* Jofa Studios, Berlin-Johannisthal. *Running time:* 74 minutes. *Premiere:* December 19, 1941, Lübeck; December 29, 1941, Berlin. *Distributed by* Tobis Filmverleih G.m.b.H., Berlin.

Menschen ohne Vaterland
(People Without a Fatherland)

1936–37. *Director:* Herbert Maisch. *Screenplay:* Walter Wassermann, C. H. Diller, Ernst von Salomon, Herbert Maisch from the novel "Der Mann ohne Vaterland" by Gertrud von Brockdorff. *Cinematography:* Konstantin Irmen-Tschet. *Music:* Harold M. Kirchstein.

Cast: Willy Fritsch, Maria von Tasnady, Willy Birgel, Grethe Weiser, Siegfried Schürenberg, Werner Stock, Josef Sieber, Alexander Golling, Erich Dunskus, Nikolai Kolin, Willi Schaeffers, Lissy Arna, Hans Stiebner, Luis Rainer, Aribert Grimmer, Maria Loja, Valy Arnheim, Werner Kepich, Johannes Bergfeldt, Karl Meixner, Hermann Mayer-Falkow, Jakob Sinn, Hans Meyer-Hanno, Hellmuth Passarge, Gustav Püttjer, Arthur Reinhardt, Albert Venohr.

Produced by Universum-Film A.-G., Berlin. *Staatsauftragsfilm. Premiere:* March 3, 1937. *Distributed by* Universum-Filmverleih G.m.b.H. (Ufaleih), Berlin. *Subject:* German volunteer corps soldiers fighting the "Red Terror" in the Baltic 1918–19.

Morgenrot (Dawn)

1932. *Director:* Gustav Ucicky. *Producer:* Günther Stapenhorst. *Location Manager:* Ernst von Neusser. *Screenplay:* Gerhard Menzel from an idea conceived by E. Freiherr von Spiegel. *Cinematography:* Carl Hoffmann. *Assistant Cameraman:* Günther Anders. *Stills Photographer:* Horst von Harbou. *Music:* Herbert Windt. *Songs:* "...denn wir fahren, denn wir fahren gen Engeland"; "Muss i denn, muss i denn zum Städtele hinaus"; "Nun danket alle Gott." *Art Directors:* Robert Herlth, Walter Röhrig. *Make-Up Artist:* Wilhelm Weber. *Wardrobe:* Fritz Schilling. *Sound:* Hermann Fritzsching. *Naval Adviser:* Kapitänleutnant a.D. Fürbringer. *Editor:* Eduard von Borsody.

Cast: Rudolf Forster (commander-lieutenant Liers), Adele Sandrock (Mrs. Liers, his mother), Fritz Genschow (sub-lieutenant Fredericks), Franz Niklisch (Petermann, sailor), Paul Westermeier (Jaul, radio operator), Camilla Spira (Grete, Jaul's daughter), Gerhard Bienert (Böhm, helmsman), Hans Leibelt (mayor of Meerskirchen), Else Knott (Helga, the mayor's daughter), Friedrich Gnass (Juraczik, torpedo sailor), Eduard von Winterstein (Major Kolch), Charles Bush, Frank Perfitt, William Cavanagh, G. W. Stroud, A. A. F. Trebes (British sailors), Oscar Aigner, Gerhard Dammann, Kate Kühl, Walter Kuhle, Gerhard Menzel, Rudolf Platte, Hedwig Schlichter, Ludwig Stoessel, Elsa Wagner, Gertrud Wolle. *Produced by* Universum-Film A.-G. (Ufa), Berlin. 35mm. *Laboratory:* Afifa. *Shooting:* October 10, 1932 (exteriors), October 17, 1932 (interiors). *Interiors:* Ufa Studios, Neubabelsberg (Stage North). *Sound System:* Tobis Klangfilm. *Running time:* 85 minutes. *Premiere:* January 31, 1933, Essen Schauburg February 2, 1933, Berlin Ufa-Palast am Zoo. *Distributed by* Universum-Filmverleih G.m.b.H. (Ufaleih), Berlin.

Musketier Meier III (Musketeer Meier III)

1937–38. *Director:* Joe Stöckel. *Screenplay:* Karl Bunje, Axel Eggebrecht. *Cinematography:* Hugo von Kaweczynski. *Music:* Marc Roland.

Cast: Rudi Godden, Günther Lüders, Hermann Speelmans, Hildegard Barko, Liselott Schaack, Edith Meinhard, Beppo Brem, Aribert Mog, Gustl Stark-Gstettenbaur, Gerhard Bienert, Adolf Fischer, Hella Tornegg, Ernst Legal, Harry Gondi, Carl de Vogt, Alfred Naack, Erich Haussmann, Erich Nadler, Jeanette Bethge, Erich Bartels, Josef Karma. *Produced by* Germania-Film G.m.b.H., Munich. *Staatsauftragsfilm. Premiere:* March 17, 1938, Dresden; March 24, 1938, Berlin. *Distributed by* Forum-Film G.m.b.H., Berlin; Rheinische Film G.m.b.H., Dusseldorf; Kopp-Filmwerke, Munich; local distributors. *Subject:* Military comedy Western Front 1917.

Ohm Krüger (Uncle Krüger)

1941. *Director:* Hans Steinhoff. *Second Unit Directors (mass scenes):* Herbert Maisch, Karl Anton. *Assistant Directors:* Roland von Rossi, Rudolf Külüs, Sieg Krügler, Georg Alfred Profe. *Assistant Directors Second Unit:* Adolf Jansen, Heinz Opitz, Oskar Haarbrandt. *Producer:* Emil Jannings. *Production Chief:* Ewald von Demandowsky. *Production Manager:* Fritz Klotzsch. *Screenplay:* Harald Bratt, Kurt Heuser, inspired by the novel *Mann ohne Volk (Man Without People)* by Arnold Krieger. *Words:* Hans Fritz Beckmann, Günther Schwenn. *Cinematography:* Fritz Arno Wagner. *Second Unit Camera:* Friedl Behn-Grund, Karl Puth, Herbert Körner, Claus von Rautenfeld, Karl Loeb, Wilhelm Schmid, Willy Gerlach. *Assistant Cameramen:* Karl Plintzner, Ernst Elsigan, Franz von Klepacki, Horst Orgel, Ernst Weiss, Erich Nitzschmann, Walter Ruge. *Stills Photographer:* Richard Wesel. *Music:* Theo Mackeben. *Art Director:* Franz Schroedter. *Assistant Art Directors:* Paul Markwitz, Hans Minzloff, Artur Nordmann, Mathieu Oostermann, Erich

Schweder, Theo Zwierski. *Costumes Consultants:* Herbert Ploberger, Hans Strohbach, Eillroda, Ursula Zilss. *Ballet-master:* Hanns Gérard. *Sound:* Hans Grimm. *Production staff:* Walter Zeiske, Gustav Rathje, Alfred Kern, Ernst Mattner, Willi Morree, Max Paetz, Rolf Geile, Wolfgang von Padberg, Alfred Arbeiter, Karl Heinz Bock, Rolf von Botesku, Ernst Braun, Erich Voigt. *Editors:* Hans Heinrich, Martha Dübber.

Cast: Emil Jannings (Paul Krüger), Lucie Höflich (Sanna Krüger, his wife), Werner Hinz (Jan Krüger), Ernst Schröder (Adrian Krüger), Gisela Uhlen (Petra Krüger, Jan's wife), Friedrich Ulmer (Joubert, general commander of the Boer Army), Eduard von Winterstein (Cronje, army commander), Hans Adalbert von Schlettow (de Wett, army commander), Fritz Hoopts (Colson, field cornet), Max Gülstorff (Reitz, permanent secretary), Walter Werner (Kock, deputy of People's Chamber), Elisabeth Flickenschildt (Mrs. Kock), Hedwig Wangel (Queen Victoria), Alfred Bernau (Prince of Wales, her son), Gustaf Gründgens (Chamberlain), Ferdinand Marian (Cecil Rhodes), Flockina von Platen (Flora Shaw, Rhodes' agent), Karl Haubenreisser (Dr. Jameson), Franz Schafheitlin (Kitchener, chief of the general staff, British South African Army), Otto Wernicke (commander of British concentration camp), Hans Herrmann Schaufuss (medical officer), Kart Martell (British officer), Walter Süssenguth (sergeant), Hilde Körber (Boer woman), Louis Brody (Chief Lobenguela), Hans Stiebner (reporter), Harald Paulsen, Otto Graf, Paul Bildt (secretary of state), Armin Schweizer (receptionist), Rudolf Blümner (professor), Werner Pledath, Friedel Heizmann, Ernst Dernburg, Georg Heinrich Schnell, Gertrud Wolle, Gerhard Bienert, Wolfgang Lukschy, Aribert Grimmer, Theodor Thony, Werner Stock, Erich Hecking, Paul Rehkopf, Viktor Gehring, Käte Jöken-König, Artur Reinhardt, Charlotte Vetrone, Willi Grunwald, Astrid Seiderer, Ingeborg Johannsen, Joe Münch-Harris, Ferdinand Terpe, Wolf Trutz, Walter Schramm-Duncker, Jack Trevor, Heinrich Schroth, Louis Ralph, Josef Reithofer.

Produced by Tobis Filmkunst G.m.b.H., Berlin. *Production Group:* Fritz Klotzsch. *Staatsauftragsfilm.* 35mm. *Laboratory:* Geyer. *Running time:* 124 minutes. *Interiors:* Jofa Studios, Berlin-Johannisthal. *Budget:* RM 5,477,000. *Premiere:* April 4, 1941. *Distributed by* Tobis Filmverleih G.m.b.H., Berlin. On the occassion of IFF 1941 in Venice *Ohm Krüger* was awarded the Cup Mussolini for best foreign film.

Panik (working title: *Panik im Zoo;* reissued in 1953 as *Gesprengte Gitter/Die Elefanten sind los)*

1940–43. *Producer-Director:* Harry Piel. *Production Managers:* Hans von Wolzogen (1st version); Willy Wiesner, Conrad Flockner (2nd and 3rd versions). *Location Managers:* Fritz Anton, Alfred Poste, Fritz Cornell (1st version); Heinz Abel, Harry Dettmann (2nd and 3rd versions). *Assistant Director:* Erwin Biswanger. *Screenplay:* Harry Piel, Erwin Biswanger, Dr. Herbert Nossen, from an idea conceived by Harry Piel and Erwin Biswanger. *Collaborators:* Erwin Kreker (2nd draft), Alexander Lix (3rd draft). *Cinematography:* Ernst Willi Fiedler, Erich Schmidtke; Karl Puth, Klaus von Rautenfeld (2nd and 3rd versions); Gotthardt Wolf, Ewald Daub, Willy Peter Bloch. *Stills Photographer:* Anton Augustin. *Music:* Werner Bochmann (scheduled for 1st version); Nico Dostal (2nd and 3rd versions). *Art Directors:* Max Seefelder (1st version); Max Knaake, Erich Grave, Hans Minzloff (2nd and 3rd versions). *Make-Up Artist:* Arnold Jenssen. *Sound:* Ferdinand Haubmann. *Editor:* Hildegard Grebner.

Cast: Harry Piel (Peter Völker), Herbert A. E. Böhme (Fr. Kröger, Peter's friend), Hans Zesch-Ballot (Dr. Joh. Thiele, manager of Zoo Ulmenau), Dorothea Wieck (Hella, Thiele's wife), Wilhelm P. Krüger (A. R. Brinkmann, farmer in East Africa), Ruth Eweler (Christa Brinkmann, his daughter), Fritz Hoopts (H. Sander, farmer), Maria Krahn (Mrs. Küppers, farmer), Julius Riedmüller (Alois Leitner), Julius Frey (F. Müller), L. Krüger-Roger (J. Huber), Joe

Münch-Harries, Beppo Brem, Elfriede Haase, Karl Heinz Peters, Karl Hellmer, Maria Hofer, Maria Henning-Roth, Eva Klein-Donath, Michael Lang, Albert Parsen, Rudolf Vogel. Cast from the 1st version not used in release version: Anneliese Uhlig, Olga Limburg, Charlott Daudert, Walter Janssen.

Produced by F.D.F. Fabrikation deutscher Filme G.m.b.H., Berlin. 35mm. *Shooting:* September 16–beginning November 1940: Arri Atelier and Tierpark Hellabrunn Munich; July–September 1941: Tierpark Hellabrunn Munich; November 1941–February 1942 and April 1942: Scalera Studios Rome, near Foligno and Nettuno; June–ca. October 1942: Tierpark Hellabrunn Munich; additional footage: January–February 1943. *Running time:* 95 minutes (reissue: 102 minutes). *Banned* October 1943. *Finally premiered* on December 13, 1953, Frankfurt/Main. *Distributed by* Herzog Film.

Patrioten (Patriots)

1937. *Producer-Director:* Karl Ritter. *Assistant Director:* Friedrich Karl von Puttkamer. *Location Managers:* Ludwig Kühr, Willi Marchant, Gert Kautzer. *Screenplay:* Philipp Lothar Mayring, Felix Lützkendorf, Karl Ritter, from an idea conceived by Karl Ritter. *Cinematography:* Günther Anders. *Assistant Cameraman:* Karl Plintzner. *Stills Photographer:* Willi Klitzke. *Music:* Theo Mackeben. *Song:* "Paris, du bist die schönste Stadt der Welt." *Music Publisher:* Ufaton-Verlag. *Lyrics:* Hans Fritz Beckmann. *Art Directors:* Franz Koehn, Walter Röhrig. *Costumes Designer:* Arno Richter. *Wardrobe:* Paul Haupt, Maria Ellner-Kühr. *Make-Up Artists:* Willi Weber, Maria Arnold. *Sound:* Ludwig Ruhe. *Dances:* Sabine Ress. *French Military Adviser:* Lieutenant Colonel René Phelizon. *Editor:* Gottfried Ritter.

Cast: Mathias Wiemann (Peter Thomann), Bruno Hübner (Jules Martin, director of a front theater), Lida Baarova (Thérèse, called Jou-Jou), Hilde Körber (Suzanne), Paul Dahlke (Charles), Nikolai Kolin (Nikita), Kurt Seifert (Alphonse), A. F.

Eugens (Jean Baptiste, Suzanne's 5 year old son), Edwin Jürgensen (commander of town), Willi Rose (office officer), Ewald Wenck (policeman), Otz Tollen (chairman of court-martial), Ernst Karchow (prosecutor), André Saint-Germain (defense counsel), Paul Schwed, Lutz Götz (German prisoners of war), Karl Hannemann (medical orderly), Gustav Mahncke (Sergeant), Karl Wagner (bellboy), Jim Simmons (pilot), Hans-Reinhard Knitsch (machine gunner).

Produced by Universum-Film A.-G. (Ufa), Berlin. *Production Group:* Karl Ritter. *Staatsauftragsfilm.* 35mm. *Laboratory:* Afifa. *Sound System:* Tobis Klangfilm. *Shooting:* January 20–March 1937. *Interiors:* Ufa Studios Neubabelsberg. *Running time:* 96 minutes. *Premiere:* August 14, 1937, IFF Venice; September 4, 1937, Paris (opening of German Kulturwochen); November 24, 1937, Berlin, Ufa-Palast am Zoo. *Distributed by* Universum Filmverleih G.m.b.H. (Ufaleih), Berlin.

Petermann Ist Dagegen! (Petermann Objects)

1937. *Director:* Frank Wysbar. *Production Manager:* Fred Lyssa. *Screenplay:* Otto Bernhard Wendler, Frank Wysbar, inspired by the stage play *Petermann fährt nach Madeira* by August Hinrichs. *Cinematography:* Erich Claunigk.

Cast: Ernst Waldow, Franz W. Schröder-Schrom, Fita Benkhoff, Johannes Bathel, Olaf Varnhorn, Berthold Ebbecke, Walter Gross, Hilde Schneider, Beppo Brem, Hugo Fischer-Köppe, Karl Platen.

Produced by Neucophon-Tonfilm Produktion und Vertriebs G.m.b.H., Berlin. *Production Group:* Hans Tost. 35mm. *Premiere:* January 14, 1938. *Distributed by* Terra Filmverleih G.m.b.H., Berlin. Comedy by director Frank Wysbar who later worked in the United States: A bookkeeper wins ticket in firm's lottery for "Strength through Joy" cruise to Madeira.

Pour le Mérite

1938. *Producer-Director:* Karl Ritter. *Location Manager:* Ludwig Kühr. *Assistant Director:* Gottfried Ritter. *Screenplay:* Fred Hildenbrand, Karl Ritter. *Cinematography:* Günther Anders. *Aerial Cinematography:* Heinz von Jaworsky. *Assistant Cameraman:* Adolf Kühn. *Stills Photographer:* Kitzinger. *Music:* Herbert Windt. *Art Director:* Walter Röhrig. *Explosives:* Erwin Lange. *Wardrobe:* Paul Haupt, Charlotte Bornkessel. *Make-Up Artists:* Hermann Rosenthal, Kurt Neumann, Paul Lange. *Sound:* Werner Pohl. *Editor:* Gottfried Ritter. *Editorial Assistant:* Friedrich Karl von Puttkamer.

Cast: Paul Hartmann (Calavry Captain Prank), Jutta Freybe (Isabel Prank), Albert Hehn (Lieutenant Fabian), Herbert A. E. Böhme (First Lieutenant Gerdes), Carsta Löck (Gerda Fabian), Fritz Kampers (Officer's Deputy Moebius), Paul Otto (Major Wissmann), Josef Dahmen (Zuschlag, noncommissioned officer), Willi Rose (Private Krause), Heinz Welzel (Lieutenant Romberg), Gisela von Collande (Anna Moebius), Clemens Hasse (uhlan), Heinz Engelmann (cuirassier), Malte Jäger (Lieutenant Overbeck), Otto Graf (lieutenant commander), Theo Shall (Captain Cecil Brown), Lothar Körner (Father Fabian), Elsa Wagner (Mother Fabian), Kate Kühl (Bar singer), Paul Dahlke (Herr Schnaase), Marina von Ditmar (young Frenchwoman), Friedrich Ettel (chairman), Ernst Dernburg (prison governor), Otz Tollen (Captain Reinwald), Wilhelm Althaus (wing adjutant), Wolfgang Staudte (Lieutenant Ellermann), Walter Bluhm (hussar), Heinz Wieck (sapper), Hans Rudolf Ballhausen (Lieutenant Reuter), Hans Joachim Rake (Lieutenant Heuser), Heinz Sedlak (Lieutenant Langwerth), Erik Radolf (Lieutenant Bülow), Gustav Mahncke (Vice Sergeant), Carl August Dennert (Kruschke), Heinrich Schroth (staff officer of airship division), Gerhard Jeschke ("Kofl" adjutant), Hadrian Maria Netto (major of infantry), Otto Krone (captain of artillery), Franz Andermann (artillery observer), Jim Simmons (radio operator), Adolf Fischer (infantry messenger), Herbert Lindner (reserve officer), Georg Georgi, Nico Turoff, Hans Bergmann (three soldier counsellors), Walter Lieck (Baumlang, deuce), Reinhold Pasch (American cavalry officer), André Saint-Germain (French capitaine), Waltraud Salzmann (Fabian's sister), Oskar Aigner (jeweller), Ernst Sattler (slaughterhouse inspector), Irene Kohl (wife of slaughterhouse inspector), Otto Sauter-Sarto (Bavarian bass), Martha von Kossatzki (Barbara, housekeeper), Fritz Petermann (landing pilot), Hildegard Fränzel (Frau Müller), Heinrich Krill (Father Kunkel), Gaston Briese (Herr Raffke), Valerie Borstel (Frau Raffke), Herbert Schimkat (Herr Meier), Aribert Grimmer (Pachulke), Fritz Klaudius, Arthur Reppert, Karl Haubenreisser, Willy Gerber (four black marketeers), Elvira Erdmann, Hanna Lussnigg (two little ladies), Serag Monier (owner of an inflations cabaret), Marianne Kiwitt (Mia), Dolly Raphael (Kitty), Lilly Schönborn (cleaning lady), Lutz Götz (gendarme from Darmstadt), Oskar Höcker (gendarme from the countryside), Ilva Günten (landlady), Fritz Marlitz (police officer), S. O. Schoening, Herbert Weissbach, Max Hiller, Josef Peterhans (four deputies), Friedrich Gnass (Herr Holzapfel), Werner Stock (Herr Holzapfel's companion), Eduard Bornträger (senior inspector Weiss), Gerhard Bienert (prison governor), Hellmuth Passarge (prison guard), Gerhard Dammann (Herr Zörgiebel), Heinz Rippert, Theo Brandt, Heinz Otte (young officers), Egon Barlogh, Kurt Hinz, Martin Baumann (three glider trainees), Franz Weber, Karl Meixner, Josef Gindorf, Bernhard Kaspar, Karl Friedrich Burkhardt, Ferdinand Reich, Willy Witte, Heinz Jungklaus, Heinz Look, Erik von Loewies [i.e., Erik Richard Michael Adalbert von Loewies of Menar], Walter Jensen.

Produced by Universum-Film A.-G., Berlin. *Staatsauftragsfilm.* 35mm. *Laboratory:* Afifa. *Interiors:* Ufastadt Babelsberg. *Exteriors:* Mecklenburg, Scharmützelsee, Rhön. *Shooting:* June 14–beginning of September 1938. *Budget:* RM 974,000. *Running time:* 121 minutes. *Premiere:* December 22, 1938,

Berlin, Ufa-Palast am Zoo. *Distributed by* Universum Filmverleih G.m.b.H. (Ufaleih), Berlin.

Quax, der Bruchpilot (Quax the Crash Pilot)

1941. *Director:* Kurt Hoffmann. *Producer:* Heinz Rühmann. *Production Manager:* Robert Leistenschneider. *Location Manager:* Fritz Anton. *Assistant Director:* Toni Thermal. *Screenplay:* Robert A. Stemmle, inspired by Hermann Grote's story. *Cinematography:* Heinz von Jaworsky. *Assistant Cameramen:* Georg Bronec, Peter Röhrig. *Music:* Werner Bochmann. *Song:* "Heimat, deine Sterne." *Lyrics:* Erich Knauf. *Art Directors:* Otto Moldenhauer, Rudolf Linnekogel. *Miniatures and Process Photography:* Gerhard Huttula. *Process Technician:* Willi Körner. *Explosives:* Erwin Lange. *Sound:* Alfred Zunft. *Editor:* Walter Fredersdorf.

Cast: Heinz Rühmann (Otto Groschenbügel a.k.a. Quax), Lothar Firmans (Hansen, flying instructor), Karin Himboldt (Marianne Bredow), Hilde Sessak (Adelheid), Harry Liedtke (Bredow, landowner), Elga Brink (Mrs. Bredow), Franz Zimmermann (Harry Peters), Kunibert Gensichen (Walter Ottermann), José Held (Karl Bruhn), Günther Markert (Gottfried Müller), Manfred Heidmann (Ludwig Mommsen), Leo Peukert (mayor), Lo Ethoff (the mayor's wife), Georg Vogelsang (old man Krehlert), Beppo Brem (Bavarian farm-hand), Lutz Götz (Mr. Busse), Irene Fischer (Hilde), Arthur Schröder (physician), Walter Holten (manager of airport), Helmut Weiss (journalist), Alfons Teuber (journalist), Erich Kestin (mechanic), Markus Staffner (mechanic), Walter Lieck (teacher), Otto Braml (travel agent), Karl Etlinger (manager of savings bank), Karl Heidmann (police officer), Wilhelm Bendow (passenger), Gertrud Wolle (passenger), Walter Bechmann (weather station member), Gerhard Dammann (photographer), Eamnuel Matousek (sports pilot), Werner Stock (trainee pilot).

Produced and distributed by Terra-Filmkunst G.m.b.H., Berlin. *Production*

Group: Heinz Rühmann. 35mm. *Interiors:* Ufastadt Babelsberg. *Running time:* 97 minutes. *Premiere:* December 16, 1941, Hamburg, Ufa-Palast; December 22, 1941, Berlin, Capitol and Babylon.

Die Reiter von Deutsch-Ostafrika (The Riders of German East-Africa)

1934. *Director:* Herbert Selpin. *Production Manager:* Walter Zeiske. *Location Managers:* Arno Winkler, Günther Pflegenberg. *Screenplay:* Marie-Luise Droop, based on her novel *Kwa heri. Story Editor:* Wilhelm Stöppler. *Cinematography:* Emil Schünemann. *Assistant Cameraman:* Bernhard Hellmund. *Stills Photographer:* Kurt Wunsch. *Music:* Herbert Windt. *Art Directors:* Robert Dietrich, Bruno Lutz. *Sound:* Fritz Seeger. *Advisor:* Resident retd. Willibald von Stuemer, Geheimer Regierungsrat. *Editor:* Lena Neumann.

Cast: Sepp Rist (Peter Hellhoff, farmer), Ilse Stobrawa (Gerda, his wife), Ludwig Gerner (Lossow, Hellhoff's assistant), Rudolf Klicks (Wilm Klix, Hellhoff's trainee), Georg Heinrich Schnell (Colonel Black, British general staff officer), Peter Voss (Captain Robert Cresswell, British officer), Vivigenz Eickstedt (British officer), Arthur Reinhardt (Charles Rallis, safari leader), Louis Brody (Hamissi, overseer), Mohamed Husen (Mustapha), Emine Zehra Zinser (Milini, servant), Gregor Kotto (Selemani, Hellhoff's boy), Andreas Aglasinger, Herbert Rudolf Ebel, Erwin Fichtner, Adolf Fischer, Willi König.

Produced by Terra-Film A.-G., Berlin. *Production Group:* Walter Zeiske. *Staatsauftragsfilm.* 35mm. *Shooting* started in August 1934. *Interiors:* Terra Glass stage, Berlin-Marienfelde. *Exteriors:* Africa. *Sound System:* Tobis Klangfilm. *Premiere:* October 19, 1934, Hamburg; November 2, 1934, Berlin, Ufa-Palast am Zoo. *Distributed by* Terra-Filmverleih G.m.b.H., Berlin. On December 19, 1939, all further screening of this film was forbidden.

...reitet für Deutschland (...Riding for Germany)

1940–41. *Director:* Arthur Maria Rabenalt. *Producer:* Richard Riedel. *Production Manager:* Hans Schönmetzler. *Location Managers:* Willy Hermann-Balz, Arndt Liebster. *Assistant Director:* Hans Müller. *Screenplay:* Fritz Reck-Malleczewen, Richard Riedel, Josef Maria Frank, from the biography of Baron von Langen adapted by Clemens Laar. *Cinematography:* Werner Krien. *Music:* Herbert Windt, Alois Melichar. *Art Directors:* Otto Hunte, Karl Vollbrecht, Herbert Nitzschke. *Costumes:* Gerda Leopold, O. Liebusch, Walter Salemann. *Sound:* Dr. Erich Leistner. *Military Adviser:* E. von Düring. *Editor:* Kurt Hamp.

Cast: Willy Birgel (Cavalry captain von Brenken), Gerhild Weber (Thoms), Herbert A. E. Böhme (Olav Kolrep), Gertrud Eysoldt (Aunt Ulle), Willi Rose (Karl Marten), Hans Zesch-Ballott (brigadier commander), Paul Dahlke (Dolinski), Rudolf Schündler (Brenner), Walter Werner (privy councillor), Herbert Hübner, Walter Lieck, Ewald Wenck, Armin Schweitzer, Gerhard Dammann, Hans Quest, Marianne Stanior, Wolfgang Staudte, Cavalry School Krampnitz, *Director:* Major Momm.

Produced by Universum-Film A.-G., Berlin. *Production Group:* Richard Riedel. 35mm. *Laboratory:* Afifa. *Shooting:* started August 26, 1940. *Interiors:* Ufastadt Babelsberg. *Running time:* 92 minutes. *Premiere:* April 11, 1941; May 30, 1941, Berlin, Capitol. *Distributed by* Universum-Filmverleih G.m.b.H. (Ufaleih), Berlin.

Rivalen der Luft. Ein Segelfliegerfilm (Rivals of the Air)

1933. *Director:* Frank Wysbar. *Producer:* Karl Ritter. *Location Manager:* Fritz Koch. *Screenplay:* Walter Forster, from an idea conceived by Philipp Lothar and Lothar M. Mayring. *Cinematography:* Hans Schneeberger. *Music:* Herbert Windt. *Musical Director:* Franz Friedl. *Art Director:* Erich Czerwonski. *Sound:* Jochen Thurban. *Aerial Consultants:* Wolf Hirth (director, Segelflughochschule Hornberg), Hanna Reitsch, Edgar Dittmar, Heini Dittmar, Alfred Böhm, Otto Arndt, M. Bohlan, Oblt. Tamm, Hans Deutschmann, Rittmeister Röhre, Fritz Stamer, Franz Orthbandt. *Editor:* Willy Zeyn.

Cast: Claus Clausen (Willi Frahms, flying instructor), Wolfgang Liebeneiner (Karl Hofer, trainee pilot), Hilde Gebühr (Christine Steeger, trainee pilot), Sybille Schmitz (Lisa Holm, sports pilot), Walter Gross (Palmström), Guzzi Lantschner (Pippin from Bavaria), Werner Stock (Otto from Saxonia), Franz Zimmermann (Corduan, trainee pilot from Berlin), Volker von Collande (Hanne, trainee pilot from Hamburg), Hans Henninger (Schnitt, trainee pilot from East Prussia), Florian Zeise-Gött (Haberkorn, trainee pilot from the Palatinate), Wolff von Wernsdorff (Ox, trainee pilot from Britain), Cavalry Captain, retd., Röhre (head of glider school Rossitten), Karl Zutavern (pilot), Dr. Lübbesmeyer (pilot), Paul Henckels, Ingolf Kuntze.

Produced by Universum-Film A.-G., Berlin. *Production Group:* Karl Ritter. *Protektorate:* Captain ret. Bruno Loerzer, President, Deutscher Luftsport-Verband e.V. 35mm. *Laboratory:* Afifa, Berlin. *Sound System:* Tobis Klangfilm. *Shooting:* August–October 1933. *Interiors:* Ufa Atelier Neubabelsberg. *Exteriors:* Rhön, Rossitten/Kurische Nehrung. *Premiere:* January 19, 1934, Berlin (Ufa-Palast am Zoo). *Running time:* 98 minutes. *Distributed by* Universum Filmverleih G.m.b.H. (Ufaleih), Berlin.

Robert und Bertram (Robert and Bertram)

1939. *Director:* Hans Heinz Zerlett. *Production Manager:* Helmut Schreiber. *Screenplay:* Hans Heinz Zerlett, based on an idea by Gustav Raeder. *Cinematography:* Friedl Behn-Grund. *Music:* Leo Leux. *Special Photographic Effects:* Ernst Kunstmann. *Art Titles:* Trickatelier Radius. *Editor:* Ella Ensink.

Cast: Rudi Godden (Robert), Kurt Seifert (Bertram), Carla Rust (Lenchen), Fritz Kampers (Strambach), Heinz Schorlemmer (Michel), Herbert Hübner (Nathan Ipelmeyer), Inge von der Straaten (Mrs. Ipelmeyer), Tatjana Sais (Isidora Ipelmeyer), Ursula Deinert (dancer), Robert Dorsay (Jacques), Alfred Maack (Lips), Arthur Schröder (Biedermeyer), Hans Stiebner (Blank), Fritz Hoopts (Flint), Walter Lieck (Dr. Kaftan), Arnim Münch (Bendheim), Erwin Biegel (Forchheimer), Eva Tinschmann (ballad-singer), Willi Schur (ballad-singer), Friedrich Beug, Peter Bosse, Fred Goebel, Harry Gondi, Aribert Grimmer, Otto Henning, Kurt Keller-Nebri, Franz Jan Kossack, Gustl Kreusch, Manfred Meurer, Lucie Polzin, Franz Walter Schröder-Schrom, Rudolf Schündler.

Produced by Tobis-Filmkunst G.m.b.H., Berlin. 35mm. *Laboratory:* Geyer. *Sound System:* Tobis Klangfilm. *Interiors:* Jofa Studios, Berlin-Johannisthal. *Premiere:* July 7, 1939, Hamburg; July 14, 1939, Berlin. *Budget:* RM 1,219,000. *Running time:* 93 minutes. *Distributed by* Tobis Filmverleih G.m.b.H., Berlin.

Die Rothschilds. Aktien auf Waterloo (The Rothschilds: Stocks in Waterloo)

1940. *Director:* Erich Waschneck. *Producer:* C. M. Köhn. *Production Manager:* Hans Gerhard Bartels. *Assistant Director:* Friedrich Westhoff. *Screenplay:* C. M. Köhn, Gerhard T. Buchholz, from an idea conceived by Mirko Jelusich. *Cinematography:* Robert Baberske. *Stills Photographer:* Willi Klitzke. *Music:* Johannes Müller. *Art Directors:* Hanns H. Kuhnert, Willy Depenau. *Costumes:* Otto Liebusch, Vera Mügge. *Sound:* Alfred Zunft. *Dances:* Fritz Böttger. *Editor:* Walter Wischniewsky.

Cast: Erich Ponto (Mayer Amschel Rothschild), Carl Kuhlmann (Nathan Rothschild, his son), Albert Lippert (James Rothschild, his son), Ludwig Linkmann (Leib Hersch, Mayer Amschel's courier), Hans Stiebner (Bronstein, Nathan's agent), Bruno Hübner (Ruthworth, Nathan's agent), Rudolf Carl (Rubiner, Nathan's agent), Michael Bohnen (Kurfürst Wilhelm IX, landgrave of Hesse), Herbert Hübner (Turner, banker), Albert Florath (Bearing, banker), Herbert Gernot (Clifford, banker), Theo Shall (Selfridge, banker), Hilde Weissner (Sylvia, Turner's wife), Gisela Uhlen (Phyllis, Bearing's daughter), Herbert Wilk (George Crayton), Waldemar Leitgeb (Lord Wellington), Ursula Deinert (Harriet, his love interest), Walter Franck (Harries, British treasurer), Bernhard Minetti (Duke Fouché, Napoleon's minister of police), Hans Leibelt (Louis XVIII, King of France), Hubert von Meyerinck (Baron Vitrolles, his court marshal), Roma Bahn, Erwin Biegel, Erwin Brosig, Rudolf Essek, Kunibert Gensichen, Fred [Selva-]Goebel, Carl Hannemann, Hansgeorg Laubenthal, Walter Lieck, Hadrian Maria Netto, Werner Pledath, Klaus Pohl, Eugen Rex, Ernst Rotmund, Hans Herrmann-Schaufuss, Hans Adalbert Schlettow, Georg Heinrich Schnell, Dr. Ernst Stimmer, Otz Tollen, Herbert Weissbach, Eduard Wenck, Ewald Wenck, Ruth-Ines Eckermann, Hilde Sessak, Günther Ballier, Conrad Curd Cappi, Walter Schramm-Duncker, Paul Westermeier, Walter Brückner (servant), Egon Vogel (aide).

Produced by Ufa-Filmkunst G.m.b.H., Berlin. *Staatsauftragsfilm.* 35mm. *Laboratory:* Afifa. *Shooting:* April 12–beginning of July, 1940. *Interiors:* Froelich-Studio Berlin-Tempelhof. *Budget:* RM 951,000. *Running time:* 97 minutes. *Premiere:* July 17, 1940, Berlin, Capitol am Zoo. *Distributed by* Universum Filmverleih G.m.b.H. (Ufaleih), Berlin.

SA-Mann Brand

1933. *Director-Producer:* Franz Seitz. *Location Managers:* Fritz Sorg, Theo Kaspar. *Screenplay:* Joseph Dalman, Joe Stöckel. *Cinematography:* Franz Koch. *Assistant Cameraman:* Josef Illig. *Stills Photographer:* Rudolf Reissner. *Music/Musical Director:* Toni Thoms. *Music Titles:* "Badenweiler Marsch"; "Die Fahne hoch" ("Horst Wessel Song"). *Art Director:* Max Seefelder. *Make-Up Artist:* Heinrich Beckmann. *Wardrobe:* Hermann Dor, Dorothea Saumweber. *Sound:* Friedrich

Wilhelm Dunstmann. *Editor:* Gottlieb Madl.

Cast: Heinz Klingenberg (Fritz Brand), Otto Wernicke (Father Brand), Elise Aulinger (Mother Brand), Rolf Wenkhaus (Erich Lohner), Hedda Lembach (Mrs. Lohner), Joe Stöckel (Anton Huber, house-owner), Helma Rückert (Genoveva Huber, his wife), Fritz Greiner (Father Baumann), Magda Lena (Mother Baumann), Wera Liessem (Anni Baumann), Ottheim Haas (Max Baumann), Adolf Lallinger (Ludwig Baumann), Max Weydner (Turow, Soviet Agent), Manfred Kömpel-Pilot (Schmitt, SA leader), Theo Kaspar (Spitzer, Communist), Philipp Weichand (landlord of SA pub), Wastl Witt (landlord of Café "Diana"), Rudolf Frank (Neuberg, Jewish industrialist), Rudolf Kunig (Rolat, state official), Josef Eichheim (Säbelmeyer), Agnes Straub.

Produced by Bavaria-Film A.G., Munich. *Staatsauftragsfilm.* 35mm. *Sound System:* Tobis Klangfilm. *Shooting:* mid–April–end of May, 1933. *Interiors:* Bavaria Studios, Geiselgasteig. *Exteriors:* Munich. *Distributed by* Bayerische Filmgesellschaft m.b.H., Munich.

Schicksal *(Destiny)*

1941–42. *Director:* Geza von Bolvary. *Screenplay:* Gerhard Menzel. *Cinematography:* Hans Schneeberger. *Music:* Anton Profes.

Cast: Heinrich George, Gisela Uhlen, Will Quadflieg, Werner Hinz, Christian Kayssler, Walter Lieck, Heinz Ohlsen, Heinz Wöster, Wilfried Seyferth, Karl Ehmann, Josef Dahmen, Adalet.

Produced by Wien-Film G.m.b.H., Vienna. *Staatsauftragsfilm. Premiere:* March 18, 1942. *Distributed by* Universum Filmverleih G.m.b.H. (subsequently DFV), Berlin. *Subject:* Life Story of a Bulgarian servant from 1919 to 1938.

Ein Schöner Tag *(A Beautiful Day)*

1943–44. *Director:* Philipp Lothar Mayring. *Producer:* Bernhard F. Schmidt. *Location Manager:* Ernst Körner. *Screenplay:* Philipp Lothar Mayring, Harald Röbbeling.

Cinematography: Richard Angst. *Music:* Franz Doelle, Franz Marszalek. *Art Directors:* Arthur Nortmann, Hans Joachim Maeder. *Sound:* Gerhard Froboes. *Editor:* Walter von Bonhorst.

Cast: Gertrud Meyen (Barbara), Sabine Peters (Mrs. Schröder), Carsta Löck, Volker von Collande, Günther Lüders, Jupp Hussels, Karl Dannemann, Ethel Reschke, Eduard Wenck, Ilse Fürstenberg, Ruth Buchardt, Margarete Kupfer, Lotte Werkmeister, Elsa Wagner, Leo Peukert, Egon Vogel.

Produced by Tobis Filmkunst G.m.b.H., Berlin. *Production Group:* Bernhard F. Schmidt. 35mm. *Laboratory:* Geyer. *Interiors:* Jofa Studios, Berlin-Johannisthal. *Premiere:* January 27, 1944, Berlin, U.T. Kurfürstendamm, Elysium Prenzlauer Allee. *Distributed by* DFV (Deutsche Filmvertriebs G.m.b.H.), Berlin.

Schwarzer Jäger Johanna *(Black Hunter Johanna)*

1934. *Director:* Johannes Meyer. *Screenplay:* Heinrich Oberländer, Heinz Umbehr, from the novel by Georg von der Vring. *Cinematography:* Alexander von Lagorio. *Music:* Wilfried Zillig.

Cast: Marianne Hoppe, Paul Hartmann, Gustaf Gründgens, Fita Benkhoff, Genia Nikolajewa, Paul Bildt, Margarete Albrecht, Harry Hardt, Erich Fiedler, Rudolf Biebrach, Karl Dannemann, Friedrich Ettel, Oskar Sima, Jakob Tiedtke, Gustav Püttjer, Angelo Ferrari, Ida Perry, Harry Frank, Heinz Berghaus, Gerhard Dammann, Erich Hausmann, Margot Köchlin, Gertrud Wolle, Olga Limburg, Wolfgang Staudte, Hella Tornegg, Hans Albin, Eduard Bornträger, Karl Platen, Paul Rehkopf.

Produced by Terra-Film A.G., Berlin. *Production Group:* Rudolf Fritsch. *Staatsauftragsfilm. Premiere:* November 6, 1934, Mainz; November 19, 1934, Berlin, Capitol. *Distributed by* Terra-Filmverleih G.m.b.H., Berlin. *Subject:* Underground resistance to Napoleon.

Sensationsprozess Casilla (The Sensational Trial of Casilla)

1939. *Director:* Eduard von Borsody. *Production Manager:* Erich Holder. *Location Manager:* Alfred Henseler. *Assistant Director:* Walter Steffens. *Dialogue Director:* Werner Bergold. *Screenplay:* Ernst von Salomon, Eduard von Borsody, Robert Büschgens, from a novel by Hans Possendorf. *Cinematography:* Werner Bohne. *Assistant Cameramen:* Kurt Schulz, Werner Lehmann-Tandar. *Stills Photographer:* Willi Klitzke. *Music:* Werner Bochmann. *Song:* "Wenn Du einmal ein Mädel magst..." *Lyrics:* Erwin Lehnow. *Art Director:* Carl Ludwig Kirmse. *Costumes:* Vera Mügge. *Wardrobe:* Max König, Bertha Schindler. *Make-Up Artists:* Hermann Rosenthal, Charlotte Pfefferkorn. *Sound:* Bruno Suckau. *Editor:* Hildegard Grebner.

Cast: Heinrich George (Vandegrift, attorney-at-law), Jutta Freybe (Jessie Vandegrift), Dagny Servaes (Sylvia Casilla), Albert Hehn (Peter Roland), Richard Häussler (Adams, prosecutor), Erich Fiedler (Salvini), Käte Pontow (Billie Casilla, the girl), Siegfried Schürenberg (James, butler), Hans Mierendorff (Corbett, judge), Herbert Weissbach (spokesman of the jury), Ernst Stimmel (physician), Alice Treff (Ama Galliver, secretary), Leo Peukert (Pick, general manager), Karl Klüsner (president of Court of Appeal), Lissy Arna (Inez Brown, maid), Josef Dahmen (pilot), Walter Lieck (American broadcaster), Willi Rose (New York City guide), Charlotte Kolle, Renée Stobrawa, Valy Arnheim, Fritz Eckert, Robert Forsch, Walter Gross, Josef Kamper, Hans Kettler, Otz Tollen, Klaus Pohl, Josef Reithofer, Ernst Rotmund, Max Schramm-Duncker, Walter Steinweg.

Produced by Universum-Film A.-G., Berlin. *Production Group:* Erich Holder. 35mm. *Laboratory:* Afifa. *Interiors:* Froelich Studio, Berlin-Tempelhof. Shooting: beginning of April–beginning of May 1939. *Running time:* 108 minutes. *Premiere:* August 8, 1939, Cologne; September 22, 1939, Berlin, Capitol am Zoo. *Distributed by* Universum Filmverleih (Ufaleih), Berlin.

Sieg des Glaubens. Der Film vom Reichsparteitag der NSDAP (Victory of Faith)

1933. *Director:* Leni Riefenstahl. *Executive producer:* Arnold Raether. *Cinematographers:* Sepp Allgeier, Franz Weihmayr, Walter Frentz, R. Quaas, Paul Tesch. *Technical Director:* R. Quaas. *Music:* Herbert Windt. *Sound:* Siegfried Schulze. *Sound Editor:* Waldemar Gaede. *Editors:* Leni Riefenstahl, Waldemar Gaede.

Produced by Reichspropagandaleitung der NSDAP, Hauptabteilung IV (Film), Berlin. 35mm. *Sound System:* Tobis Klangfilm. *Running time:* 64 minutes. *Premiere:* December 2, 1933, Berlin, Ufa-Palast am Zoo. *Distributed by* Universum Filmverleih G.m.b.H. (Ufaleih), Berlin; Landesfilmstellen der NSDAP.

Sieg im Westen (Victory in the West)

1940–41. *Directors:* Svend Noldan, Fritz Brunsch. *Screenplay:* Lieutenant Colonel Dr. Kurt Hesse, Captain Professor Erich Welter. *Cinematography:* Hans Ertl, Sepp Allgeier, Heinz Kluth. *Music:* Herbert Windt. *Animated Maps:* Svend Noldan.

Produced by Noldan-Produktion (Svend Noldan), Berlin. *Supervised by* Fritz Hippler. 35mm.

Soldaten—Kameraden (Soldiers—Comrades)

1935–36. *Director:* Toni Huppertz. *Screenplay:* G. O. Stoffregen, R. Schneider-Edenkoben, Hans Helmuth Fischer, Toni Huppertz. *Cinematography:* Bruno Timm. *Music:* Robert Küssel.

Cast: Franz Niklisch (Gustav, carpenter from Hamburg), Franz Zimmermann (Willi, spoiled young man), Ralph Arthur Roberts (photographer), Herti Kirchner, Hans Richter, Vera Hartegg, Günther Vogdt, Gustl Stark-Gstettenbaur, Walter Jensen, Heinz Pelzer, Hugo Flink, F. J. Kossak, Adolf Fischer, Menta Egies, Hans Jöckel, Vicky Werckmeister, Siegmar Schneider, S. O. Schoening, Gerhard Dammann, Franz Stein, Franz Weber, Annemarie Korff.

Produced by Cinephon-Film G.m.b.H. *Staatsauftragsfilm.* 35mm. *Interiors:* Ufa Studios Berlin-Tempelhof. *Premiere:* February 21, 1936, Munich; February 28, 1936, Berlin, Primus-Palast, Titania Palast. *Distributed by* Hammer-Tonfilm-Verleih G.m.b.H.

Spähtrupp Hallgarten. Ein Film vom Kampf und Einsatz unserer Gebirgsjäger (Hallgarten Patrol. A Film about Fighting and Action of Our Mountain Soldiers)

1940–41. *Director:* Herbert B. Fredersdorf. *Production Managers:* Ernst Garden, Alfred Bittins. *Location Manager:* Fritz Renner. *Screenplay:* Kurt E. Walter, Herbert B. Fredersdorf. *Cinematography:* Eduard Hoesch. *Stills Photographer:* Alexander Schmoll-Weisse. *Music:* Anton Profes. *Art Directors:* Alfred Bütow, Heinrich Beisenherz. *Sound:* Eugen Hrich. *Military Adviser:* Lt. Knöpfler. *Editor:* Walter Fredersdorf.

Cast: René Deltgen (Hannes Hallgarten), Paul Klinger (Sepp Eberle), Maria Andergast (Christa Hambacher), Gustav Waldau (Father Hambacher) Ursula Herking (Leni), Alexa von Porembsky (Toni), Karl Martell (Captain Pfennig), Hans Kettler (Weissgerber, staff sergeant), Rudolf Prack (Unterkirchner, rifleman), Ernö René (Schlemm, mountain soldier), Beppo Brem (Böhninger, mountain soldier), Gustav Püttjer (Tökenbrink, mountain soldier), Rudolf Carl (Ostermann), Karl Etlinger (Senfkorn, schoolmaster retd.), Hill Larsen (waitress), Franz Lichtenauer (postman), Richard Ludwig (1st British officer), Reginald Pasch (2nd British officer), Franz W. Schröder-Schrom (medical officer), Hermann Mayer-Falkow (captain), Otz Tollen (major), Rudolf Platte (candidate Wagner), Rudolf Schündler (candidate "optician"), mountain troops from Mittenwald.

Produced by Germania-Film G.m.b.H., Munich-Berlin. *Staatsauftragsfilm.* 35mm.

Premiere: March 14, 1941, Vienna; May 13, 1941, Berlin. *Distributed by* Herzog-Film G.m.b.H. (Berlin/Leipzig) — Rheinische Film G.m.b.H. (Düsseldorf) — Süddeutsche Commerz-Film G.m.b.H. (Munich) — Germania-Filmgesellschaft (Vienna).

Der Stammbaum des Dr. Pistorius (The Family Tree of Dr. Pistorius)

1939. *Director:* K. G. Külb. *Assistant Director:* Boleslav Barlog. *Screenplay:* K. G. Külb, Reinhard Köster, from the novel by Waldemar Reichardt. *Cinematography:* Robert Baberske. *Music:* Lothar Brühne. *Editor:* Hans Heinrich.

Cast: Ernst Waldow, Käthe Haack, Heinz Wieck, Carsta Löck, Otto Wernicke, Ingolf Kunze, Hans Leibelt, Renée Stobrawa, Rudolf Schündler, Trude Haefelin, Helga Mayer, Günter Brackmann.

Produced by Universum-Film A.-G. (Ufa), Berlin. 35mm. *Premiere:* December 5, 1939. *Distributed by* Universum Filmverleih G.m.b.H. (Ufaleih), Berlin. *Subject:* The coming ideas of Nazi Germany and the son's membership of the Party contribute to an appraisal of human values in the household of a minor government official.

Starke Herzen (reissued in 1953 as Starke Herzen im Sturm)

1937. *Director:* Herbert Maisch. *Producer:* Ulrich Mohrbutter. *Location Manager:* Alexander Desnitzky. *Screenplay:* Walter Wassermann, C. H. Diller [i.e., Lotte Neumann]. *Cinematography:* Günther Rittau. *Assistant Cameramen:* Gerhard Peters, Ekkehard Kyrath. *Stills Photographer:* Horst von Harbou. *Music:* Herbert Windt. Scenes from the opera *Tosca* by Giacomo Puccini. *Art Directors:* Max Mellin, Hermann Asmus. *Wardrobe:* Erwin Rosenfelder, Max Knospe, Elisabeth Kuhn. *Make-Up:* Atelier Jabs, Waldemar Jabs. *Sound:* Erich Leistner. *Editor:* Walter Fredersdorf.

Cast: Gustav Diessl (Alexander von Harbin), Maria Cebotari (Marina Martha, opera singer), Albert Hörrmann (Georg von

Harbin), Hermann Wolder (René Vareno, tenor), Otto Wernicke (Ludwig Raddat, bass buffo), Karl Hellmer (Miller, stage-manager), Ewald Wenck (prop master), Lucie Höflich (Resika Husser, wardrobe mistress), René Deltgen (Viktor Husser, Resika's son), Walter Franck (Simoni), Elisabeth Flickenschildt (Ille), Reginald Pasch (policeman), Ellen Becker, Katja Bennefeld, Kurt Dahn, Jac Diehl, Wilhelm Fassbinder, Alice Franz, Hans Henninger, Oskar Höcker, Karl Hofmann, Herbert Hübner, Willy Kaiser, Josef Karina, Ursula Krieg, Walter Lieck, Karl Meixner, Hans Meyer-Hanno, Kai Möller, Hellmut Passarge, Claus Pohl, Arthur Reinhardt, Walther Süssenguth, Walter Steinweg, Egon Stief, Erika Streithorst, Albert Venohr, Max Vierlinger, Eduard Wenck.

Produced by Universum-Film A.-G. (Ufa), Berlin. *Production Group:* Ulrich Mohrbutter. 35mm. *Laboratory:* Afifa. *Shooting:* mid–March–end of April 1937. *Interiors:* Ufa Studios Neubabelsberg; Ufa Studios Berlin-Tempelhof. *Exteriors:* backlot Neubabelsberg. *Running time:* 80 minutes. Forbidden in November 1937. *Premiere:* January 13, 1953, Stuttgart. *Distributed by* Super Film.

Stosstrupp 1917 (Shock Troop, 1917)

1934. *Directors:* Hans Zöberlein, Ludwig Schmid-Wildy. *Producers:* Franz Adam, Franz Geretshauser, Alfred Oberlindober. *Production Manager:* Marian Kolb. *Screenplay:* Franz Adam, Marian Kolb, Hans Zöberlein, inspired by the novel *Der Glaube an Deutschland* (1931) by Hans Zöberlein. *Cinematography:* Karl Hasselmann, Ludwig Zahn, Franz Barthl Seyr, Josef Wirsching, Carl Dittmann. *Assistant Cameramen:* Gustl Arno Weiss, Karl Buhlmann. *Sound:* Eugen Hrich, Siegfried Schulz. *Editors:* Karl Otto Bartning, Else Baum, Martha Dübber.

Cast: Ludwig Schmid-Wildy (Hans Steinbauer), Albert Penzkofer (non-commissioned officer), Beppo Brem (Girgl), Karl Hanft (Martl), Max Zankl (Heiner), Hans Pössenbacher (Anderl), Hein Evelt (Max), Ludwig ten Kloot (commander), Hans Schaudinn (sergeant), Hanns Erich Pfleger

(Karl), Georg Emmerling (Gustl), Toni Eggert (Toni), Hermann Schlott (Beni), Franz Schröder (Fritz), Karl Müller (Wolfgang), Emil Matousek (Michel), Hans Franz Pokorny (Major), Harry Hertzsch (Lieutenant), Matthias Olschinsky (General), Eberhard Kreysern (staff major), Leopold Kerscher (radio operator), Nestor Lampert (dying man), Georg Heinrich Lange (sapper), Josef Heilmeier (orderly), Franz Wagner (medical orderly), Heinz Burkart, Peter Labertouche, members of the Reichswehr.

Produced by Arya-Film G.m.b.H., Munich/Berlin. 35mm. *Sound System:* Tobis Klangfilm. *Interiors:* Bavaria Studios, Geiselgasteig. *Premiere:* February 20, 1934, Berlin, Ufa-Palast am Zoo. *Distributed by* Union-Film Co.m.b.H., Munich. In the United States released in 1935 as *Shock Troop*.

Stukas

1940–41. *Producer-Director:* Karl Ritter. *Assistant Director:* Conrad von Molo. *Directorial Aide:* Carl von Merznicht. *Production Manager:* Gustav Rathje. *Location Managers:* Fritz Schwarz, Wilhelm (Klinck-)Karras, Arthur Ullmann. *Screenplay:* Karl Ritter, Felix Lützkendorf. *Cinematography:* Heinz Ritter. *Aerial Cinematography:* Heinz Ritter, Walter Meyer, Walter Rosskopf, Hugo von Kaweczinski. *Miniatures and Process Photography:* Gerhard Huttula. *Process Technician:* Willi Körner. *Optical Cinematography:* Theodor Nischwitz. *Music:* Herbert Windt. Lyrics of Stuka Song: Geno Ohlischläger. *Art Director:* Anton Weber. *Assistant Art Director:* Erich Nickel. *Explosives:* Erwin Lange. *Costume Consultant:* Karl Heinz Grohnwald. *Sound:* Werner Maas. *Choreography:* Ursula Deinert. *Aerial Consultants:* Captain Nöller, First Lieutenant Hans Meffert. *Editor:* Conrad von Molo.

Cast: Staff III. Group of a Stuka Squadron — Carl Raddatz (Captain Heinz Bork, flight commander), Albert Hehn (First Lieutenant Hesse, adjutant), Egon Müller-Franken (First Lieutenant Jordan, technique officer), Günther Markert (First Lieutenant Helmers, intelligence officer),

Otto Ernst (O. E.) Hasse (Assistant Medical Director Dr. Gregorius, medical officer), Josef Dahmen (Sergeant Traugott, first mechanic of commander's plane), Erich Stelmecke (Sergeant Rochus, radio operator of commander), Georg Thomalla (Matz, non-commissioned officer, the adjutant's radio operator); 7th Squadron ("Bullenstaffel") — Hannes Stelzer (First Lieutenant H. Wilde, staff captain), Ernst von Klippstein (First Lieutenant von Bomberg, nicknamed "Patzer"), Heinz Wemper (Heinze, master craftsman), Lutz Götz (Staff Sergeant Niederegger), Beppo Brem (First Sergeant Putzenlechner, bomb guard), Fritz Wagner (Sergeant Franz, radio operator of squadron captain), Karl Münch (radio operator of First Lieutenant von Bomberg); 8th Squadron ("Kavalierstaffel") — Carl John (First Lieutenant Lothar Loos, squadron captain), Adolf Fischer (Sergeant Fritz, radio operator of squadron captain); 9th Squadron — Herbert Wilk (First Lieutenant Günther Schwarz), Johannes Schütz (Lieutenant Prack, nicknamed "Küken" [Chick]); the women — Else Knott (Ursula, nurse), Marina von Dittmar (young Frenchwoman), Lilli Schönborn (old French peasant), Ethel Reschke; Eduard von Winterstein, Gothart Portloff, Otz Tollen, Erik Radolf, Hans Wallner, Paul Mehler, John Pauls-Harding, Willy Witte, Botho Kayser, Ronald Werkenthin, Willi Schulte-Vogelheim, Georg Profe, Theodor Rocholl, Tima Stuloff, Bill-Bocketts, Arthur Kühn, Michael von Newlinski, Niki (Niko?) Turoff, Ludwig Wolfram, Werner Faust, Herbert Gärtner, Josef Gindorf, Oskar Kinne, Wolfgang Molitor.

Produced by Universum-Film A.-G (Ufa), Berlin. *Production Group:* Karl Ritter. *Staatsauftragsfilm.* 35mm. *Laboratory:* Afifa. *Interiors:* Ufastadt Babelsberg. *Exteriors:* surroundings of Berlin. *Shooting:* November 18, 1940–mid–February 1941. *Sound System:* Klangfilm. *Budget:* RM 1,961,000. *Running time:* 101 minutes. *Premiere:* June 27, 1941, Berlin, Ufa-Palast am Zoo. *Distributed by* Universum Filmverleih G.m.b.H. (Ufaleih), Berlin.

Tag der Freiheit: Unsere Wehrmacht (Day of Freedom: Our Army)

1935. *Producer-Director:* Leni Riefenstahl. *Cinematography:* Willy Zielke, Guzzi Lantschner, Walter Frentz, Hans Ertl, Kurt Neubert, Albert Kling. *Music:* Peter Kreuder. *Supervising Editor:* Leni Riefenstahl.

Produced by Reichsparteitagfilm der L. R. Studio-Film, Berlin. 35mm. *Sound System:* Tobis Klangfilm. *Running time:* 28 minutes. *Premiere:* December 1935 as short before a major UFA film screening. *Distributed by* Universum-Filmverleih G.m.b.H. (Ufaleih), Berlin.

Titanic

1942. *Director:* Herbert Selpin (movie finished by Werner Klingler). *Production Manager:* Willy Reiber. *Location Manager:* Fritz Schwarz. *Assistant Director:* Erich Frisch. *Screenplay:* Walter Zerlett-Olfenius, Herbert Selpin, from a sketch by Harald Bratt. *Dialogue Supervisor:* Walter Zerlett-Olfenius. *Cinematography:* Friedl Behn-Grund. *Stills Photographer:* Karl Ewald. *Music:* Herbert Pataky, Werner Eisbrenner. *Supervising Art Director:* Fritz Maurischat. *Art Directors:* Robert A. Dietrich, Fritz Lück, August Herrmann. *Costumes:* Max von Formacher. *Special Photographic Effects:* Ernst Kunstmann. *Sound:* Adolf Jansen. *Script Girl:* Hansi Köck. *Editor:* Friedel Buckow.

Cast: Sybille Schmitz (Sigrid Oole), Charlotte Thiele (Mrs. Astor), Kirsten Heiberg (Gloria), Monika Burg (Hedi, manicurist), Lieselotte Klingler (Anne), Hans Nielsen (Petersen, 1st officer), Karl Schönböck (Lord Astor), Ernst Fritz Fürbringer (Sir Bruce Ismay), Otto Wernicke (Captain Smith), Franz Schafheitlin (Henderson), Sepp Rist (Jan), Theo Shall (Murdock, 1st officer), Karl Meixner (Hopkins, Astor's 1st secretary), Theodor Loos (Private Councillor Bergmann), Fritz Böttger (Lord Douglas), Walter Steinbeck (Franklin), Georg Heinrich Schnell (Morrison), Werner Scharf (Mendoz), Karl Fochler (1st steward), Peter

Elsholtz (Bobby, farm hand), Aruth Wartan (Levantine), Hans Schwarz, Jr. (athletic guy), Toni von Bukovics (duchess), Herbert Gernot (detective), Karl Dannemann (Philipps, 1st radio operator), Heinz Welzel (Breede, 2nd radio operator), Charlotte Tiedemann (young woman with child), Jolly Marée [Bohnert] (Marcia, dancer), Fritz Genschow (Henry, farm hand), Walter Steinweg (officer on deck), Just Scheu (Bergmann's secretary), Josef Kamper (Romain, 1st engineer), Alexander Wuma (Hesketh, assistant engineer), Hermann Brix (Gruber, musical director), Peter Voss (physician), Ernst Stahl-Nachbaur (judge), Herbert Tiede (Lightholder, 2nd officer), Susa Jera (child), Erich Dunskus (captain of freighter), Claus Holm (sailor on freighter), Egon Vogel (employee at Stock Exchange).

Produced by Tobis Film, Berlin. 35mm. *Interiors:* Jofa Studios, Berlin-Johannisthal. *Exteriors:* Gotenhafen ("Cap Arcona"); Scharmützelsee (miniatures). *Shooting:* February 23, 1942–October 31, 1942. Banned in April 1943 in German territories. *Premiered in Paris. Released* on February 7, 1950, in Stuttgart by Central-Europäischer Filmverleih. *East German distributor:* Progress Filmverleih, Berlin. *In 1955 reiussed by* Filmverleih Südwest G.m.b.H., Frankfurt/Main.

Togger

1936–37. *Director:* Jürgen von Alten. *Production Manager:* Curt Prickler. *Location Managers:* Adolf Essek, Conny Carstennsen (a.k.a. Friedrich Wirth). *Screenplay:* Walter Forster, Heinz Bierkowski. *Cinematography:* Reimar Kuntze, Benno Stinauer. *Stills Photographer:* Karl Lindner. *Music:* Harold M. Kirchstein. *Songs:* "Ich bin in das Leben verliebt"; "Die Liebe ist ein Spiel mit dem Feuer" (sung by Hilde Seipp). *Lyrics:* Hans Fritz Beckmann. Art Directors: Gustav Knauer, Alex Mügge. *Sound:* Hans Rütten.

Cast: Renate Müller (Hanna), Paul Hartmann (Togger), Mathias Wiemann (Peter Geiss), Heinz Salfner (Professor Breitenbach), Hilde Seipp (Maria de Costa), Paul

Otto (Breitenbach), Fritz Odemar (Mariano), Walter Franck (Berg, managing editor), Karl Hellmer (Polle), Dr. Ernst Dernburg (Wölfer), Fritz Rasp (Dublanc), Ernst Waldow (Rakovicz), Volker von Collande (Hallmann), Alfred Kiwitt (Weber), Just Scheu (NS journalist), Oscar Höcker (worker), Paul Westermeier (first-aid man), Ewerth (general manager), Walter Werner (Father Andreas), Ursula Herking (Tiffi), Carl Auen (detective), Hans Meyer-Hanno (malicious agitator), Franz W. Schröder-Schrom, Maria Krahn.

Produced by Minerva-Tonfilm GmbH., Berlin. *Staatsauftragsfilm.* 35mm. *Sound System:* Tobis Klangfilm. *Premiere:* February 12, 1937. *Distributed by* Syndikat-Film G.m.b.H. (Tobis), Berlin.

Triumph des Willens (Triumph of the Will)

1934–35. *Producer-Director:* Leni Riefenstahl. *Production manager:* Walter Traut. *Location Manager:* Arthur Kiekebusch. *Assistant Directors:* Erna Peters, Guzzi Lantschner, Otto Lantschner, Walter Prager. *Volontary:* Wolfgang Brüning. *Director of Photography:* Sepp Allgeier. *Cinematographers:* Sepp Allgeier, Karl Attenberger, Werner Bohne, Walter Frentz, Hans Gottschalk, Werner Hundhausen, Herbert Kebelmann, Albert Kling, Franz Koch, Ernst Kunstmann, Herbert Kutschbach, Paul Lieberenz, Richard Nickel, Walter Riml, Arthur von Schwertführer, Karl Vass, Franz Weihmayr, Siegfried Weinmann, Karl Wellert. *Assistant Cameramen:* Sepp Ketterer, Wolfgang Hart, Peter Haller, Kurt Schulz, Eugen Oskar Bernhard, Richard Kandler, Hans Bühring, Richard Böhm, Erich Stoll, Josef Koch, Otto Jäger, August Beis, Hans Wittmann, Wolfgang Müller, Hans Linke, Erich Küchler, Wilhelm Schmidt, Erich Grohmann. *Special Photography:* Arbeitsgemeinschaft Svend Noldan, Fritz Brutsch, Hans Noack. *Stills Photographer:* Rolf Lantin. *Still Reproductions:* Gisela Lindeck-Schneeberger. *Aerial Cinematographer:* Albert Kling. *Pilots:* Captain Rolf Hanasch (Luftschiff T/PN 30), Anton Riediger (Klemm airplane). *Music:* Herbert Windt. Musikkorps der SS-Leibstandarte Adolf Hitler [Band of the SS Bodyguard of Adolf Hitler] directed by Bandmaster Müller-John. *Sets:* City Councilor Burgmann, Architect Seegy. *Sound:* Siegfried Schulze, Ernst Schütz. *Supervising Editor:* Leni Riefenstahl. *Editors:* Erna Peters and others. *Sound Editors:* Bruno Hartwich, Alice Ludwig.

Produced by Reichsparteitagfilm der L.R. Studio-Film, Berlin. "*Produced by* order of the Führer." *Suggested by* Leopold Gutterer, senior civil servant, Department II, Reich Ministry for People's Education and Propaganda. 35mm. *Sound System:* Tobis Klangfilm. Incorporated newsreel footage: Ufa, Deulig, Tobis-Melo, Fox, Paramount. *Running time:* 114 minutes [original version: 140 minutes]. *Premiere:* March 28, 1935, Berlin, Ufa-Palast am Zoo. *Distributed by* Universum-Filmverleih G.m.b.H. (Ufaleih), Berlin.

U-Boote Westwärts! (U Boats Westwards/U Boats to the West!)

1940–41. *Director:* Günther Rittau. *Assistant Director:* Wolfgang Wehrum. *Producer:* Ulrich Mohrbutter. *Location Managers:* Alexander Desnitzky, Joe Rive, Wilhelm Albert Marchand. *Original Idea and Screenplay:* Georg Zoch. *Cinematography:* Igor Oberberg. *Stills Photographer:* Otto Schulz. *Music:* Harald Böhmelt. *Lyrics:* Bruno Balz. Matrosenchor der MKK, Berlin. *Art Directors:* Hans Sohnle, Wilhelm Vorwerg. *Costume Consultant:* Gertrud Steckler. *Sound:* Bruno Suckau. *Editors:* Wolfgang Wehrum, Johanna Meisel.

Cast: Ilse Werner (Irene Winterfeld), Herbert Wilk (Lieutenant Commander Hoffmeister), Heinz Engelmann (Wiegandt, naval first lieutenant), Joachim Brennecke (von Benedikt, naval lieutenant), Ernst Wilhelm Borchert (First Lieutenant Griesbach, engineer), Josef Sieber (Warmbusch, bosun), Carsta Löck (Käte Merk), Karl John (Drewitz, first sailor private), Clemens Hasse (Sonntag, machine mate), Herbert Klatt (Buttgereit, bosun mate), Clementina Egies (Mrs. Hoffmeister), Willi Rose (Fliepusch, sailor), Jens von Hagen (captain of a Netherlands steamer), Ingeborg Senkpiel (Agnes Schenk), Agnes Windeck (Mrs. von Benedikt), Claire Reigbert (Mrs. Hahn), Theo Shall (English Officer), Erich Stelmecke (Willig, radio operator), Friedrich Karl Burkhardt (Bergmann, first steersman), Hans Hessling (Wackerle, sailor private), Heinz Goedecke, Margarete Sachse, Elsbeth Siegurth, Ruth Tuxedo, Hans Bergmann, Erwin Biegel, Eduard Bornträger, Karl Harbacher, Albert Karchow, Franz List, Günther Markert, Hans Mierendorf, Gustav Püttjer, Wolfgang von Schwindt, Hans zum Sande, Hans von Uritz, Herbert Weissbach, Ewald Wenck.

Produced by Universum-Film A.-G. (Ufa), Berlin. *Production Group:* Ulrich Mohrbutter. *Production supported by* Oberkommando der Marine (Supreme Command of Navy). *Staatsauftragsfilm.* 35mm. *Laboratory:* Afifa. *Sound System:* Klangfilm. *Interiors:* Ufastadt Babelsberg. *Exteriors:* Kiel and surroundings. *Shooting:* June 14, 1940–beginning of February 1941. *Running time:* 100 minutes. *Premiere:* May 9, 1941, Berlin, Ufa-Palast am Zoo. *Distributed by* Universum Filmverleih G.m.b.H. (Ufaleih), Berlin.

Über Alles in der Welt (Over Everyone in the World)

1940–41. *Producer-Director:* Karl Ritter. *Assistant Director:* Gottfried Ritter. *Location Manager:* George Dahlström. *Screenplay/Original Idea:* Karl Ritter, Felix Lützkendorf. *Cinematography:* Werner Krien. *Miniatures and Process Photography:* Gerhard Huttula. *Process Technician:* Willi Körner. *Music:* Herbert Windt. *Art Director:* Walter Röhrig. *Costumes:* Karl Heinz Gronwald, Vera Mügge. *Sound:* Erich Leistner. *Editor:* Gottfried Ritter.

Cast: Carl Raddatz (Carl Wiegand), Hannes Stelzer (Hans Wiegand), Marina von Ditmar (Brigitta), Fritz Kampers (Fritz Möbius), Berta Drews (Anna Möbius), Carsta Löck (Erika Möbius), Joachim Brennecke (Willy Möbius), Paul Hartmann (Colonel-Lieutenant Steinhart), Carl John (First Lieutenant Hassenkamp), Josef Dahmen (Weber, non-commissioned officer), Georg Thomalla (Krause, non-commissioned officer), Herbert A. E. Böhme (Captain Hansen), Wilhelm König (Boysen, radio operator), Oskar Sima (Leo Samek), Karl Haubenreisser (Sally Nürnberg), Maria Bard (Madeleine Laroche), Andrews Engelmann (Captain John Stanley), Hans Baumann (Robert Brown), Ernst Sattler (Rainthaler), Lutz Götz (Hofer), Franz Lichtenauer (Grassegger), Albert Janschek (Reindl), Marianne Straub (Walburga), Peter Elsholtz (Dr. von Kriesis), Kurt Gensichen (Glockenberg, government assistant), Eva Tinschmann (Isolde, senior nursing officer), Oskar Sabo (Friedrich Wilhelm Hoppe), Gerhard Dammann (master craftsman at Siemens factory), Beppo Brem (Putzenlechner), Hermann Günther (Alsatian mayor).

Produced by Universum-Film A.-G., Berlin. *Production Group:* Karl Ritter. *Staatsauftragsfilm.* 35mm. *Laboratory:* Afifa. *Interiors:* Ufa-Stadt Babelsberg. *Exteriors:* surroundings of Danzig, Greifswald, Grossglockner area. *Shooting:* May 3–end of September 1940. *Running time:* 85 minutes. *Premiere:* March 19, 1941, Posen, Deutsche Lichtspiele; March 21, 1941, Berlin, Ufa-Palast am Zoo. *Distributed by* Universum Filmverleih G.m.b.H. (Ufaleih), Berlin.

Um das Menschenrecht: ein Filmwerk aus der Freikorpszeit/Sturmtage 1919 (For the Rights of Men)

1934. *Director-Production Manager:* Hans Zöberlein. *Supervisor and Assistant Director:* Ludwig Schmid-Wildy. *Producers:* Franz Adam, Franz Geretshauser, Alfred Oberlindober. *Location Manager:* Anton Höhn. *Screenplay/Treatment:* Hans Zöberlein. *Cinematography:* Ludwig Zahn, Franz Barthl Seyr. *Stills Photographer:* Rudolf Reissner. *Art Directors:* Max Seefelder, Josef Franz Strobl. *Sound:* Eugen Hrich. *Editor:* Friedel Buckow.

Cast: Hans Schlenck (Hans), Kurt Holm (Fritz), Hilde Horst (his wife), Ernst Martens (Max), Beppo Brem (Girgl), Rose Kugler (his wife), Ludwig ten Kloot (the Captain), Hans Erich Pfleger (Paul, volunteer corps man), Paul Schaidler (Christian, volunteer corps man), Franz Loskarn (Höllein, volunteer corps man), Leopold Kerscher (Martin, volunteer corps man), Werner Scharf (leader of the Reds), Ludwig Körösy (second leader of the Reds), Trude Haefelin (Petratka, Russian agent), Katja Specht (Natasha, Russian agent), Hans Pössenbacher (Spartacist), Ludwig Schmid-Wildy (old man Krafft), Lydia Alexandra (Berta Schön), Elise Aulinger, Beppo Benz, Georg Emmerling, Hans Engelhardt, Heinz Evelt, Erwin Fichtner, Hans Herbert Fiedler, Minna Höcker-Behrens, Adolf Lallinger, Hermann Pittschau, Franz Polland, Elisabeth Reich, Josef Reithofer, Else Reval, Ernst Günther Schiffner, Hermann Schlott, Ludwig Schmitz, Heddo Schulenburg, Kaspar Sedlmayer, Alfred Stratmann, Toni Thoms, Philipp Veit, Franz Vogl, Franz Wagner, Ludwig Wengg, Wastl Witt, Kurt Zwanziger.

Produced and distributed by Arya-Film G.m.b.H., Munich/Berlin. 35mm. *Sound System:* Tobis Klangfilm. *Shooting:* beginning-end of October 1934. *Interiors:* Jofa Studios, Berlin-Johannisthal. *Exteriors:* Munich. *Premiere:* December 28, 1934, Berlin, Ufa-Palast am Zoo.

Der unendliche Weg (The Endless Way)

1943. *Director:* Hans Schweikart. *Screenplay:* Walter von Molo, Ernst von Salomon, from the novel "Ein Deutscher ohne Deutschland" by Walter von Molo. *Cinematography:* Franz Koch. *Music:* Oskar Wagner.

Cast: Eugen Klöpfer, Eva Immermann, Hedwig Wangel, Alice Treff, Kurt Müller-Graf, Friedrich Domin, Ernst Fritz Fürbringer, Lisa Hellwig, Viktor Afritsch, Josef Offenbach, Adolf Gondrell, Günther Hadank, Gustav Waldau, Herbert Hübner, Walter Holten, Oskar Höcker, Fritz Reiff, Philipp Manning, Walter Lantzsch, Walter Buhse, Heinz Burkart, A. von Cortens, Wolfgang Dohnberg, Peter Doming, Karl Graumann, Karl Hanft, Hannes Keppler, Herbert Kroll, Else Kündinger, Eduard Loibner, Emil Matousek, Julius Riedmüller, Sonja-Gerda Scholz, Franz W. Schröder-Schrom, Anni Trautner, Otz Tollen.

Produced by Bavaria, Munich. *Staatsauftragsfilm. Premiere:* August 24, 1943, Stuttgart; August 27, 1943, Berlin. *Distributed by* DFV, Berlin. *Subject:* Live story of Suabian Economist Friedrich List in the first half of 18th century.

Unternehmen Michael (The Michael Action/ The Private's Job)

1937. *Producer-Director:* Karl Ritter. *Location Manager:* Ludwig Kühr. *Assistant Director:* Friedrich Karl von Puttkamer. *Screenplay:* Karl Ritter, Mathias Wiemann, Fred Hildenbrandt, from the stage play by and with the cooperation of Hans Fritz Zwehl. *Cinematography:* Günther Anders. *Stills Photographer:* Willi Klitzke. *Music:* Herbert Windt. *Art Director:* Walter Röhrig. *Wardrobe:* Paul Haupt, Otto Zander. *Make-Up Artist:* Willi Weber. *Sound:* Ludwig Ruhe. *Editor:* Gottfried Ritter.

Cast: Heinrich George (commanding general), Mathias Wiemann (Major zur Linden, general staff officer Ia), Willy Birgel (Major Count Schellenberg), Hannes Stelzer (Lieutenant Prince Erxburg), Paul Otto (Lieutenant Colonel Hegenau), Ernst Karchow (Captain Noack, Ib), Otto Graf (Captain von Groth, Ic), Christian Kayssler (cavalry captain von Wengern), Kurt Waitzmann (first lieutenant Weber), Paul Schwed (non-commissioned officer of staff guard), Arthur Wiesner (guard of carrier pigeons), Otto Wernicke (Colonel Berg), Heinz Welzel (Lieutenant von Treskow), Josef Renner (Captain Hill), Jim Simmons (Lieutenant Mertens), Karl John (Lieutenant Hassenkamp), Otto Krone (first company commander), Malte Jäger (second company commander), Friedrich Berger (Henke, non-commissioned officer), Beppo Brem (Private Kollermann), Lutz Götz (musketeer Raspe), Josef Dahmen (moaner), Adolf Fischer

(combat orderly), Hans Bergmann (*Sturmmann*), Franz Ernst Bochum (old Frenchman), Elsa Wagner (old Frenchwoman), Otz Tollen (batallion commander of infantry), Max Hiller (British prisoner of war).

Produced by Universum-Film A.-G., Berlin. *Production Group:* Karl Ritter. *Staatsauftragsfilm.* 35mm. *Laboratory:* Afifa. *Sound System:* Tobis Klangfilm. *Shooting:* May 12–end of June 1937. *Interiors:* Ufa Studios Neubabelsberg. *Running time:* 82 minutes. *Premiere:* September 7, 1937, Ufa-Palast Nürnberg on the occasion of the 9th Party Rally of NSDAP; November 19, 1937, Berlin, Ufa-Palast am Zoo. *Distributed by* Universum Filmverleih G.m.b.H. (Ufaleih), Berlin.

Urlaub auf Ehrenwort (Holiday on Parole/ Furlough on Parole/ Leave on Parole)

1937. *Producer-Director:* Karl Ritter. *Location Managers:* Ludwig Kühr, Dietrich von Theobald, Heinz Karchow, Wilhelm Marchand. *Assistant Director:* Friedrich Karl von Puttkamer. *Screenplay:* Charles Klein, Felix Lützkendorf, from an idea conceived by Kilian Koll [i.e., Walter Julius Bloem, Jr.] and Charles Klein and inspired by a novel by Walter Bloem. *Cinematography:* Günther Anders. *Assistant Cameraman:* Curt Fischer. *Stills Photographer:* Eugen Klagemann. *Music:* Ernst Erich Buder. *Song:* "Die Liebe ist das Element des Lebens." *Lyrics:* Franz Baumann. *Art Director:* Walter Röhrig. *Wardrobe:* Hauk, Maria Hellmer-Kühr. *Make-Up Artists:* Fredy Arnold, Jutta Lange, Wilhelm Weber. *Sound:* Ludwig Ruhe. *Editor:* Gottfried Ritter.

Cast: Ingeborg Theek (Inge), Fritz Kampers (Private Hartmann), Rolf Moebius (Lt. Walter Prätorius), Berta Drews (Anna Hartmann), René Deltgen (Emil Sasse, infantryman), Heinz Welzel (Jahnke, recruit), Carl Raddatz (Dr. Jens Kirchhoff, infantryman), Jakob Sinn (Schmiedecke, infantryman), Ludwig Schmitz (Ludwig Pichel, infantryman), Hans Reinhardt Knitsch (Kurt Hellwig, recruit), Willi Rose (Julius Krawutke, infantryman), Wilhelm König (Ullrich Hagen, infantryman), Kurt Waitzmann (Dr. Wegener, infantryman), Franz Weber (Schnettelker, non-commissioned officer), Otz Tollen (Captain Falk), Hadrian Maria Netto (First Lieutenant von Treskow-Dyrenfurth), Heinrich Schroth (Lieutenant Colonel), Käte Haack (Maria, nurse), Evi Eva (Dolores Schulze), Iwa Wanja (Ilonka), Ruth Störmer (Vera Georgi), Otto Graf (Prof. Knudsen), Eduard Bornträger (Prof. Hasenkamp), Lotte Werkmeister (Mrs. Krawutke), Ewald Wenck (Hans-Georg Krause), Christine Grabe (Adelheid), Margot Erbst (Fritzi), Elisabeth Wendt (Lulu Frey), Herbert Weissbach (Hektor Hasse Hellriegel), Herbert Gernot (Rostowski), Karl Wagner (Karl Lemke), Ilse Fürstenberg (Mrs. Schmiedeke), Fritz Claudius, Josef Dahmen (two crooks), Beppo Brem (man from Bavaria), Gustav Mahnke (man from the Mark), Charlie Kracker (man from Hamburg), Heinz Förster-Ludwig (man from Cologne), Walter Schramm-Duncker (man from Saxony), Martha von Kossatzki (landlady), Trude Lehmann (cook), Oscar Sabo, Kai Möller, Karl Hannemann, Klaus Pohl, Aribert Grimmer, Horst Teetzmann, Hildegard Fränzel. *Produced by* Universum-Film A.-G., Berlin. *Production Group:* Karl Ritter. *Staatsauftragsfilm.* 35mm. *Laboratory:* Afifa. *Shooting:* end of August–end of October 1937. *Interiors:* Ufa Atelier Neubabelsberg. *Budget:* RM 598,000. *Running time:* 88 minutes. *Premiere:* January 11, 1938, Cologne, Ufa-Palast; January 19, 1938, Berlin, Ufa-Palast am Zoo. *Distributed by* Universum Filmverleih G.m.b.H. (Ufaleih), Berlin.

Venus vor Gericht
(Venus on Trial)

1941. *Director:* Hans H. Zerlett. *Screenplay:* Hans H. Zerlett. *Cinematography:* Oskar Schnirch. *Music:* Leo Leux.

Cast: Hansi Knoteck, Hannes Stelzer, Siegfried Breuer, Paul Dahlke, Charlott Daudert, Ernst Fritz Fürbringer, Josef Eichheim, Erhard Siedel, Carl Wery, Hans Brausewetter, Hubert von Meyerinck, Justus

Paris, Fritz Reiff, Peter Elsholtz, Adolf Gondrell, Liesl Karlstadt, Eva Tinschmann, Elise Aulinger, Heini Handschumacher, Martin Urtel, Gabriele Reissmüller, Albert Hôrrmann, Fritz Hoopts, Rudolph Vogel, Wastl Witt. *Produced by* Bavaria Filmkunst, Munich. 35mm. *Premiere:* June 4, 1941. *Distributed by* Bavaria. A so-called comedy: In 1930 a Jewish art dealer sells a presumed antique statue found in a Bavarian field for a fantastic sum to the government. A young Nazi sculptor proves that he has made and buried that "artifact" to show up the degeneracy of modern art.

Der verlorene Sohn
(The Prodigal Son)

1933–34. *Director:* Luis Trenker. *Production Manager:* Fred Lyssa. *Location Manager:* Rudolf Fichtner. *Assistant Directors:* Werner Klingler, Reinhart Steinbicker. *Screenplay:* Luis Trenker assisted by Reinhart Steinbicker, Arnold Ulitz. *Cinematography:* Albert Benitz, Reimar Kuntze. *Assistant Cameraman:* Klaus von Rautenfeld. *Music:* Dr. Giuseppe Becce. *Art Directors:* Fritz Maurischat, Hans L. Minzloff. *Property Men:* Max Klar, Paul Gaeble. *Costumes:* Herbert Ploberger. *Make-Up Artists:* Martin Gericke, Adolf Braun. *Sound:* Hans Grimm. *Editors:* Waldemar Gaede, Andrew Marton.

Cast: Luis Trenker (Tonio Feuersinger), Eduard Köck (his father), Maria Andergast (Barbl Gudauner), Bertl Schultes (her father), Melanie Horeschowsky (Rosina), Marian Marsh (Lilian Williams), Franz W. Schröder-Schrom (her father), Paul Henckels (teacher), Emmerich Albert, Hans Jamnig, Luis Gerold (woodcutters and mountain guides), Lore Schützendorf (a girl), Jimmie Fox (Tonio's American friend).

Produced by Deutsche Universal-Film A.-G., Berlin. 35mm. *Sound System:* Tobis Klangfilm. *Shooting* September 1933–April 1934. *Interiors:* Jofa Studios, Berlin-Johannisthal. *Exteriors:* Waidbruck and Ortisei near Bozen; New York. *Running time:* 102 minutes. *Premiere:* September 6, 1934, Stuttgart, Universum; October 3, 1934, Berlin,

Capitol. *Distributed by* Rota-Film A.-G. (Tobis), Berlin.

Verräter (working title: *Achtung, Verräter!*) *(The Traitor)*

1936. *Producer-Director:* Karl Ritter. *Associate Director:* Hans Weidemann. *Location Manager:* Ludwig Kühr. *Assistant Director:* Karl Friedrich von Puttkamer. *Screenplay:* Leonhard Fürst, from an idea and a script conceived by Walter Herzlieb, Hans Wagner. *Cinematography:* Günther Anders. *Aerial Cinematography:* Heinz von Jaworsky. *Assistant Cameraman:* Karl Plinzner. *Stills Photographer:* Willi Klitzke. *Music:* Harold M. Kirchstein. *Art Directors:* Max Mellin, Franz Koehn. *Prop Masters:* Otto Rülicke, Otto Arndt. *Wardrobe:* Paul Haupt, Ida Revelly. *Make-Up Artists:* Willi Weber, Maria Arnold. *Sound:* Ludwig Ruhe. *Editor:* Gottfried Ritter.

Cast: Willy Birgel (Agent Morris), Lida Baarova (Marion), Irene von Meyendorff (Hilde Körner), Theodor Loos (Dr. Auer), Rudolf Fernau (Fritz Brockau), Herbert A. E. Böhme (Agent Schulz), Heinz Welzel (Hans Klemm), Paul Dahlke (Geyer, a spy), Josef Dahmen (helper), Hans Zesch-Ballot (Dr. Wehner), Sepp Rist (Kilian, commissioner), Volker von Collande (Kröpke, candidate), Ernst Karchow (Major Walen), Siegfried Schürenberg (Lieutenant Colonel Naumann), Carl Junge-Swinburne (commander of a tank division), Otto Graf (Captain Dressler), Heinrich Schroth (general manager T-Metallwerke), Hans Henninger (Max), Carl Auen (Assmann, detective), Ewald Wenck (Schober, detective superintendent), Willi Rose (Ede, crook), Gisela von Collande (Trude), Wolfgang Uecker (son of Ede and Trude), Ernst Behmer (suburban photographer), Reinhold Hauer (pilot), Max Hochstetter (master craftsman), Hans Meyer-Hanno (first assistant mechanic), Hans Schneider (second assistant mechanic), Hellmuth Passarge (third assistant mechanic), Kurt Daehn (secret courier), Käthe Buchwalder (maid), Paul Schwed, Egon Brosig, Karl Hannemann, Paul Rehkopf.

Produced by Universum-Film A.-G. (Ufa), Berlin. *Production Group:* Karl Ritter. *Staatsauftragsfilm.* 35mm. *Laboratory:* Afifa, Berlin. *Shooting:* beginning of May–end of July 1936. *Interiors:* Ufa Studios Neubabelsberg. *Exteriors:* tank regiment in Wünsdorf. *Premiere:* August 24, 1936, Venice IFF; September 9, 1936, Nürnberg Ufa-Palast on the occasion of 8th party rally of NSDAP; September 15, 1936, Berlin Ufa-Palast am Zoo. *Running time:* 92 minutes. *Distributed by* Universum Filmverleih G.m.b.H. (Ufaleih), Berlin.

Die vier Musketiere *(The Four Musketeers)*

1934. *Director:* Heinz Paul. *Screenplay:* Sigmund Graff, Hella Moja, Heinz Paul from the play by Sigmund Graff. *Cinematography:* Bruno Timm. *Music:* Herbert Windt.

Cast: Hans Brausewetter, Fritz Kampers, Paul Westermeier, Erhard Siedel, Hermann Speelmans, Werner Schott, Fritz Odemar, Friedrich Ettel, Lieselott Schaack, Käthe Haack, Agnes Straub, Carsta Löck, Arthur Reinhardt, Gustav Püttjer, Martha Ziegler, Peter Erkelenz, Leo Peukert, Ernst Behmer, Willy Mendau, Hans Albin, Renée Burzat.

Produced by Terra-Film A.-G., Berlin. Production Group: Heinz Paul. *Staatsauftragsfilm. Premiere:* April 27, 1934, Berlin, Primus-Palast and Titania-Palast. *Distributed by* Terra-Filmverleih G.m.b.H., Berlin. *Subject:* Comradeship of four front-line officers in World War I.

Volldampf voraus *(Full Steam Ahead)*

1933. *Director:* Carl Froelich. *Screenplay:* E. von Spiegel, Carl Froelich. *Cinematography:* Emil Schünemann, Karl Vass, Paul Lieberenz, Karl Sesselmann. *Music:* Harald Böhmelt.

Cast: Karl Ludwig Diehl, Peter Erkelenz, Hans Junkermann, Margot Wagner, Karl Dannemann, Christine Grabe, Max Koske, Rudolf Koch-Riehl, Will Kaufmann, Walter Supper, Ludwig Andersen.

Produced by Carl Froelich-Film G.m.b.H., Berlin. *Staatsauftragsfilm. Premiere:* January 3, 1934, Berlin, Ufa-Palast am Zoo. *Distributed by* Europa-Filmverleih A.-G., Berlin. *Subject:* German Navy, torpedo boats and a love story.

Weisse Sklaven (White Slaves)

1936. *Producer-Director:* Karl Anton. *Location Managers:* Hans Schönmetzler, Karl Heinz Bock. *Screenplay:* Karl Anton, Arthur Pohl, Felix von Eckardt, based on a factual report by Charlie Roellinghoff. *Cinematography:* Herbert Körner. *Stills Photographer:* Richard Wesel. *Music:* Peter Kreuder, Friedrich Schröder. *Art Directors:* Erich Zander, Bruno Lutz. *Sound:* Emil Specht. *Editor:* Ludolf Griesebach.

Cast: Camilla Horn (Manja), Theodor Loos (Governor), Werner Hinz (Boris Wolinski), Karl John (Kostja), Agnes Straub (Sinaida), Fritz Kampers (Ivan), Albert Florath (physician), Alexander Engel (Turbin), Hans Stiebner (commissioner), Willi Schur (Nikotin), Karl Meixner (executioner), Werner Pledath (Panin), Tatjana Sais (chansonette).

Produced by Lloyd-Film. *Staatsauftragsfilm.* 35mm. *Running time:* 110 minutes. *Rereleased as Panzerkreuzer Sebastopol (Battleship Sebastopol)* by ASCO-Film Alexander S. Scotti, Wiesbaden; EFU Europäische Film-Union Filmgesellschaft m.b.H., Frankfurt/Main.

Wetterleuchten um Barbara (Storms Over Barbara)

1941. *Director:* Werner Klingler. *Producer:* Rolf Randolf. *Location Manager:* C. L. Löffert. *Assistant Director:* Adolf Schlissleder. *Screenplay:* Hanns Sassmann, Harald G. Petersson, based on the novel by Irmgard Wurmbrand. *Cinematography:* Sepp Allgeier. *Music:* Herbert Windt. *Art Directors:* Heinrich Richter, Gabriel Pellon. *Sound:* Ewald Otto. *Editor:* Roger von Norman.

Cast: Sybille Schmitz (Barbara Stammer), Attila Hörbiger (Martin Stammer), Maria Koppenhöfer (Mother Stammer), Viktor Staal (Anton Walcher), Oskar Sima (Gansterer, commander of militia), Eduard Köck (Rottbichler), Heinrich Heilinger (Dr. Heiderer), Hans Jamnig (Sergeant Kratzer), Georg Vogelsang (Aegyd, farm-hand), Maria Stadler (Wettl, milkmaid), Leopold Esterle (Hansbauer), Ilse Exl (his wife), Leopold Kerscher (Ödbauer, farmer), Liselotte Berker, Hugo Flink, Louis Gerold, Carl Günther, Hans Hanauer, Franz Lichtenauer, Karl Meixner, Waldemar Moosbacher, Magnus Stifter, Erich Teibler, Rudolf Vones.

Produced by Rolf Randolf-Film. 35mm. *Sound System:* Tobis Klangfilm. *Interiors:* Althoff Studios Babelsberg. *Export:* Deutsche Filmexport G.m.b.H., Berlin. *Distributed by* Märkische-Panorama-Schneider-Südost.

Wien 1910 (Vienna 1910)

1942. *Director:* E. W. Emo. *Production Manager:* Karl Künzel. *Assistant Director:* Karl Goritschan. *Location Manager:* Felix René Fohn. *Screenplay:* Gerhard Menzel. *Cinematography:* Hans Schneeberger. *Assistant Cameraman:* Sepp Ketterer. *Stills Photographer:* Hans Natge. *Music:* Willy Schmidt-Gentner. *Art Director:* Karl Weber. *Costumes Advisor:* Professor Remigius Geyling. *Sound:* Otto Untersalmberger. *Editors:* Arnfried Heyne, Muni Obal.

Cast: Rudolf Forster (Dr. Karl Lueger), Heinrich George (Ritter von Schönerer), Lil Dagover (Marie Anschütz), Carl Kuhlmann (Lechner, Sr.), O[tto] W[ilhelm] Fischer (Lechner, Jr.), Otto Tressler (Count Paar), Heinrich Heilinger (Dr. Gessmann), Harry Hardt (Dr. Weisskirchner), Alfred Neugebauer (Pumera), Auguste Pünkösdy (Hildegard Lueger), Rosa Albach-Retty (Rosa Lueger), Eduard Köck* (Prof. Dr. Pupovach), Herbert Hübner (Dr. Viktor Adler), Karl Hellmer (Schmöger), Hans Unterkircher (Panzinger), Oskar von Duniecky (Burchard, secretary of German National

---

Originally cast for this part was Paul Hörbiger.

Party), Kurt von Lessen (Neumayer), Erik Frey (Birkner).

Produced by Wien-Film G.m.b.H., Vienna. *Staatsauftragsfilm.* 35mm. *Interiors:* Studio Rosenhügel, Vienna. *Running time:* 87 minutes. *Distributed by* DFV (Deutsche Filmvertriebs Gesellschaft m.b.H.), Berlin.

Wunder des Fliegens
(Miracle of Flight)

1935. *Director:* Heinz Paul. *Screenplay:* Peter Francke, Heinz Paul. *Cinematography:* Hans Schneeberger, Heinz von Jaworsky. *Music:* Dr. Giuseppe Becce.

Cast: Ernst Udet (himself), Jürgen Ohlsen (Heinz), Käthe Haack (Heinz' mother).

Produced by Terra-Film A.G., Berlin. 35mm. *Premiere:* May 14, 1935, Munich; May 22, 1935, Berlin. *Distributed by* Terra-Filmverleih g.m.b.H., Berlin.; from September 1937: Degeto-Kulturfilm G.m.b.H.

Wunschkonzert
(Request Concert)

1940. *Director:* Eduard von Borsody. *Producer:* F. Pfitzner. *Assistant Producer:* Erich Roehl. *Location Managers:* F. A. Brodersen, Willi Rother, Günther Andrae. *Screenplay:* Felix Lützkendorf, Eduard von Borsody. *Cinematography:* Franz Weihmayr, Günther Anders, Carl Drews. *Music:* Werner Bochmann. *Art Directors:* Alfred Bütow, Heinrich Beisenherz. *Costumes:* Gertrud Steckler. *Sound:* Walter Rühland. *Editor:* Elisabeth Neumann.

Cast: Ilse Werner (Inge Wagner), Carl Raddatz (Herbert Koch), Heinz Goedecke (himself), Joachim Brennecke (Helmut Winkler), Ida Wüst (Frau Eichhorn), Hedwig Bleibtreu (Frau Wagner), Hans Herrmann-Schaufuss (Herr Hammer), Hans Adalbert Schlettow (Herr Kramer), Malte Jaeger (Friedrich, teacher), Walter Ladengast (Herr Schwarzkopf), Albert Florath (physician at Friedrich), Elise Aulinger (Frau Schwarzkopf), Wilhelm Althaus (Captain Freiberg), Walter Bechmann (waiter), Günther Lüders (Zimmermann, mechanic),

Erwin Biegel ("Justav," mechanic), Ellen Hille (Frau Kramer), Vera Hartegg (Frau Friedrich), Vera Complojer (Frau Hammer), Rolf Heydel (pilot aide-de-camp), Wilhelm König (Sergeant Weber), Erich Stelmecke, Ewald Wenck (controller), Willi Rose (mechanic), Oskar Ballhaus (Peters, mechanic), Gustav Püttjer (sailor), Wolf Dietrich, Werner Schott, Fritz Angermann, Max Wilmsen, Hans Sternberg, Franz List, Reinhold Bernt, Erik Radolf, Rudolf Vones, Fred [Selva-]Goebel, Oscar Sabo, Berta Drews. Appearing in the broadcast of *Request Concert:* Marika Rökk, Heinz Rühmann, Paul Hörbiger, Hans Brausewetter, Josef Sieber, Willy Fritsch, Weiss-Ferdl, Wilhelm Strienz, Albert Bräu, Philharmonic Orchestra Berlin, Eugen Jochum (conductor).

Produced by "Cine-Allianz" Tonfilm Produktionsges. m.b.H. for Universum-Film A.-G. (UFA), Berlin. *Staatsauftragsfilm.* 35mm. *Laboratory:* Afifa. *Interiors:* Ufastadt Babelsberg, Ufa-Atelier Berlin-Tempelhof. *Shooting:* July 16–beginning of October 1940. *Budget:* RM 905,000. *Running time:* 103 minutes. *Premiere:* December 30, 1940, Berlin, Ufa-Palast am Zoo. *Distributed by* Universum-Filmverleih G.m.b.H. (Ufaleih), Berlin.

Ziel in den Wolken
(Target in the Clouds)

1938. *Director:* Wolfgang Liebeneiner. *Screenplay:* Philipp Lothar Mayring, Eberhard Frowein, from a novel by Hans Rabl. *Cinematography:* Hans Schneeberger. *Music:* Wolfgang Zeller.

Cast: Leny Marenbach, Brigitte Horney, Albert Matterstock, Werner Fuetterer, Volker von Collande, Christian Kayssler, Willi Rose, Margarete Kupfer, Gisela von Collande, Franz Weber, Heinrich Schroth, Hans Junkermann, Elsa Wagner, Gertrud de Lalsky, Werner Schott, Hadrian N. Netto, Günther Hadank, Olga Limburg.

Produced by Terra-Filmkunst G.m.b.H., Berlin. *Staatsauftragsfilm. Premiere:* December 1, 1938, Hamburg; March 10, 1939, Berlin. *Distributed by* Terra-Filmverleih

G.m.b.H., Berlin. *Subject:* The first steps towards German Air Force in 1909.

Zwielicht (Twilight)

1940. *Director:* Rudolf van der Noss. *Screenplay:* Arthur Pohl from an idea conceived by Willy Fleischer. *Cinematography:* Walter Pindter. *Music:* Michael Jary. *Editor:* Else Baum.

Cast: Viktor Staal, Ruth Hellberg, Carl Raddatz, Ursula Grabley, Fritz Genschow, Paul Westermeier, Willi Schur, Erich Dunskus, Kate Kühl, Lotte Rausch, Gerhard Dammann, Ernst Rotmund, Walter Lieck, Bob Bolander, Otto Braml, Kurt Cramer, Kurt Dreml, Erich Haussmann, Paul Hildebrandt, Hellmuth Passarge, Hermann Stetza.

Produced by Universum Film A.-G. *Distributed by* Universum Filmverleih G.m.b.H. (Ufaleih), Berlin. *Subject:* The criminal police are called in to fight poachers in a country district near the German capital. No genuine propaganda but full of Nazi badges, Hitler and Göring pictures and Hitler salutes.

APPENDIX

A Who's Who of Hitler Era Filmmaking

ALLGEIER, SEPP

Born February 6, 1895, in Freiburg/Breisgau. Became a cameraman in 1911 photographing documentaries and newsreels. In 1913 Allgeier was recruited for the first time by Dr. Arnold Fanck with whom he later made pioneering Alpinist films: *Das Wunder des Schneeschuhs* (1919–20); *Der Berg des Schicksals* (1924); *Der heilige Berg* (*The Sacred Mountain*, 1926); *Der Kampf ums Matterhorn* (1928); *Die weisse Hölle vom Piz Palü* (1929); *Stürme über dem Montblanc* (1930). He then worked with two protégés of Fanck's. Under the direction of Luis Trenker in 1931 he photographed *Berge in Flammen* and in 1932 one of Hitler's favorite movies, *Der Rebell*, and in 1934 he was assigned as Leni Riefenstahl's chief cinematographer on *Triumph des Willens*. Was also involved in shooting *Der ewige Wald* in 1936. Behind the camera of several nationalist movies: *Standschütze Bruggler* (1936); *Der Westwall* (1939). In the pressbook for the 1941 *Wetterleuchten um Barbara* (Tyrol peasant drama about militia before unification of Germany and Austria) he is described as "medium-sized and mobile, an open face with very bright eyes—this is Sepp Allgeier, a mountain dweller as one would imagine him…. He descended from the Black Forest though his ancestors belonged to the Tyrolean mountain people. He liked to draw and paint. Entered the movies before World War. The premiere newsreels were made by him. Sepp Allgeier's favorite subject became nature and sports films. As a war volunteer he was twice decorated with the Iron Cross…. His expedition films led him to Canada, Spitsbergen, Greenland, Lapland—and even to Africa. He is most devoted, however, to the regionally more severe, serious North, particularly Norway. An eventful life—dedicated to the art of film and sports! His skill in the field of sport he demonstrated as an audacious skier and ski-jumper. During the Polish campaign Sepp Allgeier did his duty, too. He later belonged to the propaganda companies in the West and did a painstaking and dangerous camera job for war newsreels." He did special photography in the Dolomites for Riefenstahl's *Tiefland*. After the war Allgeier returned to documentaries (*Heimat, die uns blieb; Olympia Helsinki; In der Heimat der Welse*) and became a t.v. cameraman in Baden-Baden. He died on March 11, 1968, in Ebnet (Freiburg).

ALTEN, JÜRGEN VON

Born on January 12, 1903, in Hannover. Stage career in his home town, as well as in Detmold, Allenstein, Leipzig and Gera. In 1929 Alten came to Berlin. Entered the movie industry as an actor in the 1931 production *Yorck*. Directed *Togger* (1936–37); *In geheimer Mission* (1938); *Das Gewehr über* (1939); *Sechs Tage Heimaturlaub* (1941). After the war he was in charge of Kammerspiele Hannover. In the early '60s he returned to Berlin. Died on February 28, 1994, in Lilienthal.

BEHN-GRUND, FRIEDL

Leading German cinematographer. Born on August 26, 1906, in Bad Polzin. Got into the movie business right after World War I as an actor, then became assistant to Erich Waschneck. Eventually turned to cinematography in 1924. Photographed several Nazi films: *Robert und Bertram* (1939); *Ohm Krüger* (1940) starring Emil Jannings; *Ich klage an* (1941); *Titanic* (1942). After World War II Behn-Grund first worked for East-German Defa: *Die Mörder sind unter uns* (1946); *Ehe im Schatten* (1947); *Affäre Blum* (1948); *Die Buntkarierten* (1948); *Der Rat der Götter* (1949–50). Then he came to West Germany. Last movie: Wolfgang Staudte's *Ganovenehre* in 1965–66. Died on August 2, 1989, in Berlin.

BERTRAM, HANS

Born on February 26, 1906, in Remscheid. Studied ship building and aircraft construction at Technische Hochschule in Munich. Apprenticeship at Blohm & Voss, a Hamburg shipyard, and at aircraft factory Bäumer. For six years from 1927, consultant to the Chinese aviation authorities. With the Nazis' seizure of power former air ace Bertram returned to Germany and immediately published a best-selling book: *Flug in die Hölle* (Flight to Hell). Directed documentary *Feuertaufe* (1939) and wrote screenplays for *D III 88* (1939); *Der Fuchs von Glenarvon* (1939–40); *Kampfgeschwader Lützow* (1940). Wounded in the right eye during the shooting of one of his films. Eventually Bertram incurred Goebbels' wrath and was excluded from the Reichskulturkammer (Reich Chamber for Culture) in October 1942 for alleged false statements and slander. Died on January 8, 1993, in Munich.

BIRGEL, WILLY

Since starring in Arthur Maria Rabenalt's ... *reitet für Deutschland* (*Riding for Germany*) in 1941 Birgel was regarded as "the noble horseman of German cinema." Born on September 19, 1891, in Cologne. In 1913 entered the stage in Bonn. After the war he appeared on the stages of Aachen, Mannheim and finally Berlin. Seeing him in Paul Joseph Cremer's war play *Marneschlacht* (*Battle of Marne*) as Lieutenant Colonel Hentsch in 1934, actor-director Paul Wegener immediately offered him the part of a British officer in *Ein Mann will nach Deutschland* (*A Man Wants to Reach Germany*). State's actor since 1937. On the screen he appeared in *Feinde* (1940) and *Kameraden* (1941). "Birgel was not really suited for the role of the National Socialist hero, but his style ingratiated him with conservatives who were disappointed by the National Socialist state and who mourned the destroyed or abused values of an old tradition" (Kreimeier, *The Ufa Story*, p. 294). In 1959 Birgel became a member of the Zurich Schauspielhaus. Died on December 29, 1973, in Dübendorf near Zurich.

BOCHMANN, WERNER

Composer. Born on May 17, 1900, in Meerane. Scores for *Sensationsprozess Casilla* (1939); *Kongo Express* (1939); *Wunschkonzert* (1940); *Quax, der Bruchpilot* (1941); *Himmelhunde* (1941); *Fronttheater* (1941). Died on June 3, 1993, in Schliersee.

BÖHME, HERBERT A. E.

Born on September 7, 1897, in Breslau. Studied Germanic philology before he entered the theater in his home town in 1922. Films: *Verräter* (1936); *Pour le mérite* (1938); *Ein Robinson* (1938–39); *Legion Condor* (1939); *Über alles in der Welt* (1940); *...reitet für Deutschland* (1940); *Panik* (1940–43); *Kolberg* (1943–44). After the war for some years worked in Italy (*Il mulino delle donne di pietra*). Finally he appeared on the stage and in front of t.v. cameras (*Hafenpolizei*) in Hamburg where he died on June 29, 1984.

BÖHMELT, HARALD

Born on October 23, 1900, in Halle. In 1940 he composed the scores for *Kopf hoch, Johannes* and *U-Boote westwärts*. Died on October 15, 1982, in Munich.

BOHNEN, MICHAEL

Baritone. Born on May 2, 1887, in Cologne. Appeared in *Die Rothschilds* and *Achtung! Feind hört mit!* (both in 1940). Feared as avid informer. Died on April 26, 1965, in Berlin.

BORGMANN, HANS-OTTO

Composer. Born on October 20, 1901, in Hannover-Linden. Music-master, organist and conductor. In 1928 Borgmann joined UFA. In 1931 he became musical director for producer Erich Pommer. A melody of his that was originally scheduled for a short about Spitzbergen was chosen by Reich Youth Leader Baldur von Schirach instead to become the song of the Hitler Youth in *Hitlerjunge Quex* (1933). Scores for *Ein Mann will nach Deutschland* (1934); *Jugend* (1938); *Der grosse König* (1940–42); *Jakko* (1941); *Die goldene Stadt* (1941–42); *Junge Adler* (1943–44). In 1959 Hilde Körber appointed him lecturer at the Max Reinhardt School in Berlin. In 1970 he became an honorary professor. Died on July 26, 1977, in Berlin.

BORSODY, EDUARD VON

Born on June 13, 1898, in Vienna. After World War I, in which he served as officer 1916–18, he became assistant to cameraman Willy Winterstein. Director of photography from 1921 when he lensed *Das tapfere Schneiderlein*. In 1930 assistant director and film editor for director Gustav Ucicky (*Yorck; Morgenrot; Flüchtlinge*). Switched to directing in 1935 with several shorts. Feature films from 1937: *Sensationsprozess Casilla* (1939); *Kongo Express* (1939); *Wunschkonzert* (1940). Died on January 1, 1970, in his birthplace.

BRAUER, PETER PAUL

Born on May 16, 1899, in Wuppertal-Elberfeld. His film career started in 1928 in the Netherlands. In the same year he returned to Germany and made some shorts. Strongly sympathized with NSDAP. As production chief of Terra Company he helped to get *Jud Süss* (1939–40) on the screen (which he had hoped to direct, too). Feared as informer by colleagues. After the war he directed some unimportant movies. Died on April 28, 1959, in Berlin.

BRAUN, ALFRED

Born on May 3, 1888, in Berlin. Trained as an actor under Max Reinhardt. Started professionally on the stage of Schillertheater. From November 1924 his voice became famous in radio broadcasts. His career was interrupted by the Nazis' seizure of power. For some time confined to an early concentration camp. Then went to Turkey and Switzerland, but to everybody's surprise returned to Germany at the beginning of World War II. Narrated a propaganda air film, *Himmelsstürmer*. Collaborated with Veit Harlan on several screenplays: *Die goldene Stadt* (1942–43); *Immensee* (1942–43); *Opfergang* (1942–43); *Kolberg* (1943–44). Died on January 3, 1978, in Berlin.

BRAUN, CURT JOHANNES

Born on September 11, 1903, in Guttstadt. Screenwriter: *Der Herrscher* (1936–37); *Auf Wiedersehen, Franziska* (1940–41); *Die Entlassung* (1942). In the beginning was assigned to *Titanic* screenplay. Died on June 5, 1961, in Munich.

BREM, BEPPO

Bavarian folk actor who was often seen in *Heimat* films. Born on March 11, 1906, in Munich. Apprenticeship as cabinet-maker. On the stage from 1927. Supporting actor: *Stosstrupp 1917* (1933); *Um das Menschenrecht* (1934); *Standschütze Bruggler* (1936); *Urlaub auf Ehrenwort* (1937); *Unternehmen Michael* (1937); *Musketier Meier III* (1938); *Spähtrupp Hallgarten* (1940); *Stukas* (1940); *Quax, der Bruchpilot* (1941) as a farm-hand getting an involuntary lift by crashed pilot Heinz Rühmann; *Quax in Fahrt* (1943–44). From the 1970s was mostly seen on TV. Died on September 5, 1990, in Munich.

BREUER, SIEGFRIED

Austrian actor, born on June 26, 1906, in Vienna, son of opera singer and actor Hans Breuer. On the stage at age 18. On Nazi screens he was typecast as slimy blackmailer (*Leinen für Irland*—1939), ruthless seducer and in antisemitic parts (*Der Weg ins Freie*—1940; *Venus vor Gericht*—1941). Tested for but not cast as *Jud Süss*. Appeared in Carol Reed's post-war classic *The Third Man* (1949) as Popescu. He died in February 1, 1954, in Weende/Germany.

BUCH, FRITZ PETER

Screenwriter and director. Born on December 21, 1894, in Frankfurt/Oder. Wrote and directed *Jakko* (1940), directed *Menschen im Sturm* (1941). Died on November 6, 1964, in Vienna.

BÜTOW, ALFRED

German art director. Born on July 28, 1902, in Berlin. Started in the theater as scenic painter in 1916, then attended a *Kunstgewerbeschule* (technical art school) and took courses in perspective architecture and stilkunde. In movies from 1934: *Moskau-Shanghai* (1936);

In geheimer Mission (1938); *Wunschkonzert* (1940); *Spähtrupp Hallgarten* (1940). Died on April 3, 1986, in Herrsching.

CARSTENSSEN, CONNY

Born as Friedrich Wirth on December 8, 1888, in Colmar. Began as actor. 1914–18 soldier. After the war in silents and vaudeville (in Germany and abroad). Location manager for Communist-influenced Prometheus Films. With director Jürgen von Alten he did *Togger* (1936–37). After *Jud Süss* (1940) he worked exclusively for Veit Harlan: *Der grosse König* (1941–42); *Die goldene Stadt* (1942) and *Kolberg* (1943–44). Died on June 14, 1957, in Wiesbaden.

CASPAR, HORST

Born on January 20, 1913, in Radegast. Famous as youthful hero on the stage from the thirties to the early fifties. In 1940 he played the title role in *Friedrich Schiller—Triumph eines Genies*. In 1943 Goebbels and Harlan cast him as Gneisenau in *Kolberg*. Died on December 27, 1952, in Berlin.

CLAUSEN, CLAUS

Born on August 15, 1899, in Eisenach. After matriculation in 1920 he entered the Weimar National Theatre. 1929 film debut in the patriotic *Scapa Flow*. Georg Wilhelm Pabst gave him a part in *Westfront 1918* (1930), and Luis Trenker did so in *Berge in Flammen* (1931). From 1933 to 1945 he was seen in several nationalist and propaganda films: *Hitlerjunge Quex* (1933); *Rivalen der Luft* (1933); *Der alte und der junge König* (1934); *Mein Leben für Irland* (1940); *Der grosse König* (1941–42); *Kolberg* (1943–44). In an American post-war film, *The Devil Makes Three* (1952), he played a fanatical old Nazi, who intends to build up a new fascist organization in the American Zone. Clausen died on November 25, 1989, in Essen.

COLLANDE, VOLKER VON

Born on November 21, 1913, in Dresden. Originally wanted to become an architect but then decided in favor of acting. Youthful actor in some tendentious films: *Rivalen der Luft* (1933); *Verräter* (1936); *Togger* (1936–37); *Kopf hoch, Johannes* (1940). Member of NSDAP. Died on October 29, 1990, in Hannover.

DAHLKE, PAUL

Born on April 12, 1904, in Gross-Streitz/Pomerania (now Poland). Dahlke started in mining before he turned to acting in 1927. His career in Nazi films includes parts in: *Verräter* (1936); *Fridericus* (1936); *Patrioten* (1937); *Mein Sohn, der Herr Minister* (1937); *Pour le mérite* (1938); *Friedrich Schiller—Triumph eines Genies* (1940); *...reitet für Deutschland* (1940); *Venus vor Gericht* (1941); *Kameraden* (1941); *Heimaterde* (1941); *Andreas Schlüter* (1941–42). Tested for the title role in *Jud Süss*. Remained a popular star after the war on the screen and on t.v. Died on November 21, 1984, in Salzburg, Austria.

DAHMEN, JOSEF

Bulldog actor, born on August 21, 1903, in Solingen. From 1930 he had supporting parts in the movies: *Der Choral von Leuthen* (1932); *Flüchtlinge* (1933); *Verräter* (1936);

Unternehmen Michael (1937); *Urlaub auf Ehrenwort* (1937); *Pour le mérite* (1938); *Legion Condor* (1939); *Über alles in der Welt* (1940); *Ohm Krüger* (1940); *Stukas* (1940); *Besatzung Dora* (1942–43); *Kolberg* (1943–44). Became a regular on post-war t.v. screens. Died on January 18, 1985, in Hamburg.

DAMMANN, GERHARD

Heavyweight comedian, born on March 30, 1883, in Cologne. Started as acrobat in international vaudeville. Movie work since 1911: *Pour le mérite* (1938); *...reitet für Deutschland* (1940); *Quax, der Bruchpilot* (1941). Died on February 21, 1946, in Bad Ischl, Austria.

DANNEMANN, KARL

Born on March 22, 1896, in Bremen. Had been an artist before the Nazis made him a movie actor: *Schwarzer Jäger Johanna* (1934); *Mit versiegelter Order* (1937); *Blutsbrüderschaft* (1939); *Der Fuchs von Glenarvon* (1939–40); *Achtung! Feind hört mit* (1940); *Mein Leben für Irland* (1940); *Carl Peters* (1940); *Ich klage an* (1941); *Titanic* (1942); *Die goldene Spinne* (1943); *Junge Adler* (1943); *Ein schöner Tag* (1943). Shot himself when the Red Army occupied the German capital in April 1945.

DELTGEN, RENÉ

Born on April 30, 1909, in Esch-sur-Alzette, Luxemburg. Stage actor from 1929; on the screen from 1935: *Urlaub auf Ehrenwort* (1937); *Kongo Express* (1939); *Achtung!, Feind hört mit!* (1940); *Mein Leben für Irland* (1940); *Spähtrupp Hallgarten* (1940); *Fronttheater* (1941). Screen test for *Jud Süss*. In Fritz Lang's German exotic post-war melodramas *Der Tiger von Eschnapur* and *Das indische Grabmal* (1958), he played Fürst Ramigani. Died on January 28, 1979, in Cologne.

DEMANDOWSKY, EWALD VON

"Along with Fritz Hippler, Ewald von Demandowsky, editor of the *Völkischer Beobachter* until 1937, then Reichsfilmdramaturg until 1939, crops up most frequently as the most important colleague and regular attendee at Goebbels' countless discussions in the most intimate circle. Born in 1906, he was the first party man in the post of production chief. In that capacity he directed Tobis Filmkunst from February 1939 to 1945. At first Demandowsky was not able to deliver what the minister had expected from him in terms of political dynamism and acquiescence.... the production chief even wanted to abandon the super-expensive anti–British propaganda film *Ohm Krüger* that Goebbels had demanded. Such weaknesses and other 'mishaps' in film planning even brought Goebbels, in June 1940, to threaten Demandowsky with being called up into the Wehrmacht. But from mid 1940 Tobis developed and came to be the film studio with the highest proportion of political and 'national' material and war films" (Felix Moeller, *The Film Minister*, p. 59). On February 28, 1944, Goebbels noted with satisfaction: "He is the actual Nazi among our production chiefs." Up-and-coming film star Hildegard Knef for some time was Demandowsky's mistress. Demandowsky died in 1945 during the fight for Berlin.

DREWS, BERTA

Born on November 19, 1901, in Berlin. Wife of actor Heinrich George. On the screen from 1932: *Hitlerjunge Quex* (1933); *Urlaub auf Ehrenwort* (1937); *Über alles in der Welt*

(1940); *Heimkehr* (1941). After the war she assisted with the stage and screen career of her son Götz. Died on April 10, 1987, in Berlin.

ECKARDT, FELIX VON

Born on June 18, 1903, in Berlin. Worked as journalist for several Munich and Berlin newspapers. Through director Fritz Wendhausen he got screenwriting assignments starting in 1935. Besides comedies, musicals and detective films he wrote screenplays for some nationalist propaganda efforts: *Kopf hoch, Johannes* (1941); *Menschen im Sturm* (1941) which subsequently "justified" the invasion of Yugoslavia; the Bismarck film *Die Entlassung* (1942). In February 1952 West German Chancellor Konrad Adenauer appointed him head of the Press and Information Office of the German government. Government spokesman of longstanding. Member of German parliament from 1961 to 1972. Died on May 11, 1979, on the Isle of Capri, Italy.

ENGELMANN, ANDREWS

German-Baltic actor, born on March 23, 1901, in St. Petersburg. In 1921 fled to Finland and Berlin. American director Rex Ingram cast him as merciless German submarine commander in *Mare Nostrum* (1925–26). From then on mostly seen as villain: *Flüchtlinge* (1933); *Kadetten* (1939); *Legion Condor* (1939); *Über alles in der Welt* (1940); *Carl Peters* (1940); *GPU* (1941–42) which he also co-scripted. Died on February 25, 1992, in Basel, Switzerland.

ENGELMANN, HEINZ

Born on January 14, 1911, in Berlin. First movie role in 1938 in Karl Ritter's *Pour le mérite*. The dashing young officer in *Drei Unteroffiziere* (1938–39); *Kongo Express* (1939); *U-Boote westwärts* (1940). After the war he portrayed plain-clothes men in the t.v. series *Stahlnetz* (German version of *Dragnet*) and dubbed movie actors like William Holden, Randolph Scott, John Wayne, and Erroll Flynn. Died on September 26, 1996, in Tutzing.

ERTL, HANS

Born on February 21, 1908, in Bavaria. Documentarist and cinematographer. Worked on Leni Riefenstahl's short *Tag der Freiheit* (1935), on *Olympia* (1936) and on *Sieg im Westen* (1940) for which he filmed the sequence of a sapper, under heavy fire, jumping into the Marne, grabbing a rope and pulling a rubber boat across the river. Newsreel cameraman on the front. After the war made expedition films which eventually led him to South America where he later lived. His daughter, Monika, ended up as a terrorist. Hans Ertl died on October 23, 2000, in Chiquitania, Santa Cruz, Bolivia.

FERNAU, RUDOLF

Actor member of NSDAP. Born on January 7, 1898, in Munich. Started as an extra and amateur on the stage before debuting professionally in 1918 as Don Carlos. First film part in 1936: *Verräter*. Pictures include *Im Namen des Volkes* (1938); *Falschmünzer* (1940); *Auf Wiedersehen, Franziska* (1940–41); *Kameraden* (1941); *Die Affäre Roedern* (1943). After seeing him in a sensitive portrait as a murderer on the run in *Dr. Crippen an Bord* (1942), Goebbels called him a "destructive type." After the war he was often seen in Edgar Wallace and Dr. Mabuse films. Died on November 4, 1985, in Munich.

FLICKENSCHILDT, ELISABETH

Distinguished actress, the "magic lady" of German stage and film. Certainly not who you would expect to enter a beauty contest. Born as Elisabeth Ida Marie Flieckenschildt on March 16, 1905, in Blankenese near Hamburg. Became NSDAP member in 1932. Films include Veit Harlan's *Jugend* (1937–38) and *Der grosse König* (1940–42); Max W. Kimmich's *Der Fuchs von Glenarvon*; Hans Steinhoff's *Ohm Krüger* (1940–41), *Rembrandt* (1941–42) and the unfinished *Shiva und die Galgenblume* (1945). Often in partnership with Gustaf Gründgens. In 1965 was appointed professor by the federal state of Nordrhein-Westfalen. In 1964 was awarded Deutscher Filmpreis: Filmband in Gold (German Film Prize in Gold) and in 1975 Grosses Verdienstkreuz des Verdienstordens der Bundesrepublik Deutschland (Order of Merit of the Federal Republic). Died on October 26, 1977, on her farm in Guderhandviertel near Stade.

FORSTER, RUDOLF

Grand seigneur of German-language films. Born on October 30, 1884, in Gröbming, Austria. Debuted on the stage aged 16. In 1919 Forster went to Berlin to work for Max Reinhardt and Leopold Jessner. Played Mackie Messer in the film version of *Die Dreigroschenoper/The Threepenny Opera* (1930). Was in Gustav Ucicky's *Yorck* (1931) and played the submarine commander in *Morgenrot* (1932) by the same director. At the end of the thirties he played in New York and was even offered two small screen parts in Hollywood but decided to return to Germany when the war broke out. Portrayed Hitler's antisemitic idol Vienna mayor Dr. Karl Lueger in *Wien 1910* (1941–42). Goebbels envisaged Forster in a picture about the famous German military strategist *Schlieffen* but that particular picture was not made. Died on October 25, 1968, in Bad Aussee.

FROELICH, CARL

Born on September 5, 1875, in Berlin. Began as cameraman in 1906. In 1912 became a director, and in 1920 started producing on his own. From the beginning Froelich positioned himself with the Nazis. In *Reifende Jugend* (1933) he interceded for the "new spirit." In Zarah Leander's Maria Stuart drama *Das Herz der Königin* (1939–40) he supported anti–British propaganda (although Goebbels, in a diary entry dated August 21, 1940, saw it differently: "Was intended to be anti–English and anti-church, and has ended up pro both.") In 1937 Froelich was promoted to professor, and in 1939 Goebbels appointed him president of Reichsfilmkammer. Died on February 12, 1953, in Berlin.

FRÖHLICH, GUSTAV

Born on March 21, 1902, in Hannover. First big screen part as Freder in Fritz Lang's *Metropolis* (1925–26). There was a rumor that he had boxed Joseph Goebbels' ears when he lost his fiancée, Lida Baarova, to the minister, but in fact he was an opportunist. Fröhlich, who had divorced his first Jewish wife, Gitta Alpar, was seen in several nationalist films: he was Corporal Treskow in Veit Harlan's *Der grosse König* (1941–42). "In Gustav Fröhlich, the pose of the sentimental or pleasure-seeking but always moderate cavalier had an element of puerile simplicity, which may well account for why he became the idealized figure of the 'direct, honest, and sympathetic German man' with whom a politically immature movie-going public could identify" (Klaus Kreimeier, *The Ufa Story*, p. 294). He died on December 22, 1987, in Lugano, Switzerland.

GEBÜHR, OTTO

Born on May 29, 1877, in Kettwig. On the stage from age 20. Debuted in Berlin in 1907; in front of the camera for the first time as an extra before World War I. The eternal Friedrich the Great of the movies, from 1922 to 1942 when he reprised the role for Veit Harlan's *Der grosse König*. 1940: *Bismarck* and *Kopf hoch, Johannes*; 1943: *Die goldene Spinne* as the grandfatherly industrialist in charge of a tank factory. Died on March 13, 1954, in Wiesbaden.

GENSCHOW, FRITZ

Born on May 15, 1905, in Berlin. Stage debut in 1924. In 1927 with Erwin Piscator at Theater am Nollendorfplatz in Berlin. With his wife, Renée Stobrawa, Genschow founded a children's theater. On the screen: *Morgenrot* (1932–33); *Flüchtlinge* (1933); *Hundert Tage* (1934); *Ein Volksfeind* (1937); *13 Mann und eine Kanone* (1938); *Drei Unteroffiziere* (1938); *Titanic* (1942). After the war he was engaged in radio (as Uncle Tobias) and produced and directed children's fairy tales for the screen. Died on June 21, 1977, in Berlin.

GEORGE, HEINRICH

Born on October 9, 1893, in Stettin (now Szczecin, Poland) as Georg August Friedrich Hermann Schulz. Established himself as one of Germany's leading stage and film actors. Before the Nazis came to power he was active in pro–Communist *Revolutionäre Gewerkschaftsopposition* (revolutionary union opposition). After 1933 sympathized with the brown regime. On the screen in a trio of the worst Nazi propaganda films: *Hitlerjunge Quex* (1933); *Jud Süss* (1940); *Kolberg* (1943–44). Also in Carl Froelich's *Reifende Jugend* (1933); *Unternehmen Michael* (1937); *Ein Volksfeind* (1937); *Sensationsprozess Casilla* (1939); *Friedrich Schiller—Triumph eines Genies* (1940); *Wien 1910* (1942); and in Wolfgang Liebeneiner's unfinished *Das Leben geht weiter* (1944–45). Manager of the Schiller Theater in Berlin. Denounced by a former colleague he died on September 25, 1946, in Sachsenhausen, a former concentration camp then occupied by the Russians, where he was mistreated and fell ill with appendicitis. His younger son, Götz, in 1977 appeared in Theodor Kotulla's extraordinary *Aus einem deutschen Leben* as Rudolf Höss, commander of the concentration camp Auschwitz.

GÖTZ, LUTZ

Born in 1891. Was in *Patrioten* (1937); *Unternehmen Michael* (1937); *Legion Condor* (1939); *Sechs Tage Heimaturlaub* (1941); *Stukas* (1941); *Quax, der Bruchpilot* (1941); *Himmelhunde* (1942); the unfinished *Shiva und die Galgenblume* (1945). Died in 1958.

GRÜNDGENS, GUSTAF

Born on December 22, 1899, in Dusseldorf. Acting debut in 1918, at the end of World War I. Since the mid–'20s primarily on stages in Berlin. In 1934, supported by Göring's wife, actress Emmy Sonnemann, Gründgens became a protegé of Hermann Göring, and in 1934 manager of the Staatliches Schauspielhaus (State Theater) in Berlin. From 1937 to 1945 general manager of every Prussian state theater. In 1934 he became State's Actor, in 1936 Prussian Privy Councilor. His most famous role on the stage was as Mephisto in *Faust*. In films from 1929, for instance in Fritz Lang's *M* (1931) with Peter Lorre. He was rarely seen in outspoken nationalist films: in *Hundert Tage* (1934), the German movie version of Benito Mussolini's Napoleon epic; in the title role in *Friedemann Bach* (1940–41); and as Chamberlain in *Ohm Krüger* (1940–41). Goebbels found Gründgens "cold, intellectual, overpointed and with an icy wit" (diary entry: July 14, 1937). Died on October 7, 1963, in Manila.

HANNEMANN, KARL

Born on March 4, 1895, in Freiberg. Debuted in 1914 at Schiller Theater in Berlin. Sporadic movie appearances which started in 1915 and became more regular after 1930: *Hitlerjunge Quex* (1933); *Patrioten* (1937); *Urlaub auf Ehrenwort* (1937); *Der Fuchs von Glenarvon* (1939–40); *Die Rothschilds* (1940); *GPU* (1941–42). After the war in several productions of East German Defa. Died on November 6, 1953, in Berlin.

HARLAN, VEIT

Born on September 22, 1899, in Berlin. "Veit Harlan was the director Goebbels himself would have liked to be," Frank Noack states in his Harlan biography (p. 179). "That he made almost no movie without Goebbels' interference, speaks all the more for the high reputation which he enjoyed with the Propaganda Minister. The Harlan films were that dear to Goebbels that he controlled them more intensely." His father was an author and actively involved in literary circles, presiding over the Association of German Stage Writers and Stage Composers. His mother was born a Boothby. Veit Harlan was trained at the Max Reinhardt seminary. First stage parts as a sixteen year old in Berlin's Luisen Theatre. At the end of 1916 he enlisted as a war volunteer. Three years later he returned to the stage and became a member of Friedrich Kayssler's Volksbühne Berlin and of Landestheater Meiningen (until 1922). Toured with Holtorf Stock Company. In 1923 he became a member of the Staatliches Schauspielhaus (State Theater). First movie role in 1927 in the screen version of Carl Sternheim's *Die Hose* with Werner Krauss and Jenny Jugo. In 1931 he had a part in one of those sexual enlightenment movies that were a trademark of German cinema, *Gefahren der Liebe* (*Dangers of Love*). In the same year, Harlan played in *Yorck*, a glorification of Prussian militarism, a national epic, fabricated for domestic mass consumption. The film was directed by Gustav Ucicky. The cast offered such illustrious names as Werner Krauss, Rudolf Forster, Gustaf Gründgens, Theodor Loos, and Hans Brausewetter. From that time on, Veit Harlan was marked for parts of Prussian officers. In 1932 he appeared in *Die Elf Schill'schen Offiziere* and *Der Choral von Leuthen*, a Fridericus Rex film starring Otto Gebühr. On April 20, 1933, on the occasion of the Führer's birthday, he appeared as Friedrich Thiemann in Hans Johst's staging of the infamous *Schlageter* play in which he issued the notorious line: "When I hear of culture, I release the safety catch of my Browning!" UFA's *Flüchtlinge* dealt with the fate of *Wolgadeutsche* (Volga Germans) and was honored on May 1, 1935, with the Staatspreis (State Award). *Mein Leben für Maria Isabell* was a movie set on the Eastern Front of World War I. *Das Mädchen Johanna*, UFA's version of Jeanne d'Arc, again directed by Gustav Ucicky, assembled Germany's elite actors: Gründgens, Heinrich George, René Deltgen, Erich Ponto, Willy Birgel, Theodor Loos, Paul Bildt, and Albert Florath. In the meantime, Harlan also dubbed American movies, for example the great Jewish actor Paul Muni in *I Was a Fugitive from a Chain Gang*. For his directorial debut, Harlan selected the stage and the plays *Hochzeit an der Pauke* and *Krach im Hinterhaus*. The success of *Krach* inspired ABC Films to make a movie version, and for the director's chair Harlan was the obvious choice. After some comedies in 1937, he filmed Leo Tolstoi's *Kreutzersonate* for Tobis. The same year he got the assignment to direct Emil Jannings in the prestigious tale of a German industrialist, *Der Herrscher* (*The Ruler*) written by Thea von Harbou. It was awarded ratings of *staatspolitisch* (nationally political) and *künstlerisch wertvoll* (artistically worthy), as well as the National Film Prize of 1937. At the prize ceremony Harlan met Adolf Hitler for the first time: "From Hitler radiated a rather primitive, but absolutely inevitable fakir's effect. Even if one knew clearly that something was wrong with what he said, it was nevertheless right because *he* said it" (*Im Schatten meiner Filme*). Then Harlan directed an infamous persiflage on parlamentarism, *Mein Sohn, der Herr Minister* (1937), based on a play by André Birabeau. Starting with *Verwehte Spuren*, a Tobis movie from 1938, his films were announced as "Veit Harlan films." When Veit Harlan was commissioned to do *Jud Süss* (1939–40) he had already directed 14 movies. *Jud Süss* made him the leading director of the Third Reich. With screenwriter Alfred Braun, Harlan also prepared a movie version of *The Merchant of Venice* which (with Werner Krauss in the title role — he had played Shylock on the stage already) would have become another antisemitic production had he filmed it. Maybe Allied bombing or another reason prevented Harlan from making it. He directed Otto Gebühr in *Der grosse König* (1941–42); the anti–Czech *Die goldene Stadt* (1941–42); the all-star epic *Kolberg* (1943–44). Harlan was married three times: to Jewish actress Dora Gerson (who was gased in Auschwitz in 1943), actress and later CDU politician Hilde Körber, and Kristina Söderbaum, who appeared in most of his Nazi films. After the war, he met Stanley Kubrick who married his niece Susanne Christiane Harlan and was interested in making a film biography of Harlan's life. On April 13, 1964, Veit Harlan died on the Isle of Capri.

HARTMANN, PAUL

Born on January 8, 1889, in Fürth. Actor on the German stage (from 1908) and film (from 1914). After the Nazis' seizure of power his heroic characters on the screen had an increasingly nationalist bias: *Schwarzer Jäger Johanna* (1934); *Mit versiegelter Order* (1937); Karl Ritter's *Pour le mérite* (1938), *Legion Condor* (1939) and *Über alles in der Welt* (1940). He starred in Wolfgang Liebeneiner's *Ich klage an!* (1941) as the physician who develops into an apologist of euthanasia. From 1934 Hartmann supported Nazi cultural programs. In 1942 he became president of Reichstheaterkammer. Paul Hartmann died on June 30, 1977, in Munich.

HEHN, ALBERT

Born on December 17, 1908, in Lauda, Brasilia. Attended missionary school. A baker's apprentice before he became an actor in 1929. In Nazi films he was often seen as the exemplary smart officer: *Pour le mérite* (1938); *Legion Condor* (1939); *Jungens* (1940); *Stukas* (1940); *Annelie* (1941). Father of actor Sascha Hehn. Died on July 29, 1983, in Hamburg.

HENCKELS, PAUL

Born on September 9, 1885, in Hürth near Cologne. Trainee at Krefeld theater. First success in Dusseldorf with the title role of *Schneider Wibbel* in 1913, written by his schoolmate Hans Müller-Schlösser. In 1921 Henckels co-founded Schlosspark Theater in Berlin. First film part in Robert Wiene's Christ epic *I.N.R.I.* in 1923. Henckels filmed with Hans Steinhoff (*Der alte und der junge König*, 1934–35); Veit Harlan (*Der grosse König*, 1940–42; *Kolberg*, 1943–44); Alfred Weidenmann (*Junge Adler*, 1944). In 1945 he was mistakenly arrested by Russian troops who confused him with aircraft designer Heinkel. He had some trouble clearing up the error. Died on May 27, 1967, in Kettwig.

HESSE, DR. KURT

Born in 1894. At the beginning of World War II in charge of German Armed Forces Propaganda Section V (OKW/WPr V). Supervised production of documentary *Sieg im Westen* in 1940–41. Died in 1976.

HINKEL, SS GRUPPENFÜHRER, HANS

Hinkel, general secretary to the Reichskulturkammer (RKK), was appointed to the post of *Reichsfilmintendant* (Director of Reich Films) in April 1944 as Fritz Hippler's successor. He was born in 1901. From 1920 to 1923, he was a member of the volunteer corps Oberland. On October 4, 1921, he became a member of the NSDAP, and in 1930 editor of *Völkischer Beobachter*. Hinkel died in 1960.

HINZ, WERNER

Born on January 18, 1903, in Berlin. Hinz started with Max Reinhardt at Deutsches Theater in Berlin in 1922. First film part in 1934: In *Der alte und der junge König* he played young Friedrich II at the side of Emil Jannings. Was in two Bismarck films: as crown prince in *Bismarck* (1940), and as Wilhelm II in *Die Entlassung* (1942). Involved in three anti–British productions (all released in 1940): *Der Fuchs von Glenarvon; Mein Leben für Irland; Ohm Krüger*. Died on February 10, 1985, in Hamburg. His sons Michael and Knut became actors, too.

HIPPLER, SS OBERSTURMBANNFÜHRER, DR. FRITZ

Born on August 17, 1909, in Berlin. Studied sociology and law in Heidelberg. Joined NSDAP as early as 1927. In August 1936 entered the newsreel division of the Propaganda Ministry assisting Hans Weidemann until he was appointed to succeed him as director of the Deutsche Wochenschauzentrale (the German newsreel office) in January 1939. Became a close confidant of Goebbels. Fell into disgrace with his patron over the conduct of the Baarova affair. Made a West Wall ("Siegfried Line") picture and returned in 1939 to become head of the film division of the Propaganda Ministry and *Reichsfilmintendant* (Director of Reich Films) in February 1942, a position he held until 1943. In 1939–40 supervised and compiled several "documentaries": *Feldzug in Polen (Campaign in Poland)*; Hans Bertram's *Sieg im Westen (Victory in the West)*; and the infamous *Der ewige Jude (The Eternal Jew)*. "Repeated illnesses and differences with [Max] Winkler seem to have weakened Hippler's position in 1942…. Goebbels mentions incompetence, 'mishaps,' alcoholism and family problems" (Felix Moeller, *The Film Minister*, p. 54). After the war Hippler worked as a travel agent in Berchtesgaden, where he died May 22, 2002.

HOPPE, MARIANNE

Born on April 26, 1908, in Rostock. *Grande dame* of the German stage. Married to bisexual Gustaf Gründgens. Film parts in *Schwarzer Jäger Johanna* (1934); *Der Herrscher* (1936–37) with Emil Jannings; *Kongo Express* (1939); *Auf Wiedersehen, Franziska* (1940–41); and the unfinished *Das Leben geht weiter* (1944–45).

HÖRBIGER, ATTILA

Born on April 21, 1896, in Budapest. Son of Hanns Hörbiger —creator of "Glacial Cosmology," which met with the approval of many Nazis— a member of the famous Hörbiger acting family (his older brother was popular Paul Hörbiger). During the Third Reich Attila was seen on the stages of the Vienna Burgtheater and Berlin's Deutsches Theater. Starred in *Wetterleuchten um Barbara* (1940) and the anti–Polish *Heimkehr* (1941, which co-starred his wife Paula Wessely). Died on April 27, 1987, in Vienna.

HÜBNER, BRUNO

Born on August 26, 1899, in Langenbruck. After service, in 1919, he decided to become an actor. Started on the stage in Vienna, and later moved to Berlin and Munich. On the screen in supporting parts as character actor: *Patrioten* (1937); *Der Fuchs von Glenarvon* (1939–40); *Die Rothschilds* (1940); *Bismarck* (1940); *Alarmstufe V* (1941). Died on December 22, 1983, in Munich.

HÜBNER, HERBERT

Born on February 6, 1889, in Breslau. The 18 year old started on the stage in Heidelberg. During the Nazi time he worked mostly in Berlin: *Der Herrscher* (1936–37); *Ein Volksfeind* (1937); *Robert und Bertram* (1939: as Ipelmeyer, the Jew); *Carl Peters* (1940); *...reitet für Deutschland* (1940); *Der grosse König* (1940–41); *Kameraden* (1941); *Die Entlassung* (1942); *Junge Adler* (1943–44); *Das Leben geht weiter* (unfinished: 1944–45). According to a contemporary pressbook for *Wien 1910* (1942), "Jewish impudence and lack of morals are portrayed in the character of Dr. Viktor Adler by Herbert Hübner." Died on January 27, 1972, in Munich.

HUNTE, OTTO

Scenic artist and art director. Born on January 9, 1881, in Hamburg. Worked for directors Joe May (*Die Herrin der Welt; Das indische Grabmal*) and Fritz Lang (*Dr. Mabuse, der Spieler; Die Nibelungen; Metropolis; Spione; Frau im Mond*). First sound film: *Der blaue Engel* (1929–30). Engaged in Nazi propaganda and nationalist films: *Mann für Mann* (1938); *Jud Süss* (1940); *...reitet für Deutschland* (1940); *Anschlag auf Baku* (1940–41); *Die Entlassung* (1942). In 1946, Wolfgang Staudte invited him to design the first East German Defa film: *Die Mörder sind unter uns*. Later Hunte became a portrait artist. Died on December 28, 1960, in Potsdam.

HUTTULA, GERHARD

Cameraman, expert in animation and special photography. Born on June 6, 1902, in Berlin. Started as trick photographer for his former drawing master, Wolfgang Kaskeline, in the early 1920s. First technician to work with the Truca, a crude optical printer manufactured by Debrie. Cinematographer in Argentina. In 1937 Huttula returned to Germany and took over the Babelsberg Process Department from Guido Seeber. Frequently worked with Karl Ritter: *Über alles in der Welt* (1940–41); *Stukas* (1941); Ritter's unfinished production *Das Leben geht weiter* (1944–45). As a specialist in model aircraft he also created scenes for Heinz Rühmann's *Quax* films, for Roger von Norman's *Himmelhunde* (1941) and Zarah Leander's *Die grosse Liebe* (1941–42). Second camera: *Kolberg* (1943–44). After the war, photographed Fritz Genschow's fairy tales. Died on January 15, 1996, at the home of his daughter in Düren.

JAEGER, MALTE

Born on July 4, 1911, in Hannover. Acting career began in 1937. Almost immediately the good-looking Jaeger got prominent parts in Nazi films: *Unternehmen Michael* (1937);

Pour le mérite (1938); *Drei Unteroffiziere* (1938); *Legion Condor* (1939); *Kongo Express* (1939); *D III 88* (1939); *Jud Süss* (1940); *Wunschkonzert* (1940); *Himmelhunde* (1941). Died on January 10, 1991, in Husum.

JANNINGS, EMIL

Born on July 23, 1884, in Rorschach, Switzerland. Started in 1901 in touring companies. Entered Berlin theater in 1914. Filmed with directors Ernst Lubitsch (*Anna Boleyn*) and F. W. Murnau (*Der letzte Mann; Faust*). 1926–29 in Hollywood where he was honored with the first Academy Award for male actor. In the days of early sound films, in 1929, returned to Germany and produced *Der blaue Engel*. Became a willing propagandist of the "new order." In Veit Harlan's *Der Herrscher* (*The Ruler*) (1937) Jannings portrayed a Krupp-like industrial baron. "Emil Jannings appears as a responsible entrepreneur running an enormous steelworks, which he finally leaves to the state rather than his money-grubbing family. The inefficient directors of the company are supposed to justify the 'Führer principle' in commercial life" (Felix Moeller, *The Film Minister*, p. 71). Jannings (as the film's protagonist, Matthias Clausen): "The aim of every industrial leader conscious of his responsibility must be to serve this community. This will of mine is the supreme law which governs my work. All else must be subordinated to this will, without opposition, even if in doing this I lead the firm into ruin. He who does not submit himself to this supreme law has no place in the Clausen factories!" Especially disappointed, when he saw Jannings in *The Ruler*, was exiled Berthold Viertel: "He has grown by inches, and every inch a phony prig. An Emil, diluted to fit into line, groomed as though Goebbels had been at his beard with a cat's paws, claws retracted. He has really been preened for glory, a fat goody-goody, a royal merchant, an industrial magnate" (*Das Neue Tagebuch*, 1937). From then on Jannings was type-cast in roles of authoritarian figures. Produced, partly directed and starred in the anti–British *Ohm Krüger* (1940). Goebbels was satisfied with the result: "He is working on his Boer film like a man possessed. I am seeing the rushes. They suggest it's going to be a great success" (entry in Goebbels' diary: December 17, 1940). Not made was another project that Goebbels and Jannings envisioned concerning the German general staff. A member of the Tobis board of directors in 1936 and, from 1938, its chairman, Jannings was granted "overall artistic control" of Tobis's projects by the Nazis. Died on January 2, 1950, in Strobl, Austria.

JAWORSKY, HEINZ VON

Born on May 15, 1912, in Berlin. Aerial cinematography: *Wunder des Fliegens* (1935); Leni Riefenstahl's *Olympia* (1936); *Kampfgeschwader Lützow* (1941); *Quax, der Bruchpilot* (1941); the unfinished *Das Leben geht weiter* (1944–45). Died in New York City in 2000.

JOHN, KARL

Born on March 24, 1905, in Cologne. Was trained at the State Acting School by Leopold Jessner. Stage debut in 1931. In Nazi films often as soldier: *Unternehmen Michael* (1937); *Legion Condor* (1939); *Mein Leben für Irland* (1940); *Über alles in der Welt* (1940); *U-Boote westwärts* (1940); *Stukas* (1941). After 1945 he made two other war films: Carl Zuckmayer's *Des Teufels General* (1954) and Frank Wysbar's Stalingrad epic *Hunde, wollt ihr ewig leben?* (1958). Last film part was in William Friedkin's *Sorcerer* (1976). Died on December 22, 1977, in Gütersloh.

KIMMICH, MAX WILHELM ["AXEL"]

Born on November 4, 1893, in Ulm. Joseph Goebbels' brother-in-law. One of Kimmich's propaganda films, *Der letzte Appell* (1939), was shelved when war started. But he made two (more or less) anti–British, pro–Irish propaganda films released in 1940: *Der Fuchs von Glenarvon* and *Mein Leben für Irland*. A weaker anti–British production, *Germanin*, reached the screens in 1942.

> A gifted spirit from Wurttemberg, son of a professor who taught painting, he joined the movies, his first love, in which he, passionately addicted to music and painting, saw a new, much more exciting and, in its appeal, greater means to satisfy artistic thoughts and longing for artistic direction. The outsider, who during his whole development always remained an outsider, practiced his craft thoroughly and methodically. He knew about the severe laws of the technique and knew of the intimate and indissoluble attachment of this young art to its technique. So he started to study this technique, which was connected with physics, optics, and later acoustics, chemistry and electrical engineering. He further understood that the picture play is determined by laws and that this technique, too, would have to be learned, as far as recognized, processed and confirmed by experience. That was how he started, and after his studies he began writing screenplays. Clearly, logically, someone with an artist's personality couldn't get ahead. He wore the white coat of an assistant cameraman and an assistant set designer. He learned by working his way up from the bottom. Eventually, he became story editor and production manager. Finally he was asked to go to America, where he worked in the capacities of story editor, writer, and production manager. To Americans he introduced an entirely new kind of cinematic comedy, which was destined to become characteristic for their production: the situation comedy [Tobis pressbook].

Kimmich, who had started with one of UFA's subsidiary companies, got acquainted with German-born Carl Laemmle, co-founder and president of Universal Pictures. In the United States he made comedies with Arthur Lake and wrote screenplays for stars like Laura la Plante and Reginald Denny. Before Kimmich was naturalized as an American citizen, Laemmle sent him back to Germany to direct movies for his Deutsche Universal outfit, which was headed then by Paul Kohner. Due to his work with Laemmle, Kimmich landed on the Nazis' industry blacklist in 1933. Eventually, though, he was able to help out Paul Wegener, who had run into trouble directing *Moskau-Shanghai* in 1936, and revised the screenplay. The pressbook bio, of course, glossed over that part of Kimmich's career.

> After his time in California Kimmich returned to Germany. He wrote scripts, he experienced a second time (as already in America) the change from silents to sound film. He again became story editor and finally, because of his deep knowledge of the matter, he came to directing. He already had directed in America, but in Germany he acquired a more and more mature art in directing. He made the Tobis film *Der Vierte kommt nicht* and immediately thereafter was assigned to his first big-budget work. His *Fuchs von Glenarvon* left deep impressions as a polished and thrilling work which displayed most powerful artistic efforts. Artistic as well as cinematic success was the inevitable result. But Kimmich didn't take a rest. He next tackled *Mein Leben für Irland*. Again this was a subject which

demanded from its director absolute devotion and the highest artistic enthusiasm.... Again the task did fit his character for the artist had to identify himself with the art in the most usual sense of the word. There can be no digressions, no fancy tricks, no indifference in order to remain on the slippery surface. The director has to dive into all depths of his subject. There is only absolute clarity, absolutely honest views of film and subject as means that will guarantee a work forming an integrated whole.

After the war Kimmich did mostly t.v. work. He died on January 16, 1980, in Icking.

KLINGLER, WERNER

Born on October 23, 1903, in Stuttgart. Bit parts in American movies: *City Girl* (1929); *Journey's End* (1929); *All Quiet on the Western Front* (1930). 1931 consultant for German-language versions at Universal. During the making of *The Doomed Batallion* he met director Luis Trenker and returned to Germany. Assisted Trenker (co-director of *Condottieri* and *Liebesbriefe aus dem Engadin*) and Dr. Arnold Fanck. Directed *Standschütze Bruggler* (1936) and *Wetterleuchten um Barbara* (1940). Finished Herbert Selpin's *Titanic* (1942). Last assignment was the red light district movie *Strassenbekanntschaften auf St. Pauli* in 1967. Died on June 23, 1972, in Berlin.

KLÖPFER, EUGEN

Born on March 10, 1886, in Rauhenstich-Talheim. Entered the legitimate theater in 1905 in Landshut after various bit parts in the Bavaria. Went to Berlin in 1918. Aligned himself from the beginning with the Nazis. In 1934 he was appointed manager of Volksbühne, and in 1935 vice president of Reichstheaterkammer. In the movies since 1919: *Flüchtlinge* (1933); *Jugend* (1937); *Der ewige Quell* (1939–40); *Jud Süss* (1940); *Friedrich Schiller — Triumph eines Genies* (1940); *Mein Leben für Irland* (1940); *Jakko* (1940); *Friedemann Bach* (1940–41); *Die goldene Stadt* (1941–42); Hans Steinhoff's unfinished *Shiva und die Galgenblume* (1945). Died on March 3, 1950, in Wiesbaden.

KLOTZSCH, FRITZ

Born on May 16, 1896, in Berlin. Started as an actor, then became location and finally production manager. For two years in charge of production at Bavaria. Produced *Friedrich Schiller* (1940); *Ohm Krüger* (1940); *Menschen im Sturm* (1941); *Die Entlassung* (1942). After the war worked at Defa, and finally became production manager of Edgar Wallace films. Died on January 9, 1971, in Berlin (?).

KÖRBER, HILDE

Born on July 3, 1906, in Vienna. Debuted on the stage aged 16. In 1936 was in a *Fridericus* film. Her second husband, Veit Harlan, brought her to movie prominence in *Der Herrscher* (1936–37), *Mein Sohn, der Herr Minister* (1937) and *Der grosse König* (1941–42). Karl Ritter cast her in *Patrioten* (1937), Max W. Kimmich in *Der Fuchs von Glenarvon* (1939–40), Hans Steinhoff in *Ohm Krüger* (1940). With Alfred Weidenmann she made the Hitler Youth film *Jakko* (1940), and with Wolfgang Liebeneiner the unfinished *Das Leben geht weiter* (1944–45). From 1946 to 1950/51 Hilde Körber was CDU city councilor in Berlin. In 1951 she took over the management of the Max Reinhardt Theater School. 1965 she was appointed a professor at the Hochschule für Musik. Hilde Körber died on May 31, 1969, in Berlin.

KRAHL, HILDE

Austrian actress, born on January 10, 1917, in Brod a.d. Save. Joined the party in 1936. Goebbels, the experienced womanizer, found her "extraordinarily clever" [diary entry. September 20, 1940]. Starred in the unfinished *Das Leben geht weiter* (1944–45) which was directed by her husband Wolfgang Liebeneiner. Her greatest success, ironically, became her post-war portrayal of Bertha von Suttner, a fighter for peace, in *Herz der Welt* (1951). Died on June 28, 1999, in Vienna.

KRAUSS, WERNER

One of Germany's most experienced actors. Internationally renowned for his portrayal of a hypnotist in the expressionist silent *The Cabinet of Dr. Caligari* (1919). Born on June 23, 1884, in Gestungshausen. First stage experience as an extra. Regular stage parts from 1902. In the silents he played the title roles in *Nathan der Weise* (1922) and *Der Kaufmann von Venedig* (1923), but everything he did was overshadowed by his Jewish parts in Veit Harlan's *Jud Süss* (1940). He went on to do similar characters on the stage. In a book, published in 1942, theater critic Herbert Ihering characterized Krauss' famous racist version of Shylock on the stage (which he was to repeat in a movie to be directed by Veit Harlan) as trimmed especially for use in the Third Reich. "With swinging movements and staggering steps, he swept into the arena, an evil, dangerous clown, an eerily comical Ahasver. He stumbled, collapsed and rolled onto the ground. He kicked and was kicked. He scolded and trumpeted. Werner Krauss played an antisemitic Shylock, a red, ugly, joking devil, a ghostly distorted specter. He was spat out of the hell of the Middle Ages, marked with a ghetto's dirt." In *Jud Süss* Krauss not only played the title character's aide and secretary Levy but six other small Jewish parts, too, including that of Rabbi Loew. "It shall be shown how all these different temperaments and characters, the faithful patriarch, the cunning impostor, the haggling merchant, after all originated from the same roots." His NS documentation listed him as "*deutschblütig*" (of German blood). In fact after *Jew Suss* Krauss asked Goebbels to announce publicly that he was not Jewish but a loyal Aryan merely playing a part as an actor in the service of the state. Nevertheless, whenever he befriended Jews he did so only after telling them that he didn't consider them Jews. After some initial trouble after the war he was awarded the Bundesverdienstkreuz (Order of Merit of the Federal Republic) in 1958. In his autobiography, *Das Schauspiel meines Lebens*, he mentioned *Jud Süss* only once: "...I refused, no, not refused, I said: I did not feel like doing it." Krauss died on October 20, 1959, in Vienna.

KUNSTMANN, ERNST

Born in Babelsberg (Nowawes) on January 25, 1898. Started at the pioneering Bioscop company in 1918. Specialized in miniatures and trick shots and became assistant to Eugen Schüfftan (Eugene Shuftan), with whom he worked on *Metropolis* (1925–26). For a short period he accompanied Schüfftan to Hollywood and Universal City where they made *Love Me and the World is Mine* in 1926. Special photography: *Triumph des Willens* (1934); *Ewiger Wald* (1935); *Olympia* (1936). From 1937 to 1945 he was in charge of photographic effects at Tobis Studios: *Robert und Bertram* (1939); *D III 88* (1939); *Kampfgeschwader Lützow* (1940–41); *Annelie* (1941); *Titanic* (1942–43). After the war he joined East German Defa in Babelsberg. Among his many contributions were several fairy tales like the 1950 *Das kalte Herz* (*A Heart of Stone*) and in 1959 the first G.D.R. sci-fi epic, *Der schweigende Stern*, released in the U.S. as *First Spaceship on Venus*. In 1956 he was awarded the National Prize 3rd Class. He retired in 1963 and died on May 30, 1995, in Potsdam-Babelsberg.

LANGE, ERWIN

Born on March 24, 1913, in Berlin. From 1931, an expert in mechanical effects and explosives: *Pour le mérite* (1938); *Stukas* (1941); *Quax, der Bruchpilot* (1941); *Kolberg* (1943–44) and the unfinished *Das Leben geht weiter* (1944–45). After the war, he was still involved in many war films: *Der Stern von Afrika* (1957); *Paths of Glory* (1957); *Die grünen Teufel von Monte Cassino* (1957–58); *Hunde, wollt ihr ewig leben?* (1958); *Die Brücke* (1959); *Division Brandenburg* (1960). Worked on *The Vikings* (1957) as well as *Cleopatra* (1960–62). Died on October 25, 1982, in Munich.

LEDEBUR, FREIHERR LEOPOLD VON

Born on May 18, 1876, in Berlin. Started as jurist before he entered the theater in 1906. In the movies since 1916, often in Prussian parts: *Alte Kameraden* (1934); *Befehl ist Befehl* (1936); *Der grosse König* (1940–41); *Ich klage an* (1941); *Die grosse Liebe* (1941). Died on August 22, 1955, on his Bockhorn estate.

LEHMANN, HANS

Born on March 5, 1906, in Berlin. After training as a merchant, he got into the moving picture business in 1926. He was a producer and production manager: *Der Fuchs von Glenarvon* (1939–40); *Mein Leben für Irland* (1940); *Germanin* (1942). After the war he worked for producers Artur Brauner and Kurt Ulrich. If Lehmann is dead, when and where he died is not known.

LEHMANN, OTTO

Born on January 22, 1889, in Berlin. Was production manager at Terra-Filmkunst: *Jud Süss* (1940); *Fronttheater* (1941). Died on April 28, 1968, in Munich.

LIEBENEINER, WOLFGANG

Directed and co-wrote the euthansia film *Ich klage an* in 1941. Born on October 6, 1905, in Liebau. Studied philosophy, Germanic philology and history in Germany and Austria. Debuted on the stage in 1928 in Munich with Otto Falckenberg. In 1936 he was appointed *Staatsschauspieler* (State's Actor), in 1937 he became member of the board at Terra-Filmkunst, in 1938 head of the artistic faculty of Babelsberg Film Academy, in 1939 head of *Fachschaft Film* at Reichsfilmkammer. In 1942, along with Veit Harlan, he was made a professor by Goebbels. In 1943 he became chief of productions at Ufa-Filmkunst. He directed *Bismarck* (1940) and *Die Entlassung* (1942), and supervised Harlan's *Kolberg* (1943–44). In 1944–45 he left the last *Durchhaltefilm* (holdout picture), *Das Leben geht weiter*, unfinished. Goebbels called him "young, modern, ambitious, industrious and fanatical" in a diary entry of June 11, 1937. "Hitler was also very keen on the actor and director Wolfgang Liebeneiner. He expressly forebade Liebeneiner from being called up into the armed forces. The dictator and his Propaganda Minister even involved themselves in the marital problems of this creator of important propaganda material. While Goebbels was still discussing 'a number of personal matters that are depressing him very much and that could potentially cause a personal crisis for him' with Liebeneiner and his partner Hilde Krahl (29.11.1942), Hitler had already cleared up 'the matters': he agreed that after Liebeneiner's divorce from the Jewish actress Ruth Hellberg, her son from a previous marriage, who grew up as Andreas Liebeneiner, should not be sent to the extermination camp" (Felix Moeller, *The Film Minister*, p. 167). As a director, Liebeneiner was not too keen on visuals. He compared the movies with poetry. For him Hollywood and Goethe were equal in UFA. He felt he didn't need any theorists to explain the basics of filmmaking. "You cannot develop art from theory. The example of expressionism was the most recent, striking proof. The German film will get from its *Führung* [leadership] what is within human power regarding innovations in organization, technical improvements, and spiritual directions" (*Film-Kurier*, January 29, 1941). Liebeneiner died on November 28, 1987, in Vienna.

LÜCK, FRITZ

Born on December 20, 1880, in Berlin. Artist and art director: *Carl Peters* (1940); *Ich klage an* (1941); *Titanic* (1942). Lück worked in the movies up to his 80th birthday. He died on April 8, 1967, in Geretsried.

LÜTZKENDORF, FELIX

Screenwriter. Born on February 2, 1906, in Leipzig. Often associated with Karl Ritter: *Patrioten* (1937); *Urlaub auf Ehrenwort* (1937); *Kadetten* (1939); *Legion Condor* (1939); *Über alles in der Welt* (1940); *Stukas* (1940); *GPU* (1941–42). Also worked on *Wunschkonzert* (1940). In 1962 he quit film work and began a second career as a novelist. Died on November 19, 1990, in Munich.

MACKEBEN, THEO

One of the leading German composers of the '30s and '40s. Born on January 5, 1897, in Stargard. In 1928 conducted the premiere of Brecht and Weill's *Dreigroschenoper* in Berlin. In 1938 scored Willi Forst's *Belle Epoque* work *Bel Ami*. Films include: Karl Ritter's *Patrioten* (1937); *Das Herz der Königin* (1939–40) starring Zarah Leander; *Ohm Krüger* (1940) with Emil Jannings. Left an opera (*Rubens*) which was never staged. Died on January 10, 1953, in Berlin.

MAISCH, HERBERT

Born on December 10, 1890, in Nürtingen. Studied the history of art and attended *Technische Hochschule* in Stuttgart. A career soldier until 1919, then stage director and manager of a theater. In 1933 he began to direct nationalist movies working with the cream of German acting talent (Horst Caspar, Emil Jannings, Heinrich George). His first propaganda effort, however, the strongly anti–Soviet *Menschen ohne Vaterland* (1936), was not passed by the censors. In his memoirs, *Helm ab, Vorhang auf* (Emsdetten 1968, p. 274), Maisch assumed that it was consideration of the German-Soviet Nonaggression Pact which prevented the screening, but in September 1937 Hitler was still swearing at "worldwide Bolshevism." Other pictures include: *D III 88* (1939); *Friedrich Schiller* (1940); parts of *Ohm Krüger* (1940); *Andreas Schlüter* (1941–42). Originally assigned to direct *Titanic* in 1942. Last movie: *Die Zaubergeige* in 1943. Died on October 10, 1974, in Cologne.

MANNING, DR. PHILIPP

Born on November 23, 1869, in London. After quitting school, he went to Germany. Studied law in Freiburg and Berlin. Entered the theater in September 1891. Dubbed various British films. In the Third Reich he also participated in anti–British films *Carl Peters* and *Jungens* (both in 1940). Died on April 9, 1951, in Waldshut.

MARIAN, FERDINAND

Played the title role in Veit Harlan's *Jud Süss* (1939–40). Born as Ferdinand Heinrich Johann Haschkowetz on August 14, 1902, in Vienna. As a seventeen year old he left home. Used the connexions of his father who was an actor, too, in order to build up a stage career in Graz, learning by doing. In the beginning he appeared by his father's stage-name Fritz, then as Ferdinand Marian. In 1927 he moved to the German Rhine Province with its towns of Trier, Aachen, Mönchengladbach, Odenkirchen, Viersen, and Rheydt, birth town of Joseph Goebbels. Then came Hamburg, and eventually there were movie offers, first in Munich. In 1933, in Kurt Bernhardt's *Der Tunnel*, Marian played an agent provocateur. In Berlin he made a film with director Erich Engel, *Der Hochzeitstraum*. In 1939, he made an impression as a South American in Zarah Leander's *La Habanera*. Jews he had played already on the stage; in Trier he even had appeared as Ahasver. In 1940 a Jewish part became his fate: that of Joseph Süss Oppenheimer. About his role in *Ohm Krüger* (1941) the reviewer of *Neue freie Volkszeitung* wrote: "...Ferdinand Marian as Cecil Rhodes, best remembered for his *Jud Süss*, did understand his role again to give an exceptionally accurate portrayal." Marian's last film part was in the unfinished *Die Nacht der Zwölf*, in which he played Leopold Lanski, an obviously Jewish killer of women. He died on August 9, 1946, near Dürneck. The authorities registered his death as an accident.

MAURISCHAT, FRITZ

Born on April 27, 1893, in Berlin. One of Germany's leading art directors and production designers. Started in 1907 as a scenic painter on the stage. Worked in the film industry from 1922. Became an expert in the Schüfftan technique. At Tobis he did several nationalist or anti–British pictures: *Carl Peters* (1940); *Ich klage an* (1941); *Titanic* (1942); *Die Degenhardts* (1944). Maurischat died on December 11, 1986, in Wiesbaden.

MAYRING, PHILIPP LOTHAR

Born on September 19, 1879, in Würzburg. Stage debut in 1898 in Heidelberg. Screenplays for *Ein Mann will nach Deutschland* (1934); *Patrioten* (1937); *Blutsbrüderschaft* (1939); *Himmelhunde* (1941); *Ein schöner Tag* (1943) which he also directed. After the war he worked in radio. Died on July 6, 1948, in Leipzig.

MEISEL, KURT

Born on August 18, 1912, in Vienna. Baldheaded actor and director. First studied law, then became an actor. Veit Harlan cast him as weak characters: *Der grosse König* (1940–42); *Die goldene Stadt* (1941–42); *Kolberg* (1943–44). Also appeared in *Der Weg ins Freie* (1940) and *Menschen im Sturm* (1941). Died on April 4, 1994, in Vienna.

METZGER, LUDWIG

Wrote the screenplay for *Jud Süss* (1940), a subject he had been interested in since 1921. In 1937 he wrote a spy film for Viktor Tourjansky: *Geheimzeichen LB-17*. There is a rumor that he was murdered.

MIERENDORFF, HANS

Born on June 30, 1882, in Rostock. Early star of the silents. In sound films: *Fridericus* (1936); *Der Fuchs von Glenarvon* (1939–40); *Carl Peters* (1940); *Jakko* (1940); *U-Boote westwärts* (1940). After the war he ran a pension. He died on December 26, 1955, in Eutin.

MOG, ARIBERT

Born on August 3, 1904, in Berlin. Wanted to become a career officer. Member of a volunteer corps aged 15. Studied public law and economy, traveled around the world. In the movies from 1928: *Ewiger Wald* (1935–36); *Der Fuchs von Glenarvon* (1939–40); *Wunschkonzert* (1940). Served as a corporal on the Eastern Front where he died on November 16, 1941, not far from Moscow.

MOHRBUTTER, ULRICH

Born on January 4, 1889, in Oldenburg. Submarine commander during World War I. From 1929 affiliated with UFA, first as theater manager, then production manager and producer. In 1940 produced *U-Boote westwärts* (and was seen in it as commander of a British destroyer). Died on January 21, 1971, in Birkenstein.

MONDI, BRUNO

Born on September 30, 1903, in Switzerland. In film industry from 1918. Veit Harlan's favorite cinematographer: *Jud Süss* (1940); *Der grosse König* (1940–41); *Kolberg* (1943–44). Photographed East German Defa's first Agfacolor film, *Das kalte Herz* (1950). Died on July 18, 1991, in Berlin.

MÜGGE, VERA

Born on April 14, 1911, in Zgierz, Russia. Costume designer for UFA from February 1939: *Die Rothschilds* (1940); *Über alles in der Welt* (1940); *Fronttheater* (1941–42); *Junge Adler* (1943–44). After the war she primarily worked for Defa and Artur Brauner's CCC Studios. Died on March 9, 1984, in Berlin.

NIELSEN, HANS

Born on November 30, 1911, in Hamburg. Stage debut in 1932. In the movies from 1937: *Friedrich Schiller* (1940); *Der grosse König* (1940–41); *Ich klage an* (1941); *Titanic* (1942). Died on October 11, 1965, in Berlin.

NOLDAN, SVEND [SVEN]

Born on April 25, 1893, in Bad Nauheim. School friend of director Erwin Piscator. After the war in 1919 Piscator asked him to come to Berlin and design the sets for his stage plays. Dada artist John Heartfield then put him in touch with UFA's animation department. In 1922 Noldan founded his own studio and produced documentaries about World

War I. Belonged to Leni Riefenstahl's production teams for *Triumph des Willens* (1934) and *Olympia* (1936). During World War II the Noldan studio was in charge of army training films. Noldan had been an expert in animated effects and animated maps and continued to do snake-like arrows and lines on animated maps in *Feldzug in Polen* (1939–40), *Der ewige Jude* (1940), and *Sieg im Westen* (1940–41), which was produced by his company. After the war he suffered some years of *Berufsverbot* (career blacklisting) before resuming his work on documentaries. Died on May 1, 1978, in Darmstadt.

OERTZEN, JASPAR VON

Born on January 2, 1912, in Schwerin. Debuted on the stage in 1933. Movie parts from 1934: *Bismarck* (1940); *Der grosse König* (1940–41); *Die goldene Spinne* (1943); *Junge Herzen* (1943); *Kolberg* (1943–44). Also in Wolfgang Liebeneiner's unfinished *Das Leben geht weiter* (1944–45).

PAULSEN, HARALD

Born on August 26, 1895, in Elmshorn. Stage debut in 1913 in Hamburg. In the movies from 1920: *Der Herrscher* (1936–37); *Bismarck* (1940); *Ohm Krüger* (1940); *Ich klage an* (1941); *Die goldene Spinne* (1943). Died on August 4, 1954, in Hamburg.

PETERSSON, HARALD G.

German-Swedish screenwriter, born on October 16, 1904, in Weimar. Tobis press chief in the 1930s. Wrote *Blutsbrüderschaft* (1939) and *Wetterleuchten um Barbara* (1940). After the war he was involved in highly successful Edgar Wallace and Karl May series and scripted the remake of the *Nibelungen*. Was married to Sybille Schmitz, star of Herbert Selpin's *Titanic*. Died on July 8, 1977, in Berlin.

PLEDATH, WERNER

Born on April 26, 1898, in Berlin. Discovered by Max Reinhardt in 1921. Movie parts from 1923: *Die Rothschilds* (1940); *Bismarck* (1940); *Ohm Krüger* (1940); *Ich klage an* (1941); *Die Entlassung* (1942); *Die goldene Spinne* (1943). Died on December 5, 1965, in Berlin.

PLOBERGER, HERBERT

Costume designer. Born on April 6, 1902, in Wels, Austria. Started in the movie business with Luis Trenker. Worked on *Ohm Krüger* (1940); *Paracelsus* (1942); *Kolberg* (1943–44). Died on January 22, 1977, in Munich.

PONTO, ERICH

Was one of Germany's leading stage and screen actors. Born Erich Johannes Bruno Ponto on December 14, 1884, in Lübeck. Apprenticeship as pharmacist, then attended pharmaceutical school and studied pharmacy in Munich. Ten months of actors' school. After engagements on the stage in Passau, Nordhausen, Bad Elster, Reichenberg, and Dusseldorf, he became member of the Dresden ensemble. In 1928, in the premiere of *The Beggar's Opera/The Three Pennies Opera* by Bertolt Brecht and Kurt Weill, he played Jonathan Peachum, the beggar's king. First film part in 1920. With sound films he became a versatile supporting actor. Played banker patriarch Mayer Amschel Rothschild in *Die Rothschilds* (1940). Was in *Am seidenen Faden* (1938); *Dreizehn Mann und eine Kanone* (1938); *Achtung! Feind hört mit!* (1940); *Blutsbrüderschaft* (1940); *Anschlag auf Baku* (1940–42) and *Ich klage an* (1941) by Wolfgang Liebeneiner. Last movie part in Alfred Weidenmann's *Der Stern von Afrika* (1956–57). Last stage part as Shylock in *The Merchant of Venice* on January 16, 1957, in Stuttgart where he died on February 4, 1957.

RABENALT, ARTHUR MARIA

Born on June 25, 1905, in Vienna. Directed several tendentious films: *Flucht ins Dunkel* (1939); *Achtung! Feind hört mit!* (1940); *...reitet für Deutschland* (1940); *Fronttheater* (1941). Directorial consultant to Leni Riefenstahl: *Tiefland* (1940). Died on February 26, 1993, in Wildbad Kreuth, Bavaria.

RADDATZ, CARL

Leading man in German movies. Born on March 13, 1912, in Mannheim. Private actors' training with Willy Birgel in 1930–31. In 1937 Raddatz won a film contract with UFA and made: *Wunschkonzert* (1940); *Über alles in der Welt* (1940); *Stukas* (1940); *Heimkehr* (1941). Later dubbed American stars Kirk Douglas, Burt Lancaster, and Robert Taylor.

REINECKER, HERBERT

Born on December 24, 1914, in Hagen. Screenwriter. After the war Germany's leading producer of teleplays for the series (*Der Kommissar* and *Derrick*). Career started as NS journalist. Editor of Hitler Youth magazine *Jungvolk*. Authored National Socialist pamphlets like "Das Dorf bei Odessa" (published in 1942). 1940–45 war reporter for *Waffen-SS*. In 1943 he joined forces with Alfred Weidenmann in producing *Junge Adler*.

REX, EUGEN

Born on July 8, 1884, in Berlin. Stage debut in 1905. In the movies from 1918: *Die Rothschilds* (1940). In 1933 became member of NSDAP. Functionary for stage and film. Died on February 21, 1943, in Berlin.

RIEFENSTAHL, LENI

Born on August 22, 1902, as Helene Bertha Amalie Riefenstahl in Berlin. Her father, Alfred Riefenstahl, was a wealthy merchant; her mother, Bertha Ida (born Scherbach), cared for her daughter's education in the arts. In June 1924, Leni attended a screening of Arnold Fanck's *Der Berg des Schicksals*. She met actor Luis Trenker and director Fanck and convinced them to allow her to play the female lead in their next adventure, *Der Heilige Berg* (*The Sacred Mountain*). She made some other films with Dr. Fanck: *Die weisse Hölle vom Piz Palü* (1929) and *S.O.S. Iceberg* (1932–33). She directed her first movie in 1931–32: *Das blaue Licht*. Then she made propaganda films: *Der Sieg des Glaubens* (1933); *Triumph des Willens* (1934); *Tag der Freiheit!—Unsere Wehrmacht* (1935); *Olympia—Fest der Völker, Fest der Schönheit* (2 parts; 1936). In one of the most revealing scenes of his portrait film *Die Macht der Bilder* author Ray Müller

asks his willful interviewee whether in retrospect she is distressed by having made *Triumph des Willens*. Ardently, she hears the question as an accusation. Of course she isn't proud of the film. The editing made her seriously ill and after the Second World War she had only been "abused" for the work: "I'm terribly unhappy I made it. If I had known what it would bring me, I'd never have made it." But then while watching it on screen, she begins to rave again about her own montage skills and is pleased that she managed to get the troop of men in uniform to descend a monumental flight of stairs in step to the march music we hear. She insists that although she had been politically blind, she had been absolutely lucid with respect to her composition of the images. To her it was at all times only a question of the material and its formal treatment: lighting, mise en scène, movement, montage. Müller's portrait, which sees itself as a cross between the dismantling of a myth and the revision of a prejudice, ends abruptly. When he mentions that he has the impression people expect an admission of guilt from her, she responds as if by rote: "What do you mean by that? In what way am I guilty? I regret that I made the film on the Reich Party Convention in 1934. I regret..., but I can't regret that I was alive at the time. I never once made an anti–Semitic remark, ... I didn't drop an atomic bomb, I never slandered anyone. In what way am I guilty?" Even Müller is floored by this stubborn refusal to understand or inability to understand [Elisabeth Bronfen in *Filmmuseum Berlin*, p. 184].

Riefenstahl's final feature film was released after the war: *Tiefland* (1940–44). In her later years she became a famous photographer and scuba diver. In her 100th year she finished the deep-sea film *Impressions Under Water* [Impressionen unter Wasser].

RIML, WALTER

Born on September 23, 1905, in Innsbruck, Austria. Skier, carpenter and interior decorator. Assisted cinematographers Hans Schneeberger and Richard Angst from 1929 and became acquainted with Arnold Fanck. Fanck used him in the beginning as a skier, then as a cameraman. In 1934 Riml worked for Leni Riefenstahl and did some photography on *Triumph des Willens*. During the war Riml was a war reporter and produced several documentaries: *Josef Thorak—Werkstatt und Werk* (1943); *Harte Zeit, starke Kunst—Arno Breker* (1943–44); *Atlantik-Wall* (1944). He died on June 21, 1994, in Steinach.

RITTER, KARL

Born November 7, 1888, in Würzburg. His father was professor at the conservatory, his mother an opera singer. In World War I, Ritter served in the *Luftwaffe* (air force) and was promoted to major. "Young men today," Ritter said in a letter dated July 20, 1971, to film historian Peter Hagemann, "always want to immediately get world-famous with their first attempts at literature and film. I myself became successful on short notice as a soldier: in 1909 as lieutenant, in 1910 highly decorated as life-saver during a flood, then I constructed my own airplane, in 1911 I got a pilot's licence (at the present I am the oldest Bavarian pilot and one of the eight oldest in all Germany) etc. etc." After the war he started studying architecture but switched to painting and graphics. Through his father-in-law (according to Dorothea Hollstein a "fanatical anti–Semite"), a remote relative of Richard Wagner, he came in touch with Wagner's house, Wahnfried, and with Bayreuth, Hitler, and National Socialism. Joined the party in the mid-twenties. Production manager from 1925. "Karl Ritter's career as a Nazi propagandist began soon after the end of World War I. When national socialism came to power many years later, it started a search for its party members in radio and movies. Ritter was discovered. Between 1934 and 1938 he advanced to become, finally, the leading director of Ufa's war-propaganda series of 'pure' Nazi films. A safe estimate of how many young boys— the future soldiers of Adolf Hitler in World War II — had seen Ritter's films between 1936 and 1939 is about 6,000,000" (Dr. John Altmann). In 1932 Ritter was appointed production chief of Reichsliga-Film (Reich League Films) in Munich. But with Reichsliga on the verge of bankruptcy Ritter applied for a job with UFA in Berlin and was immediately hired (on probation) by Ernst Hugo Correll, who was in charge of production, and general manager Ludwig Klitzsch. "UFA at that time was in need of *Ersatz* (replacements) for their departing Jewish employees" (Ritter on October 22, 1976).

With *Hitlerjunge Quex* Ritter supervised one of the first propaganda films of the Third Reich. In 1936 he started to direct movies himself and produced several war films: *Pour le Mérite* (1938; Ritter received a congratulatory telegram from Adolf Hitler on December 1, 1938); *Kadetten* (1939); *Legion Condor* (in 1939, with son Heinz as cinematographer, unfinished); *Über alles in der Welt* (1940–41); *Stukas* (1941); *Besatzung Dora* (1942–43, not released). Ritter belonged to the board of UFA. In 1939, on the occasion of Hitler's 50th birthday, he was promoted to professor by Hitler's grace. At the end of the war, Ritter, although placed on Göring's *Gottbegnadetenliste* (list of national comrades who weren't drafted), returned to an air force squadron, which had to fight tanks. Made a prisoner of war by the Russians, he escaped to Bavaria. In his denazification trial he was termed a *Mitläufer* (supporter). In 1949 he went to Argentina where, as the result of an arrangement by Winifred Wagner, he got the chance to make another movie: *El paraiso*. In June 1953, for a short time he returned to West Germany (before finally settling in Argentina). His last movie, *Ball der Nationen* (1954), starred Zsa Zsa Gabor. "If Karl Ritter had had better screenplays," says Polish film historian Jerzy Toeplitz, "and if he had been more aware of the dangers of declamatory dialogue, his works would have gained immensely. They are lively and usually interesting but lack artistic profundity. They never go beyond rather loud, importunate propaganda" (p. 1201). Ritter died April 7, 1977.

RÖHRIG, WALTER

Born on April 13, 1892, in Berlin. Scenic painter on the stage; art director in the movies from *Das Cabinet des Dr. Caligari* in 1919. Sound films: *Morgenrot* (1932); *Flüchtlinge* (1933); *Patrioten* (1937); *Unternehmen Michael* (1937); *Urlaub auf Ehrenwort* (1937); *Pour le mérite* (1938); *Kadetten* (1939); *Über alles in der Welt* (1940); *Heimkehr* (1941). Died on December 6, 1945, in Caputh near Potsdam.

ROSE, WILLI

Born on February 4, 1902, in Berlin. Son of a theater director. First acting engagement in 1919 in Berlin. Movies from 1935: *Verräter* (1936); *Patrioten* (1937); *Urlaub auf Ehrenwort* (1937); *Pour le mérite* (1938); *Legion Condor* (1939); …*reitet für Deutschland* (1940); *U-Boote westwärts* (1940); *Ich klage an!* (1941); *Fronttheater* (1941). Died on June 15, 1978, in Berlin.

ROTMUND, ERNST

Born on November 26, 1886, in Thorn. On the stage from 1907. Intensive film activities in the Third Reich: *Hitlerjunge Quex* (1933); *Ein Mann will nach Deutschland* (1934); *Ein Volksfeind* (1937); *Kongo Express* (1939); *Die Rothschilds* (1940). Died on March 2, 1955, in Munich.

RUTTMANN, WALTER [WALTHER]

Born on December 28, 1887, in Frankfurt/Main. Famed movie documentarist and experimental filmmaker: *Berlin—die Sinfonie der Grossstadt* (1926–27). During the Third Reich he engaged in Nazi propaganda. Consultant to Leni Riefenstahl (*Triumph des Willens; Olympia*). Documentaries: *Metall des Himmels* (1934); *Deutsche Panzer* (1941). "Iron and steel foundries, munitions factories working day and night making big guns, shell cases, rifles, cartridges. Soldiers and airmen on parade. Planes. Tanks. Battleships. Munition dumps." Wounded while filming *Sieg im Osten*. Died on July 15, 1941, in Berlin.

SCHAUFUSS, HANS HERRMANN

Born on July 13, 1893, in Leipzig. Diminutive supporting actor, on the stage from 1910. Sound films: *Ein Volksfeind* (1937); *Kongo Express* (1939); *Die Rothschilds* (1940); *Achtung! Feind hört mit!* (1940); *Wunschkonzert* (1940); *Ohm Krüger* (1940); *Der grosse König* (1940–41); *Kolberg* (1943–44). Died on January 30, 1982, in Munich.

SCHLETTOW, HANS ADALBERT

Born Hans Adalbert Droescher on June 11, 1888, in Frankfurt/Main. Began as actor trainee at Schauspielhaus, Frankfurt, in 1908. On the silent screen he became famous as Hagen von Tronje in Fritz Lang's *Die Nibelungen* (1922–24). Sound films: *Hundert Tage* (1934); *Mit versiegelter Order* (1937); *Kongo Express* (1939); *Die Rothschilds* (1940); *Wunschkonzert* (1940); *Ohm Krüger* (1940) as Boer commander de Wett. Feared by his actor colleagues as an eager denouncer. Died during the battle of Berlin, on Führer's death day, April 30, 1945.

SCHULTZE, NORBERT

Born on January 26, 1911, in Braunschweig. Composer ("Lili Marlene," "Bomben auf Engelland"). Films: *Feuertaufe* (1939); *Bismarck* (1940); *Kampfgeschwader Lützow* (1940); *Ich klage an* (1941); *Kolberg* (1943–44); *Das Leben geht weiter* (unfinished; 1944–45). After 1945 he was involved in two more war films: *U 47—Kapitänleutnant Prien* (1958) and *Soldatensender Calais* (1960). He died October 14, 2002, in Bad Tölz, Bavaria.

SEITZ, FRANZ

Bavarian film director and producer. Born on April 14, 1888, in Munich. Expert in *Heimat* (home) films and German folklore. In 1933 he produced and directed *SA-Mann Brand*. Died on March 7, 1952, in Schliersee. His son, Franz Seitz, Jr., continued the family tradition.

SHALL, THEO

Born on February 24, 1894, in Metz, the son of German-French parents. Debuted on the screen in 1920. Sound films: *Pour le mérite* (1938); *Kadetten* (1939); *Die Rothschilds* (1940); *Achtung! Feind hört mit!* (1940); *Carl Peters* (1940); *U-Boote westwärts* (1940); *GPU* (1941–42); *Titanic* (1942); *Kolberg* (1943–44). Died on October 4, 1955, in Berlin.

SIEBER, JOSEF

Born on April 28, 1900, in Witten. Apprentice locksmith, then a seafarer (1915–21). Stage debut in 1924; in the movies from 1933: *Menschen ohne Vaterland* (1936); *Mann für Mann* (1938); *U-Boote westwärts* (1940); *Paracelsus* (1942); *Die goldene Spinne* (1943). Died on December 3, 1962, in Hamburg.

SIMA, OSKAR

Heavyweight Austrian comedian, born on July 31, 1896, in Hohenau. His stage career began when he was 18. In 1920 he came to Vienna; a year later he appeared in front of a camera for the first time. Often played slimy, unsympathetic parts: *Schwarzer Jäger Johanna* (1934); *Leinen aus Irland* (1939); *Über alles in der Welt* (1940); *Wetterleuchten um Barbara* (1940). Died on June 24, 1969, in Langenzersdorf.

SIMSON, MARIANNE

Born on July 29, 1920, in Berlin. Began career as dancer in 1935. First film part in *Friesennot* in the same year. For producer Hubert Schonger she played the princess in fairy tale *Schneewittchen und die sieben Zwerge* in 1939. Miss Simson was one of those actresses who deliberately took the Nazi route. In UFA's big 1943 Agfacolor extravaganza *Münchhausen* her head (*sans* body) served as the woman in the moon. Veit Harlan cast her in *Pedro soll hängen* (1939) as the partner of Heinrich George. With George she was also in *Andreas Schlüter* (1941–42). From 1945 she spent seven years in Soviet captivity. No parts awaited her in German post-war movies. Simson died on July 15, 1992, in Füssen.

SÖDERBAUM, KRISTINA

Born on September 5, 1912, in Stockholm, third of four children. Daughter of Dr. Henrik Gustav Söderbaum, President, Royal Swedish Academy of Sciences and chairman of the committee that awarded the Nobel Prize in 1901. A movie buff from youth. Learned German language by seeing films starring Elisabeth Bergner. Her favorite directors were Ernst Lubitsch, Carl Froelich, and G. W. Pabst. After the death of her parents Kristina left for Berlin in September 1934, accompanied by the sister-in-law of her sister, with the notion to see and possibly enter her favorite film studios. The Swedish film industry at that time was in turmoil, not capable of holding big talents like Ingrid Bergman or Zarah Leander. She took speech lessons with Margarethe Wellhoener. First small part in Erich Waschneck's *Onkel Bräsig* in 1936. Met Veit Harlan, who was married to Hilde Körber only on paper. First part in a Harlan movie in *Jugend* (1937). Söderbaum married Harlan and became his favorite actress. In *Jud Süss* (1939–40) she was raped by Ferdinand Marian, in *Die goldene Stadt* (1941–42) by Kurt Meisel. In *Der grosse König* (1941–42) and *Kolberg* (1943–44) she played the respective love interest in otherwise male movies. Second career after the death of her husband as portrait and fashion photographer. Died on February 12, 2001, in Hitzacker, Nether Saxonia, after a long illness.

SPEELMANS, HERMANN

Born on August 14, 1902, in Krefeld. Studied philosophy, history of art and sociology in Heidelberg and Berlin. Acting career started in 1924 in Cologne. In 1926 Max Reinhardt brought him to the Deutsches Theater in Berlin. Sound films: *Hitlerjunge Quex* (1933); *Ein Mann will nach Deutschland* (1934); *Mann für Mann* (1938); *Kongo Express* (1939); *Falschmünzer* (1940); *Auf Wiedersehen, Franziska* (1940). Died on February 9, 1960, in Berlin.

STEINHOFF, HANS

German film director, one of the outspoken Nazis. Born on March 10, 1882, in Marienberg, Saxony. Birth name: Johannes Reiter. In 1933 he directed *Hitlerjunge Quex* and

Mutter und Kind, and in 1937 *Ein Volksfeind*. In 1940 he helmed Emil Jannings' anti–British *Ohm Krüger*. Steinhoff died during the last weeks of the war, when he tried to flee the set of a mystery movie he was shooting with Hans Albers and Ferdinand Marian [*Shiva und die Galgenblume*] in Prague. With Russian troups virtually on the outskirts of the city, Steinhoff immediately closed the set and let two SS men escort him to a waiting plane which was to take him to safety. But the plane never got to Berlin. It is a common belief that it was shot down near Luckenwalde on April 20, 1945. Later, there were unfounded rumors that Steinhoff escaped with false papers.

STELZER, HANNES [HANS]

Born on June 20, 1910, in Graz, Austria. The 14 year old attended an actors' school in Vienna. In 1928 debuted on the stage of Neues Theater in Frankfurt/Main. In 1934 screen-tested for Emil Jannings' *Der alte und der junge König*, but didn't land the part. In 1935 film debut in another Jannings production, *Traumulus*. The Nazis used Stelzer's North Germanic profile to the best advantage in Jannings' *Der Herrscher* (1936–37); as an Arno Breker-like sculptor in Hans H. Zerlett's *Venus vor Gericht* (1941) as well as in Karl Ritter's *Unternehmen Michael* (1937); *Über alles in der Welt* (1940); *Stukas* (1941); *Besatzung Dora* (1942–43). Hannes Stelzer himself served in an air corps and died when his plane crashed near Szimö, Hungary, on December 27, 1944.

STEMMLE, ROBERT ADOLF

Born on June 10, 1903, in Magdeburg. Screenwriter and director, who started in puppeteering. In 1930 he became scenario editor with Tobis Film. In 1938 he made a propaganda film about the building of the *Reichsautobahn* (interstate highway): *Mann für Mann*. In 1940 he scripted and directed *Jungens*. His career ended with second-rate Dr. Mabuse, Karl May and Edgar Wallace films. A proposed post-war Heinz Rühmann satire, *Ich war nur ein kleiner PG* (*I Only Was a Little Party Member*), was shelved. Died on February 24, 1974, in Baden-Baden. Was married to actress Gerda Maurus (1903–1968), who had appeared in two of Fritz Lang's silents, *Spione* and *Frau im Mond*.

STOLZ, HILDE VON

Born on July 8, 1903, in Schässburg, Austria (today Sighisoara, Romania), daughter of an Austrian-Hungarian officer. Trained at Max Reinhardt School. Planned to leave the country, which was rendered impossible by the outbreak of World War II. Screen presence from 1928: *Jud Süss* (1940); *Der grosse König* (1940–41); *Fronttheater* (1941–42). Died on December 16, 1973, in Berlin.

TIEDTKE, JAKOB

Born on June 23, 1875, in Berlin. On the stage from 1899. Film veteran who began in front of the camera in 1913. Sound films: *Falschmünzer* (1940); *Jud Süss* (1940); *Der grosse König* (1940–41); *Kolberg* (1943–44). Died on June 30, 1960, in Berlin.

TOLLEN, OTZ

Born on April 9, 1882, in Berlin. Debuted in 1906 in *A Midsummer Night's Dream* in Konstanz. In May 1912 entered the Berlin theater. First movie part in 1912. Sound films: *Unternehmen Michael* (1937); *Pour le mérite* (1938); *Sensationsprozess Casilla* (1939); *Die Rothschilds* (1940); *Jud Süss* (1940); *Spähtrupp Hallgarten* (1940); *Stukas* (1940); *Der grosse*

König (1940–41); *Besatzung Dora* (1942–43); *Kolberg* (1943–44). Died on July 19, 1965, in Berlin.

TOURJANSKY, VIKTOR

Born on March 4, 1891, in Kiev. Son of an artist. Was trained by Stanislavski. Debuted on the Moscow stage. In the movies from 1912. In 1918 emigrated to Paris and even worked in the United States (involved in a film starring John Barrymore). In 1936 he accepted an offer by UFA. In the same year he directed the acclaimed *Stadt Anatol*, and in 1941 the anti–Polish *Feinde*, one of the most aggressive propaganda films. Tourjansky died on August 13, 1976, in Munich.

TRAUT, WALTER

Born on September 19, 1907, in Innsbruck. An accomplished skier. In 1927 the winter sportsman joined Dr. Arnold Fanck. Skier in *Der grosse Sprung*. Eventually became Leni Riefenstahl's production manager: *Das blaue Licht* (1931–32); *Triumph des Willens* (1934); *Olympia* (1936); *Tiefland* (1940–44). After the war producer for Ilse Kubaschewski's Divina Films. Died on September 6, 1979, in Munich.

UCICKY, GUSTAV

Born July 6, 1899, in Vienna. Son of artist Gustav Klimt. Entered the film industry as cameraman in 1920. Became a director in Austria in 1925. Got to Germany in 1928. Even before the Nazis' seizure of power Ucicky directed several nationalist films for UFA that set the tone of what would come later: *Das Flötenkonzert von Sanssouci* (1930), a Fridericus Rex film starring Otto Gebühr; *Yorck* (1931) with supporting actor Veit Harlan; the submarine epic *Morgenrot* (1932). His first film under the NS regime was *Flüchtlinge* (1933). In 1939, in *Mutterliebe*, he hailed the role of female national comrades as "serving, waiting wives and mothers at the beginning of the war" and presented "self-sacrifice in favor of husband and children as the greatest good. An enormous propaganda campaign was mounted for this film. Goebbels appeared among mothers of outstanding merit in a newsreel report on the Berlin première" (Felix Moeller, *The Film Minister*, p. 91). In 1941 Ucicky directed the anti–Polish *Heimkehr*. Among his *oeuvre* were also two remarkable adaptations from literature, *Der zerbrochene Krug* (1937) with Emil Jannings and *Der Postmeister* (1940) with Heinrich George. Ucicky died on April 27, 1961, in Hamburg.

UHLEN, GISELA

Born as Gisela Friedlinde Schreck on May 16, 1919, in Leipzig. Short acting and ballet training with Mary Wigman, then first movie part in *Annemarie* (1936). Landed further parts in *Mann für Mann* (1938); *Die Rothschilds* (1940); *Ohm Krüger* (1940); *Schicksal* (1941); *Rembrandt* (1941). Married to Hans Bertram, Wolfgang Kieling and Herbert Ballmann. Mother of actress Susanne Uhlen.

VOLLBRECHT, KARL

Born on January 16, 1886, in Rügenwalde. Joiner, scenic artist, and from 1919 art director in the movie industry, working on several of Fritz Lang's films with colleague Otto Hunte: *Dr. Mabuse, der Spieler* (1921–22); *Die Nibelungen* (1922–23); *Metropolis* (1925–26); *Spione* (1927–28); *Frau im Mond* (1928–29); *M* (1931); *Das Testament des Dr.*

Mabuse (1932–33). In 1939 (after having worked on *Mann für Mann*) Vollbrecht resumed his collaboration with Hunte: *Jud Süss* (1940); *...reitet für Deutschland* (1940); *Die Entlassung* (1942). Died on January 10, 1973, in Schladen.

WAGNER, FRITZ ARNO

Veteran cinematographer, born on December 5, 1889, in Schmiedefeld am Rennsteig. Work with F. W. Murnau (*Nosferatu*), Fritz Lang (*Spione; M; Das Testament des Dr. Mabuse*), and G. W. Pabst (*Westfront 1918*). After 1933 he was involved in shooting *Der letzte Appell* (unfinished, 1939); *Der Fuchs von Glenarvon* (1939–40); *Feinde* (1940); *Friedrich Schiller* (1940); *Ohm Krüger* (1940); *Die Entlassung* (1942). Died on August 18, 1958, on the set of *Ohne Mutter geht es nicht* in Göttingen.

WASCHNECK, ERICH

Born on April 29, 1887, in Grimma. First came in contact with the film business in 1905. In 1915 photographed documentaries and war newsreels. Feature films as cameraman from 1920, as director from 1924. In 1940 directed *Die Rothschilds*. Died on September 22, 1970, in Berlin.

WEGENER, PAUL

Born December 11, 1874, in Arnoldsdorf (later Jarantowice, Poland). After breaking off his law studies Wegener entered the German theater in 1895. In 1906 he was selected by Max Reinhardt and became a leading stage actor in Berlin. In movies from 1912. Became Germany's most prominent actor and originator of fantastic films and fairy tales: *Der Student von Prag* (1913); *Der Golem* (1914); *Der Yoghi; Rübezahls Hochzeit; Hans Trutz im Schlaraffenland; Der Rattenfänger von Hameln; Der Golem, wie er in die Welt kam* (*in the U.S., Monster of Fate*) in 1920; Rex Ingram's *The Magician* as sort of an evil Alisteir Crowley; *Ramper der Tiermensch* (*in the U.S., The Strange Case of Captain Ramper*) in 1927, as animal man; *Unheimliche Geschichten*. Immediately after the Nazis' seizure of power he became acquainted with them. In 1934 directed *Ein Mann will nach Deutschland* and starred in such epics as *Hans Westmar* (1933) (as the Muscovite) written by his friend Hanns Heinz Ewers; Max W. Kimmich's *Mein Leben für Irland* (1940); Veit Harlan's *Der grosse König* (1941–42) as Russian general Chernichev; and *Kolberg* (1943–44) as defeatist colonel von Loucadou. In 1945 he emersed himself in democractic activities, became president of "Kammer der Kulturschaffenden" and impressed many on the stage of Deutsches Theater as "Nathan der Weise." Died on September 13, 1948, in Berlin-Wilmersdorf. His grave is decorated with a buddha sculpture since Wegener had been a Buddhist.

WEIDENMANN, ALFRED

Born May 10, 1916, in Stuttgart, son of an industrialist. While still a pupil, he shot his first 16mm films. In 1936, at an amateur film competition, he won first prize for a children's movie. After studying three semesters of art history, he became a journalist and traveled for two Stuttgart newspapers, then for the Reichsjugendführung (RJF) of the NSDAP to right-wing countries. In 1938–40 he edited a 13-volume book series *Bücher der Jugend* (*Books of the Youth*). After the outbreak of war, Weidenmann went to Berlin and produced severals shorts for RJF. His youth novel, *Jakko*, was turned into a movie by Tobis Film. In 1942, he directed his first feature film (for Reichspropagandaleitung,

Hauptamt Film): *Hände hoch!* The same year saw him as director of the Hitler Youth film *Junges Europa* (Young Europe). In 1943–44 he made *Junge Adler* in association with his writer comrade Herbert Reinecker. Both became successful in the West German movie and television industries after the war for which they turned out a film biography of *Canaris* (1954), *Der Stern von Afrika* (1956–57), and solid episodes of the crime series *Kommissar* and *Derrick* (Second Channel TV), again from Reinecker scripts. Died on June 9, 2000, in Zurich.

WEIHMAYR, FRANZ

Born on December 31, 1903, in Munich. Helped his father who was a portrait photographer. In the early 1920s he became a cinematographer: *Hans Westmar* (1933); *Sieg des Glaubens* (1933); *Triumph des Willens* (1934); *Wunschkonzert* (1940). Died on May 26, 1969, in Munich.

WERNICKE, OTTO

In Fritz Lang's first sound features, *M* (1931) and *Das Testament des Dr. Mabuse* (1932), Wernicke played the role of fatherly criminal investigator Lohmann. He was born September 30, 1893, in Osterode/Harz and debuted on the stage in March 1911. 1915–18 war service. Belonged to that breed of actors, who appeared almost constantly in Nazi movies up to the end: *SA-Mann Brand* (1933); *Unternehmen Michael* (1937); *Starke Herzen* (1937); *Dreizehn Mann und eine Kanone* (1938); *D III 88* (1939); *Ohm Krüger* (1940–41, as the sadistic British concentration camp commander); *Heimkehr* (1941); *Der grosse König* (1941–42); *Titanic* (1942–43); *Kolberg* (1943–44); and in the unfinished *Kamerad Hedwig* in 1944–45. Died on November 7, 1965, in Munich.

WESTERMEIER, PAUL

Born on July 9, 1892, in Berlin. Acting debut at age 17. Films from 1915. Sound films: *Die Rothschilds* (1940); *Jakko* (1940); *Der grosse König* (1941–42). Died on October 17, 1972, in Berlin.

WIEMANN, MATHIAS

Born on June 23, 1902, in Osnabrück. Studied history of art and philosophy, then toured with a stock company before coming to Berlin in 1924. He early on came to terms with the new regime. Films: *Togger* (1936–37); *Patrioten* (1937); *Unternehmen Michael* (1937); *Kadetten* (1939); *Ich klage an!* (1941). In 1951 he portrayed Alfred Nobel in *Herz der Welt*. Died on December 3, 1969, in Hamburg.

WINDT, HERBERT

Composer. Born on September 15, 1894, in Senftenberg/Niederlausitz. War volunteer in 1914, severely wounded at Verdun in 1917, his face distorted, his left eye lost. Became member of the NSDAP in November 1931. Composed the national tunes for Gustav Ucicky's *Morgenrot* in 1932. For Leni Riefenstahl's *Triumph of the Will* (1934–35) he added studio-recorded march music to the actual sound in order to enhance the vitality of the images and the dynamic editing. "Windt's music plays a key role in forming the audience response to the [opening] titles, '20 years after the outbreak of World War, 16 years after German woe and sorrow began,' the character of the music changes to an uplifting, triumphant nature with the appearance of the title '19 months after the beginning of Germany's rebirth.' This is the first indication of the important role to be played by Windt's music throughout the film" (David B. Hinton, *The Films of Leni Riefenstahl*, p. 39). Windt's music accompanied Riefenstahl's *oeuvre*: *Sieg des Glaubens* (1933); *Olympia* films (1936–38); and *Tiefland* (1940–44). Windt was Karl Ritter's favorite composer, too: *Unternehmen Michael* (1937); *Pour le Mérite* (1938); *Im Kampf gegen den Weltfeind* (1939); *Legion Condor* (1939, unfinished); *Kadetten* (1939); *Über alles in der Welt* (1940–41); *Stukas* (1941); *GPU* (1941–42); *Besatzung Dora* (1942–43). Dr. Günther Sawatzki on *Stukas*: "Herbert Windt's music banishes the pure[ly] demoniac [aspects] of combat high up in the bright sky into sound and culminates in a Stuka song with impressive melody (and lyrics: Gero Ohlischlaeger)." Scores for *Flüchtlinge* (1933); *Die vier Musketiere* (1934); *Die Reiter von Deutsch-Ostafrika* (1934); *Standschütze Bruggler* (1936); *Starke Herzen* (1937); *Am seidenen Faden* (1938); *Feldzug in Polen* (1939–40); *Friedrich Schiller* (1940); *Der Sieg im Westen* (1940–41); *Wetterleuchten um Barbara* (1940–41); *Die Entlassung* (1942); *Die Degenhardts* (1943–44). In German post-war cinema Windt's compositions illustrated two other so-called anti-war movies: the episode film *Heldentum nach Ladenschluss* (1955) and the Stalingrad epic *Hunde, wollt ihr ewig leben?* (1958–59) by Frank Wysbar with whom Windt had collaborated on *Rivalen der Luft* in 1933. He died on November 23, 1965, in Deisenhofen near Munich.

WINKLER, MAX

Retired mayor of the City of Graudenz.

> As a fiduciary of the government from 1920 on, Winkler had a reputation as a discreet and skillful financial expert. He had expertise in the media from government work he had done on behalf of the German-language press and for the "preservation of German culture" in neighboring countries. After 1933, Winkler offered his services to the Ministry of Propaganda and the Reich Press Officer of the NSDAP, Max Amann, to help do away with private ownership of newspapers and to bring print under state control. Prohibitions and political chicanery had pushed many newspaper publishers so close to the brink of financial ruin that they had no choice but to sell on terms dictated by the National Socialist "buyers."
>
> This process became the model for the film business. With the first steps toward "nationalization" of Tobis in 1935, a chain of state usurpations began that ended in the early 1940s with the almost total nationalization of Germany's film companies. Working through Cautio Trust Company, which he had formed in 1929, Winkler discreetly negotiated with senior executives to acquire the majority of stock in all the major companies. Without himself being a board member or company executive, he could then make them comply with his directives. His objective was what Ufa described in its publications as the 'concentration of economic power,' and he considered the political and ideological consequences as mere side effects [Klaus Kreimeier, *The Ufa Story*, p. 258].

Winkler, who was appointed *Reichsbevollmächtigter für die deutsche Filmwirtschaft* (the Reich's authorized agent for the German film industry) after the nationalization process was concluded, "had immense powers in terms of economic and personnel questions, and his reports formed the basis of statements about the film industry in the Propaganda Minister's notes" (Felix Moeller, *The Film Minister*, p. 40).

WISCHNIEWSKY, WALTER

Born on September 16, 1912, in Berlin. Film editor from 1932: *Fridericus* (1936); *Die Rothschilds* (1940); *Annelie* (1940); *Jungens* (1940); *Junge Adler* (1943–44). Later for many years under contract with producer Artur Brauner. Died on February 1, 1995, in Berlin.

ZANDER, ERICH

Born on June 17, 1889, in Berlin. Artist. Collaborated with Paul Leni on silents. Worked with colleague Karl Machus on several prestige productions of the Third Reich: *Robert und Bertram* (1939); *Bismarck* (1940); *Der grosse König* (1940–41); *Kolberg* (1943–44). After the war worked for East German Defa. Died on September 15, 1965, in Regenstauf.

ZELLER, WOLFGANG

Born on September 12, 1893, in Biesenrode. Composer who first worked on Lotte Reiniger's full-length silhouette film, *Die Abenteuer des Prinzen Achmed*, in 1924–25. Soundtrack for propaganda and nationalist films: *Der Herrscher* (1936–37); *Jud Süss* (1940); *Menschen im Sturm* (1941); *Andreas Schlüter* (1941–42). After the war first worked for Defa, then for West German productions. Last time he was seen was in a cameo in Günter Grass' *Katz und Maus* in 1966. Died on January 11, 1967, in Berlin.

ZERLETT, HANS HEINZ

Born on August 17, 1892, in Wiesbaden. Debuted on the stage in 1911. War volunteer in 1914. Screenplays from 1927. Started directing in 1934. In 1936 he made a documentary about German boxing champion Max Schmeling, *Max Schmelings Sieg—ein deutscher Sieg* (*Max Schmeling's victory: a German victory*); in 1939 the antisemitic *Robert und Bertram*; in 1941 the antidemocratic *Venus vor Gericht* which attacked the art world of the Weimar Republic. *Filmwelt* magazine (No. 16, April 18, 1941) used blunt and brutal language to describe the milieu in which "real artists" like the movie's struggling hero Peter Brake (similarities to Nazi star sculptor Arno Breker were quite deliberate) have to survive. Of the art exhibitions of the Weimar Republic, the reviewer wrote that unfortunately "only the pictures had been hung and not the painters" and no one "outside a lunatic asylum" would ever try to understand them. The article continued that it was a matter here of pictures "that we have eliminated as *entartet* [degenerate]." There had been a defamatory touring exhibition "Entartete Kunst" in 1937, from which Zerlett borrowed a few originals for his movie. Zerlett was a close friend of Hans Hinkel. In 1946 he was arrested by Red Guards because they had mistaken him for the director of *Hitlerjunge Quex*. Confined to several Soviet camps. Suffering from TB, he died on July 6, 1949, in Buchenwald internment camp.

ZÖBERLEIN, HANS

World War I veteran. Volunteer corps. Early member of the NSDAP. Member of Munich City Council in 1933 and 1934. Produced and directed *Stosstrupp 1917* (1933) and *Um das Menschenrecht* (1934). Commanded a terror raid in Hausham in late April 1945 in which several striking miners were murdered. After the war, sentenced to death. His life was saved by the abolition of the death penalty in 1948 and his sentence was commuted to 20 years in prison.

ZOCH, GEORG

Born on September 2, 1902, in Danzig. Screenwriter and sometime director. Screenplays for *U-Boote westwärts* (1940) and *Menschen im Sturm* (1941). Died on March 31, 1944, in Berlin.

Notes

Introduction: All Quiet on the Western Front

1. Zbigniew Brzezinski, *The Grand Chessboard: American Primacy and Its Geostrategic Imperatives*, New York: Basic Books, 1997.
2. Oswald Spengler, *The Hour of Decision*, New York: Alfred A. Knopf, 1934, pp. 172–173.
3. Ernst von Salomon, *Der Fragebogen*, Reinbek: Rowohlt Verlag, 1961, p. 363.
4. *Film-Kurier* No. 287, December 5, 1930.
5. *Film-Kurier* No. 288, December 6, 1930.
6. Völkischer Beobachter, December 19, 1930.
7. Völkischer Beobachter, December 13, 1930.
8. John A. Leopold, *Alfred Hugenberg. The Radical Nationalist Campaign against the Weimar Republic*, New Haven and London: Yale University Press, 1977, p. 168.
9. Entry in Goebbels' diary: May 21, 1931.

1. "Martyrs" of the Nazi Movement

1. From the files of Filmmuseum Berlin–Deutsche Kinemathek. Alas, in most cases the clippings are not labeled or dated.
2. Entry in Goebbels' diary: June 14, 1933.
3. Cf. *Völkischer Beobachter*, September 13, 1933.
4. In the files of Filmmuseum Berlin, there is a copy of a guest list for that opening. Among the attendees were mayor Piehler, minister-president Siebert, ministers Schlemm, Wagner, Esser, Himmler, and Dr. Gürtner, SA chief of staff Ernst Röhm (a year later liquidated by Hitler), Rudolf Hess, Baldur von Schirach, vice chancellor Franz von Papen, Gen-

267

eral von Blomberg, Reich governor Ritter von Epp, Dr. Robert Ley, and Dr. Hjalmar Schacht, the president of the German National Bank, one of Hitler's declared backers.

5. Contemporary English-language review, not identified in the files of Filmmuseum Berlin.

6. Cf. *Völkischer Beobachter*, September 16, 1933.

7. German original:

> Die Fahne hoch! Die Reihen dicht geschlossen
> SA marschiert mit ruhig festem Schritt.
> Kameraden, die Rot-Front und Reaktion erschossen
> Marschier'n im Geiste in unser'n Reihen mit.
> Die Strasse frei den braunen Bataillonen
> Die Strasse frei dem Sturmabteilungsmann.
> Es schau'n auf's Hakenkreuz voll Hoffnung schon Millionen
> Der Tag für Freiheit und für Brot bricht an.
> Zum letzten Mal wird jetzt Alarm geblasen
> Zum Kampfe steh'n wir alle schon bereit.
> Bald weh'n Hitlerfahnen über alle Strassen
> Die Knechtschaft dauert nur noch kurze Zeit.
> Die Fahne hoch! Die Reihen dicht geschlossen,
> SA marschiert mit ruhig festem Schritt.
> Kameraden, die Rot-Front und Reaktion erschossen
> Marschier'n im Geiste in unser'n Reihen mit.

8. Hanfstaengl, *The Missing Years*, London, 1957, p. 233.

9. RM is the abbreviation for the German currency *Reichsmark*.

2. Triumph of the Will: The Odd Case of Leni Riefenstahl

1. Second Channel TV, 2001.
2. Leni Riefenstahl, *A Memoir*, p. 178–179.
3. From the files of Filmmuseum Berlin–Deutsche Kinemathek.
4. Riefenstahl, *A Memoir*, p. 158.
5. "How Leni Riefenstahl Became Hitler's Girlfriend," Part III, in: the *Hollywood Tribune*, May 12, 1939, p. 12.
6. *Hollywood Tribune*, May 5, 1939.
7. *How Leni Riefenstahl Became Hitler's Girlfriend*, Part II, May 5, 1939, p. 12.
8. *Ibid.*, Part I, April 28, 1939, p. 12.
9. *Ibid.*, Part I, p. 14.
10. *Ibid.*, Part III, May 12, 1939, p. 12.
11. *Ibid.*, Part IV, May 19, 1939, p. 12.
12. Cf. Series "Hitler's Frauen," Second Channel TV, 2001.
13. Riefenstahl, *A Memoir*, p. 142.
14. *How Leni Riefenstahl Became Hitler's Girlfriend*, Part II, May 5, 1939, p. 13.
15. Rainer Rother, *Leni Riefenstahl: Die Verführung des Talents*, p. 57.
16. Cf. Kevin Brownlow, "Leni Riefenstahl," *Film — The Magazine of the Federation of Film Societies*, No. 47, London 1966.
17. Cf. Jeanpaul Goergen, ed., *Walter Ruttmann*, p. 41.
18. Riefenstahl, *A Memoir*, pp. 136.
19. *How Leni Riefenstahl Became Hitler's Girlfriend*, Part II, May 5, 1939, p. 13.

20. *Die Zeit*, No. 48 (November 24, 1978).

21. *How Leni Riefenstahl Became Hitler's Girlfriend*, Part II, May 5, 1939, p. 13.

22. *Illustrierter Film-Kurier*, No. 2302.

23. Cf. Audrey Salked, *A Portrait of Leni Riefenstahl*, pp. 142–143.

24. *How Leni Riefenstahl Became Hitler's Girlfriend*, Part I, p. 13.

25. September 9, 1934.

26. William L. Shirer, *Berlin Diary*, New York: Popular Library, 1940, pp. 20–21.

27. Riefenstahl, *A Memoir*, p. 159.

28. *How Leni Riefenstahl Became Hitler's Girlfriend*, Part III, May 12, 1939, p. 13.

29. *Ibid.*, p. 13.

30. *Ibid.*, Part IV, May 19, 1939, p. 12.

31. Riefenstahl, *A Memoir*, pp. 353–354. (The late Paul Falkenberg, however, remembers antisemitic undertones in the original treatment of *Triumph of the Will* but couldn't produce any documents to support this.)

32. Cf. David B. Hinton, *The Films of Leni Riefenstahl*, pp. 150–153.

33. John Simon, *The New York Times Book Review*; cf. jacket of Leni Riefenstahl's *A Memoir*.

34. *How Leni Riefenstahl Became Hitler's Girlfriend*, Part V, May 26, 1939, p. 12.

35. *Ibid.*, Part I, p. 13.

36. Sokal manuscript from the files of Filmmuseum Berlin–Deutsche Kinemathek.

37. Felix Moeller, *The Film Minister*, p. 177.

3. The Eternal Forest: Blood, Soil, and Euthanasia

1. *Licht-Bild-Bühne*, June 8, 1936.

2. From a contemporary review by Dr. Günther Sawatzki, filed in Filmmuseum Berlin–Deutsche Kinemathek. (In the beginning a still distrustful Mussolini described National Socialism as the "revolt of the old German tribes of the primeval forests.")

3. Screenplay filed at Filmmuseum Berlin–Deutsche Kinemathek.

4. *Der Spiegel*, No. 7/1965.

5. Report dated January 15, 1942.

6. Felix Moeller, *The Film Minister*, pp. 99–100.

7. Karl Ludwig Rost, *Sterilisation und Euthanasie im Film des "Dritten Reichs,"* med. diss, Berlin 1986, p. 204.

8. *Film-Kurier*, September 22, 1941.

4. Hitler Youth: Soldiers for the Führer

1. From a contemporary review filed at Filmmuseum Berlin–Deutsche Kinemathek.

2. Text by Hans-Walther Betz from Tobis pressbook.

3. Text by Wilhelm Hackbarth.

4. Text by Felix Henseleit.

5. Made by Alfred Weidenmann.

6. Circular letter dated June 1, 1943.

7. GO, dnb.

6. Baptism of Fire: Nazi Germany at War

1. Roger Manvell, *Films and the Second World War*, p. 51.

2. Cf. UFA pressbook filed at Filmmuseum Berlin–Deutsche Kinemathek.

3. From the files of Filmmuseum Berlin–Deutsche Kinemathek.

4. Cf. UFA pressbook.

5. Cf. contemporary review filed at Filmmuseum Berlin–Deutsche Kinemathek.

6. Cf. pressbook.

7. Cf. contemporary review filed at Filmmuseum Berlin–Deutsche Kinemathek.

8. Cary Nathenson, "Fear of Flying: Education to Manhood in Nazi Film Comedies: Glückskinder and Quax, der Bruchpilot," in: Robert C. Reimer, ed., *Cultural History through a National Socialist Lens*, Rochester and Woodbridge, Suffolk: Camden House, 2000, p. 95.

9. Cf. Contemporary ads filed at Filmmuseum Berlin–Deutsche Kinemathek.

10. Cf. Tobis pressbook.

11. *Deutsche Reichspost*:

HERRN HANS BERTRAM

SACHSENPLATZ 1 BERLINCHARLOTTENBURG 9

ICH HABE SOEBEN DEN FILM "FEUERTAUFE" GESEHEN

ICH BEGLÜCKWÜNSCHE SIE ZU DER HERSTELLUNG DIESES

HERVORRAGENDEN FILMS ADOLF HITLER

> I just now have seen the film "Feuertaufe"
> I congratulate you on the production of this
> extraordinary picture Adolf Hitler

HERRN BERTRAM

SACHSENPLATZ 1

BERLIN NEUWESTEND

ICH BEFLUECKWUENSCHE SIE ZU DEM HERVORRAGENDEN FILM

DER EINE WIRKLICHE HOHE KUENSTLERISCHE LEISTUNG DARSTELLT

MIT BESONDEREM BEDAUERN HABE ICH VON DEM SCHWEREN UNFALL

GEHOERT DER SIE DABEI BETROFFEN HAT

IN DANKBARER ANERKENNUNG

GOERING

REICHSMARSCHALL

> I congratulate you on the extraordinary film
> which represents a really great artistic achievement
> I regret to have learned of the severe casualty
> you have contracted in the making
> In grateful appreciation
> Göring
> Reich Marshall

(*Both telegrams filed at Filmmuseum Berlin–Deutsche Kinemathek*)

12. Cooper C. Graham, Library of Congress, "'Sieg im Westen' (1941): interservice and bureaucratic propaganda rivalries in Nazi Germany," in: *Historical Journal of Film, Radio and Television*, Vol. 9, No. 1, 1989.

13. Promotional brochure for *Sieg im Westen* from the files of Filmmuseum Berlin–Deutsche Kinemathek.

14. H.O., UFA pressbook for *Besatzung Dora*.

15. Cf. *Illustrierter Film-Kurier*, No. 3186.

16. Cf. contemporary review by Dr. Günther Sawatzki, filed at Filmmuseum Berlin–Deutsche Kinemathek.

17. Cf. contemporary review by Heinrich Stahl, filed at Filmmuseum Berlin–Deutsche Kinemathek.

18. Howard K. Smith, *Last Train*, pp. 121–122.

19. Cf. Tobis pressbook.
20. Filed at Filmmuseum Berlin–Deutsche Kinemathek.
21. Cf. UFA pressbook for *Besatzung Dora*.
22. Entry in Goebbels' diary: March 29, 1943.
23. Letter by Karl Ritter dated June 3, 1971, cf. Kraft Wetzel, Peter Hagemann, ed., *Zensur: Verbotene deutsche Filme 1933–1945*, p. 62.
24. Herbert Reinecker, *Ein Zeitbericht unter Zuhilfenahme des eigenen Lebenslaufs*, Erlangen; Bonn; Wien: 1990.
25. Issue March 10, 1944.

7. Surrounded by Enemies

1. Slogans from Bavaria pressbook.
2. Cf. contemporary magazine review filed at Filmmuseum Berlin–Deutsche Kinemathek.
3. David Stewart Hull, *Film in the Third Reich*.
4. Cf. Emil Jannings' screenplay, filed at Filmmuseum Berlin–Deutsche Kinemathek.
5. *Ibid.*
6. Entry in Goebbels' diary: April 17, 1940.
7. Cf. Bavaria pressbook.
8. Cf. contemporary review, filed at Filmmuseum Berlin–Deutsche Kinemathek.
9. *Illustrierter Film-Kurier*, No. 3336.
10. Pacific Film Archive, Berkeley, 1972.
11. David Stewart Hull, *Film in the Third Reich*, p. 227.
12. *Ibid.*, pp. 228–229.
13. Published by Filmverleih Südwest.
14. Cf. contemporary review by Fritz Olimsky.
15. Georg Herzberg, *Film-Kurier*, No. 190, August 15, 1942.
16. Felix Moeller, *The Film Minister*, p. 69.
17. Cf. *Offenbach Post*, February 7, 1953.
18. *Allgemeine Zeitung*, February 7, 1953.
19. Cf. pressbook published by ASCO-Film Alexander S. Scotti, Wiesbaden.
20. *Zensur: Verbotene deutsche Film 1933–45*.
21. Entry in Goebbels' diary: June 24, 1937.
22. *Ibid.*, September 22, 1937.
23. Cf. UFA pressbook.
24. Cf. dialogue list filed at Filmmuseum Berlin–Deutsche Kinemathek.
25. By Dr. W. Hofmann.
26. Entry in Goebbels' diary, July 3, 1942.

8. The Eternal Jew: Anti-Semitic Films

1. Daniel Jonah Goldhagen, *Hitler's Willing Executioners. Ordinary Germans and the Holocaust*, New York: Alfred A. Knopf, 1996, pp. 67–68.
2. Cf. Hans Günther Seraphim, ed., *Das politische Tagebuch Alfred Rosenbergs 1934/35 und 1939/40*, Göttingen 1946, p. 91.
3. Cf. UFA pressbook.
4. Ernest Betts in: *Jew Süss*. New York & London: Garland Publishing, Inc., 1978, p. xiii.
5. Lion Feuchtwanger, *Ein Buch nur für meine Freunde*, Frankfurt am Main, 1984, p. 526.
6. From the files of Filmmuseum Berlin–Deutsche Kinemathek.

7. Veit Harlan, *Im Schatten meiner Filme*, p. 113.
8. October 20, 1940.
9. Friedrich Knilli, *Ich war Jud Süss*, pp. 122–123.
10. *Ibid.*, p. 125.
11. Veit Harlan, *Im Schatten meiner Filme*, p. 116.
12. Cf. Leonhard F. Schmidt, *Der Fall Veit Harlan*, in: *Film- und Mode-Revue*, No. 18/1952.
13. Cf. Friedrich Knilli, *Ich war Jud Süss*, pp. 155–156.
14. Courtade/Cadars, *Histoire du cinéma nazi*.
15. Issue May 5, 1933.
16. Fritz Hippler, *Die Judenfrage*, November 28, 1940.
17. Entry in Goebbels' diary, November 5, 1937.
18. John Clinefelter, "A Cinematic Construction of Nazi Anti-Semitism: The Documentary Der ewige Jude," *in Cultural History through a National Socialist Lens*, p. 135.
19. Entry in Goebbels' diary: October 7, 1939.
20. Entry in Goebbels' diary: October 17, 1939.
21. Entry in Goebbels' diary: December 12, 1941.
22. Daniel Jonah Goldhagen, *Hitler's Willing Executioners. Ordinary Germans and the Holocaust*, pp. 424–425.

9. The Great King

1. Entry in Goebbels' diary: January 23, 1942.
2. Felix Moeller, *The Film Minister*, p. 120.
3. Veit Harlan, *Im Schatten meiner Filme*.
4. Linda Schulte-Sasse, *Entertaining the Third Reich*, pp. 121–122.
5. Entry in Goebbels' diary: January 28, 1942.
6. *Ibid.*: March 20, 1942.

10. Black-Out: The Home Front, or, "That's Not the End of the World"

1. Review from an unidentified press clip filed at Filmmuseum Berlin–Deutsche Kinemathek.
2. The interviewer was Rolf Marben.
3. By Hanns Maria Braun.
4. Reviewed by Paul Ickes.
5. David Stewart Hull, *Film in the Third Reich*, p. 204.
6. Cf. Wolfgang Jacobsen, Hans Helmut Prinzler, ed., *Käutner*, Berlin: Edition Filme/Wissenschaftsverlag Volker Spiess, 1992.
7. Felix Moeller, *The Film Minister*, p. 107.
8. From a contemporary review filed at Filmmuseum Berlin–Deutsche Kinemathek.
9. Entry in Goebbels' diary: March 5, 1944.

11. Götterdämmerung: Kolberg and the Fall of the Third Reich

1. Klaus Kreimeier, *The Ufa Story*, p. 350.
2. Veit Harlan, *Im Schatten meiner Filme.*
3. Issue 73.
4. Harlan, *Im Schatten meiner Filme.*
5. Curt Riess, *Das gab's nur einmal.*
6. Cf. *ibid.*
7. Entry in Goebbels' diary: December 3, 1944.
8. Dated March 16, 1944.
9. Cf. Schirlitz telegram.
10. Medved, *The Hollywood Hall of Shame*, pp. 60–65.
11. Issue January 31, 1945.
12. Cf. Holger Theuerkauf, *Goebbels' Filmerbe*, p. 37.
13. Entry in Goebbels' diary: March 30, 1944.
14. On April 21, 1951.
15. Cf. afterword of Harlan, *Im Schatten meiner Filme*, p. 227.
16. Cf. Kristina Söderbaum, *Nichts bleibt immer so. Erinnerungen*, p. 194.
17. Noack, *Veit Harlan. "Des Teufels Regisseur."*

Bibliography

Albrecht, Gerd. *Nationalsozialistische Filmpolitik: Eine soziologische Untersuchung über den Spielfilm des Dritten Reichs.* Stuttgart: Ferdinand Enke Verlag, 1969.

_____. *Der Film im 3. Reich.* Karlsruhe: Doku Verlag, 1979.

Bauer, Alfred. *Deutscher Spielfilm Almanach 1929–1950.* Berlin: Filmblätter-Verlag, 1950. Reissued Munich: Filmladen Christoph Winterberg, 1976.

Berg-Pan, Renata. Leni Riefenstahl. Boston: Twayne Publishers, 1980.

Beyer, Friedemann. *Die Ufa-Stars im Dritten Reich.* München: Wilhelm Heyne Verlag, 1991.

Bezirksamt Tempelhof Abteilung Volksbildung (ed.). *Die UFA — auf den Spuren einer grossen Filmfabrik.* Berlin: Elefantenpress Verlag G.m.b.H., 1987.

Blumenberg, Hans-Christoph. *Das Leben geht weiter. Der letzte Film des Dritten Reichs.* Berlin: Rowohlt, 1993.

Bock, Hans-Michael (ed.). *CineGraph. Lexikon zum deutschsprachigen Film.* München: edition text + kritik, 1984ff.

Bock, Hans-Michael, and Michael Töteberg (eds.). *Das Ufa-Buch.* In Association with Cine-Graph — Hamburgisches Centrum für Filmforschung e.V. Frankfurt/Main: Zweitausendeins, 1992.

Cadars, Pierre, and Francis Coutarde. *Le cinéma nazi.* Paris: Le terrain vague/Eric Losfeld, 1972. German edition: *Geschichte des Films im Dritten Reich.* Munich: Hanser, 1975; Munich: Wilhelm Heyne Verlag, 1975.

Catalogue of Forbidden German Feature Film Productions held in Zonal Film Archives of Film Section, Information Services Division, Control Commission for Germany (BE). Original text by John F. Kelson. This edition edited with a new introduction and material selected by K. R. M. Short. In association with the Imperial War Museum. Studies in War and Film — 4. Trowbridge, Wiltshire: Flicks Books, 1996.

Dahlke, Günther, and Günter Karl (eds.). *Deutsche Spielfilme von den Anfängen bis 1933. Ein Filmführer.* Berlin/DDR: Henschelverlag Kunst und Gesellschaft, 1988.

Fanck, Dr. Arnold. *Er führte Regie mit Gletschern, Stürmen und Lawinen.* Munich: Nymphenburger Verlagsbuchhandlung, 1973.

Fetscher, Iring. *Joseph Goebbels im Berliner Sportpalast 1943 "Wollt ihr den totalen Krieg?"* Hamburg: Europäische Verlagsanstalt/Rotbuch Verlag, 1998.

Fröhlich, Elke, ed. *Die Tagebücher von Joseph Goebbels. Sämtliche Fragmente. Teil 1, 1924 bis 1941.* 4 vols. Munich, 1987.

Fröhlich, Elke, ed. *Die Tagebücher von Joseph Goebbels. Teil II. Die Diktate 1941–1945.* 15 vols., Munich, 1993.

Giordano, Ralph. "Im Zeichen des Hakenkreuzes." In: *Die Weltbühne*, Berlin, May 10, 1950.

Goebbels, Joseph. *Tagebücher 1945. Die letzten Aufzeichnungen.* Introduction by Rolf Hochhuth. Hamburg: Hoffmann & Campe, 1977.

Goergen, Jeanpaul, ed. *Walter Ruttmann. Eine Dokumentation.* Berlin, 1989.

Goldhagen, Daniel Jonah. *Hitler's Willing Executioners. Ordinary Germans and the Holocaust.* New York: Alfred A. Knopf, 1996.

Harlan, Veit. *Im Schatten meiner Filme. Selbstbiographie.* Herausgegeben und mit einem Nachwort versehen von H. C. Opfermann (Edited and with an appendix provided by H.C. Opfermann). Gütersloh: Sigbert Mohn Verlag, 1966.

Hinton, David B. *The Films of Leni Riefenstahl.* Second edition. Filmmakers, No. 29. Metuchen, N.J., & London: The Scarecrow Press, Inc., 1991.

Hippler, Fritz. *Betrachtungen zum Filmschaffen.* Berlin: Max Hesse Verlag, 1942.

_____. *Die Verstrickung.* Düsseldorf: Verlag Mehr Wissen, 1981.

Hitler, Adolf. *Mein Kampf.* München: 1941.

Hofer, Walther (ed.). *Der Nationalsozialismus Dokumente 1933–1945.* Frankfurt am Main: Fischer Taschenbuch Verlag, 1957.

Hoffmann, Hilmar. *"Und die Fahne führt uns in die Ewigkeit": Propaganda im NS-Film.* Frankfurt: Fischer Taschenbuch verlag, 1988.

Hollstein, Dorothea. *"Jud Süss" und die Deutschen. Antisemitische Vorurteile im nationalsozialistischen Spielfilm.* Frankfurt/M; Berlin; Wien: Ullstein, 1983.

Hull, David Stewart. *Film in the Third Reich: A Study of the German Cinema 1933–1945.* Berkeley and Los Angeles: University of California P, 1969; reprint, New York: Simon and Schuster, 1973.

Jacobsen, Wolfgang, ed. *Babelsberg: Das Filmstudio.* Berlin: Argon Verlag, 1994.

Jacobsen, Wolfgang, Hans Helmut Prinzler, and Werner Sudendorf, eds. *Filmmuseum Berlin.* Berlin: Nicolaische Verlagsbuchhandlung, 2000.

Kalbus, Dr. Oskar. *Vom Werden Deutscher Filmkunst: Der Tonfilm.* Altona: Cigaretten Bilderdienst, 1935.

Klaus, Ulrich J. *Deutsche Tonfilme: Filmlexikon der abendfüllenden deutschen und deutschsprachigen Tonfilme nach ihren deutschen Uraufführungen.* Volumes 4 and 5: Jahrgang 1933/Jahrgang 1934. Berlin-Berchtesgaden: Klaus-Archiv, 1992.

Knilli, Friedrich, et al., eds. *"Jud Süss": Filmprotokoll, Programmheft und Einzelanalysen.* Reprints zur Medienwissenschaft. Berlin: Spiess, 1983.

_____. *Ich war Jud Süss. Die Geschichte des Filmstars Ferdinand Marian.* Foreword by Alphons Silbermann. Berlin: Henschel Verlag, 2000.

Kracauer, Siegfried. *From Caligari to Hitler: A Psychological Study of the German Film.* Princeton, NJ: Princeton University Press, 1947.

Kreimeier, Klaus. *The Ufa Story: A History of Germany's Greatest Film Company.* Translated by Robert and Rita Kimber. New York: Hill and Wang, 1996.

Leiser, Erwin. *Deutschland, erwache! Propaganda im Film des Dritten Reiches.* Reinbek: Rowohlt Taschenbuch Verlag, 1968.

_____. *Nazi Cinema.* Trans. G. Mander and D. Wilson. New York: Macmillan, 1974.

Leopold, John A. *Alfred Hugenberg, The Radical Nationalist Campaign against the Weimar Republic.* New Haven and London: Yale University Press, 1977.

Lévy, Bernard-Henri. *La pureté dangereuse.* Paris: Éditions Grasset & Fasquelle, 1994.

Manvell, Roger. *Films and the Second World War.* South Brunswick and New York: A. S. Barnes and Company; London: J M Dent & Sons Ltd, 1974.

Medved, Harry, and Michael Medved. *The Hollywood Hall of Shame. The Most Expensive Flops in Movie History.* New York: Perigee Books/The Putnam Publishing Group, 1984.

Moeller, Felix. *The Film Minister. Goebbels and the Cinema in the "Third Reich."* With a foreword by Volker Schlöndorff. Translated from the German by Michael Robinson. Stuttgart/London: Edition Axel Menges, 2000.

Noack, Frank. *Veit Harlan. "Des Teufels Regisseur."* Munich: Belleville Verlag, 2000.

Prinzler, Hans Helmut. *Chronik des deutschen Films 1895–1994.* Stuttgart/Weimar: Verlag J. B. Metzler, 1995.

Rabenalt, Arthur Maria. *Film im Zwielicht: Über den unpolitischen Film des Dritten Reiches und die Begrenzung des totalitären Anspruches.* Hildesheim: Olms Presse, 1978.

_____. *Joseph Goebbels und der "Grossdeutsche Film."* Munich-Berlin: F. A. Herbig, 1985.

Reimer, Robert C. (ed.). *Cultural History through a National Socialist Lens: Essays on the Cinema of the Third Reich.* Rochester, NY: Camden House, 2000.

Reinecker, Herbert. *Ein Zeitbericht unter Zuhilfenahme des eigenen Lebenslaufs.* Erlangen-Bonn-Vienna: Verlag Dr. Dietmar Straube G.m.b.H., 1990.

Rentschler, Eric. *The Ministry of Illusion: Nazi Cinema and Its Afterlife.* Cambridge, Massachusetts, and London, England: Harvard University Press, 1996.

Riefenstahl, Leni (and Ernst Jaeger). *Hinter den Kulissen des Reichsparteitagsfilms.* Munich: Zentralverlag der NSDAP/Franz Eher Verlag, 1935.

_____. *A Memoir.* New York: St. Martin's Press, 1992; reprint, New York: Picador, 1995.

Riess, Curt. *Das gab's nur einmal: Die große Zeit des deutschen Films.* Vienna/Munich: Molden-Taschenbuch-Verlag, 1977.

Rother, Rainer. *Leni Riefenstahl: Die Verführung des Talents.* Berlin: Henschel Verlag, 2000.

Salked, Audrey. *A Portrait of Leni Riefenstahl.* London: Random House, 1996.

Scheugl, Hans. *Sexualität und Neurose im Film. Die Kinomythen von Griffith bis Warhol.* München: Wilhelm Heyne Verlag, 1974.

Schulte-Sasse, Linda. *Entertaining the Third Reich. Illusions of Wholeness in Nazi Cinema.* Durham, N.C., and London: Duke University Press, 1996.

Shirer, William L. *Berlin Diary.* New York: Popular Library, 1940.

_____. *The Rise and Fall of the Third Reich.* New York: Simon and Schuster, 1959.

Söderbaum, Kristina. *Nichts bleibt immer so. Erinnerungen.* Munich: F. A. Herbig Verlagsbuchhandlung, 1992.

Taylor, Richard. *Film Propaganda: Soviet Russia and Nazi Germany.* London: Croom Helm; New York: Barnes & Noble Books, 1979.

Theuerkauf, Holger. *Goebbels' Filmerbe: Das Geschäft mit unveröffentlichten Ufa-Filmen.* Berlin: Ullstein, 1998.

Traub, Hans. *Die UFA: Ein Beitrag zur Entwicklungsgeschichte des deutschen Filmschaffens.* Berlin: Ufa-Buchverlag G.m.b.H., 1943.

Welch, David. *Propaganda and the German Cinema, 1933–45.* Oxford: Clarendon Press, 1983.

Weniger, Kay. *Das grosse Personenlexikon des Films.* Berlin: Schwarzkopf & Schwarzkopf Verlag, 2001.

Wetzel, Kraft, and Peter A. Hagemann, eds. *Zensur — Verbotene deutsche Filme 1933–1945.* Berlin: Verlag Volker Spiess, 1978.

Wulf, Joseph (ed.). *Theater und Film im Dritten Reich. Eine Dokumentation.* Reinbek bei Hamburg: Rowohlt, 1966.

Zielinski, Siegfried. *Veit Harlan. Analysen und Materialien zur Auseinandersetzung mit einem Film-Regisseur des deutschen Faschismus.* Frankfurt/Main: Rita G. Fischer Verlag, 1981.

Index

279